TAKING HEAT

In Washington, I regularly sat in on meetings in the Oval Office. I dropped in to see President Bush whenever I needed to ask him a question or get guidance on an issue. I was invited by the President to spend time in his home, the residence on the third floor of the Mansion, and at Camp David. I traveled on Marine One and Air Force One. I was also a regular in little Crawford, Texas, where I got my hair cut for five dollars.

I briefed the White House press corps three hundred times on camera. My job was to stay at that podium until the senior wire reporter said, "Thank you." Only then could I retreat to the safety of my office. I got to know the people in the White House press corps well, very well.

I spent days and nights at the White House, doing my job during a recession, September 11, two wars, and an anthrax attack.

I learned to get by on little sleep and little free time.

In the little free time I had, I met Becki Davis, the woman who became my wife. She also worked at the White House.

This book is about my two and a half years in that grand mansion. It's about the President. It's about the White House press corps. It's about how news gets made, and how news gets covered.

This book attempts to capture much of what I saw behind the scenes about President Bush, his policies and his character, and I describe it so readers can have a deeper view of who he is and why he does what he does.

This book is also about the press, and that's a very complicated topic in itself. The White House press corps is one of the toughest, sharpest, most skeptical groups anyone will ever encounter. They're the best in the business, and that's why they're stationed at the White House.

They have a tough job to do, and their lives aren't easy. For all the glamour of the White House, it's not an easy beat. Except for my West Wing office and the office of my deputies, the White House is off-limits to the press. Unlike reporters who cover the Congress, White House reporters can't walk the halls and bump into good sources for news. Instead, they're chained to cramped work spaces, waiting for their phones to ring with the returned calls they are hoping for. Only

PREFACE

I LOVED MY JOB at the White House—almost every day.

Serving as the White House press secretary was the most rewarding, engaging, exciting, and enjoyable job I could ever imagine holding. It also was the toughest, hardest, most grinding and grueling job I could ever imagine holding. By definition, the job was paradoxical. To this day, I don't know how I could love so much something that often seemed so hard to do.

During my time in the White House, I traveled with President Bush almost everywhere he went. I met the Pope, twice. I met the Yankees' manager, Joe Torre, once. I stood on the Great Wall of China with President Bush. I entered closed rooms at the Kremlin that are part of President Putin's office. I observed Memorial Day on the beaches of Normandy, France, paying tribute to lost soldiers in a pristine cemetery where American lives were given so the world could be free. I was with President Bush all day on September 11, 2001, and I stood paces from him three days later, when he visited the rubble where the World Trade Center once stood. I also was with the President when he visited the mothers and fathers, and the sons and daughters, and the wives of those who gave their lives in Afghanistan and Iraq. I heard people tell him, time and again, how devastated they were by the loss, but how much their son or husband loved our military and loved our country.

CONTENTS

To anyone

who works with or talks to the press.

It may not be easy,

but at all times a free press helps keep

our nation free.

Except as noted, all photographs are courtesy of the Office of the White House Photographer.

HarperCollins books may be purchased for educational, business, or sales promotional use. For information please write: Special Markets Department, HarperCollins Publishers Inc., 10 East 53rd Street, New York, NY 10022.

FIRST EDITION

Designed by Kate Nichols

Printed on acid-free paper

Library of Congress Cataloging-in-Publication Data

Fleischer, Ari, 1960–
    Taking heat : the president, the press, and my years in the White House /
Ari Fleischer.—1st ed.
      p. cm.
    ISBN 0-06-074762-5 (acid-free paper)
    1. Bush, George W. (George Walker), 1946– —Relations with journalists.
2. Bush, George W. (George Walker), 1946– —Friends and associates.
3. Fleischer, Ari, 1960– . 4. Press secretaries—United States—Biography.
5. United States—Politics and government—2001– . I. Title.

E903.3.F55 2005
973.931'092—dc22
                                         2004063576

05　06　07　08　09　WBC/RRD　10　9　8　7　6　5　4　3　2　1

ARI FLEISCHER

TAKING

*The President, the Press, and
My Years in the White House*

HEAT

William Morrow
An Imprint of HarperCollins*Publishers*

with an appointment and an escort can they penetrate deeper into the corridors of White House power.

They're a hard-driving, competitive group. The TV reporters know a good White House beat can spring them to fame and fortune—if they can get on the air. The newspaper, wire, and magazine reporters are all looking for an edge or an angle that will make their work stand out from that of the rest of their colleagues.

When the White House press corps shows up for work each morning, there is no telling what story they will cover—which is why many of them find the White House so exciting. One day it's Social Security, the next day it's a summit meeting between two heads of state, the next day it's the President's own health, and one day it's war. And in war, some of the nation's finest reporters have lost their lives or been wounded covering the news. White House reporters are fast on their feet, and with few exceptions, they're generalists—they can't be experts in all the fields they cover because their editors ask them to cover too many fields. That's one reason why much of their reporting emphasizes conflict and politics. Conflict and politics are themes that link much of what the press cover.

In person and one-on-one, White House reporters are also some of the most engaging and enjoyable people with whom to spend time. Some of the most pleasant reporters I ever met were at the White House. I've tipped a glass and shared a meal with almost all of them— and enjoyed it every time. But when they gather together for the daily, televised briefing, a funny thing happens. Gone are the usual pleasantries that marked most of my relationships with the press. Instead, an organized feeding frenzy broke out.

White House reporters sometimes like to grumble. When I was press secretary, they grumbled about the President, they grumbled about their own industry and its weaknesses, they grumbled about their editors, and they grumbled about Congress. Every now and then, they grumbled about me. White House reporters said I was tight-lipped and secretive.

This book explains why I did my job the way I did, particularly during a time of war.

Writing about the White House press corps isn't easy. They're a complicated group that carries out a very important mission for our country. As much as the American people, myself included, sometimes grumble about the press, their work is vital to our nation's freedom.

Whatever their faults, they're a watchdog on the government, and every government—no matter what party and no matter what era we live in—needs a watchdog. They break fascinating stories that grab the attention of readers and viewers. In addition to their coverage of the White House and the government, the press provide useful, helpful news about wide-ranging topics like food safety, child care, and health care. In times of crisis, we tune in by the tens of millions. Whether it's after a natural disaster, like a hurricane or earthquake, or after the attacks of September 11, the American people turn to the media to find out what's going on.

Changes are under way in the press corps. The networks have been losing viewers for years, and their remaining viewers are typically older. Cable TV news shows, especially those on Fox, are cutting deeply into territory that used to be the exclusive domain of the broadcast networks. As newspapers lose readers, younger Americans especially are turning to the Internet and to bloggers. The media is fracturing into more choices and more diversity. While the White House briefing room is home mostly to the largest news organizations in the world representing mainstream media (CBS, ABC, NBC, the *Washington Post,* the *New York Times,* the *Wall Street Journal,* et cetera), the immediacy of the Internet and cable news has changed the way all White House reporters do their jobs—for better and for worse.

My reflections in this book are about the White House press corps. Wherever I use shorthand and refer to "the press," it is the Washington press corps, particularly the White House press corps, that I describe. There are countless press organizations across the country that can't be accurately summed up because of their diversity.

Wherever possible, I have sought to identify by name the people I write about. If I left off the name of a foreign leader or a guest of the President, it's because I'm still sensitive to the nature of my old job—I don't seek to embarrass people or cause new feeding frenzies. I hope I found the balance between writing about important public matters while maintaining confidentiality where I deemed it necessary. As with all books written by White House staffers, I submitted the text to the National Security Council to make certain I didn't inadvertently reveal any classified information. The NSC told me I did not.

I did my best to identify reporters by name as well, relying on transcripts from my briefings and, wherever obtainable, video footage. If a quote is attributed to an unnamed reporter, it's because, in almost all cases, I was unable to verify the reporter's identity. There are a few quotes from reporters whose names I decided to leave out. I think their words carry meaning, and I don't want to distract from their message if naming them would put them in an awkward spot with either their news organizations or the public.

I had the help of many people writing and editing this book. Thank you to my editor at William Morrow, Claire Wachtel. A self-described "knee-jerk liberal," Claire helped me—sometimes forced me—to carefully think through my arguments and to back them up. She challenged my assumptions and helped me to move from assertions to reasoned statements supported by evidence. What may seem self-evident to a Republican wasn't good enough for Claire. One of the most helpful and effective "prods" I ever met, I couldn't have written this without her. Thank you for your wisdom.

To Bob Barnett, my book agent, thanks for opening the doors of the publishing world to me and for ushering me through the process. You're the undisputed king of the agent business for a good reason. Thanks for your knowledge, perspective, advice, and friendship.

I also could not have written this book without the keen insights and diligent efforts of my researcher, Liz Donnan. A former member of my White House staff and a fellow Middlebury College graduate, Liz was tireless running down and verifying thousands of facts and bits of information. She helped me to write about the big picture, and she made certain the small picture was in focus as well. Always cheerful and diligent, accurate and wise, I owe Liz a debt of gratitude for a job well done.

Vickie McQuade, my assistant at the White House, who left her job there to work for me, also helped with the early research on the book and she has kept me organized in all my efforts. An invaluable helper, thanks Vickie, and thanks to Art as well for his help.

Several people read the text of my book and spent many hours giving me their thoughts, reflections, and suggested changes. To Peter Campbell, my college friend and keen observer of all things political, thanks for your time and guidance. You gave a lot of both and the book is better because you did. To former CNN bureau chief and White House reporter Frank Sesno, thanks for your efforts. You helped me to think things through and to make sure I thought about matters from the press's perspective. Your critique was invaluable and I'm grateful for your time.

Thanks also to Ken Kies and Kim Hildred for double-checking the accuracy of the portions of the book dealing with taxes and Social Security. You're both experts and I'm grateful. Thanks to Steve Scully at C-SPAN for making tapes available so I could verify the identity of reporters at the briefings. Thanks also to the public affairs office of the USS *Abraham Lincoln* for checking my facts.

A sincere thanks also to the White House press corps. As much as the job required us to clash from time to time, you're a dedicated group of professionals who provide an invaluable service to our nation. We've been through a lot together and I hope you find this book insightful. My reminiscences of standing at that podium are good ones— thank you for that.

I also want to thank the countless number of people I worked with at the White House with whom I share these memories. We worked closely together and I'm proud to have been part of such a diligent, dedicated, and professional crew. I especially thank the staff of the White House press office. You lived many of these stories yourselves. You were there and you saw them. I hope you enjoy reading about them. Thanks again for being my staff for the two and a half years I worked there. Thanks for serving your country.

And of course, thanks to the President. Thank you for the phone call on Election Day 2000. Thanks for allowing me to hold a job I will always love and remember fondly. Thank you for what you've done for America, and for the world. It was my honor to represent you.

Thanks to my loving, blue-state-living family. To my parents, thanks for your love, your lessons, and your help. It's great to be home again. Thanks to my brothers, Michael and Peter. We've talked politics together so long, you may not have realized it, but you helped prepare me for my briefings. You're both good advisers, but more important, you're family and friends. To my in-laws, Republicans one and all, thanks for your love and warmth. It's great to be part of your family and thanks for living in a red state.

Above all, thanks to my wife, Becki, and our little daughter, Liz. The best thing about writing a book is the amount of time I got to spend at home with both of you. Becki, thanks for, well, everything. You are my world. And to Liz, thanks for your smile every morning. There's no greater pleasure than holding and hugging you. You make my world complete.

THE WINDS OF WAR

September 14, 2001

THE PRESIDENT'S ARMORED LIMOUSINE turned onto New York City's Forty-second Street. Moments earlier, President Bush had hugged the last of some two hundred widows and widowers to be at the Jacob Javits Center in midtown Manhattan. On September 14, 2001, Forty-second Street could have been Main Street in any midwestern community or a small southern town. The street was lined ten deep on both sides with people holding signs reading "God Bless America" and "God Save the U.S." But this was New York City, the place where I was born and where my father commuted almost every day of his working life. It was Ground Zero, the place where America had been attacked seventy-two hours earlier. The city is not known for its outward displays of faith, but on September 14, New York City was a quiet, pious place.

During my two and a half years as the press secretary in the White House, no day was tougher than September 14. The attack of September 11 fell like a blow. My day was consumed with reacting to it, wondering how it could have happened, and learning what we were going to do about it. The suffering was tremendous, but it was somehow distant. It was on TV, on the phone, outside the so-called bubble that shields the President and the entourage around him. September 14 brought it home.

The President was scheduled for a thirty-five-minute meeting with a group of family members whose loved ones were still "missing" at the World Trade Center site. Instead, the meeting lasted almost two hours, as he walked around the room, hugging and consoling every grieving person there.

A New York City police officer came up to him with his niece in his arms and a picture in his hand. The child, who looked like she was six years old, pointed to the picture of firefighters. The man she pointed to, the cop explained, was her father, his brother. He was missing at Ground Zero, and the little girl wanted to know if the President could help her find him.

Family after family presented the President with pictures of their missing loved ones. There wasn't a person in that room who thought his or her missing wife, husband, son, or daughter wouldn't get out alive. Despite their hopes, nearly everyone in the room, President Bush included, had tears in his or her eyes. The Secret Service, which usually form a protective phalanx around the President so no one can get very close for very long, stood back. They understood the solemnity of the scene before them. I wouldn't have been surprised if there were agents with tears in their eyes.

One woman approached the President with a picture of her husband, also missing at Ground Zero. He signed it, telling her that when her husband returned she should let him know that she had met the President and had the signature to prove it. He wanted to give the families a ray of hope that their missing loved ones would be found. She thanked him and tucked the picture into her Bible.

I stood a few feet away from the President and took it in. I had never witnessed such sadness. People waited for President Bush to make his way around the room. Some cried out loud. Many sobbed softly. Several had to link arms to have the strength to stay on their feet in this makeshift room, with blue curtains acting as walls inside a giant convention hall. As people waited for their turn to talk to the President, some struck up conversations with me. One woman told me her brother had served in the United States Marine Corps during Desert Storm and had been working at the World Trade Center. She hadn't seen him since the attack. "If anyone knows how to get out," she told me, "it's him. He's a Marine. He knows how to survive for days." I told her I was sure she was right.

Moments before it was time to go, the President approached an elderly woman seated in a chair. Her name was Arlene Howard. She sat serenely, waiting for him. In her hand she held the shield of a Port Authority Police officer. The shield belonged to her son, George Howard, a Port Authority cop with the Emergency Security Unit at JFK Airport and a volunteer fireman in Hicksville, on New York's Long Island. When the towers were attacked, he rushed to the scene.

Rescue workers found her son's body the day after the attack with his shield still on his shirt. It was given to her as a loving memory. When the President arrived at her side, she took the shield and gave it to him. "This is so you remember what happened here," she said. "This is so no one will forget."

Six days later, when the President addressed the nation in a speech to a joint session of Congress, he held up the shield and said, "I will carry this: It is the police shield of a man named George Howard, who died at the World Trade Center trying to save others. It was given to me by his mom, Arlene, as a proud memorial to her son. This is my reminder of lives that ended, and a task that does not end."

As the motorcade sped down Forty-second Street, the President still clutched George Howard's shield in his hand, and I stared at the silent crowds from my vehicle, several cars back. Manhattan never felt so still. We were on our way to the Wall Street Landing Zone to catch the Marine helicopters that would take us to New Jersey's McGuire Air Force Base, where Air Force One waited. As we passed Times Square, the billboard carrying that day's news circled round—"President Bush Calls Up 50,000 Reservists," it said.

The winds of war were blowing.

AUSTIN, TEXAS

GOVERNOR GEORGE W. BUSH called me in the middle of the afternoon on Election Day 2000, the slowest day of the year. Earlier that morning I had voted and then got a back massage. I arrived at the Congress Street campaign headquarters around noon. Unless you're at the phone banks or out on the streets, there really isn't much you can do to affect the outcome on Election Day, especially in Austin. I felt pretty good about winning Texas, so there was no point in hitting the streets to wave signs. Phone banks these days are professional operations, so I did my best to relax.

I think we're in for a nice victory tonight, the governor told me, and then he added, "I'd like you to be my press secretary when I win." It was the one job I wanted, and now it was being offered to me. "I'm honored," I said. "It would be my pleasure." He told me he'd see me at the election night party and hung up.

After eighteen years as the press secretary to three congressmen and one United States senator, I thought I would soon begin the most exciting, challenging press secretary job imaginable. Little did I realize what would happen next.

Every campaign has an Election Day pool, in which staffers place bets on the outcome. Governor Bush had been beating Vice President Al Gore for more than a year in all the media polls, even though the

Vice President briefly pulled ahead in September. The polls indicated Bush would win; I thought Bush would win; who didn't think he'd win? My bet was 320 electoral votes for the governor. A solid victory I projected, given that a winning candidate needs only 270.

But the upbeat mood around the headquarters began to change as the early exit polls came in. News organizations had formed a syndicate to take supposedly secret surveys that predict state-by-state results before the polls have even closed. The polls are designed to help reporters explain the results, and they are never to be used on the air, at least not until the voting booths in the state have actually closed. Before the polls have closed, reporters also aren't supposed to share these early projections with anyone outside their newsrooms, but many do anyway. For journalists, it's one of those rare times when they have more information than the sources they depend on, and many reporters enjoy the role reversal. Events weren't looking good for my 320-electoral-vote prediction. In fact, Election Day was beginning not to look good at all. Things weren't going our way in the crucial, large state of Pennsylvania, where Al Gore was up by a big margin. Michigan looked bad, and Florida was uncomfortably close. The TV commentators accurately said that these were the likely key states to a presidential win.

At 6:50 P.M. Texas time, 7:50 Miami time, which also happens to be 6:50 Pensacola time, the networks projected Florida would go to Al Gore. No sooner had the lump formed in my throat than Karl Rove came flying to my office telling me to call the networks. "The polls in Florida aren't closed yet," Karl cried. "How can they call the race before the voting is done?" He was right. Florida's Republican-dominated panhandle was in a different time zone than the rest of the state. Voters there had more time to cast their ballots, but after they heard the state was already lost, turnout in our stronghold would likely diminish. In a close race, that could make a big difference.

None of the networks had declared Al Gore the national winner, but the mood in Austin was grim. How could this be happening? How could it be so close?

I decided to change the outcome of the election by changing my seat. Just like a superstitious baseball player who changes a part of his uniform if he's in a hitting slump, I moved offices. I moved to the office of the chief pollster, Matthew Dowd. It was already occupied by several other nervous staffers, but I found a spot on the front edge of his desk. Surprisingly enough, the longer I sat there, the better things got. Amazingly, the networks reversed their call of Florida for Gore and now reported the state was too close to call. Our internal tally, provided by staffers and Republican Party officials at Florida's polling places, showed us with a small but winning lead. I didn't budge. I wasn't going to move from my lucky spot no matter what happened.

That's when Fox News called Florida for Governor Bush, at 1:16 A.M. central time. None of us could quite believe it. We sat there stunned and silent. But minutes later, once the other networks joined Fox in predicting Bush's win, I flew off the desk, yelling, hugging, and high-fiving the couple dozen staffers who were packed into the Karl-Matt area of headquarters.

Outside, the weather was rotten. It was cold for Texas, in the forties and rainy, but it didn't matter. The staff poured out of headquarters, down Congress Street, and through the area reserved for campaign staff to wait for Governor Bush to give his acceptance speech. It was around 2:00 A.M., and we waited. Then we waited some more. I noticed that Karl Rove, who had left the headquarters with me, was missing. I didn't see Matt Dowd any longer, and someone told me the networks had again reversed course and said the race in Florida was too close to call.

I slipped down a side street so no one in the press would see me and ask me what was happening, and arrived back at the headquarters. I didn't want to be seen because I didn't know what to say if anyone asked what was happening. If it had been grim earlier, it was twice as grim now. I learned that the Vice President had retracted his concessionary phone call to Governor Bush and that the race was frozen, too close to call.

It was the middle of the night, and I didn't know what to do. Someone told me that the *Today* show was calling and needed a spokesman from the campaign to go on at 6:00 A.M. Texas time to give our side of the story. I went back into my office, curled up on my chair, got one hour of sleep, and went on the air. "We're going to go into extra innings," I told Matt Lauer, "but I think we're about to win this contest."

I had turned forty years old three weeks before Election Day, and I planned to spend the weekend after the election in Las Vegas, relaxing and catching up with friends I hadn't seen for a year. Except for the Jewish High Holy Days, I had worked seven days a week since June. I was exhausted, mentally and physically, but as of Wednesday morning, the day after the election, I thought I would still be able to meet my friends. This will take a day or two to settle, I told myself, and then I'll be in Las Vegas, anticipating my next job, as the White House press secretary.

I never made it to Vegas.

THE RECOUNT

Every time the spokesman for the Florida Supreme Court, Craig Waters, appeared on the steps of the courthouse, I shivered. During the thirty-five-day recount, I suffered through an unnerving series of ups and downs as the governor's lead shrank. Poll watchers gazed at chads through magnifying glasses, armies of partisans from both sides spread out through Florida to influence the outcome, and I watched from Austin.

Because I had been designated the White House press secretary, I didn't become part of the Florida exodus. I prepared for life at the White House by studying the transcripts of press briefings by the former Clinton press secretary Mike McCurry, and I fielded calls from reporters.

In the middle of the recount, just before Thanksgiving, the vice presidential candidate Dick Cheney suffered what later turned out to be a mild heart attack. The first medical reports received by the campaign gave no indication a heart attack had occurred. Governor Bush told the press about Cheney's hospitalization without referencing a heart attack. When they later learned that the former defense secretary did have a heart attack, they had one too.

How could you deceive us? the press cried. Why didn't you tell us he had a heart attack? Why did you try to hide it? The accusations flew.

"As Dick Cheney recuperated from a mild heart attack here today, the misinformation provided by his doctors, and passed along by Gov. George W. Bush, raises anew serious questions regarding the public's right to know about the health of candidates and the credibility of information that their doctors and their campaigns disclose," wrote *The New York Times*.

From his hospital, Cheney phoned in to *Larry King Live* to discuss what had happened. "I should be out of here in a day or two," he told King, who also had a history of heart disease. There should be "no doubt about my serving," Cheney said. "All we have to do now is get elected." He added, "I can report that when they got in there today they didn't find any pregnant chads."

Though the so-called deception controversy faded as the media's attention went back to the recount, a lesson emerged about how to deal with the national press on big, breaking news stories. It was a lesson I would often keep in mind at the White House.

When news breaks, reporters are under tremendous pressure from their editors to get the facts first, fast, and on the air. In the modern media world, marked by the Internet and three all-news, all-the-time cable networks that compete furiously with one another, the ability to digest news slowly when facts emerge and sometimes change is seriously hindered. Gone forever are the days when news would break, reporters and sources would discuss ongoing developments throughout the day, and most Americans would first hear the news in a carefully digested story hours later on the evening news. For reporters now, it's an immediate need to tell and a rush to air. The need for the public to "know" hasn't changed, but the urgency for reporters to "tell" has grown more intense.

The lesson I learned was that first reports of breaking events are often wrong because facts emerge over time, so government sources need to be guarded about what we say and how early we say it. Sometimes it's best if we don't say anything at all until additional facts can be gathered.

No matter what, it's dicey. We conceivably could have held back the news that Cheney had entered the hospital until we had more concrete medical information. But if reporters found out he was hospitalized from a hospital source or from anyone other than the campaign, they would have accused us of "withholding" the fact that the vice presidential candidate had entered the hospital. Why *didn't* you tell us? they would demand. Were you trying to hide the truth? Reporters don't want you to hold back, even if doing so is in the interest of accuracy. Tell us what it might be, they'll say. Discuss the possibilities so we can speculate on the air.

Should we have issued a statement listing multiple ailments that his illness could have become, including a heart attack? That doesn't seem responsible, particularly if none of the "potential" ailments became a reality. Should we have withheld any comment until we had more definitive word? That's a surefire way for speculation to run rampant, and it also angers reporters, who have to get something, anything, on the air. But at least no one could have accused us of saying something that turned out to be wrong. I think telling the press that Cheney entered the hospital *was* the right thing for us to do; blaming the campaign for not knowing he had a heart attack was wrong for the press to do.

Welcome to life with the press, where sometimes, no matter what you do, you get in trouble for it. When the anthrax attacks occurred one year later, the perils of early disclosure would come back to haunt us.

On November 27, 2000, within days after he checked out of the hospital, Cheney announced he had been designated by Governor Bush to move back to Washington to run the transition to the White House.

The governor had made the decision that we were losing too much valuable time waiting for the ballots to be counted. If we were going to have a serious transition, in which personnel and policy decisions could carefully be made, we needed to start. We would open our own transition office in Washington, using private funds. Just because the election was being contested in the courts, Cheney said, our obligation to govern well should not be diminished.

He announced that, at Bush's direction, Clay Johnson, the governor's chief of staff, would become executive director of the transition, and I would be the transition press secretary. After having lived in Texas for a year, I would return to Washington, and unless victory was snatched away from us during the recount, I would become the President's press secretary.

Before I left, the governor talked to me about what he expected. He told me that I would become the "face of the nation." He meant it humorously, but he also was sending me a message to be mindful of what I said as press secretary because the position, and my words, carried weight. He told me to be careful how I dealt with the press, advising me to find the right balance between being frank with reporters and allowing the White House to have a thoughtful, disciplined, private policy-making process. The press has a right to know, but the President also has a right to hold meetings without reading every detail about them in the newspapers. He told me to talk to the former President Bush's press secretary, Marlin Fitzwater, to get a sense of the relationship between the press and the press secretary. I couldn't wait to start the job.

I left Austin for Washington on December 2, but on my way out I had one final meeting at the governor's ranch. Speaker Dennis Hastert and Senate Majority Leader Trent Lott came to Crawford to discuss the transition and the work anticipated in Washington. Lott wore a hat with a funny-looking feather sticking out of it. Bush talked about warning signs on the economic horizon and his conviction that he would have a good relationship with congressional Democrats. He stressed his desire to "change the tone" in Washington and rise above the partisanship. In many ways, he was still the man from Austin, where he had the pleasure of an opposition party that indeed worked in a bipartisan way. In Washington, many things would be different from the President's hopes.

During the recount, I was struck by how the governor spent his time in Texas, especially when compared to Vice President Gore. While the Vice President worked the phones, calling county chairmen and other leaders throughout Florida in his effort to change the outcome, Bush stayed home. At that time his ranch didn't receive cable TV, so he was removed from the misery of the daily ups and downs, at least as they played out on TV. He would bide his time, working his land, receiving recount updates from former secretary of state Jim Baker, whom he had designated to lead the recount effort, and the future White House chief of staff, Andy Card. Andy often traveled one and a half hours north of Austin to meet with the governor in Crawford as they fleshed out the transition planning. The governor's hands were dirty from ranch work, but his mind was fixed on the future, in anticipation of eventual victory.

To the governor's detractors, the fact that he remained on the ranch and didn't appear regularly on TV showed he was indifferent and disengaged. It was a criticism regularly leveled at him, especially before September 11. His apparent detachment was also a first indication that led his critics to believe Dick Cheney was really in charge of the administration. With so much at stake, how could he remain so calm and secluded at his remote ranch? critics asked.

When Governor Bush lost the New Hampshire primary, he called the senior staff into his hotel room to say, Don't dwell on it, and he urged us to look ahead. He took the crushing defeat calmly, without any outward display of anger or emotion. He told us to focus on the upcoming South Carolina primary and resolutely predicted he would win there. When he was informed he had won the crucial South Carolina primary against an unexpectedly tough challenge from Senator John McCain, he was just as calm and steady as he had been in New Hampshire. He didn't high-five anyone, he didn't exalt. Observing him, I thought he wasn't a man prone to highs and lows. He somehow has the ability to remain calm in a storm while exuding confidence and leadership. If there's ever a crisis, I thought at the time, this is the type of leader I want at the helm.

I was lucky. I got to see these traits close up. Those who didn't like him, and those who were the most cynical, found what I viewed as steady determination to be noncredible, or a sign of a disinterested President. Washington is a town where the opposition party sees the worst in its opponents; Democrats do it to Republicans, and Republicans do it to Democrats. The press does it to both.

"If they're going to steal the election, they're going to steal it," Bush serenely said to me at his ranch the day I left Texas. "If they do, I'll get on with my life here."

THE TRANSITION

I returned to Washington, to the places and people I had known for almost twenty years. Our makeshift transition office was in McLean, Virginia, and I lived in a hotel nearby, since I had rented my house to a friend during my yearlong stay in Texas.

As I drove the streets of the District and got within eyesight of the White House, I averted my gaze. I couldn't bring myself to look at that historic mansion, the place where every President of the United States has lived and worked since John Adams. I didn't look because I didn't want to jinx my chances of working there. Not until the Supreme Court effectively ruled that Governor Bush had won the election could I bring myself to look at the White House and think that now I would, indeed, enter those gates and become the President's press secretary.

Transition work focused mostly on picking personnel. Even before the Supreme Court's ruling, the governor, along with Dick Cheney, Clay Johnson, and Andy Card, batted around all kinds of names for all kinds of posts. The work was done quietly, without attracting much attention, since the press was riveted on the recount. The distraction was helpful. There's nothing more difficult than a personnel selection process that is covered like a live sports event in the newspapers. "Candidate X is thought to have the inside track today, while Candidate Y is fading" was how the selection process would eventually be covered. Reporters love to speculate about who gets named to what positions, and my job was never to speculate about it. Given the fact that Bush wasn't the winner yet, my job wasn't too tough.

On December 12, the Supreme Court issued its ruling that resulted in George W. Bush winning the election. The debacle that had begun five weeks earlier had finally ended. It wasn't ten innings, like I predicted to Matt Lauer, but it was victory. Instantly, the man I called governor was President-elect, and the trappings of office sprang up. The size of Bush's Secret Service detail grew overnight. Foreign leaders called to congratulate him, the first being Britain's Tony Blair.

A charter plane took the McLean crew to Texas for the governor's acceptance speech; we joined the now President-elect and the belea-guered team of campaign workers sent to Florida during the recount. After a much-delayed late-night celebration, the charter took us back to Washington, and we prepared to welcome a much larger contingent to the taxpayer-funded, official transition headquarters, two blocks west of the White House.

In the coverage of the President's court victory, two words jumped out at me—*closely divided*. Every network and all the major newspaper accounts accurately noted that the ruling came from a closely divided Supreme Court. The Court did rule 5–4, after all. For months, all we heard about was the "closely divided" Supreme Court.

Jackie Judd of ABC discussed the ruling on the air, declaring to Charlie Gibson, "So what you have, Charlie, bottom line, is a deeply di-vided court, a very bitter minority."

"A bitterly divided court seems to have ended Al Gore's chances for the White House," NBC's Matt Lauer reported.

But four days earlier, on December 8, the Florida Supreme Court had delivered a major victory to Al Gore in a 4–3 ruling that could have made the former Vice President the forty-third President of the United States. Looking back at the coverage of that ruling, it's hard to find many references to a "closely divided" court. Most media accounts cited the 4–3 vote and then discussed what a major victory it was for the Vice President.

"It wasn't quite a celebration, but after yesterday's decision by the Florida Supreme Court—the biggest victory in his post-election struggle to win the presidency—Al Gore was in a mood to savor the moment," wrote the *Washington Post*, with no reference to a close or bitter decision.

In both rulings, the press informed their readers and viewers about the vote margin, but they dwelled on how close it was when the ruling went Bush's way. They didn't do that when it went Gore's way. "Closely divided" was the tone-setting description that lasted months for Bush. When the ruling went Gore's way, the one-vote margin of the ruling was dutifully mentioned but the emphasis was on the outcome of the Florida Supreme Court's ruling, not the divided nature of the court's action.

The Florida ruling, of course, had a shelf life of less than twenty-four hours thanks to the U.S. Supreme Court's decision to hear the case. But for one day, based on how the press was covering events, most Americans would have thought it was a unified Florida Supreme Court that put Al Gore on the doorstep of the presidency.

The transition became real, and the President's team started to come together. His first appointment to the cabinet was Colin Powell as secretary of state. Shortly after Christmas 2000, the President-elect announced the appointment of Donald Rumsfeld as secretary of defense.

At the news conference to announce Rumsfeld's nomination, someone asked Bush if he was worried he had too many powerful personalities on his defense and foreign policy team. "I wonder . . . what kind of influence Powell and Vice President–elect Cheney will have over the Pentagon, given certainly his [Cheney's] experience and Powell's stature," a reporter wanted to know.

"I think that those who follow American diplomacy and politics understand that I've assembled a team of very strong, smart people," Bush replied. "And I look forward to hearing their advice. One of the things that's really important for the American people to understand is, I'll be getting some of the best counsel possible. And so, you bet, General Powell's a strong figure and Dick Cheney is no shrinking violet, but neither is Don Rumsfeld, nor Condi Rice. I view the four as being able to complement each other."

It was a telling glimpse into how Bush governs. He is comfortable surrounding himself with strong, smart people, giving them direction, allowing them to clash in front of him, and then he enjoys making decisions—particularly on difficult and weighty matters. There are people in politics who can't surround themselves with anyone smarter or more successful than they are. They're uncomfortable if they're not the acknowledged smartest person in the room. They need to show they're the best, and they will appoint only people who pale in comparison. As a governor, Bush had little foreign policy experience, but he didn't worry for a second about the inevitable criticism that he had to surround himself with great minds because he lacked one of his own.

His appointments led to more "Cheney is in charge" stories, but like water, the criticism ran off his back.

I was observing someone I thought of as a good manager who was assembling a strong team. That's when James Warren of the *Chicago Tribune* called.

Warren is one of the nation's leading experts on the Nixon tapes. He has listened to countless hours of them and knows their content like the back of his hand. He told me that thirty years earlier, when Donald Rumsfeld was a young White House aide, he had a meeting with President Nixon in which Nixon spoke about Rumsfeld's future and his low regard for Vice President Spiro Agnew; Nixon also spoke derisively of blacks as Rumsfeld sat there without challenging the President. The former President was profane and rude, just as the tapes revealed him to be on many topics. Warren asked me to contact Rumsfeld to see what he remembered of this episode.

A story like this had the potential to make his appointment controversial. Rumsfeld, who as a young Republican congressman in the sixties had voted for the Civil Rights Act and who had a strong record on civil rights, heard Nixon's rantings on race, didn't object, and now he was being named our nation's secretary of defense. The usual pattern is for a negative story like that to come out, liberal groups to demand the nomination be withdrawn, and a controversy erupts. Democrats feel pressure from a key constituent group, and the vote is in danger. That was the worst-case scenario, and I feared it. It didn't seem right to hold Rumsfeld accountable thirty years later for something Richard Nixon said, but that's the way Washington sometimes works.

I asked Warren what his deadline was, and I tried to obtain a copy of the tape so I could hear it myself. When the tape didn't arrive quickly enough, Warren gave me more time, believing it was only fair for me to run this story to ground. Not all reporters are willing to do that, but fair ones don't allow deadlines to get in the way of letting their sources validate the accuracy of information. By contrast, some reporters will work on a story for days, or even weeks, then they'll call you at the last minute and give you an hour or two to respond, no matter how much research you have to do to find the facts. If you're unable to get back to them in time, the story will say you didn't comment. I was grateful that Warren was fair.

I called Rumsfeld at his home in New Mexico, where he was preparing for his confirmation hearings. I told him what Warren had said about the tapes, and he said he had no recollection of the conversation. I told him that I was going to get the tape and that he should listen to it when he got back to Washington.

What happened when Rumsfeld and the tape arrived in Washington was fascinating. I took my copy to his office at the transition headquarters and played it for him. There he was, listening for the first time to Richard Nixon's famous secret taping system, with his voice on the line. I had never heard the Nixon tapes myself, and I watched Rumsfeld's reaction. He had no memory, none, of the conversation. Who could blame him? It was one of many conversations he'd had with Nixon more than three decades ago. It was bizarre, however, to think that the Nixon tapes might play a role in this administration.

I called Warren and told him the secretary nominee had listened to the tape and had no recollection of the conversation. Warren and I differed on some details of what the tape actually said, and I told him that Rumsfeld was proud to have been an early supporter of civil rights, going back to his first campaign, in 1962. Then I waited for the story.

True to his reputation, Warren's story was fair and was mostly about what he called the "Good Nixon and the Bad Nixon." He described that tape's criticisms of Nixon's Democratic rivals, such as Senators Ed Muskie, Edward Kennedy, and Hubert Humphrey. He described Nixon's criticisms of Agnew, and he transcribed what Nixon said about black Americans. The story appeared, and no controversy erupted.

AS 2001 BEGAN, I did my best to establish a work routine that mimicked the White House. I began twice-a-day briefings for the press, just as I would do starting January 20, when the President-elect was sworn in. Each morning I would lead a conference call for the press that was joined by sixty to seventy reporters. The call was patterned after a White House tradition known as the "gaggle." The gaggle is an on-the-record, off-camera, official question-and-answer session for the press. Because it's on the record, it's a serious session, but because no cameras are allowed, it is more relaxed than the lunchtime, on-camera, formal briefing. Unlike how I would do it at the White House, the transition gaggle was on the phone, not in person, which also made it easier. During the transition, most of the questions were about personnel issues, scheduling updates, and the President-elect's policy plans.

The on-camera briefings also began at this time. For the first time in my life, my job was to stand at a podium to answer questions, almost always live on the cable TV news shows. When I worked on the Hill, the rule was staffers never go on TV. On occasion we could be quoted in the newspapers if that was what the congressman or senator for whom we worked wanted, but the job of a Hill press secretary was to be behind the scenes.

During the Bush campaign, Karen Hughes was the principal spokesperson, and being a former television reporter, she had plenty of experience. I had worked the phones on a regular basis with the national press corps and often appeared on political news shows like *Hardball* or *Inside Politics*, but on-camera briefings were new for me. I viewed the transition briefings as great practice for what would soon follow. My goal was to be cautious and to let the President-elect, not me, be the news. I reiterated Candidate Bush's stands on domestic issues and said he looked forward to implementing his promises. I had no background in foreign policy, but fortunately I was able to punt on all foreign policy questions, saying that Bill Clinton was still the President and our nation speaks with one voice on foreign policy. If people were looking for anything new or controversial, they would have to wait until after Bush became President. I had a steep learning curve before I would be able to tackle tricky international matters, and I knew it. I had briefing books to read and experts to talk to. Little did I know how foreign policy would dominate my work.

I paid a visit to the White House for a meeting with Jake Siewert,

President Clinton's fourth press secretary. As I walked down the north driveway of the White House, the outdoor, prepositioned press cameras that hunt for newsworthy visitors were somehow trained on me. "Ari, will you come out and talk to us when you're done?" a reporter shouted. It felt strange that the press would call *me* to the microphones that were usually occupied by visiting members of Congress or cabinet members. The vice presidential candidate Joe Lieberman had appeared at the same spot during the recount to make his case. I was still used to being a behind-the-scenes staffer, and was now making my own transition to a new role. Siewert could not have been more courteous or professional, explaining many of the mechanical nuts and bolts that make the press office run. As much as there are ideological differences between press secretaries from administration to administration, we have a common bond in dealing with a tough press corps, and Jake was a pro.

A few days before the inaugural, the incoming chief of staff, Andy Card, gathered the couple hundred of us who were working in the transition for a meeting to describe White House life. Andy was a former deputy chief of staff for former President Bush, and he had worked in a senior position in President Reagan's White House. He also is one of the nicest, most soft-spoken, yet firmest people you'll ever meet in the political business. Most of us had never worked in the White House before, and we listened eagerly.

Andy wanted to inoculate us against what he called "White House–itis." People who work in the White House who *think* they're important usually are not, he said. He urged us to be modest and to work as a team. Andy hated what he called "silos," the divisions that form in which a worker is more loyal to his immediate boss than to the President or to the broader goals of the presidency. The Reagan White House, Andy told us, was divided into three camps, loyal to the top aides Mike Deaver, Jim Baker, and Ed Meese. In the new President's White House, he said, there would be no silos. We had been chosen because we were team players, and that was how he expected it to be.

The deputy chief of staff for operations, Joe Hagin, told us about internal White House operations. There was an existing city of workers at the White House who were there before us, and they would be there long after us. "Be good to the Secret Service," he told us. "They have a hard job to do. Respect the military staff. They serve the office of the President and will make our lives easier." It was heady stuff. It was just under two years since I had left the familiarity and comfort of Capitol Hill to join the presidential campaign trail. Inauguration Day loomed, and I would shortly enter the White House as the President's press secretary.

THREE

THE EARLY DAYS

SHORTLY BEFORE NOON on a freezing cold January 20, 2001, I met President-elect Bush after he had attended a private service at St. John's Church, across the street from the White House. The President-elect's motorcade traveled on a closed road for the one-block route to the north entrance of the White House. There President Clinton and Vice President Gore greeted President-elect Bush and Vice President–elect Cheney for a ceremonial reception before the two soon to be former leaders and two soon to be leaders would depart for the swearing in on Capitol Hill.

The President seldom uses the north entrance of the White House except on Inauguration Day. Except for a public tour I took when I visited the White House as a child, it was my first time through that door. Bush, Cheney, their wives, Andy Card, and I passed through the handsome marble lobby between the six columns that separate the lobby from Cross Hall, and we entered the Blue Room, an elegant, oval-shaped space. I stepped back against the wall and watched Bush and Clinton make small talk. Vice President Gore and Vice President–elect Cheney passed their time together in what had to be a tough moment for Gore. Chelsea Clinton came up to me to introduce herself. She couldn't have been more pleasant, and I privately thought well of the press for having allowed her to grow up without the constant glare of their coverage. As tough as the press can be, they try to search for lines of privacy, and they drew them squarely around Chelsea.

I couldn't believe I was standing there, witness to a private, peaceful transition that marked the ceremonial end to the most contested election in modern American history. There were no speeches or toasts, no formal remarks. President Clinton was his usual affable self, and President-elect Bush was polite but impatient. The gathering had an air of tension. Each leader knew it was his duty to be there, but I sensed each wanted to be somewhere else.

The reception ended, four motorcades waited outside, and we would soon be on our way. As anyone who has done presidential advance knows, lining up one motorcade, with all its cars, vans, limos, and security vehicles, is a complicated procedure. A typical motorcade consists of twenty to twenty-five vehicles, all of which must be in the right order. Scores of passengers who emerge from the White House have to be directed to their vehicles, usually in just a few minutes, so when the elected officials emerge they can depart with no delays. Once every four, sometimes only every eight years, four motorcades sit on the north driveway of the White House waiting to discharge their duties. Out of earshot of the four principals, the last argument of the campaign/transition broke out as the staff discovered that there was no one in charge. The Bush advance team thought the current President's staff was in charge, and President Clinton's staff, all of whom had vacated their offices, thought the Bush people were in charge. Somehow it got straightened out, and we left for the swearing in.

The weather wasn't much better than it had been three and a half months earlier, on election night in Texas, but this time the outcome was not subject to change. George W. Bush took the oath of office, marking the beginning of a new government. It was a Saturday, and the staff had been asked *not* to enter the West Wing so workers could tear up old carpets and put in new ones, paint walls, and generally use the brief respite of the passing of the presidency to clean up while few people would be around. Washington, that day and night, was full of inaugural balls and celebrations, marking the last time the new President's staff could kick back and relax without carrying the weight of the office around with us.

On Sunday, January 21, I awoke early and drove myself to 1600 Pennsylvania Avenue for the first time. In those days, before September 11, there was only one gate to go through before I arrived on West Executive Drive, where I parked my car steps from the western entrance to the West Wing. Today the senior staff pass three gates before reaching their parking spots, all three gates strong enough to stop a truck if one were foolish enough to attempt to smash through.

I walked through the West Wing lobby, down a corridor that bordered the Roosevelt Room, opened a door on my left which took me to the Upper Press Office, and some thirty feet from the Oval Office, I entered the spacious office that belongs to the White House press secretary. I opened the door and was surprised to find a meeting under way. A group from the economic policy staff were camped inside since they couldn't yet use their own offices. Their meeting broke up; I settled in and began my job.

The President's first week in office focused on his campaign commitment to strengthen schools throughout the country. He met with scores of Democratic and Republican congressional leaders to urge bipartisan reforms. On Monday, January 22, he invited a group of Democratic elder statesmen to the White House to stress his intention to lead in a bipartisan manner, just as he had done in the far less partisan capital of Austin. Former ambassador Robert Strauss, former Illinois Senator Paul Simon, former Pennsylvania Congressman Bill Gray III, and former Senator John Glenn joined the President in the Cabinet Room to see what could be accomplished together and to discuss whether the tone in Washington could indeed be changed.

When the President met with a group of Republican congressional leaders later that day, several told him that they had been in Congress for decades but this was the first time they'd ever visited a White House occupied by a Republican President while Republicans also held a majority in the Congress. The last time the White House and both chambers in the Congress were controlled by Republicans was in 1954. The Democrats had had full power as recently as 1994. Another congressman pointed out that two-thirds of the Republicans in the House had never served under a Republican President. Bush told the group he was determined to focus on education, tax cuts, getting prescription drugs to seniors, Social Security reform, and the transformation of the military. He told them he would work with Democrats, and he asked them to do the same. It was heady stuff and an exciting beginning.

Later that day, when I met with the White House press for the first of three hundred on-camera briefings, reality from the press's point of view set in.

The briefing room was packed, with reporters squeezed in everywhere. The room has seats for forty-eight reporters in eight rows of six. Seats are assigned, with the larger news organizations in the front and the smaller, less-known organizations in the back. For opening day, there must have been an additional fifty reporters jammed into the aisles and in the back of the James S. Brady Press Briefing Room.

Why is Bush meeting with *former* Democratic officials? one reporter shouted. Helen Thomas, the dean of the press corps, who now works as a columnist for Hearst newspapers, dismissed the Democrats as a group of "has-beens," and other reporters questioned why the new President would meet with elected Republicans on his first day but not yet with elected Democrats. "They're coming this week," I explained.

Like President Clinton before him, and like the former President Bush, the new President made one of his first actions to issue an executive order dealing with family planning groups that perform abortions overseas. Former President Bush, continuing the policies of Ronald Reagan, used his executive power to prohibit taxpayer funds from going to groups that perform, pay for, or advocate abortions overseas. President Clinton, two days after his inauguration, reversed the former President Bush's action and allowed family planning groups to receive funding. Similarly, two days after George W. Bush took office, he rescinded President Clinton's order and restored the status quo.

Most of the White House press corps didn't like it.

I was pelted with forty-one questions about Bush's action. "The natives don't use the money for abortion; they use it for nutrition or other sorts of issues," one reporter protested. The timing of the President's action concerned other reporters. "Why today, on his first day?" I was asked. "Because it's something he believes in," I replied. "Is this the nation's biggest priority? So it's his top priority?" came two in a row. I silently wondered if the press had objected to the timing when President Clinton addressed the same issue, from a different point of view, on the third day of his administration.

The CBS veteran John Roberts found an interesting way to lead into the issue. "Ari, I don't want to say that this abortion executive order might be your gays in the military," he began, comparing Bush's action to Clinton's highly controversial and unsuccessful attempt to allow gays to serve openly in the military, "because it's unlikely that the Joint Chiefs of Staff would march in here and oppose it. But do you not risk being distracted in your legislative agenda by doing this right out of the box?"

"No," I replied. "I think it's something everybody expected."

Later I read the transcript of the briefing when former President Clinton had issued his executive order allowing taxpayer dollars to be used for family planning groups abroad. His spokesman, George Stephanopoulos, took six questions on the topic, including two asking if Clinton would take additional steps to have the government fund other abortions, such as those for women in the military. I took almost seven times as many, most of which were hostile to the President's action.

The difference in how ABC and CBS News covered Bush's executive order compared to Clinton's was striking.

"President Clinton kept a promise today on the twentieth anniversary of the Supreme Court decision legalizing abortion," ABC's Peter Jennings reported on January 22, 1993.

"President Bush also made anti-abortion conservatives happy, reinstalling a Reagan-era policy that prohibited the funding of family planning groups that provide abortion counseling services overseas," ABC's Terry Moran reported on January 22, 2001.

Same story at CBS.

"Today with the stroke of a pen, President Clinton delivered on his campaign promise to cancel several anti-abortion regulations of the Reagan-Bush years," Dan Rather said on January 22, 1993.

Compare it to their Bush coverage: "This was President Bush's first day at the office, and he did something to quickly please the right flank in his party," Rather told his viewers eight years later.

For a press corps that prizes its role as a neutral observer, these two important networks reported President Clinton's pro-choice action in a positive light while they reported President Bush's pro-life action in a highly political vein.

A few other skirmishes broke out the first week. California was experiencing a severe energy problem that many experts feared would lead to blackouts. I announced that a meeting had already been convened by cabinet secretaries to explore the options available to help the state and to develop a comprehensive national energy policy. "Do you mean you're just going to ignore it?" I was asked right after I'd said the meeting was held to address it.

The Associated Press's Ron Fournier tried to bait me into a fight with Bush's primary opponent, Republican Senator John McCain. "Senator McCain in his news conference today about campaign finance reform said that he has a mandate, too. Do you agree he has a mandate?" Ron asked. A mandate meant that the American people supported Senator McCain's version of campaign finance reform. If McCain *had* a mandate, I knew the questions would focus on why Bush wasn't acting on McCain's mandate.

Senator McCain has a passion for reform, and he has a right to push it, I said, ducking the mandate issue.

"Does he have a mandate to get it done the way he wants it done?" Ron asked. The process means we'll work together, I said. Ron persisted, asking a third time if McCain had a mandate. I ducked the issue again.

If I said that Senator McCain *did* have a mandate for campaign finance reform, the press would have demanded to know why Bush wasn't immediately pressing to enact the reforms into law. If I said he didn't have a mandate, a White House versus McCain clash would have been born. Bush was interested in campaign finance reform, but it wasn't as high a priority for him as it was for the Arizona senator. Ron's question was one of the first of a daily stream in which reporters tried to get me to argue with someone, anyone, the more controversial and newsworthy, the better. Usually I was alert enough to see the trap getting laid and to stay away from it. On some notable occasions, I took the bait and regretted doing so. I ducked this one all the way and kept McCain versus Bush out of the news.

It is interesting that in my very first briefing, more than two years before the war with Iraq, Major Garrett, who was with CNN at the time, asked me, "The Clinton administration apparently has recently passed on to the President, and Defense Secretary Rumsfeld, information that Iraq has rebuilt biological/chemical factories. How long have you known about this? Are you at all irritated that the Clinton administration knew this, did nothing about it? What are the intentions of the Bush administration now to deal with this particular problem?"

"I'm not going to look backward in time and reflect on anything that came before," I responded. "But I will say, in regard to what you said, that the President expects Saddam Hussein to live up to his agreements, and that deals especially with the elimination of weapons of mass destruction."

A few minutes later, Major asked again on Iraq, "You said you expect Saddam Hussein to live up to his commitments. One of the ways the world can be sure of that is to bring inspectors back in. What is the administration going to do to try to get inspectors in? Is there a timetable for that? How are you going to go about that?"

I answered, "I'm not prepared to address that today, but we will—the President will continue to make sure that we work to protect our interests in the Middle East, including, of course, Iraq. But it's too soon to address that question."

Little did I or the press know then how much this issue would come back to dominate our lives.

WHITE HOUSE LIFE

In just under twenty years working as an aide on Capitol Hill, I visited the White House on a handful of occasions, each time only briefly. I once ate lunch in the White House mess with Tim Archie, a friend who worked for then President Ronald Reagan. Under former President Bush, another friend, Cathy Jeavons, took me and some of my friends on a tour of the West Wing, where I got to stand at the press secretary's podium. I was one of three thousand people invited to the South Lawn signing of the peace agreement between Yasir Arafat and Yitzhak Rabin when Bill Clinton was President. And I once got to sit in the West Wing lobby as I waited for a former boss, Texas Congressman Bill Archer, to emerge from a meeting. But now not only was my desk thirty feet from the Oval Office but I also flew on Marine One and Air Force One. I attended meetings in the Situation Room, the Cabinet Room, the Roosevelt Room, and of course the Oval Office, where I participated in all the President's economic and domestic policy briefings and almost all his summit meetings with foreign leaders. When he made phone calls to foreign leaders, he often asked me into the Oval Office to listen. I attended cabinet meetings and almost all the President's meetings with members of Congress. National Security Council meetings and the President's CIA briefings were off-limits, but President Bush, without telling me everything, wanted me to know as much as I could about what was going on, and he trusted that I had the discretion and judgment to keep internal deliberations private while informing the press and the public about as much as I could. I had access to the Oval Office any time I needed to ask the President a question.

I ate in a small, private dining room, a mess within the White House mess that was reserved for top staff and members of the President's cabinet. It was wonderful and exciting, particularly for someone who grew up a Democrat.

I WAS RAISED a liberal by two Democratic parents. I was proud to call myself a liberal when I entered college in 1978 in Middlebury, Vermont, but thanks to Jimmy Carter, I graduated a conservative Democrat. After the Soviet invasion of Afghanistan, I became increasingly conservative, especially on foreign policy and defense-related matters. I didn't care much for Carter's foreign policies, which I found to be weak and naïve, and I became a believer in Ronald Reagan's advocacy of peace through strength. Having come of age immediately after Watergate and Vietnam, I didn't think America should feel guilty about its role in the world. It seemed to me that our government was unnecessarily apologizing for events around the world. I loved Ronald Reagan's optimism, and I started to think about becoming a Republican, even though I knew it would horrify my parents. When a speaker from the CIA came to give a speech one year, it bothered me that a Middlebury professor dismissed the CIA as "propagandists." I increasingly turned away from the Democratic Party. Six months after my graduation from Middlebury in 1982, I became a Republican.

The final straw for me was the nuclear freeze. After the Soviet Union deployed intermediate-range nuclear missiles in Eastern Europe, President Reagan proposed counterdeploying Pershing and cruise missiles in Western Europe. My Democratic Party argued that the United States already had enough nuclear weaponry to destroy the Soviet Union many times, so there was no need to counterdeploy. Respond, my party argued, with a nuclear freeze.

That made no sense to me. If the Soviets saw they could engage in a military buildup without any response from the United States, what would stop them from becoming increasingly dangerous and more provocative? Hundreds of thousands of German and French protesters took to the streets to protest Reagan's plans. They thought he was a militant and a cowboy. It didn't matter to Ronald Reagan, however. He fought for his beliefs, refusing to let the Soviet Union get away with their military buildup, and he convinced reluctant European governments to go along. He called the Soviet Union an evil empire, and I agreed with him. As a result, the Soviet Union couldn't keep up with the United States and the West, and it collapsed, bringing freedom to hundreds of millions of people, including my Hungarian aunts, uncles, and cousins, whom I'd visited in Budapest in 1974, when they lived under Communism. They live there still, but now they are free.

My first job in politics was for a New York State assemblyman who ran in 1982 against Richard Ottinger, the incumbent Democratic congressman from Westchester, where I was raised. My oldest brother had been a member of Ottinger's Washington staff. I was still a Democrat, but I thought Ottinger was too liberal, and I was content to work against him. I liked his Republican challenger, Jon Fossel, and I started to realize Republicans weren't as evil as I had been raised to believe.

We lost the election, but I got bit by the political bug. I moved to Washington, where I took a part-time job on the phone banks in the basement of the Republican National Committee raising money for the GOP. After three months searching, I landed my first full-time job as the press secretary to a congressman from Long Island, Norman Lent.

I loved what press secretaries did. Publicizing my boss's ideas and initiatives was a very measurable action. Newspapers were published every day, and newscasts aired each night. Whenever my boss got a mention, I found it exciting. Plus, I enjoyed politics and thought I had found my calling. I stayed a press secretary for most of my career, speaking on behalf of elected officials, learning the ropes, and landing jobs with more senior congressmen.

There were so few Republicans in the House of Representatives in the eighties that we really didn't count. Reporters weren't much interested in what Republicans had to say. I remember when our minority staffs published studies or reports that differed from the Democratic majority's views, the press didn't pay much attention. Our work was dismissed by most congressional reporters because they came from "House Republicans."

In 1989 I went to work for Senator Pete Domenici of New Mexico, the former chairman of the Budget Committee and one of the most respected people in Congress. From him I learned that the best press comes from the best substance. Under him I began learning policy issues, particularly on domestic matters, like the budget.

Politically, I viewed myself as conservative, but a Jewish upbringing and a family full of Democrats made me realize there is more than one way to look at issues. I thought the Democrats sounded as if they cared about people, particularly minorities and the poor, more than the Republicans. I thought Republican ideas, however, were more effective at helping people. I didn't agree with everything my new party stood for, but I was proud to call myself a Republican and never had any regrets about leaving the Democratic Party behind.

Sixteen years after I arrived in Washington, I entered my fifth year as the communications director for the House Ways and Means Committee, the most powerful committee in Congress. I enjoyed what I was doing, particularly for a boss as good as mine—Texas Congressman Bill Archer, the committee chairman. I also enjoyed the breadth of issues that Ways and Means covered. Social Security, Medicare, welfare, international trade, and taxes were my bread and butter. I liked learning the substance of these issues and discussing the committee's plans with reporters. Republicans were in the majority when I was at Ways and Means, and now the press paid us plenty of attention. In January 1999 I was approached by Kieran Mahoney, a friend who also was the chief consultant on Elizabeth Dole's presidential campaign. They needed a communications director, and he asked me if I wanted the job. The chance of working on a presidential campaign in a senior position doesn't come around too often. It was hard to leave Bill Archer, but I accepted the job. When Dole dropped out of the race in late 1999 Karen Hughes asked me to move to Austin to work for Governor Bush on his race. I wasn't sure I wanted to do it.

I had never worked for a private-sector company, and after seventeen years in government, I was ready to leave politics behind. I had two good offers in the private sector, but Karen convinced me to visit Austin to meet with Bush. I instantly took a liking to him. I found him warm, friendly, and gracious, with a great sense of humor. He struck me as an enjoyable person to be around. He also had a good chance of being elected President, and I figured I had one more race left in me. I packed my bags and moved to Texas, where I was a New Yorker living in the fun-filled city of Austin.

Perhaps because I was raised by Democrats in a very close family, I was able to enjoy my political duties without taking the differences between people too seriously. When I disagreed with someone politically, I tried to do so with respect. As deeply as I held my views, I recognized that other earnest people might hold opposite views just as deeply. And they too care about our country. I also thought being raised a Democrat helped me prepare for my briefings with the press—many of the arguments the press used against me, at my briefings, whether they were playing devil's advocate or not, were the same things my parents said to me on the phone.

PRESIDENT BUSH RUNS a very inclusive, tight ship. He is one of the most uplifting, personnel-oriented, tough, demanding, humorous bosses you'll ever find. His pat on the back is as hard as his kick in the butt. He demands good work from his aides, and he praises people when they've done well. He is fast-paced in everything he does. In my experience, he liked his briefings direct and to the point. He enjoyed a good argument between competing sides, provided the argument stayed within the walls of the Oval, as the staff calls it. He had a careful review process that allowed ample time for deliberation, debate, and consideration. Thanks to Andy Card and Deputy Chief of Staff for Policy Josh Bolten, issues were brought to his attention well before they turned into crises. He created an orderly, disciplined system in which important matters rose to his attention and lesser issues—"small ball" he called them—were handled by the staff. His briefings were lively, interesting, and informative. As the press secretary, I watched and heard the deliberations in the inner sanctum, and I took my guidance from the President about what he wanted to say publicly and when he wanted to say it. I freely offered my advice and input, particularly about the communications ramifications of any potential decision.

Once the President made his decisions on various policies, he didn't second-guess them. He understood that it's only the tough calls that make it to the Oval Office. The 90 to 10 percent decisions don't need to make their way to him. His job is to hear both sides of the 51 to 49 percent decisions and then act. When he made up his mind, he gave the staff its direction and expected us to carry it out. He didn't like what he called "hand wringers," people who could never decide or who, once they decided on a course of action, looked back and wondered why they didn't follow a different course. When former President Clinton submitted his first budget to Congress in 1993, Democrats and Republicans alike learned that he was willing to change most of it whenever they objected. The more Clinton yielded, the more he was asked to yield. When Bush made a proposal, he was known for sticking to it, getting everything he could until the last possible moment, when it came time to compromise and get things done. Some leaders can get paralyzed by the "what ifs" and never make up their minds, or once they make them up, they easily reverse course. Bush understood the nuances and the subtleties, but he also was determined to lead and implement his decisions, domestic and international.

To his critics, the President wasn't thoughtful, intellectual, or even curious. I found him to be the opposite. He was quick-witted, sharp, and he had a CEO's ability to see the big picture while keeping his experts focused on how to achieve it. Leaders can get bogged down in detail if they're not careful—it's easy to do—but then they often lose their ability to lead. For example, the President regularly told his cabinet and staff to hold off on making any compromises on the 2001 tax bill until he directed them to do so. Thanks to a rigorous briefing schedule, he stayed on top of all the congressional maneuverings, knowing the concerns of every senator or congressman who could make or break the deal. He kept in regular touch with these leaders, either on the phone or in person. He always thought Louisiana Senator John Breaux would be the key Democrat in achieving a compromise. Just like a good poker player, Bush knew when to hold his cards and when to fold them. He resisted all compromise until the last minute, and as a result, he got a tax cut that substantially matched the one he'd proposed, albeit slightly reduced in size. Presidents don't often get their way with Congress; President Bush was largely successful in getting his.

President Clinton learned this lesson the hard way. After inserting himself, often unsuccessfully, in the minutiae of countless legislative controversies in 1993 and 1994, particularly on his health care plan, he changed tactics when Republicans took the Congress and had far more success managing the big picture, empowering his chief of staff—not himself—to be his lead congressional negotiator. From that point forward, President Clinton was largely successful in negotiating with a Republican Congress. Legislators and White House staff should negotiate the details, because, Bush believed, the power of the presidency is to set the agenda and lead the nation to achieve the big picture. That's where Bush focused his efforts.

In his public speeches, Bush didn't often give people a glimpse of his thought process. Instead, he's crisp, conclusive, and to the point. He doesn't engage in self-probing doubt or public introspection. His public remarks reflect his private approach—he focuses on the bottom line and tries to lead the nation to it. He calls meetings where he directs his speechwriters about the message he wants to convey, and he demands to see drafts many days before the speech is scheduled. For States of the Union and major addresses, he would meet with the speechwriters a month or two before the speech to go over its outline. He regularly wrote all over the drafts with a black Sharpie pen, ordering one change or another. He didn't show it to the outside world, but he was plenty hands-on about his speeches.

When he makes up his mind about a policy, he sticks to it and does his best to drive others there. Critics who don't like his policies can't abide how steadfast and surely he stands by them. The combination of his policies and his decisiveness drives them crazy.

In addition to obvious differences on policy, one of the reasons Bush's detractors don't like him is his direct, to-the-point speaking style. Former President Clinton was a master of publicly intellectualizing the intricacies of an issue. He often framed the pros and the cons, walking people through his thinking process, and then he announced his stand. People could *see* him think. He was good at being deliberative in public, particularly when issues were most important, controversial, or emotional. Bush is the opposite. With one or two notable exceptions, particularly his August 2001 speech on stem cell research, President Bush would listen carefully to the pros and cons within the confines of the Oval Office, where often the debate was spirited as he pushed, probed, and prodded his staff to make certain he was hearing all sides. But when Bush made up his mind and announced it to the public, he would lay out his reasons in stark and direct terms. On stem cell, he carefully and publicly described both sides of an issue he had pondered for months, and then he announced his position. On virtually all his other policy pronouncements, he was plainspoken and direct.

Two weeks after the September 11 attack, the President visited the FBI to post a list of the world's most wanted terrorists. He said, "I see things this way: The people who did this act on America, and who may be planning further acts, are evil people. They don't represent an ideology, they don't represent a legitimate political group of people. They're flat evil. That's all they can think about, is evil. And as a nation of good folks, we're going to hunt them down, and we're going to find them, and we will bring them to justice."

When we left the FBI for the drive back to the White House, the President asked me to join him in his limo. We talked about his remarks. The issue of terrorism, I suggested to him, was more complicated than "good versus evil." I said that there were many nuances to this issue and many shades of gray. He listened to me and said, "If this isn't good versus evil, what is?" He then reminded me that Ronald Reagan didn't go to Berlin and say to Mikhail Gorbachev, "Put a gate in this wall." He didn't say, the President continued, "take down a few bricks." No, Bush reminded me, Reagan told Gorbachev, "Tear down this wall." Tear the whole thing down. Reagan was clear, concise, and he spoke to the big picture. He gave people hope, and he defined right from wrong. That was Reagan's style. It's Bush's style too.

There are millions of Americans who question how we as a country can know with such certainty what is right and wrong. When it came to the defining divide of the Bush years—his decision to use force in Iraq—his opponents seethed at the President, wondering how he could militarily impose his will on others according to what he saw as "right and wrong." Even before the failure to find weapons of mass destruction, millions of people on the left opposed his decision to use force. The President's moral judgment about the threat Saddam presented, and his willingness to depose him by force, left his critics angry and bitter. What his critics see as his greatest weakness, his supporters see as his greatest strength. Bush understood the nuances. He knew there are shades of gray, and he often gave Secretary of State Colin Powell the difficult job of dealing with them, especially with our allies.

But to his supporters, myself included, it is his willingness to call things good or evil, to make such powerful moral declarations—and to act on them—that makes him a strong leader. His approach made my job both tougher and easier. I don't think most of the White House press corps agreed with his version of right and wrong, and they regularly challenged it, calling on me to prove his statements or explain them. Conversely, the stronger the stand he took, the easier my job was. It's harder to explain indecision than it is a firm decision. I was speaking for a decisive, strong President, and I liked it.

Bush's schedule was consistent and regimented. It helped drive a disciplined, well-run White House. He would arrive in the Oval at about 7:00 each morning; there he would be greeted by Andy Card. Andy, always an early riser, usually got to work a little before 6:00. Andy would go over any overnight updates if necessary, review the day, and then the President would read his intelligence briefings, write notes, and make calls.

His mornings were devoted to national security. He typically had an 8:00 CIA briefing, and, as often as necessary, a meeting of the National Security Council; after 9/11, an FBI briefing and a homeland security briefing were added.

His approach to personnel issues was one of the least known but most important aspects of his presidency. For a typical presidential briefing, the lead expert and perhaps a deputy from the domestic or foreign policy staff would enter the Oval Office to brief the President in the company of the usual senior aides, like Andy Card, Condi Rice, Josh Bolten, Karen Hughes or Dan Bartlett, Nick Calio or David Hobbs of Congressional Affairs, Karl Rove, and myself. When it came to the personnel meetings he held a couple times a week, however, almost all the personnel office was invited to attend—about ten people.

Knowing how much work needed to be delegated to others in the government, and aware that he couldn't personally interview everyone applying for the hundreds of senior positions that needed to be filled, the President bore in on his personnel officers. He wanted to look in the eye the person who was doing the interviewing for him. "What questions did you ask? How did he or she reply? What talents does he or she have? Is this person a team player?"

The President spent a significant amount of time on personnel issues, working to hire the right people for the right jobs. He had witnessed people who he thought had let his father down, especially at the end of former President Bush's time in office, when it looked like he might lose his bid for reelection. George W. Bush thought they were at the White House to serve themselves, not the President. He stressed building a team where everyone worked well together.

To prepare for my day, I awoke at 5:00. By 5:10 A.M., I was seated at my kitchen counter, coffee in one hand and the *Washington Post* and the *New York Times* in the other. I read the papers not just to see what was in the news. I read them knowing that I would shortly take a quiz based on what was in the news—a quiz on live TV, where the questioners were the White House press corps.

I arrived at the West Wing between 7:00 and 7:15. My Secret Service code name was Matrix, and as I arrived, the uniformed division sergeants would say into the microphones tucked in their sleeves, "Matrix has arrived." My staff usually kidded me, giving me the same greeting.

At 7:15, I would meet in my office with my top deputies, Scott McClellan, Claire Buchan, and Sean McCormack. The press secretary's office is one of the largest in the West Wing—it has to be in order to cram all those reporters in there. It's about the same size as the national security adviser's office. Only the Oval Office and the chief of staff's office are larger. The office had a working fireplace that I often used in the winter and three large, floor-to-ceiling windows that look out over the driveway leading to the West Wing's front door. I had four television sets and TiVo so I could stay on top of the news.

My staff and I divided up the nation's leading newspapers, and they would brief me on what they saw in the *Wall Street Journal, USA Today,* and other papers. I also received a two-inch-thick copy of press clippings from across the country that included the network news transcripts from the night before. I always watched the network news myself before I went home, so by 7:30 in the morning I was armed with every bit of reporting I could find.

At 7:30, I attended the senior staff meeting in the Roosevelt Room, just a few paces from the front door of the Oval Office. The meeting was chaired by Andy Card, and all the top aides to the President were there, including Condoleezza Rice and her deputy, Steve Hadley. Karen Hughes, Karl Rove, Judge Al Gonzales, the President's legal counsel, and Nick Calio, the head of Congressional Affairs. My job was to speak second. The President's scheduler spoke first, describing his meetings for the day, and then my job was to describe the news the White House would face.

If the news was good, I would seldom bring it up at this meeting because I knew the press wouldn't ask me about it. If there was bad news—if there was a report out of the Pentagon that I was unfamiliar with, if there was controversy, I would raise it. I knew those were the issues that the press wanted to talk about. It didn't make me the cheeriest fellow at the morning meeting, but since all the top staff were assembled in one place at one time, it gave me a good head start to find answers to the hardest questions that I knew were an hour or two away. "Condi, is this true?" I would ask. "How would *you* respond?" "Andy, can you shed some light on this?" That was part of how I gathered my information to share with the press.

The *only* way to speak for the President is to hear from him directly. I typically spent from two to four hours of my day in meetings with him, listening to what he said, listening to what he listened to, figuring out what I would say to the press.

My first meeting with the press was the gaggle, which took place each morning at 9:45. Thirty to forty reporters, notebooks and tape recorders in hand, would cram into my office to hear me walk through the President's schedule, and then they fired away, asking questions about whatever the controversy du jour was, and anything else they wanted to ask. Every word I said was transcribed by a White House stenographer as my staff sat nearby. I sat behind my long, curved desk, looking at the mob towering above. It lasted only fifteen minutes, and then it usually took another five minutes to shoo the last reporter out since almost every one of them had "just one more question." The gaggle was serious business, but it had an informal feel to it, at least until September 11.

On September 12, 2001, I moved the gaggle into the formal briefing room, since the number of journalists covering the White House increased dramatically overnight. To keep the gaggle as informal as I could, I left my jacket in the office, but the good-natured banter that had marked the informal gaggle was slowly replaced by the seriousness of the briefing room.

Today the gaggle is more like the briefings Marlin Fitzwater used to hold before the advent of live cable TV. Marlin didn't allow television coverage of his briefings except for the first five minutes. The absence of the cameras had a remarkably calming effect on reporters, and on me. The TV-less gaggle typically lacks the contentiousness, the posturing, and the debate that often mark the televised briefing. The gaggle was mostly civilized, while the briefing increasingly turned into part business, part theater, and every now and then a good bit of nonsense.

The public never get to see the gaggle, but they hear about it almost immediately. The wire services—Associated Press, Reuters, and Bloomberg—are big enough to have one reporter at the gaggle and another in their tiny office space on the other side of the briefing room, instantly ready to move a story if anything is newsworthy. The cable television reporters would leave the gaggle and walk fifty yards to the North Lawn of the White House to go live on the air with any news that was made.

The President sometimes would sarcastically tell his staff that he was in a "news blackout" and didn't pay attention to what was in the news. I found him instead to be keenly interested in what the press were thinking. Almost every day he would ask me what was on the minds of the White House press corps. "How was the briefing?" He wanted to know what the press asked me and how I replied. He wanted to know about the controversy du jour and how the press were approaching it.

The President typically spent a portion of his morning reading the headlines, checking out articles that interested him, maintaining a healthy awareness of what the press were reporting. He wasn't consumed by it, but he paid it considerable attention. To the dismay of many TV reporters, he only occasionally watched the network news or the endless stream of political commentary on the cable TV chat shows. For the most part, he counted on me and Karen Hughes or Dan Bartlett, the communications director, to fill him in, but he didn't lose any sleep over what was on TV. He presumed most of it would be highly opinionated and largely negative, and he expected the communications staff to deal with it. Odd as it may sound to most people who depend solely on the media for information, the President is able to get his news before it's made. He doesn't need to tune in to find out what happens on any given day. When you're the President, you're often the one who makes it happen. For the President, watching the news doesn't mean learning what is happening, it more often means hearing other people's explanations of what is happening. The President's preference was to rely on his staff to inform him about "how it was playing."

Two or three times a week, a press pool of ten or so reporters would join the President before or after his meetings to listen to any public remarks he might offer, and then it was their turn to ask him whatever questions were on their minds. Before the meetings began, I would tell the President what questions I thought he would get. I had a pretty good read on what the press were thinking, having typically been asked the questions myself at the briefing or the gaggle.

Talk about accountability. Either I was right or I was wrong, and the President, and the rest of the staff who were in on the meeting, would know it. When I told Bush what questions I thought he would get, sometimes he would bounce his answers off of me or the policy expert in the room, and then he would face the music. On days when he wasn't going to see the press corps, he still asked me what was on their minds. For a man who wasn't overly worried about what the press were reporting, he sure was interested in my scouting reports about what they were working on.

Much of my day was focused on preparing for my on-camera briefing with the press corps. The press have a hard job to do, particularly in the Bush White House, where they complained they didn't have many sources for news. As glamorous as it sounds to be a White House correspondent, they work in terribly cramped quarters, but at least they have office space in the West Wing. There is enough room on Air Force One for only the revolving press pool, so most reporters fly a separate press charter that leaves Andrews Air Force Base hours before the President does, so when he travels in the early morning, as he often does, their day can begin at 4:00 or 5:00 A.M.

The White House press corps are always skeptical, and sometimes cynical. White House reporters are some of the smartest, toughest, and most experienced reporters you'll ever meet. As friendly as they can be in one-on-one settings, gather them together for the televised press briefing at the White House, and they're not the friendliest crew. They're not paid to be friendly, however. They're paid to cover the news.

White House reporters tend to set the tone for much of the media. They regularly have their stories published on the front page, the most sought after page for any reporter on any beat. They regularly kick off the evening TV newscasts. "We begin at the White House tonight . . ." is a common refrain of the network anchors. All this and more makes the White House briefing room a hotbed of confrontation and tension unlike any other briefing room in the government or anywhere else.

Unlike in most White Houses, the top staff of the Bush White House showed little interest in talking with the press, making reporters' jobs more difficult. Andy Card and Josh Bolten didn't think it was their job to answer reporters' phone calls. They preferred to focus on their governing responsibilities and thought it was the duty of the press office to work with the press. They would take calls and do interviews when I asked them to, as long as I didn't ask too often. Karl Rove knew he would never get anything else done if he answered every call reporters made to him. The press alternated between being fascinated and being perturbed by Karl's acumen and influence, and they wanted him all the time. Dan Bartlett in the Communications Office would naturally talk to the press, but many reporters complained that they couldn't get their calls returned and that everything seemed to run through the press office, although I'm sure the press had several good senior sources who I never knew about.

To much of the press, it appeared as if we were trying to manage the news and deny reporters sources. In reality, it was more the nature of the people who worked in the White House that decided whether reporters got their calls returned. If the top staff had wanted to talk to the press, they would have and they could have. No press secretary can control who picks up the phone either to make or to receive phone calls.

While I was press secretary, the President was available to the press, usually for three or four questions a day, two or three days a week. While Bush wasn't a fan of formal news conferences and rarely held any, he was regularly available to answer inquiries on the hot news of the day. He was disciplined, knew what he wanted to say, and was seldom "off message." He would often repeat the same statement to the press, no matter how many different ways they asked their questions. He seldom made mistakes or inadvertently created a controversy through what he said, and for many reporters, who are always looking for the next big story, the White House's message discipline came to be frustrating. If the President didn't slip up, and if the senior staff weren't talking all that much, that, for the most part, brought the press to me at the daily briefing.

I always did my best to remain calm at the briefings, telling myself that the press were doing their job and it wasn't personal. They were *supposed* to ask the hard questions, putting me as spokesman on the record for the President. I knew they would prod and poke, and they would repeat their questions countless times, sometimes making me feel like a piñata, hoping to get me off stride so I would make a mistake or lose my temper. I constantly reminded myself not to take the bait, to be steady, doing my job by saying what I thought.

No one can be the White House press secretary if he or she doesn't believe in the President and his policies. Believing gave me the backbone and strength to take the podium, repeating the President's message no matter how hard the questioning. I'm also calm by nature, and that helped me stand my ground as the press fired away. My discipline at times frustrated the press, but it brought me comfort. The press love press secretaries who privately criticize the President and his policies, or fill reporters in on controversies inside the Oval Office. That wasn't how I did my job, even though it meant I would take my lumps from some in the press corps.

At the beginning of the administration, I arrived at the podium with a big three-ring binder containing "talking points" arranged in alphabetical order. I relied on it especially on foreign policy issues, which were new to me. The National Security Council staff wrote up my "points," and I did my best to flip to the appropriate page and read them.

The more I attended the summits, however, the less I needed the formal points—I heard from the President directly and increasingly found my own way of expressing myself. After about six months I abandoned the notebook, which was awkward to flip through as the press sat there awaiting my answers, and instead carried one piece of paper, on which I jotted a few notes on the hot issue or issues of the day.

I would regularly touch base with Karen Hughes or Condi Rice or a senior domestic policy aide to make sure what I wanted to say meshed with their way of thinking. Karen especially would sometimes suggest a phrase or an approach to use. She is a good wordsmith, and her advice was helpful. This routine contact was also one of the ways the White House maintained its discipline. Getting along with each other and talking to each other isn't complicated, and it sure helped us sound like we were one White House that spoke with one voice.

I also relied heavily on my deputies. They routinely filled me in on what they were hearing from the various government agencies they were liaisons to. We talked countless times through the day, and they would sit down fifteen minutes before my briefings to fire questions at me in anticipation of what the press would ask. I bounced my answers off them and fine-tuned my responses depending on their advice.

When I was ready, I told my staff to give the press a two-minute warning that the briefing was about to begin.

Much of the briefing is focused on the hot news of the day, and it's a serious affair. Reporters play their role in our free society by asking the hard questions, challenging the government, and forcing the White House to think through, or at least be able to explain, the President's stands. Often at policy meetings with President Bush, I would say, If a certain policy were adopted, here's how the press will criticize it, helping the President and the staff to think through the ramifications of their decisions as well as the best way to communicate them.

On the one hand, tough questions, repetitive questions, and sometimes hostile questions are the routine, and that's territory that comes with the press secretary job. On the other hand, the briefing in the modern media era can be less than serious and informative, and can revert to a game of trip the press secretary or an attempt to lure the President into a problem or controversy anywhere around the world, even if the United States, or the President, isn't involved. If there's trouble between India and Pakistan over Kashmir, the press want to know what the President intends to do about it. If he didn't make a phone call to address the problem, the White House press corps will ask why not. If a Republican congressman made an irresponsible statement, the White House press corps would ask me if the President agreed with it, or whether he would condemn it, even if the President had nothing to do with the statement.

To me, this is a growing problem for America's political system and for the White House press corps. It's not a question of bias, partisanship, or press-driven ideology. Instead, it's a focus on conflict, particularly if it's a conflict the press corps can attach to the President. It's the nature of the White House press corps, regardless of who's in power. They are masters of being the devil's advocate, able to take with passion the opposite side of whatever issue the President supports. My job was to field their questions, no matter how pointed, calmly.

At one briefing, in the lead-up to the war with Iraq, Kelly Wallace of CNN asked me if the administration was disappointed that Syria had failed to attend a key meeting of the United Nations Security Council. In fact, Syria *was* expected to be absent, but they had shown up, a last-minute development unknown to Kelly. When I told her Syria had shown up, AP's Ron Fournier facetiously asked me if the administration was disappointed that Syria *did* show up. Ron is one of the best, most serious, and most personable reporters in the business, and he was having a little fun, but his aside shows how quickly the press can challenge whatever they want to, any time they want to.

The cameras in the briefing room have become part of the problem. Given the turmoil it would create if the White House sought a return to the old days, without the cameras rolling, there can be no turning back the clock. The first briefing ever held on live TV was poor Mike Mc-Curry's the day the Monica Lewinsky story broke. Mike allowed the cable TV cameras into the briefing room in the mid-1990s in an effort to help the start-up all-news cable networks, and he tells audiences during his speeches now that he regrets it.

Mark Knoller of CBS Radio, one of the most respected veteran reporters in the White House, told me he decided to skip the briefing and attend only the gaggle, adding he didn't know how I put up with some of the questions I was asked at the briefing.

Although I think it's too late to change, the cameras often turned many reporters and me, especially when the news was hot and we all knew people were watching, into performers. Reporters prefaced their questions with lengthy preambles; they were quick to interrupt and contradict me; they jockeyed to see who could ask the same question in a tougher way, hoping I would somehow give a different answer when I got the same question for the twelfth time; or they set traps, asking me about topics they had no intention of reporting on (will you use nuclear weapons in Afghanistan? for example), simply hoping to stump me or trip me on an issue that might turn into news if I stumbled badly enough. A good joust on TV could also make a reporter look tough and aggressive to an editor who might be watching.

"Ari, if I could just come back to the tax cut," began Corbett Daly of AFX News at a televised briefing in the spring of 2003. "Does the President consider the chairman of the Senate Finance Committee somebody who keeps his word?"

"I would never make any statement about any of the 535 members of Congress to the contrary," I responded, sensing a trip-the-press-secretary trap. The issue was whether the President's proposal for a $750 billion tax cut would be passed by Congress since many members, including Senator Chuck Grassley, the influential chairman of the Senate Finance Committee who preferred a $550 billion tax cut, thought it was too big.

How can you say yes and still believe Grassley is someone who keeps his word? Corbett asked me. "You're assuming that it's still possible to go to $750 billion, but if he [Grassley] keeps his word, it won't [be]."

I responded, "That's why it's a false choice, because many members of Congress believe in things, fight for things, and not everything everybody believes in and fights for gets agreed to. . . . If every time any one member of Congress said, This is the final outcome, well, then we would never have anything done in the Congress."

The reporter kept pressing his case, pointing out that Grassley was a powerful senator and his opinion about the size of the tax bill was influential. I pushed back, pointing out that there were several important members of Congress and the President would work with all of them to get his $750 billion tax cut passed.

"So you agree . . . that he's irrelevant?" Corbett asked; this question I chose to ignore.

That's all too often how the game is played. President Bush had proposed a $750 billion tax cut. Senator Grassley wanted to reduce it to $550 billion. Depending on which congressman or senator you talked to, you could get a quote saying the Bush plan was too big or too small. As chairman of the Finance Committee, Grassley wielded considerable weight. But so did the congressional leadership, all of whom supported the Bush tax cut. Negotiations would ensue, and an agreement would be reached.

Was this routine policy difference a matter of "honesty" and a measure of "someone's word"? Was I calling the senator "irrelevant" because he and the President differed on the size of the tax cut? Of course not. This is how normal, healthy policy debates and negotiations *should* be taking place between the executive and the legislature. Corbett was trying to create a Republican versus Republican fight, using honesty and irrelevance as his weapons, and I was pushing back.

He was arguing, and I was doing my best to reframe his questions. While much of the briefings is serious, too much of it has turned into an attempt to trip the press secretary. Not all White House reporters will argue about someone's honesty based on a policy difference. And not all White House reporters turn the televised briefing into an argument, but it happens often these days.

The cameras changed me as well. When I wanted to drive home a point, I tried to think up a one- or two-sentence statement, never longer than several seconds, and I would lean in, hold my right hand up for emphasis, and deliver my line. I knew and they knew it was the "bite" the TV networks were looking for, the pithy, short summary or explanation that would make it on the air. At other times, I would pick my words with far more caution, often repeating dull talking points in an effort to avoid making news. If the President had already addressed an issue, I wasn't going to say anything different from what he had said. Reporters had him on TV, and the only way I would make it on the air was if I said something wrong.

I DIDN'T KNOW IT THEN, but the issues the President faced at the beginning of his administration were easy compared to what happened after September 11. The sluggish economy, which experts later concluded was indeed a recession that began at the outset of 2001 and ended in the fall of 2001, the confirmation process, California's energy crisis, education reforms, and tax cuts topped the domestic agenda. The accidental sinking of a Japanese fishing boat by an American submarine, the USS *Greenville,* and a small-scale civil war in the Balkan republic of Macedonia were the top issues in foreign policy.

At a bipartisan meeting with congressional leaders during the President's first week, Senator Tom Daschle, the Democratic minority leader, told Bush that none of his nominations would be denied. Given the controversy among liberals determined to defeat the nomination of John Ashcroft for attorney general, this was a significant bipartisan statement. The President told the leaders he was going to focus his efforts on passing his educational reforms and tax cuts. He assured them his approach would be nonconfrontational. Later that day, Bush met with Senator John McCain to discuss campaign finance reform, the budget, defense spending, and tax relief. The President told me that he viewed McCain as an ally on a considerable number of issues. Everyone was reaching out to everyone that week. Call it a honeymoon. Call it a grace period. Call it whatever you want—Washington was getting along.

At my gaggle, I was asked about the congressional meeting and the status of the President's nominees. I told the press what Senator Daschle had said, without pausing to think that, one, it was a private meeting, and two, the news could cause serious problems for Daschle

with Senator Ted Kennedy and other liberals. There weren't any sub-
stantive follow-up questions to my statement, it wasn't making much if
any news, and I was enjoying a quiet day. It remained that way until
5:00 the next morning, when I got my *New York Times* at home. There
in black and white was my statement: " 'You will not be denied your
choice on nominees,' Ari Fleischer quoted Mr. Daschle as telling the
president in a White House meeting."

Instantly I knew I had stepped in it. Daschle had reached out to the
President to give him an accurate status report on his nominees, and I had
unthinkingly repaid the favor by causing the minority leader no small
amount of grief with a group of determined stop-Ashcroft senators. I
called Andy Card and turned myself in. "Did you see the *New York
Times?*" I asked him. He did, and I was told I needed to "clean it up."

When I arrived at the White House, I went straight into the Oval
Office and confessed my mistake to the President. He had already
talked to Andy, and he wanted to know if I had cleaned it up yet. At that
early hour I hadn't, but I assured him I would. Nick Calio, the director
of Congressional Affairs, was steamed. Why did you do that? he
wanted to know. My revelation would cause Nick no small amount of
discomfort. His job was to usher through each of the nominees, and
any extra controversy was not helpful.

I called the senator's press secretary and chief of staff to apologize.
I told them my job was to speak for the President and no one else. I
shouldn't have recounted what the senator said. Daschle had told the
press that I misquoted him. He said he told the President that none of
his nominees would be blocked but no one could predict whether they
would be approved. The press loved it and ribbed me for it in a good-
natured way. They appreciated the information I had shared, and they
loved the fact that I was in trouble for having shared it.

Later that day I returned to the briefing room to fill the press in on
the President's meeting with Senator McCain. Despite the good-
natured meeting in which two former rivals pledged to work together,
the White House press corps were on the hunt. Nothing makes juicier
news than a good, old-fashioned Republican versus Republican, or
Democrat versus Democrat fight. Intraparty splits make interesting

story lines, and since McCain and Bush were actually getting along—the senator told reporters the meeting was "cordial"—the press searched elsewhere.

"Did the President indicate that he had in any way changed his thinking on [campaign finance reform] since the two of them kind of discussed the issue in the South Carolina primaries?" came the first question.

I think much of the White House press corps agreed with Senator McCain that campaign finance reform was necessary to clean up a corrupt system. Those who supported McCain's proposals enjoyed the media label of "reformers," while those who had a different version of how to change campaign finance laws were typically called "opponents." On this issue, the press put a white hat on the "reformers" and a black one on the "opponents." At one briefing a reporter asked me if Bush wanted Congress to defeat campaign finance reform so the President wouldn't have to "dirty his hands" by vetoing it. That didn't strike me as an objective way to frame the issue.

Campaign finance reform gobbled up tons of news space, editors having determined that this was a highly important matter. As much as the public can get fed up with Washington, I didn't think most people outside Washington, D.C., were as interested in campaign finance reform as the press was. In fact, a return to the briefing room to report on a meeting is highly unusual for the press secretary. But since the McCain meeting involved campaign finance reform, the press clamored for news, and I obliged.

"Did the President," I was asked, "after talking with McCain, change his position on any of the differences the two of them have, and did Senator McCain indicate that he has changed his position at all?"

I said that the President thought it was a good meeting and that the process would now begin to move forward. On the fourth day of a new President's term, it would have been highly *unusual* for any nuts-and-bolts negotiations to take place, especially on a matter as complicated as this one. Hearings on Capitol Hill hadn't even been scheduled to consider the senator's proposals.

"Is it safe to say, though, that minds weren't changed?"

Aha I realized. A good meeting is not good enough. They agree on much, and they disagree on some matters, I said. "The legislative process is beginning," I said.

"On those couple differences, was there anything, any movement that would close the gap?" I was asked.

"You can't report any achievement on resolving those couple differences?" came the next challenge.

"Neither you or the President are reporting any advances on closing the differences?" another reporter asked, marking the third way to phrase the same question, which I had already answered.

"I happen to think that any time you can begin three days into your term and have a meeting with somebody who advocates something that's important on something that many people think you're far apart, and it becomes clearer and clearer you're not so far apart, and both parties say it's a good meeting, then the process is beginning on the right note," I said, trying to punch through.

"Just one more follow-up," someone began, "I just want to make sure with all the talk out there and from here that I didn't miss any advances on closing the differences that the two parties have."

"I think I've addressed it as best I can," I said, recognizing that I was at risk of spending my entire fourth evening in the White House answering the same question. I called an end to the mini-briefing.

WINTER AND SPRING 2001

Eleven days after his swearing in, the President called his first cabinet meeting. As a former CEO and the first M.B.A. to occupy the Oval Office, President Bush had a relatively open and engaging management style. The cabinet met periodically as a way for the various secretaries to hear formally what their colleagues were working on, but for the most part these meetings were ceremonial affairs and had been for decades. Much of the real work got done in the one-on-one meetings cabinet secretaries had with the President and the frequent meetings the secretaries and their aides had with top White House officials.

"Return each other's phone calls" was Bush's first command to his cabinet. He told the group he was serious about changing the tone in Washington and expected them to become a part of that mission, encouraging his top appointees to engage in a "civil dialogue" with Democrats. "Go around and see everyone in your building to thank them for working for the government," Bush said. Eric Holder, President Clinton's deputy attorney general, attended the meeting, since he was technically still in charge of the Justice Department pending Ashcroft's confirmation. A couple weeks later, he told the *Washington Post* that Bush was "formidable" and "in charge." "He has a light touch, but he fills up the space," Holder said. The story was headlined BUSH ON STAGE: DEFT OR JUST LACKING DEPTH? SOME SEE PRESIDENT AS PREPARED, DISCIPLINED; SKEPTICS FIND HIM SIMPLY SHALLOW.

Return each other's phone calls? Interesting way to begin a meeting, I thought. One thing about President Bush—the man knows how to build a team. In countless ways, large and small, Bush the CEO went to great lengths to instill a sense of comradery and teamwork among his top aides and appointees. He had seen in his father's administration debilitating fights among cabinet members who put their own agendas ahead of the President's. Often these disputes led to news stories as cabinet secretaries, and their staffs, not to mention White House aides, fed information to reporters in attempts to influence an upcoming presidential decision, or to rain on an opponent's idea.

Former Treasury Secretary Paul O'Neill contributed to a book that severely criticized George W. Bush's management style, criticisms I strongly disagreed with. He described the President at cabinet meetings as a "blind man in a roomful of deaf people." I don't know how he could have reached that conclusion, because when I observed he was always engaged and highly focused. I noticed that when the former Treasury secretary appeared on the *Today* show with Katie Couric to promote his book, he regretted his choice of words. "I used some vivid language that if I could take it back, I'd take that back because it's become the controversial centerpiece," he said. Bob Woodward's book *Plan of Attack* described debates among several principals on the foreign policy team, especially between Secretary Powell and Vice President Cheney. While there were indeed differences, Bush's cabinet remained stable and mostly kept the debates where they belonged, in private meetings where a discussion of the pros and cons of various issues would benefit the President.

In March, the President invited me to join him and his family for a weekend at the presidential retreat, Camp David. Deputy Chief of Staff Josh Bolten was also invited, making it two staffers with the President, his wife, one of his brothers, and assorted other Bush family members. There was no formal agenda—we were simply invited to enjoy the beauty and tranquillity of Camp David. We ate our meals with the President and his family. We went to movies together, bowled together, worked out in the gym together, and informally talked business. Later I learned that the President had at one time or another invited all his top staff and cabinet secretaries, along with their spouses, to "Camp," as the staff called it. The White House press corps, from time to time, would be frustrated by the cohesion and discipline of the White House staff. They weren't used to a staff that had so little internal friction or infighting. Divisions among staffers often lead to tips for reporters as one faction fights with another. Exploiting these differences is a time-honored way reporters gather news. They may not be getting a full or accurate picture of what the President may think, but one rival's tip could often be a helpful clue as reporters piece together possible future events. Our unity and desire to serve the President's agenda was formed, in part, by how well the President treated us, by the little things he did. Just like a CEO who quietly but effectively pays attention to personnel issues, Bush was building a strong team that worked well together.

Throughout this time, the President received regular updates on the economy, and none of them were good. On December 3, 2000, Dick Cheney said on *Meet the Press*, "We may well be on the front of a recession here." The Democrats jumped on him, saying he was "talking the economy down." After the cabinet meeting, Bush met with his economic advisers, and his top economic aide, Larry Lindsey, warned him that the data looked bad. A recession is likely, he added.

"Let's not blame it on Clinton. Let's solve it," the President said, directing his staff to look into the possibility of accelerating his proposed tax cuts, especially the reduction in marginal income tax rates.

All the while, Bush reached out to almost every Democrat he could find, attending the annual retreats of the House and Senate Democrats, and inviting the liberal members of the Congressional Black Caucus to the White House for a private meeting. It didn't matter that several members of the caucus had walked off the floor of the Congress when the Electoral College results were ratified to protest what they alleged was Bush's "illegitimate" election, he welcomed them to the White House. Three members from Florida, however—Representatives Alcee Hastings, Carrie Meek, and Corrine Brown—were so embittered by Bush's election that they refused to attend. At the Senate retreat where the Democrats met to plan their legislative strategy, Bush arrived to a standing ovation, and one Democrat rose to compliment him, saying, "You have your father's genetics in civility."

"Except I have half my mother in me," Bush replied to great laughter. Earlier he'd told the senators of his warm and close relationship with Texas's powerful Democratic Lieutenant Governor Bob Bullock. "Is it naïve to rid the system of rancor?" he asked. "That's my intent. I'm here to work with you, to elevate the discourse. I want people to look at the system and say what a good system it is." In the same blunt way his mother spoke, Bush also told the Democrats, "We'll argue over details, but we'll get something done." Then he left the retreat, and the Democrats planned their strategy to oppose him.

Bush also met with Defense Secretary Rumsfeld, the Joint Chiefs of Staff, and the top military field commanders, telling them not to push for increased defense spending. He had campaigned on transforming the military, making it lighter and more lethal, and he was awaiting a report from the secretary of defense on how this could be accomplished. It *was* a different world before September 11.

At 12:45 P.M. on February 7, as I was preparing to brief the press, I was summoned to Andy Card's office. Already seated at the table was the head of the Secret Service's Presidential Protective Division. There's been a shooting, I was told. Just outside the gates of the White House, a little south of the South Lawn, a gunman had appeared, multiple shots were fired, and the gunman was wounded. Traffic along E Street, immediately south of the White House, had been stopped, tours inside the White House were halted, and visitors were ushered out of the building. The President was never in any danger, I was informed, and the Park Service Police would be the lead investigative agency, because of their jurisdiction over the spot on which the shooting took place. The press had already heard about it and were reporting a shooting outside the Southwest Gate of the White House.

With this exciting twist to my day, I went out at 2:20 P.M. to brief the press. "At approximately 11:30 this morning, while the Secret Service was on routine patrol around the White House," I said, "they heard shots fired and proceeded to surround a subject who was wielding a weapon, a gun. A ten-minute standoff ensued, following at which time the Secret Service fired a shot into the suspect's leg. The suspect, as you know, is in custody. He's been taken to George Washington University Hospital, where he's being treated for injuries that do not appear to be life-threatening."

For the next twenty minutes, I was asked sixty-three questions about the shooting. Many focused on the President. Where was he? How did he learn about the shooting? Did the Secret Service take any action to protect him? How many shots were fired? What was the motive of the gunman?

I tried to limit my answers to the fact that the President was safe and that an investigation was under way. Bush had been working out in the residence at the time of the shooting and was not in harm's way. The press, trying to stay on top of, and get ahead of, the story, were hopeful I could answer all their investigative questions, which, just three hours after the shooting, I could not. I doubted the investigators would be in a position to answer so many questions so quickly.

"What was the President's reaction to this incident?" I was asked.

I answered, "The President has full faith in the Secret Service, so the President understood that he was not in any danger. . . . It's unfortunate that it ever comes to this point, but if it ever does, the Secret Service serves our nation, very, very ably." After five or ten minutes of logical questions, whose answers could be determined only by an investigation, the queries stared to swerve off into interesting places.

"Can you confirm this wasn't an act of terrorism?"

"Again, the whole matter will be under investigation, but I've seen no evidence that would suggest that," I replied.

"Was he [the gunman] menacing the tourists? Was he menacing himself, the tourists, or the White House, or all of the above?"

"Well, I think it's fair to say that anytime anybody has a weapon that they're discharging, there's a safety problem for all concerned."

"Any political impact on the happy face of the new administration?"

I wasn't sure what potential political impact the reporter could be thinking of, and I said, "Nobody ever wants to have to go through anything like this, for anybody—not for the Secret Service, who guards this building; not for the people who work here; and of course, the suspect. Nobody ever in our society wants to have these types of incidents arise. Unfortunately, as we've seen through history, they sometimes do. And that's why we're all grateful to the people who protect this building and protect our President."

But questions continued.

"Ari, what you describe as a standoff, might that be interpreted differently, might have the various officers been trying to coax him out of committing suicide, for instance? Is that part of what's being investigated?"

"I'm going to refer that question to the people who speak for the law enforcement officers. I speak for the President."

"But you used the word *standoff*."

"That's correct," I said. "I think that anytime you have law enforcement officers with drawn weapons and you have a suspect with a drawn weapon, that's a standoff."

"One more on this," came one of the final questions. "The people in other countries look at the United States as a particularly violent society. Do you think for people watching this in other countries that this says anything about the character of the United States?"

I knew someone would ask that question. "I would not engage in any such thought," I replied. "I think many nations on this earth deal with issues and the matter of protection of their presidents, and the United States does not stand alone in having to have people protect the President, protect the building in which the President resides. That's common throughout the world. There have been incidents around the world, unfortunately, where violence has taken place that we all come to regret."

Indeed, Sweden lost a foreign minister to a gunman in 2003. Israel's Prime Minister Yitzhak Rabin was slain in 1995. The United States, of course, isn't the world's only democracy that has a fence around the President's home to protect him or her from who knows whom.

After the briefing was over, I returned to my office. The press were working on a serious, breaking news story, and I tried to find the line between giving them answers and not speaking for the investigators, who would be in a more informed position to deal with the details of the shooting and the results of their investigation. One of my bosses, however, told me I went too far. You talked too much, Karen Hughes advised. You should speak for the President only and not get into *any* details about the shooting, other than what happened to the President.

On a genuine news story, the press thought I didn't tell them enough. At least one top staffer thought I went too far. Welcome to life for the press secretary, where every day you have to find the balance between how much and how little to say.

IN LATE MARCH 2001, I was sitting at my desk when I found a note from Logan Walters, President Bush's personal aide. "The President would like you to meet him on the South Lawn at 6:00 tonight to play catch."

The President, a competitive athlete, was heading to Milwaukee the following week to throw out the opening pitch for the Brewers' new baseball field, Miller Park. He wanted to get his arm loose, so he invited me to be his catcher on the South Lawn. I showed up in my business suit with my baseball glove (I always kept one in the trunk of my car), and the President, who had the advantage of living there, showed up in sweatpants with a bulletproof jacket on. He wanted to warm up the same way he would throw the pitch in front of fifty thousand baseball fans.

At one point, the President threw a pitch that scooted past me into a pack of flowers halfway down the lawn. I jogged back to look for the ball and couldn't find it. The President came down, found the ball, and we went back to playing catch on the South Lawn of the White House—a building that just three months earlier I couldn't even bring myself to look at. Now not only was I working *inside* the White House but I was also invited to play catch with the President on the South Lawn. What a great moment. What an enjoyable evening.

The next week Bush went to Milwaukee and bounced the pitch into the dirt in front of home plate. As the catcher scooped it up, he looked the President in the eye and said, "Perfect strike, Mr. President."

THE FIRST SERIOUS foreign policy crisis of the new administration began late on a Saturday night, on March 31, when a Chinese fighter pilot intercepted a routine surveillance mission of an American P-3 aircraft flying over international waters along the eastern coast of China. The Chinese pilot got too close, actually bumping planes in midair, and as the lighter Chinese jet crashed into the sea, the P-3's pilot miraculously controlled his damaged aircraft just long enough to make an emergency landing on the Chinese island of Hainan.

I spent my Sunday on conference calls gathering information about what had happened. At that time the collision was considered an accident, and the Chinese Foreign Ministry was cooperating with American authorities who were inquiring about the conditions of our crew members on Hainan Island.

On Monday morning, I was scheduled to attend opening day at Yankee Stadium with my then seventy-two-year-old father. We were guests of Mayor Rudy Giuliani, who had invited my father and me to his home, Gracie Mansion, from where we would ride with him to the game and sit next to him alongside the Yankee dugout. As a lifelong Yankee fan, I was looking forward to taking the day off to watch my team. My father and I had been to countless ball games at the stadium as I was growing up. One summer when he was in college, in the late 1940s, my father had spent a few days working as an usher at the stadium. Since I had moved to Washington in 1983, I hadn't had many opportunities to watch the Yankees at Yankee Stadium. I didn't want to miss this one.

When I left for New York, it seemed that the P-3 issue was under control. But through the morning, the situation turned for the worse. In a power struggle with the Foreign Ministry, the Chinese military flexed its muscle and ordered the detention of the crew. Phone calls to the Foreign Ministry went unanswered. At about the same time, my father, accompanying the mayor, walked down a narrow passageway below the seats that lead to the Yankee dugout, where he met his childhood hero, the former Yankee shortstop Phil Rizzuto. A tear came to my father's eye when he told Rizzuto that he was his hero growing up. Even for a seventy-two-year-old, there's something about baseball that can bring a tear to the eye.

I thought about whether I should not have come to New York, or whether I should cut the trip short and return to my post. I was receiving updates by cell phone and pager, but I also knew the White House would not have much to say until we were able to learn more from Chinese officials, and I had faith that my deputy Scott McClellan would conduct the briefing with the President's full confidence. I also knew this wouldn't be the only crisis that would hit the White House, and whatever time I could find to be with my parents was also valuable to me. I determined early on not to become a prisoner of the job, sacrificing some of the most precious moments a son can enjoy with his father just to avoid being criticized. I stayed at the game and took criticism from the press.

"The Red Chinese have captured one of our planes and are holding the crew incommunicado," wrote Lloyd Grove in the *Washington Post* the next day. Lloyd wrote the well-read "Reliable Source" column of the *Post*'s Style section. "Slobodan Milosevic has been arrested in Yugoslavia. And the Middle East, once again is falling apart. Hey, Mr. Ari Fleischer, what are you gonna do next? Not Disney World exactly. But much to the surprise of the Washington press corps, President Bush's press secretary chose yesterday—as his boss was coping with maximum crisis—to join New York Mayor Rudolph Giuliani for Opening Day at Yankee Stadium."

In the first days of the P-3 story, the President twice appeared before the press. He informed the American people of the facts as we knew them, and he called for China to return the crew and the plane.

His plan from the beginning was to keep the issue from becoming a crisis by quietly and diplomatically working with the Chinese to get our crew back. The problem was, especially at the onset, that the incident exposed deep rifts inside the Chinese government, between the generally pro-Western diplomatic corps and the tough-minded military. During the first few days of the crisis, the United States government couldn't find anyone in charge in China to talk to.

Bush tried to avoid talking to the press about the incident, and when he did, he tried his best not to let matters escalate. "Our approach has been to keep this accident from becoming an international incident," the President explained. He was determined to keep the temperature low, allowing Chinese officials enough time and space to sort out their internal issues. He was confident from the beginning that common sense would prevail and our crew would be returned if China didn't get forced into a corner.

His handling of the P-3 standoff is another reason I find Bush's critics off the mark when they call him a cowboy or a unilateralist. Whether the issue is domestic or foreign, Bush isn't locked into only one approach. He is decisive and has a strong sense of what he wants done, but he is a pragmatist when it comes to finding the most effective way to carry out his goals. Domestically, that meant working with Democrats on the education bill because he judged they wanted to work with him and could together get the bill passed. On the tax bill, he knew the liberal Democratic leadership would oppose him at all costs, so he worked with a smaller group of centrist Democrats like Senator John Breaux to muscle through his proposals. On foreign policy, Bush's default position is to let the diplomats do their jobs, backed up by his forceful and direct statement of America's intentions. Believing that diplomacy does work, that's the approach he's taken in dealing with Libya, North Korea, Iran, and with China during the P-3 crisis. Because he believed diplomacy wouldn't work with Saddam Hussein, the use of force in Iraq became an exception, but his critics mistakenly think it's been the rule.

The press were determined to make the detention of our crew a full-blown crisis, and who could blame them? An air-to-air military interception and the detention of a Navy crew isn't exactly an act of peace or an everyday event. The cable TV news networks blared their logos, describing events as if they were the names of TV shows. US/CHINA STANDOFF read CNN's omnipresent logo. The White House press asked me when it would be accurate to call our detained servicemen and women "hostages." Would China be denied the chance to host the Olympics? Would the President accept Jesse Jackson's offer to help resolve the issue?

A couple of days into the crisis, NBC's David Gregory asked, "Two days ago, the President made a very clear statement saying, give us the crew, give us the plane, in essence, saying time is running out. Two days later, we've got nothing—no crew, no plane, and no greater access to the crew. Shouldn't the public be concerned that China is not meeting any of these requests or demands?"

In words that became harder to stand by the longer the crew's detention endured, I said, "In the President's approach on this, he is not going to act or react based on news cycles. He's going to continue to lead in the manner that he thinks is the most productive way to bring our men and women home. And that's why, again, you've seen this pace of diplomacy that we are engaged in with China, and that is continuing."

In less than two weeks, the President's quiet diplomacy worked. The Chinese diplomats who prized good relations with the United States eventually won out over the Chinese military. Bush had privately predicted that would be the outcome, and he was content to give them the time and space they needed to do their maneuvering. The P-3 crisis ended with the safe return of our crew. We even got the plane back, in pieces in an assortment of shipping crates. When Bush visited China six months later, the P-3 crisis wasn't even an issue.

The President's second trip out of the country was in April, to the Summit of the Americas in Quebec City, Canada. There he gathered with the leaders of virtually every nation in North, Central, and South America, except for Fidel Castro. Much of the discussion was centered on increasing trade, aiding development, and fostering democracy. The meeting was also marked by the presence of anti–free trade protesters, who showed up and engaged in violence. This was my first taste of tear gas.

Throughout the three-day gathering, tens of thousands of protesters advocating on behalf of labor and the environment gathered to denounce capitalism and international trade. Two years earlier in Seattle, left-wing protesters, with the help of a large number of anarchists, had succeeded in shutting down an international free trade meeting. They rioted, broke windows, and were jubilant about their impact. Their protests, and the police in riot gear, were made for TV. How could any editor ignore the footage, complete with water cannons and tear gas?

From his hotel room, the President had a good view of the barricades erected to protect the meetings from the protesters. He watched the gathering throngs attempt to breach barricade after barricade as the police fired tear gas to disperse the mobs. One evening, as the world leaders met for dinner, the tear gas was taken by the wind to the streets next door to our hotel. Paul Morse, a White House photographer, flew into the lobby screaming, with his eyes shut tight in pain. A round of tear gas aimed at the protesters had caught him. A group of us ran to his side to help. A military nurse who travels with the White House came to Paul's aid, and I noticed that just being close to him hurt my eyes.

Gatherings of world leaders these days are regularly interrupted by left-wing, antitrade protesters, some of whom resort to violence, especially against the police. It's reached the point where international summits are held in remote places like Kananaskis, Canada, in 2003, or in cities that are shut down as though they were battle zones, like Genoa in 2001. Despite the opposition Bush stirred by his decision to invade Iraq, the protests predated his presidency and unfortunately are now a way of life. After the President left a European Union summit meeting in Stockholm, during the summer of 2001, more than a year before the Iraq war, the protesters arrived en masse for the rest of the meeting. Violence ensued, and 118 people, including 56 police officers, were injured.

The protesters' aim is to object to free trade, and they're overwhelmingly liberal. Somehow, these left-wing activists are still mainly described by the press as "protesters," with an occasional reference to "anarchists." It's funny because when the press covers protests by conservatives, they're quick to use the label "right-wing protesters" or "conservative opponents." That's routinely the way the press described protesters against the former First Lady Hillary Clinton's health care reforms, and it's the usual lexicon used to describe right to life marchers or traditional family groups. But when it comes to describing labor and environmental activists who regularly disrupt summit meetings, destroy millions of dollars' worth of property, injure the police, and on occasion cause death, the press withhold any political label, except for an occasional anarchist.

In Quebec, CNN called them "protesters" that included "big environmental and labor groups." They didn't call them liberal. In Genoa, ABC's Peter Jennings called them "demonstrators" who were "angry with the world's wealthiest governments and this was their chance for them to say so." Sometimes they're called militant, but they're not called liberal. Isn't the coverage missing something? Violence is now a standard part of these protests, and it's carried out by left-wing extremists that the press are reluctant to describe as left-wing. I wish the press used the same standard in judging conservatives as they do in judging liberals. If a right to life march turned violent, I have a hard time believing the press wouldn't refer to the participants as "right-wing" or "conservative." If the media are going to label one side of a debate, they ought to label all sides. Similarly, if they won't call one group of protesters "liberal," then they shouldn't call a different group "conservative."

ONE HUNDRED DAYS into his presidency, President Bush invited all 535 members of Congress to the White House for a luncheon. He said it was to mark "our," not "his," first one hundred days. Many Democrats refused to attend, accusing the President of using them as props to show he was being bipartisan when, they alleged, he was not. Bush did the traditional heavy round of press interviews and spoke with pride about what he perceived as a productive start to his presidency. The education bill was moving, the tax cut appeared on its way to passage, even if its size might be reduced. He thought he was making progress in changing the tone in Washington.

In an interview with *Newsweek* aboard Air Force One, he was asked what the greatest difference was between Congress and the Texas legislature. In Washington, he said, everything seems to be done with an eye on public relations. Legislators in Texas, he said, never held news conferences to reveal what was discussed in their meetings with him. He preferred the way government business was done in Texas, where even the opposition party, including its leaders, still wanted to get things accomplished, while in Washington the job of the minority leader was to criticize the President and try to make himself into the next majority leader. In Washington, that's the way it works, for *both* parties.

Much of the President's focus when he took office was on the struggling economy and his plan to cut taxes. During the campaign, he'd promised a $1.6 trillion tax cut for three reasons. One, he said, because we have a surplus and it's the people's money, not the government's money, and taxpayers deserve to keep more of what they make. Two, as an insurance policy against an economic downturn, since the stimulus of a tax cut would boost the economy. And three, if we didn't cut taxes, the money would be spent anyway by the politicians in Washington.

From the moment the Supreme Court declared him the winner, pundits speculated about whether Bush would shrink his tax cut because of the close election. He didn't have a mandate, they said, so how can he stand by his tax cut? I wondered why these observers didn't question whether he would abandon his commitment to getting senior citizens prescription drugs because of the close election. Or his plan to improve education. Or his proposal to rebuild the military. It was only his tax cut they called into question.

Bush's plan called for lowering marginal income tax rates for all Americans. The top rate, he said should be reduced from 39.6 percent to 33.0 percent, a 16.6 percent reduction for those at the top. The bottom rate should drop from 15 percent to 10 percent, a 33.3 percent reduction for those at the bottom. All rates in between would drop as well, and the marriage penalty would be reduced, the five-hundred-dollar per child tax credit would double to a thousand dollars per child, and the death tax would be abolished. In 1992, then Candidate Clinton successfully ran on a "middle-class tax cut" without ever defining it. Bush's plan was specific and concrete, and had its costs attached. For a campaign, it was more detailed and specific than usual.

From the early days of his administration forward, the President made it plain he was not going to reduce his tax cut. In a meeting with congressional leaders in the Cabinet Room in early February, Bush said, "I'm not going to let the tax plan get pencil-whipped. Are you ready to change the numbers? No I'm not."

There was one change he was willing to make. Given the weakness in the economy, he wanted to get as much stimulus into the system as early as possible, which opened the door to making the tax cut retroactive, effective January 1, 2001.

When it came to retroactivity, Bush told the group, "Start at the bottom of the economic ladder and work our way up." In other words, drop the 15 percent rate to 10 percent and then see if taxes could be cut retroactively for those in higher brackets.

The economic news throughout the winter and spring continued to get worse. "Every piece of economic data is a disaster," Larry Lindsey, his top economic adviser, warned the President in February.

In another February meeting, with congressional Republicans, Bush asked them to hold the line on spending. His budget director, Mitch Daniels, had briefed him on how the surplus had led to far higher expenditures than were warranted. Mitch said the government had been on a "binge" for the last three years, with spending rising at 6 percent a year, $1.4 *trillion* above target over a ten-year period. Indeed, as congressional Republicans and President Clinton wrestled over spending priorities in the late nineties, the taxpayers always seemed to get the short end of the stick. Republicans, battered from the government shutdown fight of 1995, were afraid President Clinton would veto their spending bills, saying they underfunded key priorities, threatening another shutdown, for which the GOP would be blamed. Lacking the leverage to defeat the popular President during a time of surpluses, congressional Republicans negotiated higher than desired spending levels in return for President Clinton's signature on the bills. An "exit fee," congressional Republicans called it, the price to be paid for successfully adjourning the Congress without shutting down the government. As for taxes, Bush told members of his own party to "stay tough," don't negotiate now.

President Bush understood the process. Any concession he made on the level of the tax cut this early in the budget season would be pocketed by those who didn't like the tax cut anyway, and his new, lower number would become just another starting point on the way to an even smaller tax cut. Like any good negotiator, Bush wanted his opponents to raise their figures before he lowered his. The real work of negotiating would come later in the spring, when the bill went to a conference committee between the House and the Senate. That's always been the way Congress works, and Bush wasn't about to unilaterally betray his own plan, or cut it back, if he didn't have to. He did run on it, after all.

In late February, Bush still wouldn't budge. "The key on the tax cut," he told his cabinet, "is never blink or flinch. It's needed." He added a moment later, "I assure you, if we don't cut taxes, it will be spent." In addition to helping stimulate the economy, Bush always viewed the tax cut as a struggle between people who wanted to increase the size of government and those who wanted to limit it.

The White House press corps, meanwhile, were itching for the tax fight to begin. They continuously pressed the President on when he would negotiate and what level tax cut he was willing to accept. "I won't negotiate with myself" was his favorite refrain. Two reporters from NBC cleverly tried to squeeze him on the topic. At a meeting with reporters in early March, Campbell Brown asked Bush when he would start to negotiate on the tax bill. David Gregory asked if accepting any level of tax cut below his requested level would constitute a "failure."

"Now is not the time, that's not the way it's going to work," the President told Brown. "There's a lot of work to be done in the Congress and they need to know they're dealing with someone firm." As for Gregory's question, Bush replied, "It's too early to tell how a president will be judged." He suggested a president's success or failure is better viewed through a long-term prism, not based on the final level of one particular tax cut proposal.

At my briefings, the questions followed the usual course of Aren't these tax cuts for the rich? The Democratic leadership in Congress said they were, and the press pointed their criticisms out to me.

"On the tax cut," one question began, "the Democrat leaders are up on the Hill today with a car and an automobile part, and they're saying that millionaires under the Bush plan would get a tax cut sufficient to buy a Lexus, and working people would get a tax cut sufficient to buy a muffler. Is their arithmetic wrong, or do you disagree with their emphasis and argument?"

"I think both their arithmetic and their emphasis is wrong," I said. "What the Democrats are proposing to do is collect almost $1 trillion in higher taxes than President Bush has proposed; that way they can spend the money on bigger government. Under the Democrats' plan, the government will get put in the driver's seat, and the taxpayers get stuck in the back."

"But their numbers are not wrong, are they, that a millionaire will get a $46,000 tax cut, and that's enough to buy a car?"

"The numbers are incomplete," I responded. "The real numbers are that the biggest percentage gainers in this tax plan are people at the middle and the low end of the income scale. They will benefit the most from President Bush's proposed tax cut. . . . But I think what you're going to really see is a growing group—a smaller group, it won't be all the Democrats, but there will be a smaller number of Democrats who want to work with us to cut taxes for all Americans. And that's how we're going to achieve a bipartisan government coalition to get taxes cut."

"One more question on this. This example has a kind of visceral appeal, that people would get so much money they could buy this luxury car. Is it a fair argument to make against the President's plan, to make an argument on that basis?"

"I think the fairer argument is that there are some tax-and-spend Democrats who every time they see a car start thinking about building a toll booth," I replied.

The argument over the so-called fairness of tax cuts drove me crazy. The Democrats' charge was simple and lent itself to easy pictures, like the stunt with the luxury car. The Republican argument, which centered on growth as a result of tax cutting, was complicated and esoteric. It was easier for the press to summarize the Democrats' message.

As for fairness, because of the progressive nature of the American tax code, almost half the workers in our country pay virtually no federal income taxes. Instead, income taxes are increasingly paid by a shrinking group of Americans, namely middle- and upper-income workers. The top 1 percent, people with incomes in excess of $285,000 in 2002 (the most recent year data are available), paid 33.7 percent of all income taxes that year, the taxes that pay for the defense department, welfare payments, educational spending, national parks, everything other than Social Security and Medicare. The top 10 percent, people with incomes greater than $92,000, paid 65.7 percent of all income taxes.

Think about that. Ten percent of the people pay nearly two-thirds of the income taxes.

The top 50 percent, those making roughly $28,000 or more, paid 96 percent of all income taxes. In other words, half the people in our country pay virtually no federal income tax, yet they receive many federal services and benefits.

Above and beyond income taxes, almost every worker in the country pays about 8 percent of his or her income for Social Security and Medicare, and in return they get their Social Security and Medicare benefits. Social Security, whose payment structure is very progressive, allows low-wage workers to get benefits that well exceed the taxes they pay in. For example, today on average, males are expected to live seventeen years after they reach the retirement age of sixty-five. A low-wage earner would recoup the Social Security taxes, plus interest, he and his employer paid into the system within twelve years of retirement. In contrast, a high-wage worker, who pays more in Social Security taxes, would need to live five years *beyond* his life expectancy to recoup his Social Security taxes plus interest.

In other words, payroll taxes for Social Security and Medicare are indeed regressive, but the benefits are progressive, and no discussion of fairness can consider the tax side without accounting for the benefit side. Many White House reporters frequently objected to my focus on how much *income* tax people paid, asserting that low-income workers also pay their share of payroll taxes. I could never get the press to focus on the fact that low-income Americans often get their payroll taxes, and then some, back thanks to the way Social Security works.

Given the progressive nature of the income tax code, when taxes are reduced, upper-income workers *will* receive more money back from Uncle Sam, because they pay so much more to begin with. But as a percentage of what they pay, the Bush tax cut gave most of the relief to lower-income workers.

According to the IRS, a married couple with a taxable income of $20,000 in 2003 paid $2,304 in income taxes. A couple whose taxable income was $100,000 in 2003 paid $18,620. A single taxpayer with $20,000 in taxable income in 2003 paid $2,654. His $100,000 counterpart paid $22,746 in income taxes.

2003	TAXABLE INCOME	TAXES DUE
Married Couple	$20,000	$2,304
	$100,000	$18,620
Single Taxpayer	$20,000	$2,654
	$100,000	$22,746

Simply put, the $100,000 family made five times as much as the $20,000 family, but they paid more than *eight* times as much in taxes. The single "rich" guy made five times as much, and paid almost *nine* times more in income taxes. Democrats, and much of the press it seemed to me, pointed out the "rich" taxpayer got a tax cut larger in dollar amounts than the lower-income worker. A tax break for the rich! they cried. They typically forgot to point out that the upper-income worker paid and will continue to pay more, much more in taxes. Plus, when it comes to changing people's lifestyles and helping them to pay their bills, a $500 drop in taxes for someone who owed $2,000 is a 25 percent reduction, while a $3,000 drop for someone who owes $20,000 is only a 15 percent reduction.

The numbers allow both sides to make their cases, but the arguments made by the Democrats were typically the ones the White House press corps seemed to agree with. Maybe that's why some reporters put their questions to me in the form of statements.

"Do you honestly think it's okay for Bill Gates and the like to transfer all of his wealth to his kids? There's so much money there." I was asked in February 2001, about Bush's proposal to abolish the death tax.

The President has also proposed to drop the top tax rate of 39.6 percent to 33 percent, and the bottom rate from 15 percent to 10 percent.

"Why is he cutting the rich people's tax by 6.6 percent, and the poor people's tax 5 percent?" asked another reporter whose forte wasn't math. The accurate numbers are that dropping the top rate from 39.6 percent to 33 percent is a 16.6 percent reduction, while dropping the bottom rate from 15 percent to 10 percent is a 33.3 percent reduction.

If you go into a store and the price of a sweater is reduced from $39.60 to $33.00, you're saving 17 percent, or $6.60. If the price of a pair of socks drops from $15.00 to $10.00, you saved 33 percent, or $5.00. Last time I looked, 33 percent off is bigger and better than 17 percent off. The biggest winners from the tax cut, as a percentage of taxes paid, were low-income workers.

"As you know from your time in Congress, those with the most influence get what they want. And the people with the most influence tend to be corporations and upper-income earners," a reporter asked me, sounding very much like a Democrat. "What will this President do to ensure that middle- and lower-income Americans do get their tax relief as this process goes through on the Hill?"

Corporations and upper-income earners? I guess labor unions, environmental groups, and trial lawyers don't have any influence in the Democratic Party according to that reporter's thinking. And if the fact that 50 percent of the country pay only 4 percent of the income taxes isn't a form of assistance to those on the lower end of the income scale, then I don't know what is. Not all reporters take the Democrats' side of an issue, but on taxes, it sure felt to me as if most of the White House press corps were more inclined to see the issue through the eyes of Democrats than through the eyes of Republicans.

In early March, the House of Representatives was on the verge of passing Bush's tax cut. The President's agenda was moving, deadlock was breaking, and progress was in the air. In the briefing room, a different atmosphere prevailed. If reporters couldn't criticize the President for having his agenda fail, they blamed him for it succeeding. True to form, almost all Republicans in the House were for the tax cut, and almost all House Democrats were against it.

"As you know," came the first of two questions, "many House Democrats are just saying all this talk of bipartisanship is a big sham, that the House Republicans are pretty much ramming this through without sort of taking into account Democratic concerns on this and other issues. So they say that any sort of bipartisanship, working together coming from here, really isn't spreading to Capitol Hill."

"In the Senate," another reporter asked, "if you only get a few Democrats voting for your plan, you won't actually stand here and say that's a bipartisan agreement, will you?"

I didn't pay the criticism much mind. I had been around Washington long enough to see several presidents who couldn't get Congress to pass their proposals, and I was glad at long last action was being taken, with however many Democrats onboard. On March 8, the House passed the Bush tax cut 230 to 198. Only 10 Democrats voted for it. I did point out that it was still early in the congressional process, and there was plenty of time for the Democrats to come onboard later. They would be welcome anytime.

Larry Lindsey's worries about weakness in the economy were turning out to be right. At a March 14 speech in New Jersey, the President said there were dark clouds on the economic horizon and "Our economy is beginning to sputter."

Senator Daschle and Congressman Dick Gephardt, the House minority leader, immediately went into attack mode, accusing the President of "talking down the economy." They charged Bush with contributing to a drop in consumer confidence and creating the economic downturn in order to drum up support for his tax plan. They knew their statements would become fodder for the press.

The White House press corps, sensing a good fight, picked up the charge. I was asked to respond.

"Number one," I said, "the President believes the most important thing for policy makers, either in the Congress or in the White House, is to be accurate, and not to withhold information from the American people, but to accurately and fully describe to the American people the state of the economy."

I had earlier told the press that the President thought it would be a failure of leadership for him to put a "Pollyanna-ish glow" on the economy if the facts indicated otherwise.

The questions kept coming, from what I thought was an odd point of view.

"Just a follow-up on that. Is there any shift, though, or change in the administration's approach in light of what we've seen in the markets this week in terms of questioning or reevaluating what the President says publicly and what you all say privately about the economy?" Wow. A reporter was wondering if it might be better for the President to believe one thing in private but say something different in public.

Another follow-up. "Isn't there a psychological impact by talking about the problems of the economy that people say, oh, I shouldn't spend money on this car, or I had better save, and that could contribute to some of the warning signs we're seeing now?"

It wouldn't be the last time I was questioned about whether Bush was "talking down the economy."

The questions about whether the President was either causing or contributing to the economic slowdown were a good illustration of the press's ability to play the devil's advocate on any issue.

Former President Bush was widely criticized by the press for ignoring the seriousness and depth of the 1991 recession. He didn't acknowledge it until it was too late, and when he did, he was criticized for not caring and treating it too lightly. Now another President Bush, who had learned the lesson of ignoring bad economic times from watching his father, was being criticized for what? For accurately describing the state of the economy! George W. Bush was being challenged by the press for causing the economy's weaknesses. What should he have done? Ignored economic facts? If, instead, he had pretended the economy was strong in early 2001, then much of the press would have faulted him for being unrealistic and missing the existing warning signs. No matter what he did, many in the press were ready to blame him.

Given the early indications that Bush was right about the state of the economy, I wondered why White House reporters didn't challenge Daschle and Gephardt for their assertions that Bush was talking down the economy, when instead he was expressing the truth. It seemed to me that much of the press preferred to cover the fight over the economy and who was to blame for its downfall, and that meant the tough questions came my way, not Congress's way. The President is almost always a bigger bull's-eye for the media than a congressional leader, with the exception of the former House Speaker Newt Gingrich, who earned and received his share of tough coverage.

It took about a year for the final data to come in, but economists concluded that Bush and Cheney were right. The economy went into recession in the first quarter of 2001 and remained there for about nine months.

At the end of March, Bush gave a speech in which he said he had faith in the long-term strength of the economy, but he was worried that the nation had entered an economic downturn. To protect against the downturn, he stepped up his push for tax cuts, arguing they would help stimulate the weak economy.

The day before his speech, I was aboard Air Force One on the way to an event in Kansas City as the press bore in on Bush and the economy.

"Is this [speech] an attempt to clarify what many regard as confusion over what the President does believe about the economy?" I had learned early on that when reporters used the term *many,* there was no telling who they were referring to, but often it meant they were referring to their own hunches.

"I'm not aware that there is any confusion," I replied.

"A lot of people have said and written that he's made conflicting statements about the state of the economy, wondering whether he's talking it up or talking it down," a reporter stated. "A lot of people" in this case really meant congressional Democrats who didn't support his tax cut anyway.

"We've always dismissed that as not a serious question," I said, trying to dismiss it once more.

Then things got really confusing.

"Is it [the economy] sputtering, or is it an economy that he [the President] is confident will recover?" I guess it didn't occur to the reporter that it very well could be both.

I explained the President was confident about the long term, but there was no dispute we were in an economic downturn now.

"A recession?" I was asked.

"Economic downturn," I said. The data showing it was a recession weren't in yet.

"How do you define a downturn?" the reporter wanted to know.

"How do you define a recession is probably the real question," I said.

"Negative growth," the reporter answered, before asking me how I defined a downturn.

"We had 5 percent economic growth and 4 percent economic growth and 2 percent economic growth and 1 percent economic growth," I replied, describing the slowdown in the economy that began early in 2000, continued through the summer, and slid further into the fall of 2000, before President Bush's election.

"What does the President think about the timing of the downturn? It was just after his coming into office," a reporter asserted, evidently not having listened to a word I said. It didn't matter that the economy was in a yearlong slide that had begun before Bush entered office. The press were now covering Bush, so Bush was going to get the blame.

I avoided the blame game and said instead, "It doesn't matter when it began; what matters is how to fix it." It was hard to hide my frustration, however, with the notion that the slowdown began on Bush's watch, and that *he* was talking the economy down.

As the President kept pressing for his tax cut on Capitol Hill, he met with a group of top Republican congressional leaders, including the Speaker of the House, Dennis Hastert, and the Senate majority leader, Trent Lott. "Senators want spending that's way too high," Bush complained in the meeting. He recognized that everyone had to deal with the reality of a Senate that was split fifty-fifty, but he added that "the tax cut is too low." Returning to his argument against more spending, he complained, "Not everyone who calls himself a Republican behaves like one." The leaders told him it might be hard to keep spending in line.

In one short month, the data grew worse. Bush met with his economic team two to three times a week to review the latest economic facts and trends as well as to receive an update about legislative action from his head of Congressional Affairs, Nick Calio. Glenn Hubbard, chairman of the President's Council of Economic Advisers, told him in early May that without a tax cut there was a real risk of recession. Unemployment was rising, and Glenn predicted it would hit 5.4 percent by the fall of 2002. "It's baked into the cake," he warned. He told the President that growth would be less than one percent for the spring of 2001. The President had previously instructed his economic and congressional aides to focus on reducing marginal income tax rates and getting as much money into the economy in 2001 as possible. The idea of sending out rebate checks came into play, and the President gave it his blessing. He told the group to stick to their guns in seeking the highest tax cut possible, holding his cards close to his vest about how much or when he was prepared to settle for less.

As spring became summer, it looked increasingly likely that the new President would emerge with most of his tax cut in place. It might be smaller than what he sought, Congress might change some of the details, but it was coming together.

In May, I entered the briefing room increasingly optimistic that good things were happening.

"Democratic leaders on the Hill," I was asked at one briefing, "seem to be growing increasingly strong in their criticism of what they call a lack of true [bi]partisanship at the White House." What's your response? I was asked.

I said the President would continue to work with all those who were willing to work with him. He would welcome the votes of Democrats who supported his policies and respect those who voted against him.

The reporter kept pressing. "If those votes come from a few moderate or conservative Democrats and the President stiffs the Democratic leadership, does that count as bipartisanship?"

I thought the question was slanted in its definition of *bipartisanship*. I bit my tongue and said, "I think that in a democracy the only thing you can ask for is for civility and for someone's ideas to be presented, where each individual member of Congress, whether a liberal, a moderate, or a conservative, can express themselves through their votes. And the President will be very pleased to create bipartisan coalitions in a nation that is governed by majority rule, so that he can sign bills into law, which is what the country wants."

"Does that mean he won't work with the Democratic leadership in forming these policies, as much as searching for votes with the moderate—"

"Well of course he'll work with the Democratic leadership," I interrupted. "But in the end, the process always comes down to a question of getting things done for the American people. And to get things done for the American people, what counts is the ability to assemble a bipartisan coalition that is called a majority."

I wondered if White House reporters ever asked Bill Clinton's press secretary if *Clinton* was being partisan when he stood up to former House Speaker Newt Gingrich or former House Majority Leader Dick Armey. The premise of the reporter's question was if liberal leaders like Dick Gephardt or Tom Daschle didn't support Bush, *Bush* was the partisan. The Democratic leadership in the Congress is so liberal that in 1996, after President Clinton announced he would sign welfare reform into law, *every* member of the House Democratic leadership voted against the reforms. Every single one. If they were too liberal to support their own party's President on welfare reform, why did the press think the Democratic leadership would be inclined to support an opposite party's President on tax policy? With Bush in the White House, I believe that for many in the White House press corps, the definition of partisanship shifted. Whereas Clinton won plaudits in the press for standing up to Gingrich and Armey, Bush was described in the briefing room as partisan when he stood up to Gephardt and Daschle.

"So the President," I said, "is going to continue to work with members of Congress, of both parties, to assemble governing, bipartisan coalitions. On some issues, there are going to be many votes. On some issues, the vote will be narrower. The point remains in the end, the legislation gets signed into law, and that's what good government is all about."

On June 7, 2001, President Bush signed into law a retroactive reduction in tax rates from 15 percent to 10 percent for low-income Americans and from 39.6 percent to 35.0 percent for upper-income Americans. Rates were also reduced for everyone in between. The child credit was doubled from five hundred to a thousand dollars, and the marriage penalty was reduced. The death tax was abolished. The tax cuts weren't permanent, but it was a singular accomplishment, achieved earlier than usual and with strong Democratic support, especially in the Senate, where twelve Democratic senators supported Bush.

FOUR

BIAS?

I S THE WHITE HOUSE PRESS corps biased?

Yes. They're biased in favor of conflict.

Much has been said and written about media bias. Many Republicans, especially conservatives, believe the press are liberals who oppose Republicans and Republican ideas. I think there's an element of truth to that, but it is complicated, secondary, and often nuanced. More important, the press's first and most pressing bias is in favor of conflict and fighting. That's especially the case for the White House press corps.

If the press find someone fighting, they love it and they cover it. If people aren't fighting, the press are pretty good at getting them to fight. If they find a small conflict, they're skilled at making it into a larger conflict, one they can increasingly cover as the sparks fly. If someone, anyone, from any political party, is in trouble, the press want to know if the person is going to be fired. If not, the press want to know why not. The political realm isn't the only place in the press where reporters love conflict; they love it anywhere they can find it. Head coaches and managers as well as athletes and, increasingly, businesspeople are often treated with the same conflict-driven focus.

The press love a scandal, no matter which politician or what party is involved. No one can claim with a straight face that the White House press corps were easy on former President Bill Clinton. They were relentless in their coverage of his scandals, his honesty, and his character. In numerous stories, for example, they blamed him for causing delays on a runway at the Los Angeles airport when, in May 1993, he got a two-hundred-dollar haircut aboard Air Force One. Yet most of the media barely mentioned it when they later found out much of that "reporting" was wrong—the haircut did not cause any serious delays.

According to a story in the *Los Angeles Times* from September 1993, four months after the haircut, "The networks covered the haircut, and it was Page 1 in the *New York Times, Los Angeles Times, Washington Post, Boston Globe* and *Dallas Morning News,* among many others." Six weeks after the haircut took place, however, a Freedom of Information Act request by *Newsday* revealed that Federal Aviation Administration records showed "no planes had been forced to circle the airport, no runways had been backed up—and only one plane was delayed . . . for two minutes." The *L.A. Times* added, "*Newsday, USA Today* and the *Houston Chronicle* gave that corrective story prominent attention. Virtually every other news organization in the country either ignored it or buried it. . . . The *Washington Post* ran one paragraph. The *New York Times,* which had editorialized about 'the haircut that tied up two runways,' ran not a word. The three major network evening news shows were equally silent."

Why? Because the White House press corps are driven to cover conflict, no matter who they cover. Conflict is juicy, conflict sells, the public is interested in conflict, and the White House press corps respond by providing it. It's also harder to cover the intricacies of major policy debates as a White House reporter. Conflict is easier to cover.

The problem is exacerbated by live cable news coverage, twenty-four hours a day. White House reporters are asked by their editors to report live from the White House lawn sometimes a dozen times a day. These reporters are pressed to give "updates," even if there's no news to update. For news organizations thirsty for fresh material, conflict is often the fire that gets stoked. Many people in politics are happy to provide it, and cable TV reporters know a juicy piece of criticism will help get them on the air. I knew that if I criticized someone on the Hill at my briefing, it would be news.

Through my first six months on the job, the press repeatedly tried to bait me into a fight with President Clinton on a wide variety of issues. I tried hard not to let them create a conflict, typically saying the President was looking forward not backward, frustrating the press's desire to kick up a little dust.

The problem with a conflict-first approach to covering news is that many significant stories are ignored or downplayed. At the White House, reporters for the broadcast networks, unlike their cable counterparts, had a hard time getting on the air if they didn't have a conflict to sell their editors. Absent a serious newsworthy announcement by the President, these reporters have to search for other stories in order to get published or aired. Their quest typically begins with a search for a conflict.

William Powers, a columnist with the respected Washington magazine *National Journal,* wrote about the media at a time when President Bush's popularity was sky-high, after the end of major conflict in the Iraqi war. "The problem, and the essential challenge for the news business right now," he wrote, "is that we are living through a moment that's inhospitable to our deepest talents and inclinations. The best journalists are troublemakers, pot-stirrers, naysayers, dirt-eaters. When the whole culture is saying 'yes, yes, yes' to some sparkly idea or popular leader, we love nothing better than to be the ones who rush in screaming 'no, no, no,' brandishing the ugly evidence. To the noble hack, there is no smell sweeter than the skunk spray of a major political scandal." I wouldn't call the press dirt-eaters, but Powers sums up what makes reporters run—it's the constant hunt for someone, somewhere who's done someone or something wrong.

As for ideology, it does play a role, typically a subtle but important one, particularly on policy-related stories.

In March 1998, when I worked as communications director for the House Ways and Means Committee, twelve students from Columbia Journalism School visited Washington for a training program that included a meeting with me. I talked to them about how a spokesman does his job and how I interacted with the national press corps. We sat around a conference table on the first floor of the Longworth House Office Building, and the talk was informal and amiable. After it was over, out of a sense of curiosity about these future reporters, I asked for a show of hands on how they had voted in the 1996 presidential election.

"Clinton first," I said. "How many of you voted for President Clinton in the 1996 election?"

Eleven hands went up.

"So only one of you voted for Senator Dole?" I asked, amazed it could be so lopsided.

"No," said the owner of the hand that didn't go up. "I voted for Ralph Nader."

Reporters will tell you it doesn't matter what they think personally, or who they voted for. It doesn't affect their coverage, they assert. They mean it, they believe it, and they say it earnestly. My twenty years of experience working with Washington reporters tells me it's not that simple. I've concluded that when it comes to policy-related stories, particularly stories involving social issues, Democrats have an easier time with the Washington press corps than Republicans. When it comes to scandals, the press are equally tough on everyone.

Give me a newsroom that consists of eleven Ronald Reagan voters and one Pat Buchanan voter, and I'll bet the news would come out differently. Stories that are today on the front page would be buried inside, or they wouldn't appear at all. Stories that are today on the inside, or don't appear, would make the front page. One-day stories about controversies involving Democrats would become feeding frenzies, while the feeding frenzies aimed at Republicans would instead be one-day stories. For example, the press turned their guns on President Bush in 2004 over his attendance record when he was stationed in Alabama as part of his National Guard Service in the 1970s, yet they largely gave Senator John Kerry a pass over his failure to show up for three-quarters of the public hearings of the Senate Intelligence Committee from 1993 to 2001 and his refusal to release his attendance record for the committee's private meetings.

In Iraq, stories about the way insurgents routinely hide weapons in mosques—a violation of the rules of war—would get far more airtime and prominent coverage. So too would the success stories in Iraq—

there must be *something* good happening in a nation of 25 million people.

On the domestic front, today's occasional story about the failure of government spending to solve the most intractable social ills would be replaced on a more frequent basis with stories showing that personal responsibility is often the difference between people making it or failing in our free society. On the economic front, stories about the power of markets to correct mistakes and improve the livelihoods of all Americans would be more common. Instead of declaring that government leaders who believe in private markets favor "doing nothing" to solve problems, stories would feature the fact that there are limits to what the government can accomplish.

If newsrooms had more balance, the very words reporters use to describe what they see would be quite different. When Republicans held congressional hearings in 1997 to criticize abuses by the Internal Revenue Service, the *New York Times* originally dismissed the effort as "IRS bashing." When Democrats criticize health maintenance organizations or large corporations, their actions are treated seriously by the Washington press corps. They're certainly not dismissed as "HMO bashing." Only after the public was gripped by the IRS hearings did much of the press take the issue seriously. This too is bias. It is subtle, common, and regrettable. It's also inevitable when newsrooms, particularly in Washington, are so heavily dominated by people who, studies show, are mostly Democratic voters. It's another reason why Republicans think the Washington press corps isn't fair to them, especially on policy-related matters.

Talk radio is dominated by conservatives. Fox News has found a large and growing niche in the news market with a largely Republican audience. By contrast, CNN has a largely Democratic audience. Outside the Washington Beltway, there's much more political diversity in the news media. There's no shortage of Republican-leaning news outlets in communities throughout America. Based on the reporters I got to know in Washington and at the White House, I believe a strong majority of them don't agree with Republicans when it comes to policy matters. They don't always agree with the Democrats, but I believe they hold a higher degree of skepticism about Republican policies. Are they able to ignore their personal views and instead objectively report the facts? That's where I found a common, subtle bias.

Subtle signs of a writer's often unthinking bias would be checked and corrected if there was a greater ideological balance in newsrooms. Evidence of a lean to the left would more likely be caught if newsrooms reflected the ideological balance in the country instead of the mostly liberal backgrounds of those who are drawn to journalism school and the professors who teach them.

According to a September 2002 article in *The American Enterprise* magazine, the Democratic bias in academia is profound. In eight academic departments surveyed at Cornell University, 166 professors were registered in the Democratic Party or another party of the left, with just 6 registered in the Republican Party or another party of the right. Similar imbalances showed up in departments at the eighteen other universities surveyed. At the University of Colorado, Boulder, the numbers were 116 to 5. They were 151 to 17 at Stanford, 54 to 3 at Brown, 99 to 6 at the University of California, San Diego, and 59 to 7 at Berkeley. At Williams College, a poll turned up only 4 registered Republicans among the more than 200 professors on campus. According to another poll taken for the American Enterprise Institute, 84 percent of Ivy League professors voted for Gore in 2000, while just 9 percent voted for Bush, who narrowly beat Nader's 6 percent.

It defies common sense to think that one year of training in journalism school can prevent a man's or woman's personal point of view from emerging in print or on the air, particularly when those who do the teaching are so uniformly Democratic themselves. Reporters are *taught* to challenge everything and to question everybody, they're *trained* to find the truth and the facts, no matter where they lie. But you simply can't erase a person's perspective, no matter how well intentioned even the best schools are.

On August 1, 2004, the *New York Times* reported a small story, buried in its "Political Points" column, revealing a sharp Democratic bias in the media. According to an unscientific survey the *Times* took of 153 journalists during a press party at the Democrats' Boston convention, the media overwhelmingly said John Kerry would make a better President than George W. Bush.

"When asked who would be a better President, the journalists from outside the Beltway picked Mr. Kerry 3 to 1, and the ones from Washington favored him 12 to 1. Those results jibe with previous surveys over the past two decades showing that journalists tend to be Democrats, especially the ones based in Washington," the *Times* reported. "Some surveys have found that more than 80 percent of the Beltway press corps votes Democratic," the paper added.

According to another survey of journalists, taken in 2004 by the Pew Research Center for the People & the Press in collaboration with the Project for Excellence in Journalism and the Committee of Concerned Journalists, 34 percent of national journalists view themselves as liberals, up from 22 percent in 1995. Only 9 percent of national journalists call themselves conservative, while 33 percent of the general public are conservative, according to Pew.

Much of the public agrees that most reporters are too liberal. When asked in a September 2004 Gallup poll, "Now thinking for a moment about the news media: In general, do you think the media is too liberal, just about right, or too conservative?" 48 percent of responding adults said "too liberal." Thirty-three percent said "just right," and only 15 percent said "too conservative."

Republicans aren't making this up. The bias is real and well documented.

The problem is accented in the modern media age, when the line between reporting and commenting is blurred, often beyond distinction. According to the Pew Research Center, 53 percent of journalists working for national news organizations in 1995 agreed with the criticism that the distinction between reporting and commentary had seriously eroded. In 1999, Pew found that 69 percent, more than two-thirds, of the national press corps thought the distinction between reporting and commentary had seriously eroded.

Appearing at the National Press Club in Washington on February 9, 2004, on *The Kalb Report*, a public affairs program sponsored by the George Washington University, the National Press Club, and the

Shorenstein Center, Bill Keller, the executive editor (the number one person) of the *New York Times,* noted that "the fact is, what goes into— what we publish on the front page of the *New York Times* today—a fair amount of it would have been regarded as excessively opinionated twenty years ago." What an amazing admission. It's also a sign of trouble in contemporary journalism. Bill Keller didn't say it because he thought it needed to be changed or fixed, though. It was instead his observation of how the *Times* has changed the way it covers the news.

When the preponderance of journalism professors and reporters are Democrats, in an era when reporting has increasingly turned into commentary, and when the top editor of the *New York Times* admits the front page of his paper is "excessively opinionated" compared with how it used to be, it's hard to deny that there's an ideological bias in the media. With so few Republican in the press corps, whose commentary and opinions *are* being reflected? The Democrats' far more than the Republicans'.

It is routine today for reporters from the biggest newspapers to appear on television shows to offer their commentary about the news they cover. A decade ago it was rare for a working journalist to do this. Columnists did it all the time, but they are paid to provide insight and opinion. Now that print reporters appear on TV to provide commentary, TV reporters edge deeper into commentary themselves. Reporters interviewing reporters is a common sight, especially on the three all-news cable networks, which have an insatiable need to fill airtime. As reporters become pundits, their own biases and points of view seep further out, out onto the air and into the news pages.

CONFLICT, CONFLICT, CONFLICT

Years ago a football player named Conrad Dobler did a commercial for Miller Lite beer. Dobler was an offensive lineman for the Saint Louis Cardinals, New Orleans Saints, and Buffalo Bills, and he enjoyed a reputation as one of the toughest players in the game, a man who stirred up fights on the field with his relentlessly aggressive play.

In the commercial, he goes up to one group of fans and says that another group of fans said their beer "tastes great." Dobler then tells the other group of fans that the first group thought their beer was "less filling." Pretty soon he gets the groups to yell at each other. "Tastes great," screams the first group. "Less filling," shouts the second. "Tastes great. Less filling. Tastes great. Less filling," both sides yell, as Dobler smiles and slides into the background to watch them fight.

In the White House briefing room, all the reporters have a little Conrad Dobler in them.

On May 1, 2003, President Bush landed on the deck of the aircraft carrier USS *Abraham Lincoln* to deliver a prime-time address to the nation about the status of the war in Iraq. Standing beneath a banner that said MISSION ACCOMPLISHED, Bush declared an "end to major hostilities" on the battlefield, and he continued, "We have difficult work to do in Iraq. We're bringing order to parts of that country that remain dangerous. . . . The transition from dictatorship to democracy will take time, but it is worth every effort."

From that day forward, the White House press corps had a marker to contrast the reality of events on the ground in Iraq with the President's speech. It was a marker drawn with conflict in mind.

After May 1, each time an American serviceman or woman lost his or her life in Iraq, press accounts contrasted the death with the President's words. An American soldier was killed in Iraq today, making him the fiftieth, the hundredth, the thousandth serviceman killed since President Bush declared an end to major hostilities in Iraq, the press would write. It's a true statement, but is it all the news, or just some of the news?

Why didn't the press report that an American soldier was killed in Iraq today, making him the fiftieth, the hundredth, or the thousandth serviceman killed since President Bush warned that Iraq remained a dangerous place? That too would have been a true statement, but it is one the press cannot bring themselves to report.

The press today all too often provide the maximum contrast, not the maximum information. Why can't they report both statements, giving readers and viewers a more accurate, richer context to controversial events? What's wrong with reporting the death of a serviceman, saying it marked the thousandth death since President Bush declared an end to major hostilities while warning that Iraq remained dangerous? The news industry typically doesn't work in such a nuanced, more accurate way, that's why. Conflict comes first.

In August 2004, Ron Insana of CNBC interviewed my brother Michael Fleischer, who lived in Baghdad for eight months working for the United States government on Iraq's economic reconstruction. A former Foreign Service officer and aide to a Democratic congressman, and a graduate of Harvard Business School, my brother is an expert in restoring to profitability American companies that are in decline. He volunteered to help Iraq and moved there because he believed improving the post-Saddam Iraqi economy was good for the Iraqi people and good for the United States.

During his live interview, he optimistically described economic conditions as he found them and stated he believed the Iraqi economy would continue to grow. As he was talking, however, someone at CNBC decided to cut away from him and instead show viewers file footage of bombs going off, large rings of fire and smoke, and mayhem in the streets. These pictures conflicted sharply with my brother's words. Why didn't CNBC show streets full of commerce or Iraqis shopping? Indeed, such scenes are everyday, common occurrences in Iraq. Why did they show any pictures at all? Why didn't they just interview their guest?

Because much of the press prizes conflict so highly, viewers were shown images selected to undercut the message of the man being interviewed. Good news about Iraq is hard to get out. But bad news flows like water.

I believe not only that the American people can handle more information but that they want it. But often—not always, but often—the press's coverage is driven by contrasts and conflicts, even if it means the American people don't get the full story. When a newsmaker says A, the press tend to focus on B. When a newsmaker says B, the press tend to focus on A. They don't just do it to Republicans, they do it to

Democrats as well. They don't just do it to government officials, they do it to many people. The media's first bias is in favor of conflict.

Such skepticism can also help the press to uncover problems. Their ability to challenge what they hear and see makes them one of society's watchdogs. Thanks to their skepticism, the government has to work harder to justify what it does and says, and thanks to their probes, many problems in corporate America, or in unions, or throughout our society are unearthed. The issue I found is, Where do they draw the line? Where does the balance lie? As the person standing at the White House podium every day, I was exposed to a unique, live, on-the-air coming together of conflict and skepticism about almost everything the White House touched. It's why my job was a paradox. I enjoyed defending the White House, and I understood the role reporters play, but it also was a grind that eventually took its toll.

RON REESE was a press secretary for two Republican members of congress before he moved to Las Vegas in 2004 to become the spokesman for the Venetian Hotel. I asked him what the difference was in working with the Washington press corps and the business press corps.

"When I worked on the Hill," Ron told me, "reporters would ask me a question and then immediately call the Democrats to say, What's your response to what I said? Here, they don't run to the Bellagio to say, What's your response to what the Venetian said? They're more inclined to take what I say and report it if they think it's newsworthy."

In Washington, people in both parties jockey against each other, often by lobbing accusations against the other side. That's not the press's fault. But the press do stir the pot, by contrasting one source against another. That also, however, is the way the public gets its chance to evaluate two competing visions for how the government should function. The press doesn't work in a vacuum. It's how Washington works, and the press is part of Washington. Both sides get to have their say, but conflicting statements are the ones reporters find the most newsworthy.

At the White House, when I wanted to avoid controversy, I learned not to accept a reporter's version of events until I could check into them myself. Often I was asked to respond to a seemingly controversial comment made by a world leader or a member of Congress. The press would sometimes omit crucial information or put an emphasis on what sounded like a conflict. A fuller read of the remarks often showed there was less conflict than the reporter had indicated.

In December 2001, Associated Press's Ron Fournier asked me, "President Putin has just said that [the United States's] pulling out of the ABM [Anti-Ballistic Missile Treaty] was a mistake. And once again reiterating that the treaty is a cornerstone of world security. What's your reaction to that?"

I told Ron I thought there was more to Putin's reaction than his short summary. "I do not believe you have all of it," I said, withholding further reaction until I could check it out. Indeed, Putin said the American withdrawal *was* a mistake. However, in the same breath he said it didn't come as a surprise to Russia, and he added, "I can say with full confidence that the decision made by the President of the United States does not pose a threat to the national security of the Russian Federation." To Putin, the treaty wasn't such a cornerstone of world stability.

In February 2003, Terry Moran of ABC asked me about a statement he claimed Bush made on the Middle East. "Last night, the President talked about resolving the Israeli-Palestinian conflict. Last June, he said, 'Israel should immediately halt—immediately—halt all settlement activities in the occupied territories. Last night, he says, 'As progress is made toward peace, settlement activity must end.' Why did he retreat on this?"

I didn't think that sounded like the President, and I had never heard him make such remarks. I told Terry I wanted to look into it.

"The language speaks for itself," he insisted. "Immediately halt all settlement activity."

I looked into it. Bush never said that. Egyptian President Hosni Mubarak did, in a meeting with Bush the previous June. It was an honest mistake, made by a usually very thorough reporter.

Reporters didn't like the fact that I didn't always accept their versions of events. They wanted me to give them an instant reply, helping to feed a frenzy or to stir things up. There were many times when members of the press *were* accurate, and then my job was to explain the President's position against whoever they cited as a source of disagreement.

George Vecsey, a well-respected sports columnist with the *New York Times,* described the conflict-driven nature of the media when he wrote about the all-star baseball player Alex Rodriguez's 2004 trade to the New York Yankees, in which Rodriguez moved from his shortstop position to third base, a new position for him, allowing the Yankee shortstop Derek Jeter to keep his spot. Using Rodriguez's nickname, Vecsey said, "A-Rod will be the lightning rod in the clubhouse. The first time Jeter misplays something at short, a posse of the news media will go running to A-Rod, trying to get him to say he would have had it. The problem is not going to be A-Rod or Jeter or [Yankee Manager Joe] Torre or maybe even [the Yankee owner, George] Steinbrenner. The problem is going to be us. It is what we do," Vecsey wrote. Remarkable. Even though his prediction turned out to be wrong and the press didn't stir up any fights between Jeter and Rodriguez, his statement shines light on how the press approach their job. Vecsey's thoughts apply too often to reporters who work for the news section.

The Pew Research Center's 1999 poll of the press corps found that reporters themselves see their industry as too cynical. Among reporters who work for national media organizations, 59 percent agreed that they were too cynical, while only 39 percent thought that was not a valid criticism. The same poll found that 60 percent of national TV and radio reporters believe their coverage of the personal and ethical behavior of public officials was driven by controversy instead of reporting the facts.

The last sentence of a television correspondent's "stand-up" from the lawn of the White House is the perfect place to see how it works. These sixty-second or ninety-second stories are still watched by millions, and they have a large impact on how the American people receive their news. Almost uniformly, reporters from all the broadcast and cable networks sum up their stories with a gloomy, negative, conflict-driven final sentence. When the entire story is bad, the last sentence is worse. When the news is largely positive, the last sentence finds someone for whom the news can't be good. I call their last sentence "the down note."

In October 2002, Democratic and Republican congressional leaders joined President Bush in the Rose Garden to announce a bipartisan agreement on the language of a resolution authorizing the use of force in Iraq. House Minority Leader Dick Gephardt and Democratic Senator Joe Lieberman, as well as Republican Senator John McCain, stood should to shoulder with Bush when he made what was then a surprise announcement. After CBS's White House correspondent John Roberts announced the major accomplishment, he closed by saying, "What's not clear at this point—is the White House seeking unanimity in the Senate, or simply enough votes to get the measure passed?"

The network had to work so hard to close its report with a conflict-ahead, negative note that it established a new standard in seeking conflict. Unanimity? There wasn't unanimity for the resolution authorizing force after September 11, 2001, or when a declaration of war was passed after Pearl Harbor. In both cases, one member of the House voted against the use of force.

Terry Moran of ABC covered the show of support for Bush by declaring that Dick Gephardt's leadership was crucial. He ended his report, saying, "His support and that of key Senate Democrats like Senator Joe Lieberman puts a lot of pressure on the Senate Majority Leader, Tom Daschle." An accurate statement, of course. But an example of how one person's good news must be someone else's bad news.

When the President announced a comprehensive energy plan, most of the White House press corps faulted the plan for lacking a short-term solution to the high price of gasoline. How come there is nothing short term in the plan? they demanded. When the President announced his Medicare plan in 2001, he included a short-term plan for a prescription drug card to lower the price of drugs. A "Band-Aid," the press mockingly labeled it. When the White House did something long term, many in the press wanted to know why we weren't doing anything short term. When we did something short term, the press wanted to know why we weren't doing anything long term.

Given the press's conflict-driven reactions to much of what the government does, the White House, regardless of which party is in power, is often damned if it does and damned if it doesn't.

In the spring of 2004, a jolt of good economic news hit when the government announced that the economy had produced 308,000 new jobs in March, almost three times higher than the "experts" had predicted. All the networks made this their lead story, all in glowing terms. The ABC anchor, Peter Jennings, called it a "strong report," and the correspondent Betsy Stark said "Today's report should put to rest fears that the jobless recovery might never end." Her last sentence, however, sounded the familiar down note. "The key, of course, is whether companies will continue to hire at this aggressive pace." On NBC, the correspondent Rehema Ellis noted the news was "far better than economists' predictions," but her last sentence was "A start, but economists say the nation needs six to twelve months like March so everyone who wants to work, can." I can't quarrel with the accuracy of either sentence, except to point out the way reporters are trained—to end many of their stories on a down note, even when the news is good.

Two months later, the good economic news continued. For the third month in a row, employment growth had surged, creating a total of 1.2 million jobs. Reporting the good news for the third month in a row, the networks' last sentences once more sounded the down note.

"The job market, finally gaining momentum. But is it enough to put over 8 million unemployed Americans back to work?" asked NBC's Anne Thompson.

"Today's employment report gives the Federal Reserve one more reason to raise interest rates later this month. The worry is no longer pumping up the economy. The job, now, is to keep it from overheating," reported ABC News.

The Pew poll of the national press corps also found that by 58 to 40 percent, national reporters agreed they "have become obsessed with intricate dynamics like being first with the big story and impressing their colleagues." The combination of impressing colleagues while finding or creating conflict played itself out every day in the on-camera White House briefing room.

In early May 2001, the President announced the appointment of John Walters as director of national drug control policy, the drug czar. In a Rose Garden speech, the President also announced an effort to combat drug abuse on both the supply and the demand sides. He talked about how drug use saps a young person's life. He added, "From the early 1980s until the early 1990s, drug use amongst high school seniors was reduced every year. We had made tremendous strides in cutting drug use. This cannot be said today. We must do, and we will do, a better job."

Three hours later I entered the briefing room.

"Ari, on drugs, the President talked about what's failed really in the drug war in this period, beginning in the early nineties. From his point of view, what's gone wrong?" a reporter asked.

"It's not clear what the exact causes of it were," I said. "But the trend is discernible and worrisome and crystal clear. We just handed out . . . the study that was done that shows the trend in how the use of drugs declined each and every year from the early eighties until the early 1990s, and then it went up consistently throughout the early 1990s. The President thinks it's essential for the government to send a simple and clear message: Don't do drugs. Doing drugs will kill you."

"But we've heard all that," a reporter replied. "What I'm asking you is why you won't be reflective here? I mean, if the President is out there saying that something has gone wrong since the early 1990s . . . so what's happened?"

I said that the President would be interested in hearing about the cause from experts and that he wanted to move forward to reverse the rise in drug use.

"Why can't you look in the past and be reflective? Why do we always have to look forward? He doesn't have any opinion about what's gone wrong and what the problem with the approach is?"

Moments later another reporter followed up.

"The President said today that acceptance of drug use is simply not an option for this administration. And afterwards, one of his domestic policy advisers said, 'The notion that drug use is okay, the notion that I didn't inhale, we're all baby boomers, we all did it, those days are over.' Does the President believe the previous administration tacitly accepted illegal drug use?"

Uh-oh. My Conrad Dobler alert went off, realizing the press wanted a Bush versus Clinton fight.

"The President is not going to look back. He's going to look forward," I said. "He does think it's very important for the government at all levels to send a consistent message that drug abuse is wrong, that people should not tolerate drug abuse, and that parents need to know that the government is working with them when they send signals to their children, that don't do drugs, don't get started on drugs, it can ruin your life, and that treatment programs are available and other methods of education are available to help those who do make the mistake and start taking drugs."

The temperature in the room started to rise.

"If you're unwilling to answer his question and say, no, we're not accusing the Clinton administration of tacitly condoning drug abuse, then, in fact, you are accusing them of doing that," a reporter stated. "You're not answering his question, yes or no—do you think the Clinton administration tacitly endorsed—"

"The President's focus is on the future," I reiterated.

"But, Ari, a fair question is that you are coming out saying, here's your solution, or what you're going to do, you don't want to look back, but isn't it fair to say, what are you all doing differently that the Clinton administration didn't do for eight years that didn't result in a reduction in drug use?"

As many times as reporters offered the bait of a Bush versus Clinton drug fight, I refused to take it. "I think sometimes in this town there's this fascination with trying to pit one politician against another, to have one person blame a predecessor—"

"You're the one bringing it up," a reporter interjected.

"That's not President Bush's style—" I started to say.

"You're the one who keeps referring back to the eighties and nineties," someone argued.

"I'm responding to questions that are asked me about the eighties and nineties," I argued back.

And on it went.

Reporters were partially right. Bush did bring up the trends as he discussed the eighties and the nineties. He did look back in an attempt to frame the future. I didn't think he looked back in an effort to blame President Clinton. It's possible to cite statistics and trends without placing blame. The aide who referred to former President Clinton's statement about "not inhaling" didn't help matters. He gave reporters reason to find a fight. The press's job that day was to find conflict; my job was to avoid it.

The briefing actually turned humorous, I suppose, when a reporter asked if the White House was drug testing its own workers.

Yes, I said, the President and the Vice President included.

"This is going to sound arcane," a reporter asked. "But when the President took this test, how was it administered? Who gave it? Was it a blood test?"

"I'll be happy to talk to you about that somewhere other than this podium," I replied, having no wish to talk about the President's bodily fluids on TV. A couple reporters, however, thought it was interesting, or perhaps funny, and they were determined to find out whether the drug test was a blood test or a urine test.

"In the usual fashion, we assume?"

"I'm sorry," I said, wondering why this was so important.

"In the usual fashion, we assume?"

"There are two ways to do it," a reporter helpfully pointed out.

"Let's take some other topics," I said.

Attempts to create conflict in the briefing room weren't limited to Bush versus Clinton. Reporters were good at finding conflict anywhere, whether it was a congressional Democrat against Bush or, better yet, a congressional Republican against Bush, or a member of the cabinet against Bush.

Often the press's target for a split with the President was Secretary of State Colin Powell. Powell, a pro-choice Republican, was seen by the press as slow to support the war with Iraq and as a moderating influence on the President. On abortion and affirmative action, Bush and Powell didn't see eye to eye, but he was the secretary of state, so there was room for the two to have those differences without causing a stir.

In February 2002, Powell, reaching out to young people, appeared on *Be Heard,* an MTV program. Joining him via satellite were youngsters from Brazil, India, Russia, Egypt, the United States, and other places. They wanted to hear the secretary's views on the war against terrorism, the peace process in the Middle East, AIDS, whatever they chose to talk about. Powell is great in these formats, and as usual, he answered every question he got.

"Hi, everyone, my name is Daniela," from Italy. "As a young Catholic woman, I would like to know from the secretary of state what he thinks of the Catholic positions on condoms, which is prohibited, and therefore, this condemns anyone who might be exposed to the [HIV] virus."

Powell responded, "I certainly respect the views of the Holy Father and the Catholic Church. In my own judgment, condoms are a way to prevent infection, and therefore I not only support their use, I encourage their use among people who are sexually active and need to protect themselves. I think it's important for young people especially to protect themselves from the possibility of acquiring any sexually transmitted disease, but especially to protect themselves from HIV/AIDS, which is a plague that is upon the face of the earth.

"And so I believe condoms is [*sic*] part of the solution to the HIV/AIDS crisis, and I encourage their use by young people who are sexually active. You've got to protect yourself. If you don't protect yourself, who is going to protect you? And you're putting your life at risk when you are having sexual relations with partners who might be infected. And you really don't know whether they are or they are not, do you?

"And this is especially the case in sub-Saharan Africa, in the Caribbean, and increasingly a problem in other parts of the world. It was a major American problem and still is. But we have gotten more control over it. But now it is raging out of control in some parts of Africa, Caribbean, elsewhere—China, India—all of these nations will be touched by it, and it is important that the whole international community come together, speak candidly about it, forget about taboos, forget about conservative ideas with respect to what you should tell young people about it. It's the lives of young people that are put at risk by unsafe sex, and therefore protect yourself."

When I walked into the briefing room the next morning for the off-camera gaggle, the press were having a field day, thinking they had a Bush-Powell split, a conservatives versus Powell split, a split over the issue of sex. And sex sells, especially on cable TV. Bush, while supporting the use of condoms for sexually active kids, typically focused his remarks on abstinence, and here the secretary was caught discussing condom use! He even took a poke at conservatives! The press assumed he was referring to American political conservatives, despite the fact he was talking to a young Italian woman who had cited the position of the church. I thought he was referring to theological conservatives, and also the conservative notion in Africa that the existence of AIDS shouldn't be acknowledged—it was taboo. Maybe he was referring to American political conservatives, but I didn't think so.

Reporters went running to social conservatives in the United States claiming that Powell had attacked them, and being no fans of the secretary to begin with, conservatives like James Dobson, president of Focus on the Family, and Ken Connor of the Family Research Council gleefully took the bait, went on the record, and voilà, a controversy was born. Conrad Dobler couldn't have been prouder. The press didn't start the fight with Dobson and Connor, but they knew that turning to them would fan its flames. Reporters could have sought quotes from many people who would have praised Powell's statement or said it was no big deal, like I did. The sought-after quotes, however, were the ones that kicked up a little dust.

Is the President frustrated by Powell's remark? I was asked. Is there a conflict with Powell? What's the White House position on condoms? The questions came rapid-fire.

"The President's position is that abstinence education and sex education, health education are important parts of preventing unwanted pregnancies. Our society has been wrestling with the issue about how to prevent unwanted pregnancies and to fight sexually transmitted diseases for a long time, particularly since the sixties. And the fact is that no social researcher has come up with any one answer to how to prevent this.

"The White House and the secretary share the same approach, which is both abstinence and, as the budget reflects, sex education, health education. As society together grapples with what works— what's happened in recent years is that there was no focus on abstinence. And the President thinks that's important. So, too, does the secretary. And the secretary has dedicated a lot of time to that." The secretary and Mrs. Powell, along with the well-known conservative activist Bill Bennett and his wife, were sponsors of the Best Friends Foundation, which stresses abstinence education.

After thirteen questions on the Bush-Powell condom "split," the gaggle came to an end.

Less than three hours later, I returned to the briefing room for the on-camera meeting. The great condom debate quickly resumed.

"Some conservative groups, hearing what you told us earlier today at the gaggle, saying that there's no daylight between the President and the secretary on this, are saying that you're— They still view it as a contradiction. They say you're undermining the President's position of abstinence. The secretary did not mention abstinence. He was talking about encouraging condom use. What's your response to that?"

I again stated there was no split between Powell and Bush, pointing out that the question and the answer were both in the context of people who *are* sexually active, people who made a decision not to practice abstinence.

Then, thinking of Powell's involvement with Best Friends, I asserted, "But let me say this—Colin Powell takes a backseat to no one when it comes to abstinence—" And the room burst into laughter. I quickly added, "Abstinence *education*."

I had just accused the married secretary of state of practicing abstinence! Uh-oh. Mercifully, the briefing moved on to other issues, and as soon as it was over, I hurried to my office, called the Situation Room, and asked to be transferred to Secretary Powell *immediately*!

He came on the line, and I said, "Mr. Secretary, I need to reach you before the press does, or before Alma [his wife] does," which left him puzzled.

I filled him in on the fact that I just told the world, on TV, that he, a married man, was abstinent. He laughed out loud, thanked me for getting to him before Alma did, and good-naturedly hung up the phone. You never know what's going to happen to you when you show up for work in the White House briefing room.

The search for conflict, the desire to expose a problem and air it so the American people can decide which side they're on, is a vital mission of journalism. But when the mission becomes lopsided to the point that the news is mostly defined by conflict and negativity, deeper, richer truths, such as the President's warning that Iraq remained dangerous, get lost. At a time when the American people yearn for positive candidates, positive campaigns, and positive leaders, the press tend to reward with coverage those who engage in negativity. Attack your opponent and you're likely to make the news, the front page, if it's juicy enough or a first-time attack. Describe who you are and what you're for, it's harder to gather day-to-day coverage.

Announce a policy on an issue about which leaders in both parties support you and you're not likely to get much coverage, even though the prospects for enacting your ideas into law may be strong. No conflict? No disagreements? No news. Pass a bill that the President threatens to veto? That's news. Negotiate for three weeks over a complicated piece of legislation before reaching an agreement. It's likely to turn into three weeks of negative coverage about splits, differences, deadlocks, and divisions that will be hard to bridge, followed by one day of positive press about the agreement. The conflict-driven negativity of the press is found almost every day in all areas of the news and especially on the front page. On August 6, 2002, the *Washington Post* ran seven stories on its front page, every one of them about something bad, wrong, or negative, not just in politics but throughout our society.

Conflict can come in many shapes and sizes, particularly in pictures. In the summer of 2002, a friend of the First Lady called to warn her that she had been approached via e-mail by a *U.S. News & World Report* editor shopping around Texas for a picture of the Bushs' then teenage daughter Jenna at a party. The magazine was willing to pay cash.

Mrs. Bush's friend was alarmed. The e-mail was from a photo editor at *U.S. News*. "We are doing a story where we could use a social type photo of Jenna Bush with friends at a party in Texas within the last year or so. Understand you have these types of photos. Our standard repro rates . . . begin at $225 for quarter page and escalate up to $500 for full page." The friend was told the story was going to be about whether the Secret Service was doing a good job protecting the presidential daughters, and they wanted the photo to fit the story.

Mrs. Bush's friend sent her the e-mail, which was then given to me. I called a top official at *U.S. News* to complain about both the invasion of the daughter's privacy and the practice of offering money for the right kind of picture. To the magazine's credit, the editor stopped this project dead in its tracks.

During briefings, I headed off the press's hunt for conflict with my determination to avoid letting them find one. Conflict in the briefing room provides great "made for TV" moments that I typically wanted to avoid. This is another reason that the briefing in the modern media age isn't as valuable as it used to be. Acknowledging a problem, taking blame for an incident, agreeing there may be a split in the cabinet would often lead to dramatic front-page stories that I thought were blown out of proportion. Too many of the press's questions exaggerated conflicts, and too many of my answers glossed over potential problems. I often felt like the press and I were talking past each other. Whether it's the cameras or the nature of the news industry today, the normal give-and-take between the press secretary and the press has turned too often into a standoff, with the press playing their aggressive role and the press secretary playing a defensive one.

Did Secretary Powell and Vice President Cheney agree on every issue? I'm sure they didn't. When asked on live TV if Powell and Cheney disagreed about an issue, was I supposed to say yes? I thought it better if the President was allowed to receive the private counsel of his advisers, especially when they disagreed, enabling him to hear all sides of an issue and reach his own conclusions. I felt no obligation to engage with the press on internal policy discussions, appreciating the value of a thoughtful and deliberative decision-making process.

In July 2002, the Pew organization took a poll of the public that asked "if the news media helps society to solve its problems, or if the news media gets in the way of society solving its problems." The results were not good for the press.

By a margin of 58 percent to 31 percent, the American people said the press got in the way of society solving its problems. Often reporters are drawn to journalism to expose what's wrong in society or government, so that problems can be aired and fixed. But the overly adversarial nature of the press and the relentless quest for conflict are creating a divide between writer and reader, reporter and viewer, journalist and source.

Having stood at that White House podium for two and a half years, I believe what's really at stake is whether the public is getting complete and accurate news, or mostly the bad news, from the press. Are they reading and seeing all sides, including the positive side, or mostly the bad side? Is good news in Iraq being covered as frequently as bad news? No, it's not. Bad news travels through the press with a greater velocity and intensity than good news. Bad news stories can stretch for days and weeks. Good news stories are often one-day events.

There *are* reporters in Washington who consciously make an effort to stand out from the pack. They're tough and they ask hard questions, but they don't seek conflict unless it's genuine. When they hear a good explanation, they accept it. Tim Russert, of NBC, is probably the most respected reporter in the business because he's tough, he's smart, but he's not overly adversarial. He doesn't assume the worst. He gives people a chance to explain, and he challenges them. He comes across as fair and thoughtful, not just conflict-driven. But for too many reporters, it's a daily overdrive toward conflict, regardless of who they cover or what party is in power.

THE LIBERAL PRESS?

Like every other institution, the Washington and political press corps operate with a good number of biases and predilections.

They include, but are not limited to, a near-universal shared sense that liberal political positions on social issues like gun control, homosexuality, abortion and religion are the default, while more conservative positions are "conservative positions."

They include a belief that government is a mechanism to solve the nation's problems; that more taxes on corporations and the wealthy are good ways to cut the deficit and raise money for social spending and don't have a negative effect on economic growth; and that emotional examples of suffering (provided by unions or consumer groups) are good ways to illustrate economic statistic stories.

The press, by and large, does not accept President Bush's justifications for the Iraq war—in any of its WMD, imminent threat, or evil-doer formulations. It does not understand how educated, sensible people could possibly be wary of multilateral institutions or friendly, sophisticated European allies.

It does not accept the proposition that the Bush tax cuts helped the economy by stimulating summer spending.

It remains fixated on the unemployment rate.

It believes President Bush is "walking a fine line" with regards to the gay marriage issue, choosing between "tolerance" and his "right-wing base."

It still has a hard time understanding how, despite the drumbeat of conservative grass-top complaints about overspending and deficits, President Bush's base remains extremely and loyally devoted to him—and it looks for every opportunity to find cracks in that base.

That's what ABC News said in its influential daily newsletter *The Note* on February 10, 2004, in a breathtakingly frank and rare internal assessment of the journalism business. The public largely agrees.

A Pew poll in October 2000 asked the public, "How often do you think members of the news media let their own political preferences influence the way they report the news? Often, sometimes, seldom, or never?"

By a margin of 89 percent to 9 percent, respondents said the press often or sometimes let their political preferences influence the way they reported the news. Only 9 percent said seldom or never. The largest response was "often," cited by 57 percent.

Asked a similar question in 1999, reporters told the Pew organization the opposite of what their readers and viewers think. In response to the question "Is it possible for journalists to develop a systematic way to cover events in a disinterested and fair way, or don't you think it's possible?" 71 percent said it was possible, while 24 percent said it was not.

Before joining Governor Bush's presidential campaign in late 1999, I was the communications director for Elizabeth Dole's presidential bid. On May 2, she traveled to New Hampshire, the first primary state, for a major meeting of the Republican Party. Hundreds of activists were present, along with many of the presidential candidates. Governor Bush was the overwhelming front-runner, and the Dole campaign was struggling. We needed to do something to break through and grab attention.

In a carefully worded speech, Dole announced to the mostly conservative audience that she supported safety locks on guns, a ban on assault weapons, and the elimination of cop killer bullets. As her unexpected words sank in, a few in the crowd booed, but most applauded. What she said was mainstream, but it had the distinction of being an unusual statement for a Republican candidate in the middle of a primary. Talk of "gun control" was typically the domain of Democrats. The press reaction followed a predictable pattern.

The initial coverage pointed out that her remarks were greeted by boos, despite the fact that most people had applauded and only a few booed. But the next day a funny thing happened. As I fielded reporters' calls at our headquarters in Rosslyn, Virginia, journalists repeatedly told me how "brilliant" her remarks were. They established her as a serious, thoughtful candidate, I was told. The press are largely pro–gun control, so they liked what she'd said. I thought to myself, This must be what it's like to do press for a Democrat. When the press are on your side, it sure is an easier job.

When it comes to policy, the Washington press corps, as the ABC *Note* reported, are more likely to see issues through the eyes of Democrats than through the eyes of Republicans. As tough as the press can be on *both* sides, Democrats enjoy a distinct advantage in how their policies are covered, especially when it comes to the way subtle but important nuances are shaded.

Every good writer understands the power of the written word. Every good television correspondent understands the power of a picture combined with the power of the spoken word. Whether someone is writing fiction or nonfiction, covering the news, or writing an e-mail or a letter home, words have weight and carry meaning. Those who pursue journalism have a special appreciation for the written word—it's how they earn their living. Their choice of words is the hallmark of what they do. They know how to pick words, shape sentences, and write an account that leaves a reader with an impression.

Reporters dismiss the notion that they're largely liberal, or they say it doesn't matter, it's not reflected in their writings. I beg to differ. The lexicon of the left is too often the natural lexicon of the press. There's no better example of how many reporters bring their bias to work than the way they label Democrats and Republicans in a policy debate. With few exceptions, the Republican side is described as "conservative" or "right-wing." The Democratic side is typically described in neutral terms and only occasionally as "liberal." As campaign 2004 heated up, I noticed an increased use by the press of the word *liberal,* but while I served as press secretary, coverage of policy debates only occasionally labeled the other side "liberal." Instead, the word *liberal* is too often replaced in the press with the Democrats' own preferred word—*progressive.* I don't really know what a "progressive" is, but I know the Democrats like the word and the press use it, particularly in their coverage of social issues.

Discussing the political views of Senator John Kerry's wife, Teresa Heinz Kerry, the *New York Times* wrote in May 2004, "Will her devotion to *progressive* [emphasis added] causes imbue her husband's campaign with badly needed passion or offend voters who expect first ladies to be obeisant sidekicks?"

The *Washington Post* the same month wrote a story citing a poll taken by Democracy Corps, a political consulting firm founded by James Carville and the Kerry campaign adviser Bob Shrum. Democracy Corps's own webpage states they were founded "out of outrage over the impeachment of President Clinton," and they accuse the Republicans in Congress of "radical partisanship." The *Post* wrote, "For a president whose credibility on national security and terrorism remains quite high, Bush's credibility on the economy is tepid. A new poll Greenberg conducted for the *progressive* [emphasis added] group Democracy Corps found 52 percent of the public saying they want to move in 'a significantly different direction' on the economy, with 43 percent saying they prefer Bush's direction." Progressive? I think *liberal* would have been a more accurate description.

In February 2004, a controversy broke out about whether President Bush had performed his duties with the Alabama National Guard. Around the same time a photo emerged of a young John Kerry sitting near Jane Fonda at an anti–Vietnam War rally. The front page of the *New York Times* ran a short piece about the issue headlined FOR KERRY AND BUSH, VIETNAM YEARS LOOM.

The piece stated, "In Mr. Kerry's case, *conservatives* [emphasis added] are working hard to shine an unflattering spotlight on his antiwar activities and his record on defense and intelligence matters in the Senate." It continued, "In the case of the president, leading *Democrats* [emphasis added] have seized on a lingering issue by hammering one simple question: If Mr. Bush served in Alabama, is there anyone he served with who remembers him?"

"Conservatives" for one side? "Leading Democrats" for the other? Why didn't the story describe Bush's opponents as "leading liberals"? Why does one side in a debate deserve an ideological label, *conservative,* when the other side enjoys the broader term Democrats, which after all can include liberals, moderates, and conservatives? Why are the press so willing to label one side and so reluctant to label the other using equal terms? Why have they largely stopped using the word *liberal*? I think it's because candidates tagged by their opponents as "liberals" began to lose their elections in the eighties and the nineties, causing the press to hesitate before calling someone a liberal, believing the word's use would reflect an echo of a Republican charge, an echo they try to avoid. Yet they show no such reluctance to label Republicans as right-wingers or conservatives, charges often made by Democrats.

What makes this small front-page piece even more important is that it was *not* a complete news story. It was a tease, a five-paragraph piece that encouraged the reader to flip to the full story on page fourteen. A tease like that is typically written not by a reporter but by a senior editor, an editor responsible for the content of the most important page in the news industry, the front page of the powerful, trend-setting *New York Times*. It's a telling snapshot into how the top minds lean on important but subtle matters. It's also a signal sent to reporters about how their bosses approach the news. And the front page of the *New York Times* has a profound influence on reporters not just in the *Times*'s newsroom but everywhere in the country. Perhaps that's why ideological labeling in the press is so one-sided and repeated so often.

In September 2004, an antibusiness group funded by organized labor, Citizens for Tax Justice (CTJ), released a study of the tax burden on American corporations. To its credit, the *Washington Post* headline read, LIBERAL GROUP DECRIES CORPORATE TAX SLIDE. The *Wall Street Journal* called the group "liberal leaning." At the *New York Times,* a different story emerged. Their headline read, STUDY FINDS ACCELERAT-ING DECLINE IN CORPORATE TAXES. Their story began, "American's largest and most profitable companies paid less in corporate income taxes in the last three years, even as they increased profits, according to a study released yesterday."

Not until the fourth paragraph were readers advised that CTJ was, according to the *Times,* "a non-profit research and advocacy group" that was funded "in part by labor unions." The *Times* wouldn't call them "liberal." Yet the same story included a rebuttal to the study from the Heritage Foundation, which the *Times* described as a "conservative research group."

In February 2002, the Bush administration proposed making fetuses eligible for low-income health insurance in an effort to deliver additional prenatal care to recipients of federal health programs. The *Washington Post* covered the story on its front page. The second paragraph read, "Administration officials said the proposal was intended purely to extend health care to more women during pregnancy, but *women's groups* [emphasis added] and abortion rights advocates denounced the move. . . . The proposed rule change was one of two administration announcements yesterday that appeared to be aimed at satisfying *social conservatives* [emphasis added] as President Bush prepared to release next year's budget on Monday. Officials said the president also would add $33 million to federal funding of programs that encourage teenagers to abstain from sex."

Women's groups on one side? Social conservatives on the other? Why does the Republican side get an ideological label while the other side has the universally appealing label "women's groups"? Why isn't one group "social conservatives" and the other "social liberals"? I don't think I've ever seen the phrase "social liberal" in the press, yet "social conservatives" is common usage. That's not balanced reporting. It is, however, a subtle but important sign of bias. Who says, by the way, that the Bush stand is supported only by conservatives? Liberals may not have liked it, but I'm sure many moderates supported the President's effort to help low-income mothers receive prenatal care, and most parents I know, regardless of political party, hope their teenage children *are* abstaining from sex. Who in the world said that a program that encourages teenagers to abstain from sex is aimed at satisfying only social conservatives?

Abortion is probably the issue that brings the press's bias into play more than any other. In 2003 the House of Representatives passed a ban on partial-birth abortions by a vote of 281 to 142. Sixty-three Democrats voted with the Republicans. Despite the large bipartisan vote, the press adopted the language of the minority, which couldn't even describe the abortion procedure as "partial birth." Instead, ABC's and CBS's evening news both fuzzed up the term, with CBS's Dan Rather describing instead what "anti-abortion groups call 'partial birth,'" and ABC's correspondent Elizabeth Vargas labeling the bill "what some critics have named partial-birth abortion."

USA Today wrote that President Bush looked forward to signing the ban, although he said the nation was not ready to prevent all abortions. The story continued, "To Gloria Feldt, president of Planned Parenthood, which advocates abortion rights, 'That's just code for "I can't outlaw all abortion yet, but I want to." The story continues, "Sandy Rios of Concerned Women for America, a *conservative* [emphasis added] group that opposes abortion says, 'It's possible that all abortions could be banned in a second Bush term.'"

Stop the presses. Why is the antiabortion side, or pro-life side, as they call themselves, labeled "conservative" while Planned Parenthood *isn't* called liberal? Why does one side earn an ideological warning label while the other side enjoys benign neutrality? It's because, as *The Note* points out, most reporters are pro-choice and they think most Americans agree with their point of view. And reporters like to think of themselves as moderates, not liberals, so their point of view can't be described as "liberal." But the other side, reporters think, surely *can* be described as "conservative." If Columbia Journalism School, and all the nation's J-schools, graduated eleven Reagan voters and one Buchanan voter, readers would see "left-wing" and "liberal" in print all the time and seldom hear about conservatives or right-wingers. And if newsrooms, especially at the top levels, were equally divided between Democrats and Republicans, then references to "liberal" would likely be offset with references to "conservative," "right-wing" with "left-wing," and "Democrat" with "Republican."

Even the Associated Press, a bastion of straight reporting without commentary, can be part of the problem. In 2002, when President Bush withheld money for UN family planning programs because of concerns about coerced abortions in China, the AP led its story, "The Bush Administration, in a victory for *social conservatives* [emphasis added], will withhold $34 million that had been earmarked for UN family planning programs overseas. 'Women and children will die because of this decision,' said Thoraya Obaid, executive director of the UN fund." The AP story described her as one of the "critics of the decision." The story's first sentence referred to "social conservatives." Why wasn't Ms. Obaid called a "social liberal"?

The story continued, "*Conservatives* [emphasis added] helped Bush win the presidency and political advisers have tended to them. But the family planning decision could damage Bush's standing with moderates and *women* [emphasis added]." I double-checked—it wasn't a news analysis or commentary. It was carried by AP as a straight news story. Conservatives on the one side, women on the other. Isn't it possible that many women supported Bush's action to prevent China from using family planning money to support its coercive abortion policies? It's more than possible, it's likely. I suspect moderate women split right down the middle, with pro-life women supporting Bush and pro-choice women opposing him. But in the case of this story, all women and all moderates must be pro-choice. Otherwise, how could Bush's action damage his standing with these groups?

Biased and unfair, and it's another reason the press are more likely to see issues through the eyes of Democrats than through the eyes of Republicans. But it doesn't stop there. The press often write about the political influence of the "religious right" or "evangelical Christians." How often do they write about the "religious left"? Seldom. There are liberal religious leaders who play important roles and have great political influence in the Democratic Party.

The antiwar movement in the United States has important and powerful backers who find moral justification in opposing war, any war, in church teachings. Many of the San Francisco–based protests against the war in Iraq were organized by a group called Interfaith Communities United for Justice and Peace. The Military Globalization Project, an organization that opposes military spending, is headed by a Lutheran pastor, Margaret Lumsdaine. The Reverend Brenda Bartella Peterson is executive director of the Clergy Leadership Network, an anti-Bush, liberal organization in Washington, D.C. The religious left exists and has clout. Black churches, whose memberships overwhelmingly support Democratic candidates, are sought-after places for Democrats to campaign. Voter registration drives led by liberal groups target many of these parishioners because they're a major base of the Democratic Party. The religious left, however, isn't covered in the press on terms equal to the religious right. A notable exception occurred in June 2004, when the *Washington Post* wrote an article headlined RELIGIOUS LEFT SEEKS CENTER OF POLITICAL DEBATE. I also saw one article in the *New York Times* during the 2004 campaign headlined LIBERAL CHRISTIANS MOBILIZE TO REACT TO RELIGIOUS RIGHT. It's a start, but it's still not balanced.

Just before the President delivered his 2003 State of the Union, the *New York Times* wrote about his chief speechwriter, Michael Gerson. "Mr. Gerson, the pencil-chewing evangelical Christian," the story said in its second paragraph. If Mike was Jewish like me, or Roman Catholic, would the *New York Times* have described him as "a pencil-chewing Jewish aide" or a "pencil-chewing Catholic"? I doubt it. I think an editor would have asked what his religion had to do with his job, and absent a direct connection, the reference would have been removed, if it even appeared in the reporter's first draft. There were no other references in the story to Gerson's faith, or to the President's for that matter. But for some reason, the *Times* thought its readers needed to know Mike was an "evangelical." Too often, the press believe that readers deserve to know if someone is a conservative Christian. If a strong majority of reporters weren't so Democratic themselves, and liberal, especially on social issues, they wouldn't view conservative Christians in such a skeptical manner. If more reporters and editors were neutral or Republican, they would spot a religious left and cover it with the same skepticism used when covering the religious right.

The White House press corps are paid to ask tough questions and to play the devil's advocate, challenging whoever is in power. As tough as they can be on both parties, every now and then the press's bias came out in the way they asked their questions. On more than one occasion, some reporters stretched the limits of the devil's advocate, exposing their own points of view and making them sound more like Democrats than like Republicans.

In the spring of 2001, questions were raised about the administration's response to the rising cost of gasoline. Standing at the podium in the briefing room, I told the press that the faster Congress took action to pass the President's tax cut, the quicker consumers would have additional money to help them pay the higher cost of gasoline. "So what you're saying," Helen Thomas asked, "is that the consumer will have more money to pay the higher prices to line the pockets of the *big oil*? [emphasis added]?"

At another briefing, I was asked about the President's plans to simplify the tax code. I said that his proposal would reduce the number of tax brackets and, by eliminating the death tax, abolish one of the most complicated provisions in the code. Abolishing the death tax, I added, would put many lawyers and CPAs out of work because they would no longer have to design loopholes for their clients to avoid paying taxes. A reporter picked up on my reference to tax lawyers and CPAs, and asked, "If you're not afraid of going after special interests, including those that supported him like *big tobacco, big pharmaceuticals . . .*"

"Big oil"? "Big tobacco"? "Big pharmaceuticals"? Aren't those former Vice President Al Gore's words? Isn't that how John Kerry speaks? "I have a message for the influence peddlers, for the polluters, the HMOs, the big oil, and the special interests who now call the White House their home: We're coming!" Kerry exclaimed upon winning the New Hampshire primary in January 2004. Democrats deride these industries, with the emphasis on *big,* as in the little guy against the big guy. The reporter's question echoed the Democrats' words, linking Republicans to special interests. Maybe these reporters were using the lexicon of the left to bait me into a fight. I doubt it. I think it's more likely that most White House reporters largely agreed with the negative way Democrats describe corporate America, and they used the Democrats' language because they were comfortable with it.

In January 2003, the President announced a plan to accelerate several of the tax cuts enacted in 2001 so they would take effect immediately, and one of his economic advisers briefed the press on the proposal.

"The President made the point that if tax relief is good enough for the American people three years from now," a reporter asked, "it ought to be good enough for them today. Then the question naturally, I think, arises as to why, when he was proposing the *scheme* [emphasis added] he had in 2001, he didn't make the tax cuts accelerated then?"

"Scheme"? That was the word Al Gore used in the 2000 campaign when he criticized the President's tax plans. It's a derisive way to describe someone's ideas, and now it was the lexicon of the press, or at least one reporter.

"Does the President really have information or figures that show that the death penalty is a deterrent?" I was asked at one briefing.

"There are many people, the President included," I said, "who believe it is a deterrent. There are many people who question whether it is or not. I'd refer to the Department of Justice specifically for their studies—"

"Well, everything I've read is that it has not been a deterrent," opined the reporter.

Time after time, the lexicon of the left is more apt to be repeated by the press than the lexicon of the right. Conservatives have their own language as well. "Death tax" is used instead of "estate tax." "Pro-life" is used instead of "opponents of abortion rights." "Tax relief" instead of "tax cuts." Are these words found in the press's vocabulary? Not often. Once again, a newsroom of twelve Reagan and Buchanan voters would talk and write a lot differently than a newsroom with twelve Clinton and Nader voters. So too would a newsroom that was split fifty-fifty, the way their readers and viewers are.

The press's natural bias sometimes showed up in stories that cast a sympathetic light on one side of the debate while the other side received greater scrutiny. I've seen this pattern repeated often when it's time to describe protesters.

On September 1, 2002, the *New York Times* ran a front-page, above-the-fold photo with a caption reading, "March on Poverty." The full caption said, "Protesters demonstrated in South Africa's Alexandra township yesterday before a United Nations meeting on development. The marchers seek help for the poor and criticized President Bush for not attending." A reader didn't have to look too hard at the photo to see a banner held by the protesters that read, "Israel is a Rogue State." Another banner said, "Israel. US. UK. The Axis of Evil," and a third read, "Ariel Sharon The War Criminal." March on poverty? What a sympathetic summary of a group that appeared to be more anti-Israel, anti–United States, and anti–United Kingdom, than a march on poverty. In fact, the only three banners that could be read were those criticizing Israel, the United States, and the United Kingdom. I wish conservative protesters received that kind of sympathetic coverage on the front page of the *Times*.

As the war in Iraq began, the *New York Times* turned its focus to the protesters against the war. In late March, ten days into the war, a story was written about the protesters in America headlined, DECADES LATER, 60s ICONS STILL LIVE BY THEIR MESSAGE. The story described what the leaders of the 1960s anti–Vietnam War protests were doing today as the nation once again was at war. It filled readers in on the activities of the folk singer Pete Seeger, Tom Hayden, and Joan Baez. Jane Fonda, along with Hayden, was shown in a 1972 picture captioned, "Experienced Old Hand." It closed with a quote from Joan Baez's manager describing her impact on audiences today. "While her message is the same and is consistent with her message of 30 years ago, 40 years ago, it seems to resonate differently with different segments of the audience," said Mark Spector. "Some of them at age 50 or 55 don't seem to be as interested in hearing her basically antiwar views as others, and yet the majority seem comforted hearing those views expressed by someone they grew up hearing express those views." The story was laced with a fond nostalgia and wrapped in sympathy. Nowhere did the words *liberal* or *left-wing* appear.

Also that week, *Time* magazine wrote its account of the protest movement. Two full pages were devoted to those who opposed the war in Iraq under the headline VOICES OF OUTRAGE. THEY'RE ENERGIZED AND ORGANIZED. BUT CAN U.S. ANTIWAR PROTESTERS SURVIVE THEIR OWN DIVERSITY?

The story began, "On the first day of Gulf War II, shock and awe came to San Francisco. Antiwar protesters had long pledged that if bombs fell on Baghdad, they would unite to 'stop business as usual' in America's major cities. Here's how they fared by the Bay: 40 intersections shut down by human blockades. Hay bales set on fire in the streets around the Transamerica Building. Police-car windows smashed all over town. A vomit-in by a small group at the base of the Federal Building to demonstrate that the war made them sick. 1,350 arrests—the highest one day total in the history of the city—and a police plea for motorists to stay away from downtown. 'Absolute anarchy,' was how San Francisco assistant police chief Alex Fagan put it."

The story wasn't sympathetic toward the protesters, but the words *liberal* or *left-wing* never made an appearance in describing those who engaged in these tactics. I doubt these people were moderates, who aren't known for shutting down intersections, or conservatives, but in this case the press didn't inform their readers about the ideology of the protesters. The closest the story came to describing them was a quote from a "liberal leaning" author who referred to the "principles of the left." *Time,* somehow, couldn't bring itself to call the protesters "left-wing" or even "liberal."

The reluctance to label the left isn't matched with a reluctance to label the right. Ideological identification is almost a given when it's time to describe conservatives.

As then First Lady Hillary Clinton toured America to promote her husband's health reform plan in 1994, she was met by protesters. "Down the street, protesters tried to be heard—anti-abortion groups and conservatives," reported ABC News's Linda Douglass. Earlier that year, a story in the *Washington Post* covered a different anti-Clinton protest: "Meanwhile, about 20 conservative protesters called for the president's impeachment."

THE RIGHT'S GRIP ON THE CAPITOL blared the headline of the *New York Times* lead editorial on September 28, 2003. Twice the editorial decried what it called the "hard-right" agenda of Republicans in Washington. It even renamed partial-birth abortions "midterm abortions," as opposed to "so-called partial-birth abortions." The editorial page is designed to be opinionated, and it's said that a wall separates editorial from news. But when the former head of the editorial page,

Howell Raines, becomes the paper's top editor, followed by Bill Keller, who wrote opinions on the op-ed page, the wall seems to have a few doors in it.

Two weeks before the editorial, a different story on a separate topic appeared on the *Times*'s front page. Headlined NEW TWIST BRINGS ANGER FROM *RIGHT* [emphasis added], the story described the latest events in the unfolding recall against then Governor Gray Davis of California. The front page described how "*right-wing* [emphasis added] radio was cranked up," and inside the paper, the story described the "liberal" precincts of San Francisco and the "liberal" Ninth Circuit court there. This story at least called someone a liberal, but when it comes to describing San Francisco's politics, it's hard not to. The front-page description of California's Republicans belonging to an "angry right," however, is reflective of the one-sided ideology that is too common in newsrooms and on editorial pages. I only wish it was balanced with similar front-page headlines about the "angry left," but that's a description that editors seldom assign to Democrats.

In the summer of 2002, President Bush traveled to Portland, Oregon, to do a fund-raiser for Senator Gordon Smith. The presidential entourage was met by hundreds of angry protesters who opposed Bush and his policies. A pool report, which is a summary of the news prepared by a print reporter from the small press "pool" that accompanies the President, describing the scene was sent to hundreds of fellow reporters.

"The most notable feature of the president's fundraiser for Sen. Gordon Smith were the riot police fending off hundreds of protesters outside. A coalition of Portland's activist community gathered outside the Portland Hilton to, as one organizer told the local press, communicate to the president, 'we want him out of town.' The demonstrators represented peace, environmental, labor and anti-poverty groups," the report said.

Peace, environmental, labor, and antipoverty groups? If a president had been met by hundreds of protesters from the National Rifle Association, various right to life groups, and the Christian Coalition, the press would have described them as "conservative protesters" or "an assembly of right-wing groups." But when the protesters are from the left, they're called "activists."

What difference does it make if the press continue to cover events accurately, even if they often give an ideological label to only one side? It does matter.

America remains a closely divided country. While both parties have ideological bases that are largely united, the search for independent-minded swing voters is a crucial part of governing. It's also a crucial part of winning elections. These voters eschew labels and often vote on the basis of a shifting series of issues. The press hold themselves out as neutral, favoring neither Republican nor Democrat. Yet when the words they use and the impressions they convey repeatedly inform readers and viewers that the Republican Party is made up of conservatives and right-wingers, many of whom are "angry," and the Democratic Party is made up of women's groups, activists, civil rights leaders, and antipoverty groups, one party sounds more fringe than the other. For better or worse, one party is ideologically branded, and one party enjoys neutrality bordering on positive labeling. It's one reason why many Americans don't have confidence that the press are as neutral as the press purport to be.

When Kate Michelman announced her resignation as the president of NARAL Pro-Choice America, formerly called the National Abortion Rights Action League, in the fall of 2003, the *New York Times* didn't call her or her group "liberal." The same day's paper ran a story about the American Civil Liberties Union's efforts to organize college campuses. The story described the ACLU as "a non-profit activist organization." The words *liberal* and *left-wing* were nowhere to be found. On September 5, 2003, the *Washington Post,* writing about Move On.org, a left-wing group that has spent tens of millions of dollars against President Bush and in favor of liberal policies, simply called it an "online advocacy group." Some *Post* reporters called MoveOn.org a liberal group but not all. It seems as if the *Post* editors leave it up to their reporters to use whatever label they like best. One year later the *New York Times,* referred to the political action committee of MoveOn.org as "Democratic leaning."

Compare the press's neutrality to the left with its descriptions of the right. In 2003, when the antitax Club for Growth ran ads in the Democratic primary accusing Vermont Governor Howard Dean of raising taxes, the *Times* showed no hesitation about affixing an ideological warning label to the club. "Eleven months before Election Day," the paper wrote, "a *conservative* [emphasis added] antitax group began television advertisements in Iowa and New Hampshire on Thursday that accuse Howard Dean, a leading Democratic presidential hopeful, of planning to raise taxes." When the *Washington Post* covered the grassroots organizing efforts of Grover Norquist, the leader of Americans for Tax Reform, they wrote, "He has crisscrossed the country, handpicking leaders, organizing meetings of *right-wing* [emphasis added] advocates in 37 states."

Debates about abortion are described by the *New York Times* as about "abortion rights," based on the 1973 Supreme Court decision declaring a woman's constitutionally based right to an abortion. Yet debates about guns are debates over "gun control" instead of "gun rights," despite the constitutionally guaranteed right to bear arms. Why do the press label the debate over campaign finance reform as a matter of "reform," not "speech rights," given the fact that the courts have found a constitutionally derived right to free speech in the political arena? Why does the constitutionally derived "right" apply only to abortions and not to guns or free speech? Reporters' denials that ideology doesn't matter don't hold up very well. In each of these controversial issues involving constitutional law, the language of the press is more similar to the language of Democrats than to that of Republicans.

Would twelve Reagan and Buchanan voters in the newsroom describe the ACLU or MoveOn.org in neutral terms? Of course not. Reporters with conservative backgrounds would call these groups "liberals," just as reporters with liberal backgrounds don't hesitate to call Republican groups "right-wing." If the mainstream press were as unbiased as they are trained to believe, they would label neither side, or both sides, but they wouldn't label just one side. The Washington press corps are largely Democratic, and their bias often seeps through. Having the ability to be tough on both sides doesn't wash away the fact that they're often more critical of one side, the Republican side.

Beyond labels, the press's bias showed up in coverage of tax cuts.

Just as I remembered from Elizabeth Dole's campaign how much easier it was to work with the press on her speech about gun safety, I often thought how much easier it would be to work with the press in opposing President Bush's tax cut. White House reporters will say they were doing their jobs by raising tough questions. To me, it often seemed like they agreed with the Democrats' view that Bush's proposal was a tax cut for the rich. They also *disagreed* with Republicans who said that any effort by the Democrats to repeal Bush's tax cut would be a tax hike.

Once again, the summary labels used are a good indication of which way the press lean. Throughout the mid- to late nineties, the press wrote often about President Clinton's 1993 budget, which passed the Congress by two votes in the House and one in the Senate. Despite the fact that its central feature was a massive tax hike that contributed to the Democrats' losing control of Congress in 1994, the press routinely described the agreement as Clinton's "deficit reduction plan," or simply "budget agreement." It was by definition a tax hike, but the press largely stopped calling it one.

The typical reaction from the Democrats to a Republican proposal to cut taxes, especially marginal income taxes, is to call it a tax cut for the rich. Despite the fact that the taxes cut are in proportion to the taxes paid, it's not surprising for one political party to use statistics to gain an advantage over the other party. What I found surprising was how willing the press were to go along with the Democrats' arguments. When it came to cutting taxes, the press's skepticism seemed to point to one side of the debate—the Republican side. It wasn't only true when they were playing devil's advocate to a Republican President. It was the same way when President Clinton was in the White House fending off Republican tax cuts.

"The pro–tax cut argument is pretty classic, trickle-down economics," ABC's Betsy Stark reported in the spring of 2003. Trickle-down? That term was used in a 1984 commercial by Walter Mondale and the Democrats against President Reagan's tax cuts. The commercial showed a champagne glass overflowing with bubbly as a rich man got out of his limousine. The champagne poured out of its glass and slowly turned into a trickle that left a scant drop or two in the cup of a working man. Surely there were other ways for ABC to describe the pro–tax cut argument. "Trickle-down" was one of the more derisive.

As the debate over tax cuts heated up in 2003, the *Washington Post* weighed in with a story examining the arguments both sides used. Democrats said Bush was offering a tax cut for the rich, and Republicans accused Democrats of engaging in class warfare, according to the story. Fair enough. But the headline couldn't have been more lopsided: BUSH BLUNTS "FAIRNESS QUESTION" ON TAXES; PRESIDENT'S "CLASS WARFARE" RHETORIC BRINGS SUPPORT FOR TAX CUTS SKEWED TO WEALTHY. The story declared that Bush's success "is all the more remarkable because the president's original $726 billion tax cut plan—and the smaller versions that passed the House and are under consideration in the Senate—*clearly do favor the affluent* [emphasis added]." The statistics can be read by either side to support their claims. Republicans can accurately state that because middle- and upper-income taxpayers pay so much more in taxes, they of course will receive a larger tax cut than do lower-income workers, who pay little or no income taxes, but as a percentage of taxes paid and taxes cut, the reductions are fair and proportional. The Democrats can point out that, thanks to our progressive income tax system, the rich receive more money when taxes are cut than do lower-income workers. What's hard to understand is how the *Post* story could take sides. Once again, I felt how much easier it would have been to discuss these policies with the press if I had been a Democrat.

In the winter of 2003, the director of the Office of Management and Budget, Mitch Daniels, briefed the press on the President's budget for the upcoming year. When question time came, he was asked, "Nearly twenty years ago, I believe it was twenty years ago, we had the big tax cuts of—which led to very high deficits, and it was only a short time after that the Reagan administration had to endure tax hikes and take back some of those tax cuts. Are you confident enough about your outlook that you could rule out that ever happening again?"

The deficit is caused by tax cuts, argue the Democrats. The deficit is caused by spending increases, argue the Republicans. Which side of the divide was that reporter on? Not the Republican one.

On the flip side, Republicans love to charge the Democrats with tax hikes. Democrats love to charge the Republicans with spending cuts, particularly for social programs, especially Social Security. The press are reluctant to go along with the Republican charge about Democrats raising taxes, but it doesn't take much to get them to write the Democratic charge that Republicans support spending cuts for vital programs.

GEPHARDT HEALTH PLAN TO COVER ALL; REPEAL OF TAX CUTS WOULD HELP PAY FOR INSURANCE, read the *Washington Post*'s front page in 2003, as former House Minority Leader Dick Gephardt geared up his unsuccessful presidential campaign. Gephardt had pledged to undo all of President Bush's tax cuts. The 10 percent tax rate on low-income Americans would have been raised to 15 percent under the Gephardt plan. Tax rates would have been raised for all taxpayers, in every income level. Married couples would have had the marriage penalty reimposed, and the thousand-dollar child credit, which reduced taxes by one thousand dollars for every child a taxpayer had, would have been replaced with only a five-hundred-dollar credit if Gephardt had his way. If ever there was a tax hike, this was it. But the *Post* couldn't call the Gephardt plan a tax hike; instead it was a "repeal of tax cuts." Often a headline is forced to have few words and letters by space limitations. In this case, the editors opted for the longer "repeal of tax cuts" description instead of the "tax hike" label.

Aboard Air Force One in the fall of 2003, my successor as the President's press secretary, Scott McClellan, was discussing how Bush would pay for his spending initiatives by focusing on policies that created growth, which would bring more revenue into the treasury. Raising taxes, Scott explained, was the worst thing that could be done. The Bush tax cut, it should be noted, was the law of the land. Because parts of it were phased in, taxpayers could look forward to future decreases in their taxes paid.

"Does that also include suspending planned decreases?" a reporter asked.

Suspending planned decreases? Now a tax hike wasn't a tax hike, or even a revenue raiser. It was, according to the euphemism employed by this reporter, a suspension of a planned decrease. I wish the press made up favorable new expressions to describe Republican proposals, but that doesn't happen when the press tends to agree more with the Democrats than they do with Republicans on policy matters.

Automatically every year, senior citizens receive increases in their Social Security checks thanks to what's called a COLA—a cost of living adjustment. The law states that the checks go up annually based on a formula. It's a promise of a future increase.

In 1986, Senate Republicans proposed a delay in providing these COLAs as a way to reduce the deficit. The press didn't hesitate, in headlines, in stories, and on the air, to say Republicans were cutting seniors' COLAs. The press didn't say the Republicans were suspending a planned increase. They didn't call it a rollback. They said it was a cut in seniors' COLAs, and the press were right. But when Democrats promise to repeal a planned tax cut, the press don't call it a tax hike. Once again, Republicans have to work twice as hard as Democrats to get to the same point in the press. Sometimes the press is with you and sometimes the press is against you. On tax policy, the Republican side ran into friction much of the time. The Democrats' arguments enjoyed a much smoother reception.

Patriotism, or the alleged lack of it, has also become a well-worn route in which the press rally to the side of the Democrats. Throughout President Bush's term, Democrats criticized his conduct of foreign policy and the judgments he had made as Commander in Chief. John Kerry said Bush "lives out a creed of greed for he and his friends . . . you know what I call that? Unpatriotic." The former Florida senator and onetime presidential contender Bob Graham said Bush's Iraq policy is "anti-patriotic at the core." Former Vermont Governor Howard Dean called Attorney General John Ashcroft unpatriotic, adding he "is a descendent of Joseph McCarthy." Former Vice President Al Gore said in a speech in 2004 that "Bush betrayed his country."

My boss, the former chairman of the Ways and Means Committee Bill Archer, was called a Nazi by Democratic Congressman Pete Stark, a Fascist by former Congressman Sam Gibbons, and his actions were likened to Adolf Hitler's by Congressman Charlie Rangel. These allegations didn't raise an outcry in the press.

Despite the overt statements by Democrats questioning the President's patriotism, the press don't fault them for their attacks. But when a Republican simply questions how a Democrat voted on a defense or foreign policy issue, some in the press are quick to label the Republican guilty of an attack on the Democrat's patriotism.

In March 2003, one day before the Iraq war began, I entered the increasingly tense briefing room for my morning gaggle.

"Ari, Senator Daschle had some very harsh words yesterday saying he was saddened by the fact of what he called the President's failure brought us to war. Can you respond to that?"

I replied, "Actually, I think Senator Daschle's words were, 'failed miserably,' to quote the senator accurately. You know, every member of Congress is entitled to their opinion, of course."

Then I pointed out that "just as recently as last fall, Senator Daschle said, 'We ought not politicize this war; we ought not politicize the rhetoric about war and life and death. We have to rise to a higher level. It's not too late to forget about the pollsters, the campaign fund-raisers, the accusations about how interested in national security different parties are.' That's what Senator Daschle said last fall. So it's hard to assess what Senator Daschle means when his remarks are so inconsistent."

My answer offended some in the press, and I was accused of somehow challenging the senator's patriotism.

"Aren't you skating on pretty thin ice again about suggesting, even at the margins, that anybody who criticizes the President or the war is being unpatriotic?" asked CBS's Bill Plante.

"Bill, that's an invention of your own. I never used such words. In fact, I began it by saying—"

Bill cut me off. "You don't have to use the words, Ari. That's my point," he said.

The one-sided debate over which party is guilty of challenging the other's patriotism had now reached the point where Republicans didn't even have to "use the words." At least one member of the press *knew* I was challenging Senator Daschle's patriotism, even while acknowledging I didn't use any such words. I said Senator Daschle's declaration that the war was caused because Bush "failed miserably" was inconsistent with his previous call for not politicizing the rhetoric and for rising to a higher level. How anyone can say calling a politician "inconsistent" is tantamount to challenging his patriotism is beyond me.

Later that day, when Senator Daschle held a news conference on the Hill, there was no uproar in the press about his "failed miserably" accusation. One reporter played softball, asking, "Senator Daschle, does there ever come a time when it is inappropriate to criticize the President? I mean, you're talking about a democratic society in which people should be able to speak openly," the reporter opined. "Does there ever come a point where you can't criticize what the President's done?"

In that reporter's judgment, I didn't challenge the senator's patriotism. I challenged the senator's right to free speech.

Three days later, Senator Daschle appeared on CBS's *Early Show* with the anchorman Harry Smith.

"You are under a certain amount of criticism, especially directly from the White House, as the day before the war actually began, you talked about the failure of diplomacy," Smith said. "Did you feel along the way, and especially in the hours after that, that some Republicans were actually challenging your patriotism?"

"Well, I did, Harry," Daschle replied.

In politics today, patriotism has become a protective cloak that too many reporters wrap around the Democrats to shield them from Republican charges which have *nothing* to do with love of country. Democrats can overtly challenge the patriotism of Republicans with impunity from the press. But newsrooms that aren't balanced between left and right find Republicans guilty of patriotic challenges far too often.

After twenty years of working closely with the Washington press corps, including two and a half years in the cauldron of the White House briefing room, I've concluded that nothing makes the press happier than a good old conflict. But absent a conflict *they* get to stir up, when the two parties start fighting over policy issues, much of the press typically see the issues more through the eyes of Democrats than through those of Republicans. They'll deny it to this day, but it's simply human nature. It's not a conspiracy. It's not a cabal, and there are no meetings where they agree to act this way. Instead, it's old-fashioned human nature. No profession can be as ideologically unbalanced as the press without it seeping into their work. The press *are* largely Democratic, and that fact shows up in their work more often than most reporters like to acknowledge.

FIVE

LESTER

T HE WHITE HOUSE briefing room has always had its share of interesting reporters who stand out from the crowd. Colorful, aggressive, and often provocative, these reporters see the briefing
room not only as a place where they can get their questions answered
but also as a place where they can get their questions, and points of
view, heard. Add live television and radio to the mix, and a stage is
born.

Lester Kinsolving added his own ring to the three-ring circus called
the White House briefing room. When it was Lester's turn to ask questions, the cable stations typically cut away from the live briefing, recognizing that his inquiries often needed to be accompanied by a
parental warning label. Lester has a talk radio show in Baltimore and
he's a contributor to WorldNetDaily, an Internet version of talk radio.
Almost every time Lester had a chance to ask a question, the briefing
room became a less than serious place. Lester was not typical of the
White House press corps—far from it. But he was a part of my day.

I first heard of Baltimore's Lester Kinsolving during the 1980s,
when I did communications and political work for Republican congressional candidates and causes. Before talk radio was big, Lester was
known in conservative circles as an important radio talk show host. He

was popular with conservative listeners, and the word was that if Lester liked your candidate, he could help to increase the candidate's name recognition in the Washington area, which would often lead to more money raised. If he approved of your cause, it would get a good airing. Having heard his name during my formative years in the business, I didn't hear it again for a decade.

I met Lester late in 2000, at our transition headquarters in downtown Washington, after the Supreme Court ruled that George W. Bush had won the election.

Help me, Lester said, collaring me after one transition briefing. The Clinton White House had pulled his press credential, he explained, and wouldn't let him in the daily briefing anymore. He had to wait for an hour or two at the front gate each day, waiting to be cleared in. If he could have his credential restored, he wouldn't have to wait.

I didn't pay his request much attention, having other, more important matters to focus on. But I must have given someone instructions to give him back his pass, because Lester, one of two or three identifiable conservatives in the briefing room, became a fixture at my briefings. I also didn't think it was my place to pick and choose which reporters were allowed into the White House. That's a slippery slope for any press secretary to walk. Lester didn't have an assigned seat like reporters from mainstream organizations, but he made his presence known.

Perhaps it was fitting that Lester tried to make the briefing room his pulpit. According to his own webpage, Lester served for fourteen years as an Episcopalian minister before becoming a reporter covering the White House under former President Nixon.

Lester had an unusual fixation on questions that involved racial issues, gays, pornography, child molestation, and the news media. An odd mix if ever there was one.

Of all the questions I ducked or dodged in my three hundred televised White House briefings, Lester's had the highest IQ, or "ignore quotient." His questions were typically so far off the wall they were easy to ignore. Usually when I ducked a question, reporters didn't like it. With Les, if I *had* answered his questions, reporters would have thought I had gone crazy.

Here's a sample of life with Les:

"Page one of the *Washington Times,*" Les began one day, "quotes Jefferson scholars at Harvard, Yale, Stanford, and George Mason, as concluding in a yearlong study, 550 pages, 'We are asked to believe that [President Thomas] Jefferson would have entrusted his reputation to the discretion of a 15-year-old child. If he did this, he was essentially a child-molesting rapist, and that is far from what we know of him.' My question is, does President Bush believe that his predecessor President Jefferson was a child-molesting rapist, or not? They raised it, from two of his alma maters, Harvard and Yale."

"That is not a view the President holds," I said.

"That's good," Lester followed up. "Then why did he—"

"Can we talk about the Middle East?" another reporter interrupted.

IN THE SPRING OF 2001, Lester told the briefing room that he was going to be away for a week at a talk radio convention, and he asked if he could have three questions. I let him proceed.

"In the President's effort to promote intelligent government spending—that is, only where it's really needed—does he believe that the Democrats on the San Francisco City Council were wise to vote to provide any city employee who wishes with $37,000 to be changed from male to female, and $77,000 to be changed from female to male?"

"Not a topic I've talked to the President about," I replied with a straight face.

"London's *Daily Telegraph,*" Les continued, "reported that Prime Minister Tony Blair is considering recommending to the Queen an honorary knighthood for Mr. Clinton. And Reuters News Agency reports that Mr. Blair, when asked about this, laughed. And since honorary knighthoods were conferred upon Presidents Reagan and [George H. W.] Bush when they left office, can you deny that anyone in the White House laughed, too, or did anyone think that Mr. Blair was wrong to laugh?"

"Try as hard as I may, I've not kept up with all the White House laughter. I don't know what my co-workers laugh at," I said.

Time for question three.

"Last one. On Sunday, the *New York Times* reported at some length from Geneva that the former runner-up for Miss America, who is now the wife of the Swiss ambassador to Germany, has been furiously criticized by the Swiss media and the Swiss foreign ministry because she posed for photographers on a horse wearing a strapless gown, among other things. Since this gorgeous young lady is Shawn Fielding, the former Miss Texas, she can surely depend on gentlemanly support from the former governor of Texas, can't she, Ari?"

"Les," I said, "I'm afraid you're 0–3 on your final round of questions. I don't have anything to offer you on this topic."

IN THE SUMMER OF 2002, Les raised an interesting topic.

"There has been nationwide media coverage of a McKees Rocks, Pennsylvania, councilwoman who has charged that racial profiling has been done by Dolpho, the borough's one police dog, for whom she has demanded the death penalty. And my question is, while I know of no law allowing the President to commute the capital punishment of a dog, as the owner of two beloved dogs, the President surely hopes that McKees Rocks will not allow this execution on such an absurd charge, doesn't he, Ari?"

"I think you just validated the point I was making to Terry [another reporter] that the President is not involved in every issue across America with everybody who does or says anything," I said.

"But he doesn't want that dog put to death, does he, Ari?"

"Lester," I said, "I think you need to bark up a different tree."

LES WAS NO FAN of Jesse Jackson, and he reveled in Jackson's woes. If a public figure on the right said something foolish or got into trouble, I knew many in the mainstream press would ask me about it, trying to insert the President into the controversy. Les was one of the only reporters in the room who pointed out some of the sayings and doings of public figures on the left.

"The Associated Press," Lester began, "quotes the Reverend Jesse Jackson as comparing President Bush's foreign policy to King Herod's. But you, Ari, told us that when Jesse was caught paying extensive money to get his impregnated mistress out of Chicago, the President telephoned him to say, 'You are in my prayers,' with no such prayers for other clergy adulterers, such as Jim Bakker or Jimmy Swaggart. My question is, does the White House have anything by way of response to the King Herod charge? Or do you think that Jesse's failure to attract more than 600 to a 15,000-seat arena at Michigan State University illustrates how discredited he is?" The briefing room broke into laughter.

"The White House is not aware of any recent statements by King Herod," I deadpanned.

AT ONE BRIEFING shortly before the war in Iraq began, Les and another reporter almost came to blows. Russell Mokhiber, of a publication called the *Corporate Crime Reporter,* was opposed to the President's actions in Iraq, and his questions made his position perfectly clear. Russell asked me one day about opposition to the war from various church leaders who, he said, were "uneasy about the moral justification for war on Iraq." I told him that the President was a deeply religious man himself and that he respected the views of others and would act as he saw fit as Commander in Chief to protect the country.

"One question on that," Russell followed up. "You just said the President is a deeply religious man. Jesus Christ was an absolute pacifist. How does the President square his militarism with Jesus' pacifism?"

Before I could even answer, Lester the minister rose from his seat like a rocket ship, exclaiming with his deep radio voice, "No he wasn't — How about the—at the temple with a whip, where he beat the hell out of those money changers? Does that sound like he's an absolute pacifist, Ari?"

Horrified that two reporters were fighting with each other at the televised briefing, Steve Holland, the senior wire reporter in the press corps, exercised his authority to call an end to the proceedings by shouting an instant "Thank you." As I walked off the podium, Russell and Lester were still yelling at each other about whether Jesus was a pacifist.

SIX

THE CALM BEFORE THE STORM

THE SUMMER OF 2001 was peaceful. The tax cut, lowering income tax rates for all Americans, reducing the marriage penalty, doubling the child credit, and eliminating the death tax, at least for a while, was signed into law. The education reform bill was heading for passage, and the typical partisanship that marked life in Washington hadn't gone away, but it wasn't as bad as usual. The United States had made clear we intended to withdraw from the Anti-Ballistic Missile Treaty, paving the way for the development of a national missile defense. The President's faith-based initiative, one of his legislative priorities, was, unfortunately, sputtering in the Congress, and negotiations on a patients' bill of rights, which had once seemed promising, broke down. The President's environmental record was highly criticized, and the White House suffered a major blow when Senator Jim Jeffords of Vermont declared himself an independent and took with him Republican control of the Senate. Legislatively it was a dramatic setback. The White House wasn't accomplishing everything the President sought, but as I approached my twentieth year in government, I still thought times were good. I accompanied President Bush on Air Force One and Marine One, and thoroughly enjoyed my work. Becki Davis, an assistant in the White House, and I started dating just before Memorial Day, and it didn't take long for me to realize I had met the woman I wanted to marry.

Troubles in Israel and Iraq made early appearances on the radar screen throughout the first nine months of 2001. During a 1999 Republican presidential debate in New Hampshire, Governor Bush was asked what he would do if it were discovered that Saddam Hussein had weapons of mass destruction. "I'd take 'em out," he said, causing an uproar about whether he said he's take "them" or "him" out. The governor later said he said "them," not "him," as in Saddam Hussein. In any case, Bush was laying down a clear marker that he would not tolerate weapons of mass destruction in Iraq.

He complained that the sanctions against Iraq had turned into "Swiss cheese," whereby the Iraqi military was able to procure military parts and the people weren't getting the food they needed. He pledged to toughen the sanctions if elected.

Iraq rudely interrupted the White House in mid-February 2001, when President Bush was in the middle of his first presidential trip out of the country, a summit meeting with President Vicente Fox at Fox's San Cristóbal ranch. Earlier at the White House, the President had authorized an air strike to enforce the no-fly zone, which Iraq had been violating on a regular basis. Iraq was building radar facilities with fiber-optic lines that would allow them to better target, and one day destroy, coalition aircraft. It was always feared that a pilot might one day be shot down and killed, or taken hostage, giving Hussein a prized American hostage.

The joint U.S.-British air strike, which was routine even though it required presidential authorization, took place close enough to the Iraqi capital that air-raid sirens went off alerting the Baghdad-based media that Iraq was under attack. The Iraqis fired antiaircraft weapons. It took seconds for the news to get from Baghdad to the traveling White House press corps.

I was with the press when the news broke and told them I would look into it. The press were buzzing, thinking Bush had gone to war. I hadn't known the strike was coming, and I hurried to find Andy Card and Condi Rice to see what was going on. They had known about the strike, but hadn't expected it so early. Condi called back to Washington and then she, Andy, and I quickly gathered in a vehicle with a secure phone, and they called the Pentagon to get the latest information, knowing the President would face the reporters in a few minutes.

As Bush and Fox stood together for their joint news conference, the first question wasn't about Mexico, it was about Iraq.

"I'm wondering," asked AP's Ron Fournier, referring to the bombing, "whether it signals a hardening of the U.S. position toward Iraq? And specifically, is it your goal to drive Saddam Hussein from power? And secondly, are you putting Saddam on notice today that American military action will be more frequent or more forceful than it was before you became President?"

"Saddam Hussein has got to understand," Bush said, "that we expect him to conform to the agreement that he signed after Desert Storm. We will enforce the no-fly zone, both south and north. Our intention is to make the world as peaceful as possible. And we're going to watch very carefully as to whether or not he develops weapons of mass destruction, and if we catch him doing so, we'll take appropriate action."

Bush deeply mistrusted Saddam and would have welcomed his removal, but tighter sanctions and tough enforcement of the no-fly zone were the policies he pursued before September 11. "Instead of standing by and having a sanctions regime that's weak, we're going to put a sanctions regime in that's strong," he told the *Washington Times* in March 2001. "And that our policy will continue to be containment of Saddam."

OF ALL THE CRITICISMS aimed at Bush, one of the most frequent was his alleged "disengagement" from the Middle East. It was almost as if the new President should have been able to step into the tortured atmosphere that existed between the Israelis and the Palestinians the day he took office and, perhaps just by sitting down, do what no President had done before.

The day Bush was inaugurated, January 20, 2001, was also eighteen days before Israel's elections to pick their new prime minister. In the wake of the breakdown of peace talks among Yasir Arafat, former Israeli Prime Minister Ehud Barak, and President Clinton, Israel's foreign policy was on hold until their elections ended. The Intifada had resumed on September 20, 2000, and Israelis were being killed almost daily by suicide bombers. The Israeli people had lost faith in Barak and placed their hopes in General Ariel Sharon, a candidate who promised security by being tough. Sharon was elected in a 19-percentage-point landslide on February 6, 2001.

In early March, Bush met with a group of White House reporters and he was asked about the prospects for peace in the Middle East. He noted the choice the Israeli people had made and said of Sharon, "Give the man a chance. I believe he'll be a proponent for peace." He added that he would be patient; encouraging, not compelling the parties on the path to peace. "They need to get their houses in order so they can come to the table."

Less than three weeks later, Sharon was Bush's guest in the Oval Office. The President had met Sharon once before, in 1998, when he toured Israel as a governor. Sharon, then an out-of-power retired general, took the future president on a helicopter ride to see Israel's 1948 and 1967 borders. As they flew over the nation's nine-mile-wide narrowest point, Bush told Sharon, "There are driveways in Texas longer than that."

Their Oval Office meeting lasted about an hour, and Bush began it by expressing his concern about the then six-month-long rise in terror. He told Sharon he wouldn't force a solution and would be realistic.

Sharon warned Bush that Arafat's presidential guard was working with Hizbollah, and he warned that the Iranians were making trouble in the region. He promised he was ready to make concessions if they would lead to peace, and he said Arafat needed to do more to end the violence.

Bush thanked Sharon again for the 1998 helicopter tour as the meeting broke up. He had earlier told the Israeli leader how much he had enjoyed his visit to Jerusalem. "It was a glorious moment," he said, remembering "the golden glow upon the curtains" in his room.

A week later Bush was asked at a news conference when he planned to invite Yasir Arafat to the White House. The President, who began his tenure doubtful that Arafat was interested in peace, wanted to give the Chairman a chance to prove himself. If he performed by cracking down on the terrorists, he would be on the receiving end of an invitation. For Bush, the jury on Arafat was out. "We're going to work with all parties," he said, sidestepping the specific question. Reporters asked the President if he was sending Arafat a signal. "The signal I'm sending to the Palestinians is, stop the violence. And I can't make it any more clear. And I hope that Chairman Arafat hears it loud and clear."

In June, Colin Powell prepared for his first trip to the region as secretary of state. Around the same time, the United Nations was preparing for its World Conference Against Racism, Racial Discrimination, Xenophobia, and Related Intolerance, to be held in Durban, South Africa. "If Israel gets bashed at the meeting, we'll raise hell about it," Bush told his secretary of state in his usual blunt way.

As violence continued in the Middle East, the President had yet to see any signs that Arafat was willing to work for peace. I entered the briefing room shortly before Powell's departure and announced that Bush had a call scheduled with Arafat later that day. He planned to tell the Palestinian leader to adhere to a cease-fire and take steps that restored confidence in the prospects for peace. Prime Minister Sharon, I said, was coming back to the White House the following week.

Helen Thomas didn't like it. "Every other American President who had dealt with the Middle East has been pretty evenhanded in the sense that [when] the President sees an Israeli official he will see the counterpart of the Palestinians. The President is breaking this kind of precedent," she said. "Why?"

"Helen," I replied, "that's not an accurate description of the history of Presidents and the meetings they've held."

"Yes, it is," she said.

"No it's—" not, I was going to say, before Helen piped up again.

"I'm sorry, I've been here a long time—" she said to great laughter.

"I know you have. And you'll be here long after I'm gone," I replied, also causing a laugh. "But that's not an accurate statement about the history of presidential meetings in the region."

"Yes, it is. I'm sorry, it is," Helen said, getting in the last word.

Indeed, Helen was wrong. President Clinton was the first president to meet with Yasir Arafat. No American president had met with a Palestinian leader until Arafat's so-called renunciation of terror in 1993. For a brief few years, the Chairman enjoyed an aura of legitimacy around the globe, especially in Europe, where he was awarded the Nobel Peace Prize. President Bush always doubted Arafat's intentions, with good reason.

In June and July 2001, the President traveled to eight European countries, and the Middle East constantly came up. Bush was relentless in his message to European leaders. "My attitude is Arafat can do a heck of a lot more," he said, urging leaders on the Continent to put pressure on the Chairman to stop the violence. Bush knew Arafat had the sympathy of many European leaders, and he hoped they would use their influence to moderate his behavior.

The President sent CIA Director George Tenet to the Middle East to see if he could restore some of the security arrangements that had existed between the Israelis and the Arabs. Senator George Mitchell had previously met with all sides in the conflict and proposed a series of steps for each party to take to restore the peace process. Despite the attention the region was receiving, the Middle East was again entering a time of conflict.

THE ECONOMY SHOWED MORE SIGNS of trouble in the summer of 2001. The revenue coming into the treasury was below expectations, even before the tax cut went into effect. The economic slowdown was taking its toll. The President met with Hill leaders and urged them to hold the line on spending. "It's not a question of tax relief," Bush said, "the issue is spending. I think my job is to help you bring fiscal restraint to the budget. What we don't do a good job of is finding savings. We're pitiful at it," he complained.

In July, the President visited Capitol Hill, where he received a tumultuous reception from Republican members of Congress. After six
years in the majority party with a Democratic President, congressional
Republicans were feeling their oats. Tired of veto fights, vicious rancor, and government shutdowns, Republicans welcomed the chance to
work with a Republican President. The President urged them to complete their work on the domestic agenda.

The biggest issue of the summer was whether Bush would allow
taxpayer funding of stem cell research. Proponents of funding argued
that breakthroughs that could lead to miracle cures might be in reach if
the President would allow funding. Opponents said other ways of doing research could be accomplished without obtaining stem cells from
live organisms, even if those organisms were fertilized eggs in a lab
that had the potential to become life. The President deliberated on the
issue for more than a month, privately meeting with leaders on both
sides. On most issues, the President heard presentations of the pros and
cons, and was quick with a decision. On this issue, he was undecided
and took his time, announcing a compromise solution from his ranch in
mid-August.

The press couldn't get enough of the debate. At every chance they
shouted, "Mr. President, have you made up your mind yet?" He
couldn't walk to Marine One or finish a speech without the shouted
question. I often thought how differently I'd approach the topic if I was
a reporter. If the press *wanted* him to ignore their questions, asking
him about stem cell first was the best way to have him walk away and
take no questions. If, instead, they had lured him into taking questions
with a different first topic, then popped the stem cell question, they
might have gotten more from him. Sometimes reporters can't help
themselves. If the issue is controversial, it's the only thing on their
minds. They missed a lot of chances to talk about other issues, and
maybe get an update on Bush's stem cell thinking, but they could at
least tell their editors they tried to get the President on the record but he
refused to speak.

The President took two trips to Europe that summer, including a summit meeting with Russia's President Putin in Slovenia in which the two leaders hit it off, beginning what has become a powerful and important relationship. In a show of support for the new democracies of east Europe, the President made a state visit to Poland and visited our troops in Kosovo. Back then, civil war in Macedonia was the most pressing military struggle on earth.

One Friday in late July, I entered the briefing room, and it wasn't long before it was Helen Thomas's turn to inquire.

"Is there any treaty since World War II that this administration is not willing to torpedo?" she said, to the press's great amusement.

"Is that what you call a leading question?" I smiled.

"Definitely leading," said a reporter helpfully.

"Every treaty, it seems, that's been made in at least twenty-five years you seem to be saying no to and tearing up. I mean, has nothing any validity that was done before you arrived?" Helen asked.

Her question was sparked by two things: the United States's withdrawal from the Kyoto treaty concerning global warming (in a test vote under President Clinton, the Senate voted 95–0 against ratifying the treaty, a point the press seldom bring up as they blame Bush for *his* stand) and reservations we had expressed about how best to enforce the treaty banning biological weapons.

After going a few more rounds with me about treaty obligations and foreign policy, Helen asked, "How can you lead when you don't have any friends or allies anymore with us on anything?"

It wouldn't be the last time I heard that charge.

AT AN EARLY AUGUST cabinet meeting, before virtually all of Washington left for the remainder of the summer, the President asked Karl Rove to outline the fall agenda. The season would mark a new initiative, the cabinet was told, focused on "communities of character." The spotlight would be on citizenship, personal responsibility, and youth development, with a special effort on education. The week of September 7 through 13 would be marked by a sustained presidential focus on the importance of reading. The President would visit elementary schools to drive home the message, and a White House assembly on reading was planned for September 13. The First Lady, a former librarian, would play an important role.

Defense Secretary Donald Rumsfeld, who was trying to transform the Pentagon into a leaner, more agile and mobile fighting force, told the cabinet that his mission was hard. Change, he said, makes people in his five-sided building nervous.

The President and other top aides left for Crawford, Texas, and I left for Nantucket. As exciting as White House life could be, it was also a tough grind, and I needed the break. After a week off, I flew to Texas and spent much of August traveling with the President as he conducted business in eleven cities throughout the country. When you're President, "working vacations" are the only kind you get. When Bush was at the ranch, I remained in one-hundred-degree Crawford and Waco. The President returned to Washington before Labor Day to get ready for the fall.

On Friday, September 7, 2001, back at the White House, I gave the press the usual "week ahead," outlining Bush's upcoming activities. "On Monday," I said, "the President will go to the Navy Yard with the Prime Minister of Australia for an event, and he'll have a working lunch and a meeting with the Prime Minister in the White House. In the afternoon on Monday, the President will continue his focus on reading and education when he travels to Jacksonville, Florida, and then on to Sarasota, Florida.

"He'll return to the White House on Tuesday afternoon [September 11], where he will host, in the evening the Congressional Barbecue on the South Lawn. Mrs. Bush will make remarks on early child cognitive development to Senator Kennedy's committee."

SEVEN

SEPTEMBER 11, 2001

T HE DAY COULD NOT HAVE BEGUN more beautifully. It was a clear, crisp late summer day along the eastern seaboard. The sun shone, and the President rose early, looking forward to his visit to the Emma E. Booker Elementary School in Sarasota, where he would lead a group of children in a reading event. Taking advantage of his scenic setting, the President went for a rare outdoor run at the Colony Beach and Tennis Resort on Longboat Key, where the traveling White House had overnighted. My room faced the Gulf of Mexico, and if ever there was a peaceful setting, this was it. I had gone running on the gym's treadmill the night before, not knowing it would be my last run for more than three months.

The President returned from his run, readied himself, and the motorcade headed off to work. As we pulled into the school's driveway shortly before 9:00, my pager went off. Brian Bravo, an assistant in the press office in Washington, had been monitoring the news as usual, but what he sent me was far from usual. One of the towers of the World Trade Center had been hit by an airplane, Brian told me in a page. There was no more information.

I hopped out of my car, which was several cars behind the President's, and followed him into the school, watching him shake hands with the teachers and staff who had lined up to greet him. As he shook the last hand, Karl Rove, whose office had also called him with the news, stepped beside the President and told him about the plane. The President's immediate reaction was that it must have been some kind of terrible accident, perhaps in bad weather a pilot had got lost or suffered from a heart attack, he thought, unaware of the weather in New York City.

Everywhere the President goes, no matter how long he's there, a "Presidential hold" is set up in case he needs to talk on a secure phone line. He has a secure phone in his limousine, a secure phone in Crawford and at Camp David, and he's surrounded by secure phones at the White House. I don't think I ever recalled seeing the President use a secure line in his hold before, but as he entered the room, his national security adviser, Condoleezza Rice, was on the line waiting for him.

In the initial minutes after the first tower was hit, there was little to report. No one yet knew it was a terrorist attack, but Dr. Rice told the President federal resources were being dispatched to help the city deal with the apparent accident, and he directed her to monitor events and keep in touch.

The President planned to make a statement to the press pool that had gathered to watch him in the reading event. It was a classic two-tiered event, a meeting in one classroom to hear the kids read, followed by a speech in the auditorium to a much larger group where the President was scheduled to talk about the importance of reading.

As Bush sat in the classroom, my pager vibrated again. The second tower had been hit by another aircraft, and I knew at once it had to be terrorism. I told the advance team to get the press out of the room as soon as the reading event was over. The last thing I wanted was for them to shout questions at the President when he didn't even know the second tower had been struck.

I started writing a note to the President in large letters on the back of my legal pad, and before I could finish I saw Andy Card, the chief of staff, enter the room. He bent down in what is now a famous photo and whispered in the President's ear, "A second plane hit the second tower. America is under attack." Andy quietly retreated, leaving the President to sit there, his face masking his emotions, pondering the meaning of those four words—America is under attack—as schoolchildren proudly read to him from their textbooks. I will always admire the President's calm and self-control, allowing the kids to keep reading without his body or his words betraying the enormity of what he had just been told.

I maneuvered in front of the President with my back to the press and held up my notebook for him to see. "Don't say anything yet," I had written. Until he could get a better briefing, I didn't think it would be wise for him to address what surely now was a nation riveted to television sets, eager for news. The President complimented the children and ended the meeting. The advance team got the press out quickly, without any questions shouted. Either the press didn't realize the second tower had been hit, or they were too numb to ask questions, even on their way out the door. The President returned to the hold to get more information.

More than two years after the attack, some criticized the President for not leaving the room to manage the crisis *instantly* after Andy whispered in his ear. Given the fact that no one told the President's traveling party that additional aircraft had been hijacked, I don't know what difference it would have made had he left the room any earlier, other than perhaps to panic a frightened nation if his first reaction was suddenly to bolt from his chair and leave the room without any explanation. Under inconceivable pressure, Bush maintained his composure and sent an image of calm to the nation.

A television set had been brought into the hold, and now the President could see what the rest of the world had been watching. He saw replays of an airliner crashing into the towers and the aftermath, with the smoke billowing before the towers fell, just like everyone else saw it. He and Andy worked the two phones in the hold, seeking what little information was available.

In longhand on five-by-eight note cards, the President wrote the remarks he would deliver to the crowd that awaited his arrival in the auditorium. He declared that the United States had been attacked and vowed to bring justice to whomever was responsible. He also told those gathered, many of whom had no idea the Twin Towers had been struck, that he was returning immediately to Washington, D.C. Later the press panned his speech, saying he looked unsure and unsteady.

As the motorcade sped to the Sarasota airport, the President learned a third plane had just hit the Pentagon. At 9:45 A.M., he boarded Air Force One, and instead of going to my usual seat in the staff cabin, I entered the President's cabin and took notes on his conversations. I always took notes of the meetings I attended, but on this day, my note taking seemed more important than ever.

Bush immediately got the Vice President, who by this time had been evacuated from his West Wing office to a bunker below the White House, on the phone. "Sounds like we have a minor war going on here. I heard about the Pentagon," the President said.

The first reports we received on Air Force One indicated that there were another three aircraft missing and presumed hijacked. Three more missiles were in the air, we thought.

Sitting behind his desk on Air Force One, the President spoke with Andy Card, Karl Rove, and the Air Force military aide whose normal duty was to carry the nuclear football but whose duty on September 11 also included activating an evacuation plan for the President in case he too came under attack. Bush stated, "We're at war. That's what we're paid for, boys. We're going to take care of this. When we find out who did this, they're not going to like me as President. Somebody's going to pay."

Shortly after we took off, the President authorized the military to shoot down any civilian aircraft that was deemed a threat. The communications equipment, he added, was good, not great, as he often had to wait to get people on the phone. After September 11, Air Force One's communications equipment received a major modernization.

Worried that Air Force One itself might become a target, I heard Andy say that we were flying at an unusually high altitude. "They claim we can outrun anybody," he added. Moments later, at 10:32 A.M., the President was on the phone with the Vice President, and he turned to his military aide and said, "A call came into the White House switchboard saying, 'Angel is next.'" Angel was the Secret Service code word for Air Force One.

The latest reports also indicated that there may have been six hijacked aircraft, and the television news reported that there was a bomb at the State Department. Early reports also came in about a car bomb at the Lincoln Memorial, a fire on the Mall in Washington, and another aircraft flying low five miles outside Washington. Even on Air Force One, in the hub of power and information, confusion was the order of the day. We knew three planes had hit their targets; we didn't know how many more were out there, or what else was threatening the country.

"We're at war, Dick," Bush said to Cheney, "and we're going to find out who did this and we're going to kick their ass."

A few minutes later, Andy reported to the President that a fourth plane had gone down, "in the vicinity of Camp David," he said. Karl Rove noted the crash was "south of Pittsburgh."

At about that time, 10:41 A.M., the President told us that the Vice President didn't think it was safe for us to return to Washington until we could get a handle on how many hijacked planes there were. All planes flying in the continental United States had been ordered to land, but it wasn't clear that all had done so. Landing Air Force One at a know location, like Andrews Air Force Base, or returning the President to the White House didn't seem sensible when someone, we didn't yet know who, had proven an ability to hit fixed targets with hijacked aircraft.

Andy Card, after talking to the military and the Secret Service, decided the plane should land at Barksdale Air Force Base in Louisiana. The President wanted to address the nation.

The press were instructed not to use their cell phones when we landed or to identify our location. Security officials didn't want whoever was behind the attacks to learn where the President was in case there was another hijacked plane which could now target him in Louisiana. The Air Force was scrambling a fighter escort, but it wasn't in place yet. As we landed, the TV sets on Air Force One tuned in to the local stations, which were showing our arrival live. Someone on the ground must have tipped the press, and Air Force One is a hard plane to hide. Pretty soon, everyone knew where we were.

From the base commander's office, the President again called the Vice President. "I think it's important for people to see the government is functioning, because the TV shows our nation has been blasted and bombed. Government is not chaotic. It's functioning smoothly," Bush said, knowing the efforts that were being made to help New York and Washington deal with the attacks, in addition to the actions the Federal Aviation Administration had taken to ground all air traffic.

"You're doing great," the President told his Vice President. "I'll stay in touch with you." Then, prefacing what would become a major theme of his war against terror, Bush added, "It's the new war. It's the faceless coward that attacks."

Moments later, in the same conference room, Bush told the small group of staffers gathered with him, "I can't wait to find out who did it. It's going to take a while, and we're not going to have a little slap on the wrist crap." Then the President spoke with Defense Secretary Donald Rumsfeld. "It's a day of national tragedy and we'll clean up the mess and then the ball will be in your court and [Chairman of the Joint Chiefs of Staff, General] Dick Myers's court to respond."

Two things struck me watching events in the early hours of September 11. One was the confusion and the lack of facts. The other was the President's instant recognition that this was war and his determination to lead our nation in winning it.

In the first moments of crisis in any organization, people look to the person at the top for direction and leadership. Whether it's the president of a country, the president of a company, or a school principal, all eyes focus on the leader in moments of peril. In this instance, I saw a President instantly decide to lead our country to war, but first he would be patient. He instilled in his Vice President and his defense secretary a sense of mission, a commitment to war as a full response to the day's awful terror. Rejecting half measures, President Bush made clear that he would stop at nothing short of victory. But he stressed patience. He wanted his team to plan for war immediately, but he told them they would have the time to do it well and do it right. He wouldn't rush into military action for short-term political gain. He set the policy—uproot and destroy those responsible for striking the American homeland.

In hindsight, what president *wouldn't* have led the nation to war after September 11? It's easy to see now why and how we went to war in Afghanistan, but I don't believe other presidents would have reacted, or led, in the manner President Bush did. Another president might have decided we would begin our reaction with sanctions, or with an international conference, ratcheting up the pressure over time. On September 11, we didn't even know who attacked us, but the President had made the decision, at least privately, to go to war. I believe one of the reasons we were so successful so quickly, with only eleven servicemen losing their lives in Operation Enduring Freedom in 2001, was because the President instilled the mission in his top planners from the very first moments of September 11. Their planning and their direction were set, and they were successful because their military objective never changed.

The President also led the world. He knew what he wanted to do, and while he consulted closely with allies and potential foes like Pakistan, he didn't wait for permission to act. The world followed *his* lead. With Pakistan he was tough. The Pakistani government was one of a handful around the world to have diplomatic relations with the Taliban, and the Pakistani intelligence service was close to the Taliban as well. Pakistan mistrusted the Northern Alliance, the group the United States had allied itself with to defeat the Taliban and Al Qaeda. Yet Bush's blunt approach to the Pakistani leader, General Pervez Musharraf, convinced the general that Bush and the United States were deadly serious. Musharraf switched sides, and his government provided vital help to the United States in routing Al Queda.

I called my parents from Barksdale. I hadn't spoken to them yet, and like those of everyone else in the country, their eyes were glued to the television. I told them I was all right and there was no reason to worry about me. Did you know anyone in the Twin Towers? I asked. I remembered years earlier we had celebrated a family birthday with a dinner at Windows on the World, the restaurant at the top of one of the towers. My parents soon found out that two good friends of theirs lost their son, daughter-in-law, and two grandchildren on the plane that hit the Pentagon. An entire family destroyed.

After nearly two hours on the ground, as we prepared to leave Barksdale Air Force Base, Andy Card pulled me aside. We have to reduce the number of people aboard the airplane, he told me. Wherever the President flies, a small army of personnel arrive ahead of him, bringing armored vehicles, including his custom-made limousine. Scores, if not hundreds, of Secret Service agents and uniformed officers are flown on-site to ensure his safety. On September 11, there was no one ahead of us. Wherever we went next, the support crew would be limited to those on the plane. Given the heightened sense of security, the Secret Service didn't want the President to wait for the normal entourage to board the makeshift motorcade that would be assembled upon landing.

The White House staff was going to be reduced, members of Congress who were onboard were to be left behind, and Andy explained, I needed to decrease the number of reporters we were taking with us. Because the entire traveling press corps can't fit onto the President's plane, Air Force One typically flies with a small, rotating pool of thirteen, who file news reports for their colleagues if anything notable happens aboard the plane. One day ABC travels, the next day NBC, the following day CNN, and so on. For the print press, one day it's the *New York Times,* the next day the *Washington Post,* the next day the *Dallas Morning News,* et cetera. I drew a sigh of relief. I had feared for a moment that Andy would tell me *no* press would be allowed, a decision I would have fought vigorously. Reduce the number to three, I was told. I asked Andy to make it five. Five, he said, just do it.

On the flight from Sarasota to Barksdale, the pool consisted of thirteen reporters: a CBS TV news crew, a *Time* magazine reporter, three reporters from the Associated Press, Reuters, and Bloomberg news wires, a print reporter from *USA Today,* and four photographers from AP, Reuters, Agence France-Presse, and *Newsweek.* Ann Compton of ABC Radio was also on the plane. I reduced the pool to Sonya Ross of the Associated Press and Ann Compton, since their organizations were the largest and thus represented the greatest number of viewers or read-ers. Ann was also an experienced TV reporter, and since CBS's crew included an off-the-air producer, Gordon Johndroe of my staff thought Ann could do the TV work with the CBS crew. Joining them would be the CBS cameraman and soundman, as well as Doug Mills, an Associ-ated Press still photographer.

As the President and I approached Air Force One, the group of re-porters who were now barred from the plane, furious and upset, watch-ing their colleagues and the President board the plane on one of the most fateful, newsworthy days of their lives, yelled at me from the tarmac.

"Ari, what about us?" shouted Reuters's senior correspondent, Steve Holland. It was difficult to leave anyone behind, especially a re-porter as gracious as Steve.

"Who's in charge here, the military or the civilians?" demanded an angry reporter. I couldn't blame the press for being upset, but it was necessary. Plus, we didn't treat them any differently from fellow White House aides who were left off the trip. It was tough, however, to leave people behind on a day like September 11. It wasn't quite a lifeboat with only five places for thirteen people, but it was uncomfortable for me to leave those eight reporters behind. Later, a military aircraft took the abandoned party back to Washington.

We left for Nebraska's Offutt Air Force Base a little after 1:00 P.M. The President told his staff in Washington he wanted to have a 4:00 meeting of the National Security Council, and Offutt had a secure video teleconference capacity. "Our focus," Bush told Cheney, "should be to find these people and get them." A moment later he added, "I can assure you I'd like to come home now. Tonight would be great."

He hung up and looked at Andy. "I want to go back home ASAP," Bush said. "I don't want whoever this is holding me outside of Wash-ington."

The head of his Secret Service detail piped up. "Our people are say-ing it's too unsteady still."

"Cheney says it's not safe yet as well," Bush said, resigning himself to the fact that he still didn't know when he could return.

"The right thing to do is let the dust settle," Andy said.

A few minutes later, the President told Andy and me, "This administration will spend whatever is necessary to find, hunt down, and destroy whoever did this."

I realized I hadn't yet spent any time with the press. A little before 2:00, I went back to the two-thirds-empty press cabin to fill them in. The President spoke to the Vice President several times from Barksdale, as well as to Secretary Rumsfeld, New York Senator Chuck Schumer, and the First Lady, I said. He continues to receive updates, and he will convene a meeting of the NSC later today, I explained.

The press asked where the President's wife and children were, and they wanted to know if we had determined who was responsible for the attacks. We didn't know yet, I said about who was repsonsible. Did we have any warnings? they asked. No, I replied.

"Is he concerned about the fact that this attack of this severity happened with no warning?"

"First things first," I said. The President's concern is with the safety of people and with the families of those who have lost their lives. "There will come an appropriate time to do all the appropriate look backs. His focus is on events this morning."

"Does the President feel hunted or in jeopardy?"

"The President is looking forward to returning to Washington. He understands at a time like this, caution must be taken; and he wants to get back to Washington."

A few minutes later I was back in the President's cabin.

He was on the phone with Mayor Rudy Giuliani and Governor George Pataki. "Our sympathies are with you and the people of New York," Bush said. "I know your heart is broken and your city is strained. Anything we can do to help, you let me know." The President warned them there might be a second wave.

As we prepared to land in Nebraska, Bush turned to the head of his Secret Service detail and exclaimed, "We need to get back to Washington. We don't need some tinhorn terrorist to scare us off. The American people want to know where their dang President is."

Moments later we were on the ground, heading for what looked like a small concrete protuberance from the ground. From the outside, it resembled a small hut. The press and some of the traveling party remained far behind as the President, Andy Card, Karl Rove, Dan Bartlett, and I entered. The hut hid a small staircase that descended, and descended, and descended some more. After a few minutes, we found ourselves deep below the earth in the command center of Offutt Air Force Base. Andy and the President went inside a large room with multiple screens on the wall for the NSC meeting, while Karl, Dan, and I were escorted to a separate room nearby. The room where the President was reminded me of the control room in the Matthew Broderick movie *WarGames*.

While at Offutt, I learned that an additional two inbound international flights had not responded to their instructions to return to their cities of origin, in Japan and either Spain or Portugal. Once again we feared there were more hijacked planes heading toward the United States. Before we left, the planes did respond.

After an hourlong meeting, the President emerged, and we headed back upward. He boarded Air Force One, called his wife, and said, "I'm coming home. See you at the White House. I love you . . . go on home." Then he added, "If I'm in the White House and there's a plane coming my way, all I can say is I hope I read my Bible that day."

En route back, the President spoke with Karen Hughes, his top communications adviser. He gave her the outline of what he wanted to say when he addressed the nation that night, his first ever address from the Oval Office. The Vice President and Condi Rice told him about the numerous calls they had received from heads of state pledging their solidarity with the United States. The President told Karen how grateful he was to hear from these leaders and how united the world was in fighting terror.

He was particularly pleased to hear Russia's reaction to the attack. On September 11, when American troops worldwide were put on DEFCON 3, the highest alert level the military had been on since the 1973 Arab-Israeli war, Russia stood down its forces. During the Cold War, Russia would have matched our alert status, raising concerns that the two superpowers might miscalculate and go to war. Putin, Bush thought, was indeed a different kind of Russian.

"We will find these people, and they will suffer the consequences of taking on this nation. We will do what it takes. Everyone must understand this will not stand," he said, echoing his father's words about Iraq's invasion of Kuwait. "No one is going to diminish the spirit of this country."

Then he called the solicitor general, Ted Olson, whose wife had died on American Airlines Flight 77. I slipped out of his cabin so he could express his condolences in private and went to the back of the plane to see the press.

The President will address the nation tonight, I said. His message will be one of "resolve and reassurance. . . . Our nation has been tested before, our nation has always prevailed." Beyond that, I didn't have much information.

"Does the President have any information about the source of the violence and the mastermind behind it?"

"I'm not going to discuss any of the intelligence information that's been provided to the President." Privately, his top advisers suspected Al Qaeda, but it was too soon to offer any speculation to the press.

"Can you give us some idea of why the stops that we made today were made?"

"For security purposes that involve the President," I said. "There are a series of plan[s] that you always hope remain on the shelf that, unfortunately, today had to be implemented."

"Why is he returning now? Who makes the decision that it is safe for his return now?"

"Well, ultimately, it's the President," I explained. "Information is provided to the President about any type of threat, and the President makes the final determination. The President wanted to get back to Washington. He understood that there can be a period of caution so that the security people can make a full and proper assessment about any threats. They were afforded that possibility. The President traveled to a secure location while they took that opportunity. And now, obviously, the President is returning home safely."

It helped that there were two fighter aircraft off the wings of Air Force One, escorting us home.

I was asked whether the Emmy Awards should go on, whether baseball should halt play, and how people should react.

"The President thinks it's important for America to return to their lives. As he indicated, this is a test of America's resolve and that no one will diminish America's spirit; and America's spirit includes a return to normal lifestyles."

Eight hours and forty minutes after leaving Sarasota for what we thought would be Washington, D.C. President Bush landed at Andrews Air Force Base, outside the nation's capital. He boarded Marine One and took off for the White House. The President's helicopter has many approach routes to the White House. On September 11, we entered Washington from the northeast, flying low over the Capitol Building, down the Mall toward the Washington Monument, where Marine One banked right for its final approach to the South Lawn.

As we banked, the President looked out his window over his left shoulder, watching the smoldering Pentagon come into view below. "The mightiest building in the world is on fire," he said aloud, to no one in particular. "That's the twenty-first-century war you just witnessed."

EIGHT

THE AFTERMATH

THE PRESIDENT SAID to act as if we are at war," Andy Card told the 7:30 A.M. senior staff meeting on September 12. Five feet from the Oval Office in the Roosevelt Room, we were assembled for our usual morning meeting, but there was nothing usual about this meeting the morning after. There were to be no loose lips, Andy said, and access to the West Wing would be restricted. I noticed an increased Secret Service presence inside the inner sanctum.

A heaviness hung over the White House, reflecting the hard, somber mood of the nation. The morning meeting, which usually combined healthy doses of seriousness and humor, now combined a somber sense of mourning and a determination to lead the nation with strength and resolve. But it was tough. Nothing I had done before prepared me for life in the White House at a time when our country had been attacked. I focused on my job and tried not to think about the pain the victims' families were feeling. On a normal day, life in the White House flows at a fast pace and I had to bear down just to keep up. After the attack, the pace quickened, the tension mounted, and there was little joy or fun to be found.

The night before, the President had addressed the American people from the Oval Office, declaring, "The pictures of airplanes flying into buildings, fires burning, huge structures collapsing, have filled us with disbelief, terrible sadness, and a quiet, unyielding anger. These acts of mass murder were intended to frighten our nation into chaos and retreat. But they have failed; our country is strong.

"A great people has been moved to defend a great nation. Terrorist attacks can shake the foundations of our biggest buildings, but they cannot touch the foundation of America. These acts shattered steel, but they cannot dent the steel of American resolve.

"America was targeted for attack because we're the brightest beacon for freedom and opportunity in the world. And no one will keep that light from shining."

Brad Blakeman, the President's scheduler, announced that Bush's calendar had been cleared for a week; no events were on it, allowing him to conduct meetings and plan his response. Already we were hearing from Capitol Hill about a possible presidential address to a joint session of Congress and the need for an emergency appropriation to fund cleanup efforts, and Andy Card stressed that Congress needed to confirm the President's appointees, especially those whose duties were required after the attack. He also said that counseling would be available to any White House worker who needed help.

Having spent September 11 with the President, I had missed what the staff in Washington went through. As the third plane approached Washington, D.C., the Secret Service scrambled. Anticipating a possible crash landing into the White House, they physically picked up the Vice President from his desk in the West Wing and ushered him to safety in the bunker below the White House, known as the Presidential Emergency Operations Center, or PEOC. The Vice President and the top staff spent the day in the safety of the windowless shelter. The rest of the staff weren't so lucky.

The West Wing staff, including many who worked for me in the press office, were told to gather in the White House mess, also an underground facility but hardly a bunker. As they assembled, wondering what was going on and when it would be safe to return to their desks, a White House aide responsible for internal administrative matters announced that everyone was to leave immediately and head for Lafayette Park, on the north side of the Executive Mansion. Walk calmly, the staff were told. As people began their orderly departure, a Secret Service agent shouted, "Run, don't walk! Women, take off your shoes and run." The Secret Service feared an aircraft was heading toward the White House.

The gates of the White House swung open, and a one-way stampede ensued. As the staff fled, the Secret Service shouted at workers to take off their ID badges, fearing gunmen might be waiting to pick off White House aides during their panicked departure.

The atmosphere on September 12, when the staff returned to work, was understandably tense.

I left the senior staff meeting to meet with my staff. In any White House, a number of young campaign workers fall in love with their work and the allure of 1600 Pennsylvania Avenue. They break their backs on the campaign and are rewarded with low-paying, eighty-hour-a-week, entry-level White House jobs. My staff were mostly in their twenties, with one nineteen-year-old and one twenty-year-old, both of whom had left college to work there.

I told them the only reason we were fortunate enough to be in the White House today was that other staffers before us had worked at our same desks, in the same West Wing, generations ago to ensure that *our* freedoms would be preserved. While this was the first attack on our soil during our lifetimes, America had been attacked before, and we owed our lives to those who had served their government during World War II and in the many other battles that had made us free. Now it's our turn, I said. What we'll do today and tomorrow will help shape the future for the next generation of Americans. I asked everyone to remember why we were there and reiterated that, if they needed help, help would be available. If the stress is too much, I said, let me know and we'll try to find something else for you. I told everyone to talk to their parents and loved ones to let them know how they felt.

Then I turned to get ready for the first of two September 12 briefings with the press.

Shortly before 10:00 A.M., I entered the briefing room, the new site for the gaggle, since my office could no longer accommodate a press corps that had doubled overnight. The President had arrived in the Oval

Office at 7:05 for briefings with the CIA and other security officials, I told them. He had spoken with several foreign leaders (British Prime Minister Tony Blair, Canadian Prime Minister Jean Chrétien, French President Jacques Chirac, German Chancellor Gerhard Schroeder, Chinese President Jiang Zemin, and twice with Russian President Vladimir Putin) and had convened a meeting of the National Security Council. Later, I told the press, he'll meet with congressional leaders, and I gave an update on what the various agencies were doing in the aftermath of the attack.

Helen Thomas started the questioning, asking if we knew who did it. Not yet, I said.

Was it state sponsored? I won't speculate, I said. One morning after the attack, it was still too soon for the White House to declare who was responsible.

Behind the scenes, intelligence officials immediately focused on Osama bin Laden and his Al Qaeda network. Since I wasn't part of the NSC meetings or the President's CIA briefings, I received most of my information from Condi Rice and her deputy, Steve Hadley. Secretary of State Powell was the first to state publicly, on September 13, that bin Laden was the principal suspect. Only after he said it did I repeat it.

Did I know anything about the Department of Agriculture being evacuated?

I hadn't heard anything about that, I said. "I do want to caution everybody— Yesterday there was a series of information provided that was aired, that turned out to be wrong. So I will do everything in my power to check, to help keep everybody accurate; but I have not heard a thing about that."

"Is there anything to suggest that this might not be over?" Would there be a second wave?

This was a well-coordinated, planned attack, I said. "We believe the perpetrators have executed their plan and, therefore, the risks are significantly reduced."

"But, Ari, considering the enormity of the information that U.S. resources did not know yesterday, why do you feel confident that you know enough today?"

Good question, I thought. "The United States will stay vigilant," I said. Beyond that, I couldn't speculate.

"Why didn't we know some things that we should have known?" one reporter asked.

"Does he [the President] consider it an intelligence failure?" Helen Thomas asked.

"But has he commissioned an analysis of what went wrong? Does he want to know what happened?" asked ABC's Terry Moran.

"Terry," I replied, "I think in all due course, all items will be looked at. The President's focus right now is on helping to save lives and take appropriate action."

From where I stood, those three questions in a row felt as if the blame game was being played within twenty-four hours of the attack. From where the press sat, however, I'm sure they thought they were holding the government accountable for what went wrong. Tension and conflict are built into the relationship between the press secretary and the press. In the aftermath of the attack, as I did my job and the press did theirs, tension and conflict started to rise.

Some reporters said the attack raised questions about why we needed a missile defense system. Simply because this attack was conducted using airplanes doesn't mean we're no longer vulnerable to a missile attack from a rogue state, I replied, wondering how September 11 could possibly be a reason to scrap our plans for a missile defense.

Then I was asked a crucial question: Does the President see the attack as "an act of war"?

Knowing what he would say to the press when he met with them later that morning, I referred reporters to the President's message from the night before, which did *not* include a reference to war, and I hinted that he would continue to express himself on this issue.

In the Bush White House, my job was *not* to make news before the President. I knew he would shortly call the attack an act of war, but it was his job to do so, not mine, so I danced around the question. The press often called me tight-lipped and secretive, but what other way should I have done my job? The President, not the staff, got elected and makes the news. Reporters would have loved me to give away his plans before he announced them himself. That just wasn't how I viewed my job.

At the end of the meeting of the National Security Council, the press were escorted into the Cabinet Room to hear from the President.

"The deliberate and deadly attacks which were carried out yesterday against our country were more than acts of terror. They were acts of war," Bush declared. "This will require our country to unite in steadfast determination and resolve. Freedom and democracy are under attack." For the first time, the President had publicly said the word *war*.

Just before noon, a bipartisan delegation of congressional leaders sat around the long table in the Cabinet Room for a briefing with the President and the Vice President. Speaker Dennis Hastert and House Minority Leader Dick Gephardt, Senate Majority Leader Tom Daschle and Minority Leader Trent Lott were present, along with a dozen other top congressional officials from both parties.

"This is the beginning of war in the twenty-first century," Bush said. "It will require a new strategy. . . . We will answer the bloodlust of the American people that is rightly at boil. We'll spend our capital wisely, and make it stick. We'll be patient. We are at war. The dream of the enemy was for us not to meet in this building. They wanted the White House in rubble."

Combat air patrols composed of AWAC aircraft and F-16s were flying over Washington, the leaders were told.

Secretary Powell told the group that he had spoken with Yasir Arafat. He told Arafat to grab the opportunity to jump-start the Middle East peace talks. Arafat, of course, would miss the opportunity.

And then Bush, speaking as only he can, gave a preview of his doctrine that those who harbor terrorists are as guilty as the terrorists. "These guys are like rattlesnakes. They'll go back into their hole. Not only will we strike the hole, we'll strike the rancher."

Around the table, each congressional leader pledged his or her support for the President. The nation had rallied, and their elected representatives rallied as well. We need to be consulted, they added, fearing that Bush would lead without them. He promised he would consult.

There was one voice of dissent in the room. One congressional leader advised Bush to be careful of his rhetoric. *"War* is a very powerful word. This war is so vastly different. Take great care in your rhetorical calculations," the President was advised.

I couldn't believe my ears. Our nation had just been attacked, and the President was being cautioned *not* to call this a "war." If an attack on our country wasn't war, what was?

"Life needs to go on," Bush said. "There will be no safe harbor for terrorism. We will build from the past and effect a positive future. We're fighting *terrorism,* not a *cell,"* he declared, previewing his assessment of the magnitude of the threat we faced. If anyone thought Bush would settle for a limited response, this meeting should have provided ample warning.

Stating something he would soon say publicly, the President told the group, "We must be mindful of the rights of Arab Americans." The United States needed to "ferret out those who nestle in and hide," Bush said, adding it would be a "balancing act of our great nation."

Several members of Congress told the President they were praying for him, and the meeting broke up.

The broadcast TV networks' news divisions were still going live without commercial interruption. Soap operas as well as sporting events were canceled, and the cable TV networks of course were covering the aftermath nonstop. A growing chorus of criticism was raised about the President's failure to return to Washington immediately after the attack.

I caucused with Karen Hughes and the Vice President to discuss whether we should respond to the criticism or let it fade away. I didn't think the American people thought ill of the President for having taken the precautions he did. But there were a lot of talking heads taking shots at him, filling time on the air.

Karen suggested I tell the press during my briefing about the threat to Air Force One. The public didn't yet know about the call using Air Force One's code word, "Angel is next." Don't respond to the charge, Karen advised, just put out the facts.

As I prepared for my briefing, I watched NBC's Brian Williams's coverage. He too was tough on Bush for not returning to Washington. I called him to fill him in. I think you're being unfair, I said, given the security situation. The last thing you should do in a crisis like yesterday's is put the President in a known location until you know the threat has gone away. Plus, there was a threat made to Air Force One, I told him.

Brian knew I had just made news. Major news. Can I use that? he asked. I didn't see why not since I was about to say it to the briefing room. Sure, I said.

Moments later the NBC screen lit up with a scroll on the bottom stating, "Fleischer says Air Force One Threatened." All hell broke loose. I knew I had made a tactical mistake. Instead of mentioning the news at the briefing, informing everyone at the same time in full and with context, I had dramatized it by giving one network an exclusive that sounded fateful.

Bill Plante of CBS was furious at me for giving an exclusive to a rival network.

The briefing bore down on the news. Was the plane that crashed in Pennsylvania supposed to hit Air Force One? When was the threat made? Was that why the White House was evacuated?

At some point in time, I'm not certain when, the White House concluded that there never was a threat to Air Force One. I learned it was a mistake from the press, who had been tipped by someone who knew. Someone in the Situation Room apparently used the code word while describing a possible threat to Air Force One. That statement set off a chain of conversations that were judged credible enough on September 11 to be passed all the way up to the President. But for all the President, the Vice President, Karen Hughes, and I knew on September 11 and 12, the threat *was* real.

Slowly the briefing drifted toward other topics. Do you know who did it yet? Has the President made up his mind to retaliate? Is his religious faith sustaining him during this crisis? Will he seek a declaration of war? When will the President visit New York City?

On September 11, Bush was criticized for his failure to return quickly to Washington. One day later, a new story line was emerging that the President didn't care enough about New York to express an interest in visiting the damaged city. I told the press of course he wanted to go, but he didn't want to do anything that would interfere with their cleanup efforts, given the distraction a presidential visit can cause as well as the manpower the city would be called on to provide when he did visit. "At the appropriate time the President will visit," I said thirty hours after the attack had begun. "But the President's first focus is on making sure that the rescue workers are able to conduct their jobs."

That evening, President Bush took an unannounced tour of the damaged Pentagon. The impact of American Airlines Flight 77's attack there was structurally far less than the impact of the attack on the Twin Towers of the World Trade Center. I boarded the motorcade in my usual vehicle several cars behind the President's, and we entered the wreckage.

All around me workers were still clearing the ground where the plane had struck. Members of the military and civilians in white, protective clothing were identifying the remains of the victims they had found. It was a somber scene. As the President inspected the damage and thanked the rescue workers, a gigantic American flag was unfurled from the top of the building, next to the deep gash torn in its side.

Inside another section of the Pentagon, the President was briefed. The fire is out, he was told. There are still 183 people unaccounted for. It will take three days to get the bodies out. No one knew how long it would take to rebuild—perhaps a year, he was told.

"It's kind of hard to make it through one of these scenes," Bush said. "The enemy is pretty cagey, but they're not cagey enough. I wish it was tomorrow and I could announce to the nation we're going to wipe it off the face of the earth."

During the senior staff meeting on Thursday, September 13, plans were made for the President to call New York's Mayor Giuliani and Governor Pataki. A national prayer service was arranged for the next day, September 14. When I returned to my office, Sean McCormack, my deputy who was also the spokesman for the National Security Council, told me he'd taken a call from the Associated Press asking if it were true the United States had bombed Iraq. Sean had told them no.

The President called the governor and mayor again that morning. After a last-minute determination that New York City could accommodate his visit, he told them, with the press watching and his call covered on live television, that he would visit Ground Zero tomorrow, September 14. He hung up, and I didn't expect he would take questions. The plan was for Bush to step out of the Oval Office after the call, and the press would then be ushered out. Instead, he stood behind his desk and took questions. Tears fell from his eyes when he was asked how *he* was feeling.

"I don't think about myself right now," he said. "I think about the families, the children. I am a loving guy, and I am also someone, however, who has got a job to do—and I intend to do it. And this is a terrible moment. But this country will not relent until we have saved ourselves and others from the terrible tragedy that came upon America."

Moments earlier, Bush had declared, "Through the tears of sadness I see an opportunity. Make no mistake about it, this nation is sad. But we're also tough and resolute. And now is an opportunity to do generations a favor, by coming together and whipping terrorism; hunting it down, finding it and holding them accountable. The nation must understand, this is now the focus of my administration."

An hour later I boarded the motorcade, this time to accompany the President as he visited survivors of the attack on the Pentagon at the Washington Hospital Center's burn unit.

Bush entered the hospital's shiny, clean lobby and was greeted by a line of physicians. As he and Mrs. Bush made their way down the corridor, a doctor turned to him and said, "I wish we had more patients." One hundred eighty-four people were killed in the attack on the Pentagon, an upward revision of one since the President's briefing. Only about eighty were wounded seriously enough to be hospitalized.

The President greeted the shaken loved ones of those who survived, making small talk, doing his best to cheer them up. "How old are you?" he said to a child. "How's she doing?" he asked a husband. "Bless your spirit. The prayers of the nation are with you," he said.

He entered the room of a Navy lieutenant who was badly burned and stood at his bedside. "You'll get the best care in the world," the President assured the young man, who was too hurt to speak. "We'll take care of you."

The lieutenant's mother pointed to another Navy officer who had rushed into the burning Pentagon after the plane struck. "This is the young man who saved my son's life," she said. Tears fell everywhere.

"This is a special place," President Bush said. "Tomorrow at noon, we'll have a prayer service. The whole nation will pray for your families," he said, referring to the planned service at the National Cathederal.

The President entered the room of a major in the Army Special Forces who was expected to make a full recovery. "Thank you for your service to our country," Bush said. "I look forward to seeing you back in uniform. Are you a Ranger?" he asked.

The major piped up, "My IQ is too high to be a Ranger." Amid calamity, the good-natured rivalry of the military was ever present.

When we returned to 1600 Pennsylvania Avenue, Andy Card called a meeting of the senior staff in the Roosevelt Room. There are continued threats targeting the White House, he announced. The Secret Service will expand the security perimeter around the building, and the Vice President will be at an undisclosed location. The rest of the day's schedule will go ahead as normal, he added.

A short time later I prepared to brief the press. As I was heading out my door for the briefing room, I was told that there was a rumor that a part of the White House, the Eisenhower Executive Office Building (EEOB), right across the street from the West Wing, was being evacuated. I turned around and headed for the deputy chief of staff's office to see if it was true. He was in charge of operations and would be in a position to know. Nothing to it, he told me. There was no evacuation.

Before I could begin the briefing, a reporter asked me about the evacuation. "There is no evacuation of the EEOB," I said.

I later found out there *was* an evacuation of the EEOB—another false alarm. First reports in this business often turn out to be wrong. The press sometimes see things on the ground that people at the top don't get briefed on until later. The push of my job was to answer reporters' questions as quickly as possible. The pull of my job was to make reporters wait for answers until events settled so I didn't say anything that turned out to be wrong. I wish I had waited before I answered that one.

I left the briefing and hurried into the Cabinet Room, where the President was about to meet with members of Congress from the regions affected by the attack, mostly New Yorkers and Virginians.

"The threat to America may not be over," Bush said. "This is a dangerous period, however America must go forward. It's a different war, a war on terrorism, not a cell. . . . When the U.S. moves, it will be deadly serious."

The President went around the room, listening to the concerns of the members of Congress. After one congresswoman talked about the need to help children who were frightened, Bush added, "It's essential we show that Arab Americans are pro-American. We must be mindful of a backlash. All of us as leaders must speak out."

The President had previously told Congress's four leaders (Hastert, Lott, Gephardt, and Daschle) that he supported a $20 billion emergency appropriation to help rebuild New York and the Pentagon. The members could not have been more grateful.

"Thank you for the $2 billion," said Westchester County's congresswoman, Nita Lowey.

"You mean $20 billion," Bush said.

"Two billion dollars is *for* Westchester," Lowey said, quickly recovering, doing a good job at fighting for her constituents' needs.

Knowing how wealthy many of the taxpayers are in suburban Westchester, Bush replied said, "Westchester is *giving* the $20 billion."

SEPTEMBER 14 promised to be a tough, emotional day from the start. The President had called a cabinet meeting at midmorning and would then speak to the nation from a prayer service at the National Cathedral. Then he would leave for Ground Zero and his visit with family members at the Javits Center in midtown Manhattan.

As the cabinet meeting began, an emotional President spoke of his feelings changing from mourning to shock to anger. "I hope it doesn't happen, but we must be mindful of a second wave of attack," he said. The fear was that any action we took would lead to additional terrorist strikes within the United States. Bush concluded his remarks, saying, "There is a God." This affirmation steeled him for what was ahead.

Each secretary took a turn describing how his or her agency was responding to the attack. Powell described his calls to foreign leaders urging them to take action. "We're making it clear to our international partners, you're either with us or not with us." The secretary of state added, "I've been so multilateral the last few days, I've been seasick." Rumsfeld, who reserved talk of his military planning for the smaller war council, updated everyone on the rescue and recovery efforts at the Pentagon. Secretary of Transportation Norman Mineta gave the welcome news that commercial aviation had resumed, although only 16 percent of scheduled flights were in the air.

The meeting broke up, and I looked forward to the prayer service. The National Cathedral, filled with several thousand people, was silent as the President's party exited the motorcade, slipping in before he did. Former Presidents Bush and Clinton were there. Former Vice President Gore as well. Four-star generals, foreign ambassadors, representatives from all major faiths joined together to pray for America and for the victims and their families.

I worried the President wouldn't be able to make it through his remarks without breaking down. Mrs. Bush and Karen Hughes had helped plan the service so it would properly commemorate the lives taken in tragedy without further draining the emotional President, especially right before he got up to speak.

"Just three days removed from these events, Americans do not yet have the distance of history. But our responsibility to history is already clear: to answer these attacks and rid the world of evil," Bush said.

"America is a nation full of good fortune, with so much to be grateful for. But we are not spared from suffering. In every generation, the world has produced enemies of human freedom. They have attacked America, because we are freedom's home and defender. And the commitment of our fathers is now the calling of our time."

In some quarters, the President was criticized for delivering from the pulpit what his critics called a strident message that bordered on bellicose. I thought it was a beautiful speech that represented the thinking of the American people.

When he sat down, the choir sang "The Battle Hymn of the Republic." It's a song I had heard many times before, but until September 14, I never paid much attention to the words. It's a Christian song, and one verse in particular struck me. "He has loosed the fateful lightning of His terrible swift sword. His truth is marching on." Whatever savior people believe in, on that day, the notion of a terrible swift sword sent a chill through me. Our nation would soon go to war.

The service ended, the traveling White House staff hustled out ahead of everyone else so we could be on our way. A short time later, we were wheels up from Andrews Air Force Base headed for McGuire Air Force Base in New Jersey, where we would board helicopters for the Wall Street Landing Zone, then make the short drive to Ground Zero.

KAREN WAS the first to smell it. She and I usually flew in Marine One with the President, but today we were on Marine Two to make room for Governor Pataki and Mayor Giuliani.

"What's that smell?" she said from somewhere over the Atlantic Ocean as we approached the city's stricken skyline. At first I couldn't smell a thing. As we got closer, I thought I smelled something wrong with the helicopter. A second later, I realized it was the smell of the burned and collapsed towers reaching toward us, preparing our senses for the wrenching experience of entering Ground Zero.

We landed, ran to the waiting motorcade, and wound our way around lower Manhattan. We drove through an opening in a newly erected mesh fence surrounding the rubble, and the President exited his limo.

Standing near the intersection of Barclay Street and West Broadway, Pataki and Giuliani pointed up, showing the President what had been two 110-floor-high towers, now reduced to a pile of debris perhaps seven stories high.

It was a sunny day, but underneath our feet were inches of what looked like a gray, dirty snow. In reality, it was the ashes of the Twin Towers, everywhere you walked. It was hard to grasp the enormity of what took place. New York City is a tough, proud place, a city where people hurry through their days, outwardly oblivious to those around them. On September 14, New York was still and downcast. As we stood feet from the outer edge of the rubble, it was hard to say a word to anyone, about anything. The silence was pierced by a roar overhead, the sound of an Air Force F-16 fighter aircraft on combat air patrol over the city in which I was born.

Growing up in New York, you're not exposed to men and women walking down the street in military uniforms the way you are in Washington. There are no military bases in Manhattan or in Westchester the way there are sprinkled throughout America, where the military way of life is a daily presence in countless communities. As a child, I strained my neck in my parents' car when I saw several Army vehicles drive past us in upstate New York. What have we come to, I thought, when the streets of New York City are being protected by fighter aircraft?

The President got back in his car and traveled a short distance to another vantage point amid the destruction. He plunged deep into the middle of the rescue workers who were trying to save anyone who might still be alive. Wearing a windbreaker and casual clothes, the President shook hands with the firemen and rescue workers, who refused to sleep. Like all New Yorkers, they wouldn't give up hope.

They were a stern group. There were no smiles, just grim looks of determination from dust-caked work crews. Several firemen pointed out to the President spots in the rubble where they thought bodies might still be found. Rescue dogs sniffed anywhere they could, looking for signs of life. Up the road stood veterinary trailers to tape the dogs' paws, which bled from the towers' jagged remains.

"Don't let us down, Mr. President. We're counting on you," the workers told him. The President told me later you could feel the testosterone flowing from these grim, vulnerable rescuers.

He didn't plan to say anything. He had already addressed the nation from the National Cathedral, and there was no place set aside here for remarks.

Andy Card pulled me aside. "The President's going to address the workers in five minutes," he said. "Get the press together."

"Where's he going to do it from?" I asked.

"See that older man standing on top of that mound over there?" Andy said. "He'll do it from there." The mound was the remains of a New York City fire truck, destroyed at the intersection of Murray and West Streets.

I found the press and told them to assemble in front of the mound because the President was going to have something to say. An advance aide, Nina Bishop, found a megaphone and gave it to the President.

As he started to speak, the firemen gathered around him started yelling.

"We can't hear you," one said loud enough for the President to hear.

"*I* can hear *you*," the President replied through the megaphone. "I can hear you. The rest of the world hears you. And the people who knocked these buildings down will hear all of us soon."

Newsweek's Jonathan Alter was standing next to me. "That will go down as a moment in history," he said.

"What do you mean?" I asked.

"What the President just did was historic. It will long be remembered by historians and the public," Jonathan said. He grasped the impact of the President's emotional reply long before I did.

The shouts of "USA, USA" echoed in our ears as the President boarded his limousine, which had to crawl out through an army of rescuers. The Secret Service always leaves a clean escape route for the President's motorcade, no matter where he is. On September 14, it was hard to make it through the crowd, and it was harder yet to endure the emotional scene at the Javits Center, where the President met with two hundred families of the "missing." En route there, the West Side Highway was lined with New Yorkers cheering the President, just as they had days earlier cheered each fire truck and police vehicle that rode past.

As Bush's grueling day came to a close, we boarded our Marine helicopters for the short ride back to Air Force One. The President would travel on a smaller aircraft since he was heading to Camp David, where he had called a meeting of the War Council. Just as it was time to leave, I got word that Congress had passed a resolution authorizing the use of force in response to the September 11 attack. As the President walked from Marine One to Air Force One, I intercepted him to let him know about the vote and to get his approval for a statement welcoming the action. A drained and weary President Bush looked at me. He told me he was "whipped" and said, "Put it out."

I NEVER ATTENDED War Council meetings, so I headed into the White House on Saturday. I briefed the press on a conference call without really answering any of their questions.

The briefings were getting tougher and tougher. The press were asking questions I could, and would, never answer.

"Were there any determinations or decisions made today?"

"I'm not going to get into any specifics of these meetings. . . . It's a Saturday and, you know, it's different because everybody is at Camp David. But this is the same ground rules that if you knew about a meeting here in the Situation Room of the President and his team, I wouldn't indicate what took place in this building, so I certainly won't indicate what's taking place at Camp David."

"Could a U.S. response come at any time?"

"Well, it depends. As the President said in his radio address this morning—'you'll be asked for patience, for the conflict will not be short; you'll be asked for resolve; the conflict will not be easy—because victory may be long.'"

Then I added, "You know, there is an enemy who wants to know, so I'm not going to give any indications about—"

"That's not us, right?" a reporter interrupted, causing laughter on the conference call. The press always worry that people in government view them as "the enemy."

"No, it's not," I said, to the press's relief. "But I'm just not going to give any indication to the enemy. Let them fret and worry about it."

Times *were* tough on the press. They wanted to know when we would counterattack, how we would counterattack, and where the counterattack would take place. They knew I wouldn't answer their questions, but that didn't stop them from asking. They again thought I was tight-lipped and secretive. I thought I was doing my job.

"Ari, when the President talks about, you know, those terrorists are going to hide in the hills and we're going to find them and we're going to smoke them out—is he preparing the American people for the possibility that U.S. ground troops may have to be used to try and have this sweeping and effective assault against terrorism?" asked CNN's Kelly Wallace.

"The President is preparing the public for all eventualities," I said, being as vague as I could.

"So we're not ruling out that ground troops might have to be used in this assault against terrorism?"

"The President has not ruled out anything."

A moment later I was asked, "When you say that the President has not ruled any options out for our response, does that include the use of nuclear weapons?"

You must be kidding, I thought.

"You know that's a subject we never even get into. You're asking me operational issues."

"Well, you said nothing has been ruled out, no eventualities. I'm asking if that's truly what you mean now."

"When I said nothing has been ruled out, it was about ground troops. But if you're asking me what type of weapons we're going to use, that's a question that— If you asked me that question in peace time, I wouldn't answer it; you're asking me today, I don't answer those questions."

No matter how many ways I told the press I wouldn't talk about operational plans, they kept asking.

"Can you give us more of a sense, Ari, of how far advanced the planning is?"

"Obviously on the planning, I'm not going to get into that."

Moments later, "Pakistanis are saying among those things that they are willing to do is allow the U.S. to store troops along its border. Can you confirm that that's one of the things you guys would like to see happen?"

"I'm not going to talk about any military movement," I said.

The reality of how the press cover military matters is complicated.

Top editors will, upon request, hold stories that they believe could endanger troops or cost lives. The press have a fair sense of responsibility, especially when they're appealed to. Immediately after September 11, I asked the top editors of the major news organizations and the White House press corps not to report the President's schedule more than forty-eight hours in advance, because of heightened concerns about a possible assassination attempt. Because the press care about our country and national security, they agreed. At the same time, however, White House reporters are so intent on getting the story, they'll say they're not asking about troop movements in the same breath they ask about troop movements. They say they don't want to reveal military plans as they ask what those plans are. It's not like the old days, when a trusted senior reporter or two might have been told inside information so history could be better served, knowing the reporter would hold the news until later. The pressure to report, the desire *not* to get beat by the competition, and the instinct of smart reporters to break significant news stories compel them to ask questions that no press secretary should answer.

We were a White House heading for war, and my relationship with the press grew more tense and complicated. Increasingly, my job on military and intelligence matters was to say nothing and take the heat.

On Sunday the President returned to the White House from Camp David. As he stepped off Marine One, he stopped to answer questions from reporters gathered on the driveway of the South Lawn.

Patsy Wilson of Reuters asked about his military plans. "Mr. President, the Taliban apparently has refused to hand over Osama bin Laden to the Pakistanis. Does this mean that the U.S. will be prepared to move militarily?"

"Patsy, I want to make it clear to the American people that this administration will not talk about any plans we may or may not have," Bush said. "We will not jeopardize in any way, shape, or form anybody who wears the uniform of the United States."

After a few questions, he entered the Mansion and summoned Karen Hughes, Dan Bartlett, and me to his office in the residence. Condi Rice was there as well. In the Treaty Room, a handsome room with creamy walls that was once the White House's waiting room as well as the Cabinet Room, the President laid down the law.

There were to be no loose lips, he said. Lives were at stake. Troops could begin to move, and he didn't want to read about it in the press. I wasn't to confirm, deny, or acknowledge any of the press's questions on military matters. He made clear he knew his job was to keep the public informed, and he would do so, not the staff.

If that was how the President was answering questions, that was how I was going to answer questions.

Later that night, Andy Card called a meeting of the senior staff. We're going to evacuate the White House's offices along Seventeenth Street, he said. Visitors won't be able to congregate in the West Wing lobby, and from this point on, there will be only one public entrance into the Old Executive Office Building. All tours of the White House are canceled. The fear was a truck bomb.

A tense White House grew even tenser.

At the next day's briefing, I was asked about an action taken by Pakistan to give the Taliban seventy-two hours to turn over bin Laden. Is that a U.S.-sponsored deadline? I was asked.

Again, I wouldn't answer, but this time I tried to explain why. "We've asked our allies to cooperate with us in military areas, in financial areas, in economic areas, in political and diplomatic. And I understand why you want to know more. But for me to indicate to you anything more than that would also be an indication to our enemy about what concrete steps allies may be taking. And one of the easiest ways for them to get around any steps our allies may be taking is for them to know about them.

"So I wish there was a way that I could share this information with people here and with the American people. But as you know, any answer I would give to that would also be directly provided to our enemy. And I will not do that."

Earlier that Monday, September 17, the President visited the Pentagon, and the press asked him about Osama bin Laden.

"Do you want bin Laden dead?"

"I want justice. There's an old poster out west, as I recall, that said, 'Wanted: Dead or Alive,'" Bush replied.

Back at the briefing, reporters followed up.

"We like to think of ourselves as a civilized world," asked the *Wall Street Journal*'s Jeanne Cummings, "so why does the administration feel that it is appropriate to encourage, globally, people to go kill someone else?"

"Our nation has been attacked and we're at war, and to win a war it is vital for the United States to engage in it," I said. "And, unfortunately, having had the first blow taken at our nation, our nation will defend itself."

Another reporter followed up.

"Speaking of civilized nations and religion, America heeded the call that President Bush gave this week, talking about going to church house or going to the place of worship and praying. Many of those who prayed this week were praying to prevent war. What does the President, who is a devout Christian, say to these people as they're praying that there is no more bloodshed?"

"One of the reasons all of us are here and enjoy what we do, and have the lifestyles we lead is because somebody in a generation before answered the call," I said. "And unfortunately in our history, there has been a call to war at times. And it's a call that a peace-loving nation and a free nation like the United States never—ever—wants to get involved in or answer.

"But make no mistake: the United States has been attacked, and the United States will answer the call."

A reporter then said, "The Bible says, turn the other cheek."

"This nation will be defended," I replied. "That way, we can have a Bible to continue to live by and to listen to, as well as a Koran . . ."

I believe these reporters were playing devil's advocate. I can't believe anyone after September 11 would *really* think the best response was no response.

When the briefing was over, I hurried to board the motorcade for the President's trip to the Islamic Center of Washington, D.C., a prominent gathering spot for the Muslim community in the nation's capital. Bush, worried about an anti-Muslim backlash in the United States, went there to show the American people the importance of respecting Muslims and Muslim Americans.

The President sat with the imam and other Muslim leaders in a meeting room as the press waited outside. The United States, Bush said to his hosts, is a "hospitable country that treasures diversity. These horrible acts do not reflect on the Muslim faith. My administration," he pledged, "will continue to speak out against violence against our fellow citizens."

The President looked at his hosts and continued, "God's way is saying to all the righteous of all faiths to come together to fight evil, and root out terrorism. I'm determined. I'm patient. I'm angry, but I'm reasoned."

The imam responded, "Jews call Jerusalem the city of peace. Christians called Jesus the prince of peace. Muslims call their religion the religion of peace. We will all stand together in peace." Another Muslim leader told the President, "We know America is a great power not only because it has the power to destroy, but the power to rebuild. In past conflicts, the U.S. transformed their enemies." Bush nodded his head in agreement.

Addressing the Middle East, the President said with his characteristic bluntness, "Arafat has to do a better job. Sharon wants peace because his people want peace. I've told Sharon to 'seize the moment.'" Jerusalem, Bush said, should be the last issue the parties discuss so they can build confidence in their ability to resolve other matters first.

And then a Muslim American woman told him she was fearful of going out in public wearing her headdress. She was scared she would be attacked. Bush was touched, and worried, that a pious woman had reason to fear if she dressed herself according to her religion. He frequently spoke out about the woman, urging Americans to be respectful of Arab Americans, who, he said, love the American flag just as much as their neighbors.

———

ROSH HASHANAH, the Jewish New Year, was the day after the President's visit to the Islamic Center.

I had never worked on a High Holy Day. Observant Jews don't work on Rosh Hashanah or Yom Kippur. How could I? But one week after the attack, I wasn't sure what to do. I called my rabbi and asked him if I could go to synagogue that morning and return to the White House after services to brief the press. Given the gravity of the times and the possibility that lives could be at stake, he said yes.

As I prepared for my briefing with my staff (Scott McClellan, Claire Buchan, and Sean McCormack), I asked them if I could say I had been in synagogue in the morning. Working on a High Holy Day sent a terrible signal to fellow Jews, and I was uncomfortable. They told me it would be better if I left it alone. Don't bring religion into the briefing room, I was advised. I agreed.

But at the briefing, I was asked a question about a meeting that had taken place in the morning. Knowing that Jews, especially Jewish children, might be watching, I took advantage of the question and said, "I was in synagogue this morning and so I did not participate in the meeting."

It felt so good to do what I never did. I spoke for myself and slipped in a message about the importance of attending services and missing work even during a time of emergency. I was glad I'd said it. Ten days later, I didn't go to work and observed Yom Kippur instead.

I called my family from home as Rosh Hashanah began to wish them a happy holiday. A cousin whose office building faced the World Trade Center told me she saw the plane approach and hit the second tower. She described how terrible it was.

I hung up the phone, and for the first time in a week, I stopped thinking about work. I broke down and cried. Somehow I had been able to do my job and calmly speak for the President about the tragedy and its aftermath. But when I finally let my professional thoughts fade and instead thought about my family, New York City, and all those who had lost their lives, all I could do was cry.

I always told myself that because of the importance of the presidency and the intensity of the press, every day at the White House is a crisis, so I might as well get used to daily crises and treat them as routine. Even on September 11 and in its aftermath, I somehow found a way to do my job calmly, without pausing to think how momentous events really were. Aboard Air Force One on September 11, I heard the President discuss shooting down commercial aircraft. I learned our military was on DEFCON 3. I heard the aircraft on which I rode was threatened.

Through it all, I knew my job was simply to report the facts to the press and explain what the President was doing and why he was doing it. Events move so fast at the White House that I never did stop to think how frightening or troubling the times had become. Even during the anthrax attacks, when the government didn't have any answers, I knew my job was to remain calm and in control. I had a responsibility to represent the President and handle whatever came my way, no matter how bad it was. Perhaps I could do this because I'm not easily excitable, but I also had faith that no matter what challenged our country, we Americans always pulled together and succeeded. I didn't worry on the outside because I was confident on the inside.

BACK AT THE WHITE HOUSE, Bush turned his attention to economic matters and the impact of the attack. Meeting with his top domestic advisers, the President reviewed how much money was being spent to rebuild New York and Washington, as well as the tax cuts that had gone into effect. "We're going to have the best of supply side and Keynesian [policies] kicking in. We need to rebuild New York," he said, realizing that the pump was being primed on both ends, spending and tax cutting.

He was shown a chart marked by a severe drop in capacity utilization of factories. "I don't care what the title of that chart is," he said. "It doesn't look very good." The airline industry, he was told, now had 60 percent of their planes back in the air, but they were mostly flying empty. The economy was bad and getting worse.

One of his advisers suggested dropping the corporate income tax rate from 35 percent to 20 percent for three years to give the economy a boost. Bush rejected the idea out of hand. On September 18, the Presi-

dent signed into law a $40 billion emergency spending package for re-
building and recovery efforts, and he was told $25 billion of it would
be spent in 2002; the remainder couldn't be spent any sooner. He had
asked for a proposal to help the airline industry and was waiting for it
to be developed. He was right, the government was getting ready to
spend a lot of money.

That evening, one week after the attack, France's President, Jacques
Chirac, met with Bush in the Oval Office. Chirac, in front of the press,
said he stood in total solidarity with the United States. Bush repeated
his mantra that this was a "new kind of war." But then Chirac, hinting
of Franco-American differences, corrected Bush.

"I don't know whether we should use the word *war,* but what I can
say is that now we are faced with a conflict of a completely new nature," he said, speaking in French. "It is a conflict which is attempting
to destroy human rights, freedom, the dignity of man. And I believe
that everything must be done to protect and safeguard these values of
civilization."

Again I thought, How can anyone say this is *not* war? Not only is
the French language beautiful but it is thought by its speakers to be a
language of nuance and diplomacy. Stark descriptions such as those
used by President Bush were met by Chirac with a vague, often nuanced, delicate reply. The difference is part of a cultural gap between
how many Americans and many Europeans, the French especially, approach world affairs. I may have minored in French during college, but
I thought President Bush's description was the more accurate one.

During their private meeting, Chirac asked the American President
what his intentions were. Bush said he expected the Taliban to hand over
bin Laden and his top aides, or there would be consequences, "grave
consequences." He added, "There was once a time when we weren't prepared to lose lives. Those days are over. We cannot talk reason to these
people. There's no diplomacy. We understand we can't bomb our way,
but we can loosen them up. Make no mistake. This is our campaign."

The European Union, Chirac told Bush, was also susceptible to terrorism. He promised the President his support with all means, and he
added, it had to be done collectively.

The press, meanwhile, had picked up reports that Mohamed Atta, one of the hijackers, had been seen meeting with the head of Iraqi intelligence in the Czech Republic earlier in 2001. Was it true? they asked me. Was there a connection between the attack and Iraq?

"I'm not in a position to confirm or give you any indication on that," I said. The Atta link to Iraq was a rumor that wouldn't go away. No one who might have known could ever tell me it happened, but I was also told we didn't know enough to say it didn't happen. I did my best to tell the press not to chase the story, but I couldn't say flat out it didn't happen.

In another sign of the press's ability to take any side of any issue, I was asked on September 19 about nations that urged the United States to exercise restraint in our pending military response. How much would we listen to foreign nations, I was asked, and how much of what we would do would be unilateral?

I said it would be a "healthy dose of both." I said that the President was going to lead and that many nations would be shoulder to shoulder with us, and some nations would be less than shoulder to shoulder.

A reporter followed up. "Are our hands tied at all by these calls for restraint? Is the United States still able to act unilaterally?" One year later, much of the press wanted to know how we possibly *could* act unilaterally.

Bill Plante from CBS picked up the theme. Sometimes Bill asked questions. Sometimes Bill shared what he was thinking. "Your answer really suggested that the United States is going to do as it sees fit, and other nations can come along to the extent that they're willing to. But it doesn't sound as though you're really talking about consultation with anyone," he stated.

"I think that the nations that the President is talking to would strongly disagree with what you said," I replied. "And that's the whole reason that the President has called more than twenty world leaders, that he's been meeting with a series of presidents and foreign ministers."

"Is it consultation, or is it telling them what we intend to do?"

"It's both," I said. "That's called leadership, and that's called consultation. And that's all, added up, called diplomacy."

Taking the oath at the swearing in ceremony for staff alongside several dozen aides, including Karen Hughes, Karl Rove, and Condi Rice (January 22, 2001).

Dropping in on the old White House swimming pool through the floor of the James S. Brady Press Briefing Room (January 27, 2001).

LEFT: Gathering facts with Condi Rice about the allied armed forces' military strike enforcing the no-fly zone in Iraq during the President's trip to President Vicente Fox's Rancho San Cristóbal in San Cristóbal, Mexico (February 16, 2001).

FACING PAGE, TOP: At the President's meeting with cable and broadcast network members of the White House press corps in the Roosevelt Room. Reporters pictured are Jim Angle of Fox, John Roberts of CBS, John King of CNN, Mark Knoller of CBS Radio, and Terry Moran of ABC (March 2, 2001).

Listening to the President at a press conference in the briefing room alongside Karen Hughes, Condi Rice, and Andy Card. The White House press corps members (from left) John Roberts (CBS), Ron Fournier (AP), and David Gregory (NBC) are visible in the first row (February 22, 2001).

ABOVE: The President shielding my head on a rainy day as we walk across the South Lawn to Marine One (March 21, 2001).

BELOW: Playing catch with the President on the South Lawn to warm him up for throwing out the first pitch at the Milwaukee Brewers' season opener. Andy Card is standing on the sidelines (April 3, 2001).

Outside the Yankees' dugout at Camden Yards with Joe Torre before the game (May 18, 2001).

BELOW: Playing the game Risk aboard Air Force One on a return flight from Kosovo (and Europe): Gordon Johndroe, Chief of Protocol Donald Ensenat, a military aide, the President, Andy Card, me, Logan Walters, and Karl Rove (July 24, 2001).

A typical gaggle with members of the White House press corps in my West Wing office before September 11, 2001. *New York Times* photo

Discussing the President's first public remarks after the terrorist attacks in his holding room at the Emma E. Booker Elementary School in Sarasota, Florida (with Scott McClellan, the President, and Dan Bartlett) (September 11, 2001).

Listening to the President in his office aboard Air Force One on September 11.

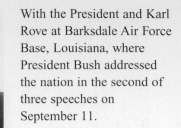

With the President and Karl Rove at Barksdale Air Force Base, Louisiana, where President Bush addressed the nation in the second of three speeches on September 11.

Watching coverage of the attack on the World Trade Center at Barksdale Air Force Base (September 11, 2001).

Meeting with members of the White House press corps in my West Wing office upon the President's return to the White House (September 11, 2001).

The President discussing his Oval Office address to the nation. In his private study off the Oval Office are Al Gonzales, Condi Rice, Karen Hughes, me, and Andy Card (September 11, 2001).

In the White House briefing room with the former press secretaries. From left: Jake Siewert (Clinton), Jerald terHorst (Ford), Ron Ziegler (Nixon), Ron Nessen (Ford), me, Mike McCurry (Clinton), Dee Dee Myers (Clinton), Larry Speakes (Reagan), Marlin Fitzwater (Reagan and George H. W. Bush), and Joe Lockhart (Clinton) (November 30, 2001).

Talking with President Musharraf of Pakistan and Karen Hughes in the Oval Office (February 13, 2002).

MEETING HEADS OF STATE

Receiving a papal coin from Pope John Paul II at the Vatican (May 28, 2002).

His Majesty King Abdullah greets me in Aqaba, Jordan. Waiting their turns are Dan Bartlett, Andy Card, Condi Rice, and Colin Powell (June 4, 2003).

Conferring with the President and Israeli Prime Minister Ariel Sharon before the press corps enter the Oval Office during the leaders' meeting on the prospects for Middle East peace. Arnon Perlman, chief spokesperson and head of communications for Sharon, whispers into his boss's ear (October 16, 2002).

The World Series champions Arizona Diamondbacks' pitcher Randy Johnson pats me on the head as the pitcher Curt Schilling looks on following my daily White House briefing (December 13, 2001). *Agence France-Presse* photo

With the President and broadcast television news anchors for lunch in the family dining room of the mansion on the day of the 2002 State of the Union. Visible are President Bush, Dan Rather (CBS), Brit Hume (Fox), Jim Lehrer (PBS), me, Tom Brokaw (NBC), Vice President Cheney, and Peter Jennings (ABC) (January 29, 2002).

Conferring with the President in the Oval Office (March 26, 2002).

Playing catch on the tarmac in Waco, Texas, beside Air Force One (April 7, 2002).

BELOW: Talking with members of the White House press corps aboard Air Force One (April 9, 2002).

ABOVE: Watching a Secret Service training exercise with the President and presidential aides at the Secret Service Training Center in Beltsville, Maryland (April 19, 2002).

BELOW: Talking with the President, Vice President Cheney, Condi Rice, and Josh Bolten in the Oval Office.

Preparing for the President and Secretary Rumsfeld to discuss security and defense issues in a press availability at the Bush Ranch (August 21, 2002).

Conferring with the President and Dan Bartlett in the Oval Office (October 16, 2002).

WHITE HOUSE *NEWS SUMMARY*

PRODUCED FOR THE OFFICE OF THE WHITE HOUSE PRESS SECRETARY

TO: THE PRESIDENT AND SENIOR WHITE HOUSE STAFF

DATE: FRIDAY, APRIL 4, 2003

CORRECTIONS

First page of the White House news summary, showing a series of media errors and corrections.

New York Times
Corrections
04/02/03

Corrections

A front-page news analysis article on Sunday about the political perils faced by President Bush over the war with Iraq misattributed a comment about Saddam Hussein's government being "a house of cards." While some American officials had used the phrase to predict a shorter conflict and a quick collapse of the Iraqi leadership, Vice President Dick Cheney was not among them. ■

New York Times
Corrections
04/03/03

Corrections

A front-page article on Tuesday about criticism voiced by American military officers in Iraq over war plans omitted two words from an earlier comment by Lt. Gen. William S. Wallace, commander of V Corps. General Wallace had said (with the omission indicated by uppercasing), "The enemy we're fighting is A BIT different from the one we war-gamed against." ■

Washington Post
Corrections
04/03/03

CORRECTIONS

An April 2 article incorrectly stated that Deputy Secretary of State Richard L. Armitage "made calls" to Capitol Hill regarding funds for relief and reconstruction in Iraq in the Bush administration's supplemental spending proposal. Armitage made no such calls.

≡

USA Today
Corrections
04/04/03

Corrections & Clarifications

USA TODAY is committed to accuracy. To reach us, e-mail editor@usatoday.com or call 800-872-0001.

Wednesday's 1A cover story reported that Commerce Secretary Don Evans had said President Bush believes he was called by God to lead the nation at this time. Evans, in fact, said only that the president believes he was called to lead at this time. The story also said Evans talks with the president every day. Evans says he talks with the president often but not every day.

Touring the USS *Abraham Lincoln* with Condi Rice and the ship's crew (May 1, 2003).

Touring Auschwitz with the President (May 31, 2003).

Celebrating my last flight aboard Air Force One, en route to Washington, D.C., from Nigeria after the President's weeklong trip to Africa. From left, Director of Presidential Advance Todd Beyers, the President, me, Andrews Air Force Base flight attendant Master Sergeant Reginald Dickson, Condi Rice, and Colin Powell (July 12, 2003).

Thanking the President during a good-bye party in the Indian Treaty Room as my wife, Becki Fleischer, looks on. Among the others pictured are Vickie McQuade (behind the President) and Josh Deckard (arms folded) (July 14, 2003).

My final daily briefing in the James S. Brady Press Briefing Room (July 14, 2003).

I was challenged again on how the President could lead if not every nation agreed to follow.

"The President," a reporter asserted, "intends to move forward knowing that there are going to be a number of countries that may not be standing shoulder to shoulder with the United States, and the United States will move ahead anyway."

"Are you saying," I replied, "that the United States should do nothing unless there's world unanimity? I'm not aware of any such doctrine."

The briefing was turning into an argument.

"Why should the American people believe that this government has such solid evidence linking Osama bin Laden to these terrorist acts when it wasn't even able to determine that there were four planes that were going to get hijacked and kill thousands of people? Why should we believe you?" asked a reporter.

I walked reporters through bin Laden's connections to the repeated terrorist attacks against the United States in the nineties, and I explained that we were sharing intelligence with other nations about who was behind September 11. "If any of the governments share your concerns, I'm sure they'll make it clear to us. We're hearing scant little of that," I said.

And again the press asked me about the movement of troops, this time a report that we had sent one hundred military aircraft to bases closer to Afghanistan. There's nothing I can tell you, I said. I later found out that we had moved aircraft, but the reporter's number was way off.

Should I get back to the reporter who asked? I wondered. He had mistaken information and he might put it on the air. How could I do that, though, without confirming the essence of his story, that we *were* moving aircraft closer to Afghanistan? The President had told me not to discuss anything military. I let it go.

My refusal, even in private, to help White House reporters sort out fact from fiction on military and intelligence issues frustrated them tremendously. They had counted on earlier White House press secretaries to steer them straight. It's often said the press secretary serves two masters, the President and the press. Increasingly the press thought I served just one—and it wasn't them.

As the military story became the looming front-page issue, many in the press faulted my failure to help them find the facts. They were, after all, in search of the truth and they wanted to report it to the American people. I knew my refusal to answer their questions about military matters, even on background, would hurt my relationship with some of them. Some complained that all I would do was read preapproved talking points. But just as their job was to cover the news and not worry about whether they were being friendly or not, my job was to refer all military matters to the Pentagon. Even if they didn't like the way I did my job, I wasn't going to change. I thought secrecy concerning military matters was the right approach to take.

The next night the President addressed the nation at a joint session of Congress. In a speech hailed by the press and by Democrats, he announced what became known as the "Bush doctrine."

"Americans should not expect one battle, but a lengthy campaign, unlike any other we have ever seen," the President said. "It may include dramatic strikes, visible on TV, and covert operations, secret even in success. We will starve terrorists of funding, turn them one against another, drive them from place to place, until there is no refuge or no rest. And we will pursue nations that provide aid or safe haven to terrorism. Every nation, in every region, now has a decision to make. Either you are with us, or you are with the terrorists. From this day forward, any nation that continues to harbor or support terrorism will be regarded by the United States as a hostile regime."

He described Al Qaeda as "the heirs of all the murderous ideologies of the twentieth century. By sacrificing human life to serve their radical visions—by abandoning every value except the will to power—they follow in the path of fascism, and Nazism, and totalitarianism. And they will follow that path all the way, to where it ends: in history's unmarked grave of discarded lies."

He finished declaring, "Freedom and fear, justice and cruelty, have always been at war, and we know that God is not neutral between them."

Vice President Cheney was not there for the speech. In a sign of the times, he was secreted away, somewhere safe. In case the Capitol was attacked, plans were made for Cheney to survive.

NINE

YOU'LL ATTACK WHEN?

I N HIS ADDRESS to the Congress, President Bush gave the Taliban an ultimatum to hand over bin Laden and all Al Qaeda leaders, permanently close Al Qaeda's camps, and give the United States access to verify that the camps were shut. He added, "These demands are not open to negotiation or discussion. The Taliban must act, and act immediately. They will hand over the terrorists, or they will share in their fate."

The President said no negotiations. The White House press corps didn't take him at his word.

"Is the President ruling out any kind of discussions with the Taliban that could ultimately lead to his goal along the lines that the United States has with Pakistan?" a reporter asked me, evidently hoping I would say in the briefing room something different from what the President had told the nation the night before.

Yes, I said, he ruled out discussions. He wants action, not words.

"But does meaningful consultation or negotiation not constitute action?"

No, I said.

"Does he believe that the Taliban wants to negotiate, or is he convinced that the response to the speech was essentially the Taliban thumbing its nose at the United States?"

The Taliban responded with defiance to the ultimatum Bush delivered. "If they want to show their might, we are ready and we will never surrender before might and force," said the Taliban ambassador to Pakistan, Abdul Salam Zaeef.

The President wants action, not words, I repeated.

Helen Thomas entered the questioning. "Do we have concrete proof, other than they hate freedom and that— This is very nebulous, simplistic stuff, because you really don't know. That doesn't really given enough of meat on the plate here. Do you have concrete proof that this man [Osama bin Laden] was guilty, and if you have it, why don't you present it?"

"The challenge that the government always faces when you ask a question like that," I said, "is the means of providing the proof provides valuable information to those who are the objects of any potential action. They would like nothing better than to be able to hide where they are hiding, and have the United States reveal what we know and how we know it, which will make it easier for them to hide, and will make it easier for them to carry out further actions if we report our sources and our methods for how we obtain information."

I had been told that when satellite phones first came on the market, Al Qaeda didn't think their calls could be monitored. But after government officials revealed publicly they could listen in on the calls, Al Qaeda changed tactics, making it harder for us to eavesdrop. I wasn't about to give them any more hints about what tracking abilities we had up our sleeve. Indeed, I was sure there were many things we were capable of that I would never know about, so it wasn't hard not to answer some questions.

Invariably, the press asked again about military operations.

"Without getting into operational details, can you tell us if that military strike or retaliation, or whatever, is coming within hours, days, weeks, or months?"

"Of course not," I said. The press laughed, and so did I. They kept asking. I kept refusing to answer.

Moments later another reporter tried again. "How long will the clock tick?"

"I'm not going to define clocks," I said.

Sometimes the press tried a bank shot to find out, and report, when our attack would begin.

"The British press, at least two newspapers, are implying today that Tony Blair says that war against the Afghani Taliban is imminent. Without getting into op-sec [operational security], is that a statement you're willing to buy?" asked the veteran radio reporter Ivan Scott, whose expertise is military issues.

"I'm not going to discuss with you the timing of any military actions," I said.

"Not timing, but just imminent as a kind of a—" Ivan followed up before I interrupted him.

"The last I looked up *imminent,* it had something to do with a sense of time," I said, to the amusement of the press corps.

At one point I grew weary of the press's repeated attempts to get me to talk about things I wasn't going to discuss. "I just want to say this with the greatest respect possible. You have the right to ask those questions. I have the responsibility not to answer them."

Ten days after military action began, a member of the Taliban was quoted in the Pakistani press seeking a bombing pause so the so-called Taliban moderates could persuade their leaders to turn over bin Laden. A Taliban moderate? I wondered what in the world that could be. Once again I said, There will be no negotiations.

"Why not any negotiations?" Helen Thomas asked. "Everything is negotiated eventually. And why not a cease-fire for a couple days?"

"Because that's not what the President announced to the American people in his speech to the Congress. The President is not pursuing such a course, because he does not think it would be constructive." I added that the Taliban had previously been given time to turn over bin Laden and meet the President's other demands, and they had failed to act.

"It isn't a question of time," Helen argued. "This is a possible opening."

"The President doesn't view it as such," I said.

After September 11, some reporters criticized their own industry, saying the press was too easy on the government and President Bush. During wartime, when the nation is rallied behind the President, it's still the press's job to ask tough questions, but some reporters didn't think the press was tough enough.

"I guess you didn't get the word that criticism of President Bush was suddenly off limits, at least during the early days of our national trauma," wrote Clarence Page, a Washington insider and a member of the *Chicago Tribune* editorial board, in October 2001.

From where I stood, they were still plenty tough.

Exactly two weeks after the attack, I entered the briefing room for the televised briefing, and questions rang out about nation building, and what form of government the United States would put in place assuming we removed the Taliban from power.

I explained that we would take whatever military action we take but always with an eye toward stability.

When Helen Thomas's turn came, she picked up the same theme. "Don't you think that the United States ought to have an answer at the end of the road? . . . You know, during World War II many promises were made, Atlantic Charter and so forth, to people who would help us, allies and so forth, North Africa, that they would find freedom at the end of the road, and so forth. And we are offering nothing, publicly."

"What we are not doing is turning a blind eye to anybody who would sponsor or harbor terrorism," I rebutted.

"All we're offering is destruction," Helen declared.

"We're offering protection," I countered.

THE NEXT DAY'S briefing marked the beginning of a controversy that, for some, continues today.

"Has the President had any communication with Representative Cooksey regarding his comments on Sikh Americans? And does he have a message for lawmakers and members of his party in particular about this issue?" a reporter asked me.

John Cooksey, a Louisiana Republican, had earlier told reporters, "I don't care what their race is or religion is, but I can tell you this—if I see someone that comes in with a diaper on his head and a fan belt around that diaper, that guy needs to be pulled over and checked out."

"It's important," I said, "for all Americans to remember the traditions of our country that make us so strong and so free, our tolerance and openness and acceptance. All Americans—and we come from a very rich cultural heritage, no matter what anybody's background in this country. And that's the strength of this country, and that's the President's message that he expressed in his speech to Congress and as he has done when he visited the mosque a week ago." The President, I added, was disturbed by Congressman Cooksey's comments.

A few minutes later, I was asked about a comment made by Bill Maher.

"As Commander in Chief, what was the President's reaction to television's Bill Maher, in his announcement that members of our armed forces who deal with missiles are cowards, while the armed terrorists who killed six thousand unarmed are not cowards, for which Maher was briefly moved off a Washington television station?"

Maher's actual statement on ABC's *Politically Incorrect* was "We have been cowards lobbing cruise missiles from two thousand miles away. That's cowardly. Staying in the airplane when it hits the building, say what you want about it, it's not cowardly."

I replied, "I'm aware of the press reports about what he said. I have not seen the actual transcript of the show itself. But assuming the press reports are right, it's a terrible thing to say, and it's unfortunate. And that's why—there was an earlier question about has the President said anything to people in his own party—they're reminders to all Americans that they need to watch what they say, watch what they do. This is not a time for remarks like that, there never is."

Not much was made of my answer until the following evening, when I received a phone call from one of the White House stenographers whose job is to faithfully record every word I say at the briefing for the official White House transcript.

I was at Dulles Airport, in northern Virginia, on my way home after spending Yom Kippur with my parents in New York.

The press is making a controversy over your remarks, she told me. But that's not all. The stenos, she said, made a mistake and left my "watch what you say, watch what you do" comments out of the transcript. Some reporters sniffed a deliberate White House cover-up to erase what I said.

Put it back in the transcript, I told her, and explain to the press what happened. The stenos are contract employees who have served numerous White Houses. They're not known for partisanship or favoritism, and their word is accepted by reporters as true and reliable. I could tell, however, this wasn't going to look good, especially in some circles.

The next day's briefing began the usual way.

"Ari, there are press reports that say Special Forces from the United States and Great Britain are on the ground in Afghanistan. Has the military war against terrorism begun?" asked Ivan Scott, a veteran newsman.

"Let me lay out one rule now and for the future," I said. "I will never comment on any military operations that may or may not be under way."

USA Today had reported on its front page that the United States had landed Special Forces inside Afghanistan. I was asked whether it was proper for the article to be published since Special Forces were covert and whether the White House would like to see the press exercise greater restraint.

"This is always a balance of our democracy," I said. "But the fact of the matter is, our democracy seems to typically get it right, and it's one of the reasons we win wars, is because we have a free people and a free press.

"And in that interesting, historical, and delicate balance, people do their part," I said. "They understand the implications about what they do, they say, they write, they publish. And history, I think, is a good guide. I think there are some challenges today in the modern communications era that didn't exist in World War II, for example, where things said today are instantly heard and can be heard by enemies around the world.

"But it's an interesting question of delicacy and balance. I've made some concerns known to the media, which I'll continue to make known on a private level about things that are done or said, and I think we're all going to work our way forward on this together."

Toward the end of the briefing, two reporters asked me about my Bill Maher statement. They wanted to know if I stood by it.

"It's always the right, and forever will be, of any American to speak out. It's always the right of an American to be wrong," I said. "I stand by what I said about what he [Maher] said, was unfortunate and should not have been said. But I understand, of course, in all times, it's everybody's right to say things, no matter how wrong they can be."

"So you don't believe what you said, that Americans ought to at this time watch what they say? Do you stand by that specific part of your statement?" asked *Congress Daily*'s Keith Koffler.

"I think that everybody always has to be thoughtful," I said. "I think everybody has to think through the repercussions, the implications of what they say."

To the White House press corps, which heard *everything* I said in full and in context, it wasn't a real controversy. As much as they were frustrated with how tight-lipped I was, they knew I wasn't the type who would deliver ominous-sounding warnings about people's right to free speech. They were there, and they heard what I said and knew my comments had focused on tolerance and I had prefaced them with a criticism of Congressman Cooksey.

But for Maureen Dowd, Paul Krugman, and other liberal columnists, who didn't hear what I said in its entirety, it was the excuse they were looking for to criticize the White House. No matter how much the nation rallied behind the President's post–September 11 leadership, these columnists didn't like Bush and never would. They jumped all over me.

Dowd accused me of acting like "Big Brother" and wrote that the White House was signaling that anyone who challenged us was "cynical, political and . . . unpatriotic."

After a week's worth of liberal criticism about my so-called attempt to strip Americans of their right to free speech, ABC's Ted Koppel spoke out on *Nightline*. "It sounded just a little nasty, even alarming. Here was the President's press secretary, Ari Fleischer, being asked at a White House briefing about Bill Maher's comment, especially the part about the U.S. having been the cowards for lobbing cruise missiles from two thousand miles away. The part of Fleischer's response that got most of the attention was this: 'The reminder is to all Americans that they need to watch what they say.' Well, here's the Fact Check," Koppel said.

He then walked through my answer about Cooksey's comments and gave my full answer to the question about Maher. "Seen in its entirety in context, it does not sound like a warning from the White House or a threat. Ari Fleischer got a bum rap on that one. And that's our Fact Check and our report for tonight. I'm Ted Koppel in Washington, and for all of us here at ABC News, good night."

IN THE OVAL OFFICE, President Bush met with Jordan's King Abdullah. I took my usual seat.

"Our nation," the President said, "is still somewhat sad, but we're angry. There's a certain level of bloodlust, but we won't let it drive our reaction." The United States, Bush said, would enforce the "no harbor" doctrine, provide a humanitarian component in our response, and work closely with Pakistan.

"Our military," Bush said, "is made to do one thing—kick ass." He said we weren't going to put the military in the business of nation building and added, "We don't want to be parked in the nations along the Afghan border. "We're steady, clear-eyed, and patient." But pretty soon, he said, we needed to produce results. Bush also said that once Al Qaeda was dealt with, the United States would address the root causes of terror.

As October began, the press and I started to wrestle over a new issue—should Americans resume their normal lives, or should they worry that America could get hit by a second wave of attacks?

The notion that it was an either/or proposition didn't make sense to me. I thought the American people were plenty capable of getting back to their normal lives while remaining aware of the fact that times had changed. We were now living in an era of potential terror.

After Attorney General Ashcroft warned that there might be other attacks coming, a reporter put me on the spot. "What [Ashcroft] specifically said is there is a very serious threat of additional problems now, and he went on to say, we've not been able to rule out plans for hijacking additional aircraft. The President has also been out there saying, Get back to work, America; get up in the skies. Which is it?"

"It's both," I said. "And that's the reality of life in America today." I explained that people were increasingly taking to the skies and resuming their normal lives. "But the one issue will always remain in our country, so long as we are free and so long as we are open, threats from terrorism remain. And that's why the President is as determined as he is to treat this as a war, in reality, and to take it to the enemy so that the cause of terrorism can be rooted out, so Americans can again find that balance between liberty and fear, and so liberty can win."

"Just to follow up on this, are administration officials unnecessarily alarming people, though, with these very strong warnings of serious threats of additional terrorist activity?"

"I think if you look at the reactions from the American people, the American people are appreciative of the forthrightness of the government. I think the government has an obligation to be forthright, and that's why you're hearing these measured statements from government leaders."

We were damned if we did and damned if we didn't. The White House press corps would have been in full uproar if the government had withheld information about potential second strikes or if we had downplayed the seriousness of a potential second terrorist attack. The press would have accused us of cover-up and deception. "Don't the American people have a right to know?" they would have cried. It's a classic example of the press's bias in favor of conflict. No matter what the government says, the White House press corps reflexively take the opposite side.

For months, the White House was accused by the press of sending "mixed messages" to the public. When the government received warnings of potential attacks and held news conferences to announce an increase in the terror alert status, the press ridiculed us for causing confusion *and* sending mixed messages. To me, it was also an example of the press going so far in playing the devil's advocate that they separated themselves from their readers and viewers. As people increasingly did go back to work and fly commercial aircraft and take their children out to play, I had no doubt the public did not think they were receiving a mixed message. They received two messages—resume your lives but be aware we're vulnerable—and the American people understood and accepted both messages. To the conflict-driven press, the government had to choose one message or another. To the public, it was never a controversial choice to make.

ANTHRAX AND WAR

O N THE MORNING OF OCTOBER 4, the President visited the
State Department to thank workers there for the jobs they were
doing and to praise the international coalition that had assembled
to fight terror. He seemed particularly emotional, and at one point in his
speech he teared up.

As we returned to the White House, I got out of my vehicle in the
motorcade, which pulled up near the Rose Garden on the driveway of
the South Lawn, and walked toward my office. As the President entered
the Oval Office from its outside doorway, he caught my eye and mo-
tioned for me to join him.

We stood alone in the Oval Office. I had never before and never since
seen the President look as tired and troubled as he did that morning.

A Florida man, he told me, has been stricken by what appeared to
be a heavy dose of anthrax. The facts were just starting to come in, but
the President feared it was a second wave of terrorist attacks, this one
using biological weapons. He had learned about it himself just that
morning.

Ten minutes later, I was back in the Oval for Bush's meeting with
Mexico's President, Vicente Fox.

Bush told Fox there was a likelihood terrorists would strike again. I
had heard those warnings before, but after what the President had said

to me about anthrax, they had a whole new meaning. Bush didn't say anything to Fox about the man with anthrax, but he did say, "If there's another incident, we'll have to dig way down in our souls to rally the world."

Knowing that Mexico wasn't going to send troops to Afghanistan but instead was helping us stop or arrest suspected terrorists, Bush also told his neighbor to the south, "The idea of catching someone is just as important as someone suiting up with a rifle."

Anticipating a major media storm when word about the anthrax got out, the President decided we should brief the press before they heard the news through the grapevine. Secretary of Health and Human Services Tommy Thompson came to the White House to brief the press with me at a delayed session of my regular briefing.

Officials in Florida and experts from the Centers for Disease Control and HHS briefed the White House throughout the day on what they were finding. It was still too early to believe the Florida case represented a second attack, and the last word we had before the briefing was this might be an isolated case and there was, at that time, no need for greater concern.

The White House press corps were surprised when I entered the briefing room with Thompson and one of his top experts, Dr. Scott Lillibridge. Apparently, they hadn't yet heard anything about the Florida case, despite a news conference held by Florida officials to report on the incident.

"The Centers for Disease Control has just confirmed the diagnosis of anthrax in a patient in a Florida hospital," Thompson began. "Based on what we know at this point, it appears it is an isolated case. . . . Officials are aggressively investigating the individual's schedule for the last two weeks and the source of the infection." The patient's name was Bob Stevens.

"Is there any reason to believe that this is a result of terrorism?" AP's Ron Fournier inquired.

"It appears that this is just an isolated case," the secretary replied. "There's no evidence of terrorism—at this—"

Before he could finish saying "point," John Roberts, a former medical correspondent for CBS News, jumped in. "Mr. Secretary, do we know if this particular individual had contact with raw wool? Was he a gardener, working in the ground?" Roberts knew anthrax could occur naturally in people who have had contact with wool, animal products, or hides. It was rare, but it had happened before.

Thompson said the FBI and the CDC were investigating that possibility.

Roberts pressed the secretary again. "Do you know if he happened to work around wool or any of the products that might have—"

"We don't know at this point in time," Thompson said. "That's entirely possible. We do know that he drank water out of a stream when he was traveling to North Carolina last week. But as far as wool or other things, it's entirely possible. We haven't got all of the investigations done."

A few moments later, the *Wall Street Journal*'s Jeanne Cummings jumped in. "Can you explain why he was drinking water from a stream?" For some reason, the press thought the question was funny, and the room broke into laughter. "Is that a reason—should we know that? Why are you giving us that detail?" Jeanne asked.

"Just because he was an outdoorsman, and there is a possibility that— There are all kinds of possibilities," Thompson said, leaving wide open the answer to how this had happened.

Despite the fact that Secretary Thompson told them the case *appeared* to be isolated and there were all kinds of possibilities, many White House reporters seemed to conclude it was indeed an isolated case, caused by a man drinking from a stream. After the secretary left, Ron Fournier asked me, "When was the government able to determine that it was an isolated incident. An hour ago? Fifteen minutes ago?"

I said the press needed to check with HHS to find out when the experts "would" make that determination, using the future tense to warn that the verdict was still out, hedging my bet on whether it really was isolated. I also told the press that we were working off "first reports," which they know are often subject to change.

Poor Tommy Thompson. He tried to help the press, but they didn't return the favor.

After several days of no news on the anthrax front, when additional letters containing bacterium showed up in New York City and Washington, he was ridiculed by many in the press for *suggesting* that the first case was caused when Bob Stevens drank water from a stream in North Carolina. He never said that *was* the cause, and he said there were many possibilities, all of which were being checked out. He did his best to answer a question from a knowledgeable reporter about whether Stevens was an outdoorsman. But it was too late. Many in the press twisted his words and put the blame on him.

"For his part, Thompson has made some missteps," reported the *Los Angeles Times*. "When the first case of inhalation anthrax was reported in Florida, he suggested that tabloid photo editor Bob Stevens had contracted the disease by drinking water from a stream."

"In the ten days since the first anthrax case was confirmed in South Florida, the flow of information made public by the federal government has been similarly inconsistent, confusing, and even wrong," wrote the *New York Times*. "Tommy G. Thompson, the Secretary of Health and Human Services, initially went so far as to suggest that Robert Stevens, the tabloid photo editor who became the first anthrax victim identified in Florida—and the only one to die—might have contracted the disease while drinking from a tainted stream."

It reminded me of the time in the transition when the Bush campaign said Dick Cheney did not have a heart attack, only to learn later that he did.

The lesson here, like the lesson with Cheney's heart attack, is to be careful about how much early information you share with the press, because if you're wrong, they will blame you for doing your best to answer their question. The secretary initially didn't answer the question about whether Bob Stevens had had contact with wool. He added the information about the stream only when he was asked a second time. Sometimes ducking a question and taking heat for saying little or nothing beats sharing everything you know. If the press don't give any leeway for being forthright with information that is limited to appearances and subject to change, then it's very hard for government officials to share information until all the facts are in. The press can create their own quandary when they drive government officials to silence, or reticence because the price to be paid by being forthright with early information can be too high.

Imagine there had been no anthrax attacks in New York or Washington, just the one case in Florida. Let's say the Florida case *was* caused by one man drinking from a stream. If Thompson had held a news conference and said everything he did, and withheld the fact that the man drank from a stream, and people had panicked, thinking a second wave of attacks was under way, the press would have had a field day after they learned the government had withheld information about the man drinking from a stream.

"You could have avoided scaring people if you had shared that information," they would have said. "Why *didn't* you tell us?" "Were you *deliberately* trying to deceive people to take attention away from the lack of success in winning the war on terror?" There's no end to where the press would have gone.

I believe Secretary Thompson tried to do the right thing by giving information to the press and hoping they would treat the sharing of *speculative* information as speculative.

The press grew tired of me saying I wouldn't speculate about a wide variety of issues. After seeing what happened to Tommy Thompson, I wasn't about to do any speculating from that podium.

THREE DAYS LATER, on Sunday, October 7, 2001, the United States struck back at the Taliban and Al Qaeda.

That morning the President had left Camp David to attend a memorial service for firefighters in nearby Maryland when I got a call from Karen Hughes suggesting I get to the White House, pronto.

I jumped into my 1992 Saab, put on the flashers, and risked a traffic ticket as I drove through several red lights. I pulled in at the White House just as the President's helicopter was landing, greeted him in the Diplomatic Reception Room, and walked with him to the Oval Office.

Karen had already prepared his remarks. Now, less than one month after the attack on our country, the United States was responding.

The President was all business—resolute, tense, and terse. He wasn't in a mood to chat, so after I greeted him, I went back to my office. I thought about the fact that we were now a nation in the middle of a shooting war, with troops on the ground and pilots in the air, and later that day I got an update on the anthrax case. Another person in Florida may have had anthrax, and the FBI had decided to evacuate the building where Bob Stevens had worked.

September 11, war, recession, and now a possible wave of anthrax attacks. These were extraordinary times, I thought to myself.

At my first briefing after the first night of bombing, Helen Thomas went first.

"The United Nations," she said, "has been informed that this is going to be a broader campaign than just Afghanistan. Where else is the United States prepared to attack?"

"What you're referring to," I said, "is a letter that was sent to the [UN] in accordance with Article 51, the charter that always gives the nations a right to self-defense. That's a communication required at the time of a nation like the United States acted in its self-defense."

"That's a pro forma communication and does not indicate plans to broaden the attack beyond Afghanistan?" Helen asked.

It's a UN requirement concerning self-defense, I said.

"And so we are putting the [UN] on notice that this campaign, could down the line, as the President has said, include other states which harbor terrorists?" Helen pressed.

The letter, I said, "made the same points that the President has made in multiple speeches about the United States reserves the right to take any action it sees fit in our self-defense."

"Does it also reserve the right to present evidence before it attacks another country?" Helen asked.

I told her I'd have to read the letter in its entirety before I could answer.

Other reporters jumped in.

"What sort of endgame does the President have in mind for the government of Afghanistan?"

"What do you do after the Taliban is gone?"

I replied, "Suffice it to say, the United States will work with those who want to create a peaceful Afghanistan, an economically developing Afghanistan, and an Afghanistan that is free from terrorism."

"But do you have a plan to reconstitute the government of Afghanistan after this is over?"

"It's not the job of the United States to engage in nation building of that manner," I said.

"So do you just walk away, or what?"

I read from our official policy. "We do not want to choose who rules Afghanistan, though we will assist those who seek a peaceful, economically developing Afghanistan, free of terrorism."

I wondered if the White House press corps, on D-Day, June 6, 1944, had asked President Roosevelt what the plan was to rebuild Germany before he invaded France to liberate its people and prosecute the war. I wasn't aware of the doctrine that said you can't defend yourself by attacking those responsible for September 11 until you have a specific plan in place for a new Afghani government. The press knew we were eventually going to attack the Taliban and Al Qaeda—they would have been shocked, as Americans let alone as reporters, if we didn't. Privately, a number of reporters told me they were glad we had taken military action. Professionally, I viewed their questions as more examples of playing the devil's advocate.

The next morning a new event was added to my schedule—twice-a-day anthrax briefings. Two days after the war began, three people appeared to have anthrax. A rumor circulated that an envelope with anthrax had been sent to Jennifer Lopez. It turned out to be detergent. That night I learned that Tom Brokaw's secretary had received an envelope containing what appeared to be anthrax.

The day of the attack on Afghanistan, Osama bin Laden released a taped video pledging defiance and urging Muslims to join his cause against the United States. A few days later, the CIA expressed concern that the tape could contain coded messages signaling an attack to sleeper cells in the United States.

The President's national security adviser, Condi Rice, called the heads of the major broadcast and cable news networks to bring to their attention the administration's concerns. Noting that bin Laden's video was pretaped, Condi told the executives, "At best, it's pretaped propaganda to kill Americans. At worst, he's actually signaling somehow."

She said airing the tape was problematic. But she also said, "You have to determine your own policies on this. It's your call, not ours."

A few hours later, the call was the talk of the briefing. Reporters wanted to know if we really thought the tape contained a hidden message. It's being analyzed, I said. We don't know.

Condi's call didn't sit well with Helen Thomas, a champion of the free press. "Do you know of a real message, or a subliminal message? And what's the response of the networks?" she asked.

"No, there is no hard indication," I said.

"Are you just guessing that it's—"

"It's a specific level of concern."

"But, I mean, on what basis?"

"I think it's fairly obvious," I told her. "The means of communicating out of Afghanistan right now are rather limited. One way to communicate outside Afghanistan is through Western media."

"But I mean, should people—should we all operate on your impressions?" Helen challenged. "Do you have concrete—"

"Those are decisions that the media makes every day," I said.

After a few more minutes on the topic, Helen had had enough.

"It seems to me that you will be well-informed if you're able to analyze these messages and so forth. It would redound to your good to know what the hell is going on," she exclaimed.

A veteran of nine administrations, Helen treasured the press's role in society. She didn't like the idea of the government asking the networks to consider the possibility of a coded message if we didn't *know* it was coded. She wanted proof. We couldn't provide proof, but I thought advising the media of our concerns was appropriate. It was, after all, their call whether to air the tapes.

The media chiefs thought about Condi's message and decided not to broadcast in their entirety any of bin Laden's pretaped messages. They might edit the video and select newsworthy portions to report, but they decided not to become forums for his messages. It was a responsible action to take, and an example of how the press does care about national security.

One month to the day after the attack, the President decided to hold a live, prime-time news conference in the august East Room of the White House. He preferred small, informal question-and-answer sessions with the press. This would be his first prime-time event.

Prepping Bush didn't take very long. I prepared a list of questions for him the day before, and he reviewed them overnight. Along with Karen Hughes, Dan Bartlett, Condi Rice, and Andy Card, I sat in the Oval Office firing questions at the President, and he gave his answers. We would typically do two half-hour to one-hour sessions the day of the news conference.

The news conference began at 8:00 P.M., exactly on time. The press asked whether the war in Afghanistan would turn into another Vietnam, whether he intended to attack Iraq ("We're watching him carefully," Bush said, referring to Saddam), why he wouldn't meet with Arafat, and on it went for forty-four minutes.

After it was over, I joined the President in the residence and told him I thought he did great. He felt good too, as he reclined in his chair and lit a cigar.

The anthrax attacks heated up as envelopes containing the powder were sent to Dan Rather's office and to a reporter from the *New York Times*. In Washington and New York City especially, people were increasingly afraid to open their mail. A USAirways flight carrying sixty passengers from Charlotte to Denver was diverted to Indianapolis after a flight attendant discovered a powdery substance on the plane. When a highly potent strain of anthrax was sent to Senate Majority Leader Tom Daschle's office in mid-October, all hell broke loose. The Senate offices were closed, and fear started to spread.

My job became increasingly difficult.

Of the three hundred televised briefings I did, none were harder than the anthrax briefings. As tragic as September 11 was, the nation rallied as the President took command. Ignoring questions about operational details was pesky, but it wasn't hard, and my job was simply to explain what the President was doing and saying. The lead-up to the Iraq war and our dealings with the United Nations were messy, controversial, and tense, but I knew each day what I was going to say. Even after the war in Iraq began, the Pentagon briefed operational details, and my job was tiring but not that complicated.

The anthrax briefings were different because I never really knew what to say. The hardest briefings are when you don't know the facts, and the government didn't have many facts to report. I gave explanations in a vacuum as best I could. As I write this book, the government still doesn't know who was behind the anthrax attacks.

Thanks to the speed of communication, when a white powder showed up in a post office anywhere in the country, the story hit the local news wires and then was read by an editor in Washington, where within minutes reporters were asking me if it was anthrax. How in the world could I know that quickly? Meanwhile, the United States was involved in a shooting war in Afghanistan. I did my best to get answers, but they were hard to come by.

Pretty soon the press started to wonder if the anthrax was being sent by a foreign power. I was asked if we had found ties to any of the September 11 hijackers, or to bin Laden, or to Iraq. In mid-October, I told the press that no determinations had been made. Privately, I had been told that none of the anthrax appeared to be sourced to known stockpiles from a foreign government, but I wasn't going to say that publicly in case the information changed. I thought it was best not to discuss appearances.

The President departed for a summit meeting in China in mid-October, and from there I did my twice-a-day anthrax calls. We were still getting reports of white powder showing up all over the place, almost all of it bogus, but all of it was time consuming and drained resources from the medical and law enforcement communities that were called on to investigate. One American had died from anthrax exposure, but several others who actually did receive anthrax in the mail were recovering.

By the time we returned to the United States, the anthrax situation had grown worse. Two postal workers at Washington, D.C.'s Brentwood Post Office died from exposure to the bacterium. The press wanted to know how that could have happened. I didn't have a good answer. They asked if any White House mail had tested positive for anthrax. I said no, but if our mail was ever affected, I promised to let the press know. I was asked again if we had found a connection between the anthrax attacks and September 11. I said no one had found any evidence linking the two.

The briefing ended at 1:19 P.M., and at 2:00 I was summoned to Chief of Staff Andy Card's office. I was told anthrax had been found at the White House remote mail facility. Workers there were being tested for exposure, but no one in the White House was in danger, because all our mail had already been cut off as a precaution. Leave it to the Secret Service, they think of everything. They even rerouted the mail to my home through the remote facility, where it could be tested before I opened it. When the remote facility was shut, they let me get my mail at home again. Even if you work at the White House, the electric and cable TV companies still want you to pay your bills.

Almost two hours later, I returned to the briefing room for an unprecedented *second* on-camera briefing, this one a surprise to the press.

"At my briefing earlier today, I said that the White House would report any new developments, should they occur. Early this afternoon, a positive anthrax culture was found at the remote mail site that serves the White House. . . . Test results showed it to be positive for a small concentration of anthrax. The facility has been closed for further testing and decontamination." A machine in the mail room that opens letters, a slitter, was found to have traces of anthrax on it. Anthrax was not found in any White House mail, but for months following, no routine Postal Service mail arrived at the White House. Giant stacks of potentially contaminated mail sat in the remote facility, waiting to be inspected and sent to the presidential correspondence office and the

White House staff. Eventually the mail was inspected and later, much later, delivered. Even after I left the White House, in the summer of 2003, I received an occasional envelope with the familiar "White House" on its top left corner containing my mail from the fall of 2001 and the winter of 2002. It was still crispy from its irradiation treatment. But at least I got it. Since I was almost never at home to sign for a package, my parents sent my birthday present to the White House in October 2001. I received it in the summer of 2003.

Later that night, just before 9:00, I was sitting in my office when Deputy Press Secretary Scott McClellan walked in. Scott was my liaison to the Department of Health and Human Services, and he helped me stay on top of the constantly changing events.

There's a potential smallpox case in Florida, he told me. A hospital there had quarantined a patient who was displaying signs of the highly contagious, deadly disease. I held my breath. A smallpox attack would panic the nation. Smallpox is a killer, and it spreads easily. I hoped this first report would turn out wrong.

I waited for the press to burst into my office asking if it were true that a Florida man had smallpox. Is the nation under attack? they'd ask. Is this an escalation? Are we suffering from a series of connected biological attacks? I was certain that news of quarantine in a Florida hospital couldn't stay private for long.

Scott and I waited for an update from HHS. Finally, we got the word. It wasn't smallpox. It was syphilis.

"Yes! It's syphilis!" I shouted. "He's got syphilis!" I said with delight. Anyone walking past my office would have thought I was crazy, shouting for joy because someone was suffering from syphilis.

A couple of days later, I received a briefing on the quality of the anthrax sent to Senator Daschle's office. The person who made it, I was told, must have had a fair degree of sophistication. A foreign source couldn't be ruled in or out, but the experts were increasingly leaning toward the theory that it was made and sent from a domestic source. The anthrax could have been made in a small, well-equipped lab by a Ph.D. or a microbiologist. It was possible he or she had learned the technique from textbooks or the Internet.

On October 26, ABC News aired what I view as the most worrisome, inaccurate story of my time in the White House. They had received a tip that led them to inform their viewers that the anthrax sent to Senator Daschle's office had characteristics that made "it a trademark of Saddam Hussein's biological weapons program." Peter Jennings told millions of Americans that "some are going to be quick to pick up on this as a smoking gun." For days I fought with ABC over the accuracy of the story.

It started at 6:15 on the night of the twenty-sixth, when ABC's White House correspondent, Terry Moran, walked into my office to explain that in fifteen minutes the network would air a story linking Iraq to the anthrax attack.

You must be kidding, I said. Terry explained he wasn't, and he needed an official reaction. In fifteen minutes? I asked incredulously. That's right, in fifteen minutes, I was told. I had no idea how long ABC had been working on the story, but they gave the White House just fifteen minutes to check it out. In fairness to Terry, it wasn't his story. He was asked only to get the White House reaction to it.

Luckily, I knew the right people to ask thanks to my anthrax conference calls. I was assured by officials at the National Security Council that ABC was wrong—we had no reason to believe, or evidence suggesting, that Iraqi anthrax had been used in the attack. I pressed the NSC hard. Networks don't make things up, I said. Someone is telling them this. Are you certain? I was told it was certain by a senior NSC staffer responsible for counterterrorism.

With five minutes until airtime, I called Terry back and told him the story was wrong. The government had no evidence Iraqi anthrax was used in the attack. I knocked it down, hard.

It did little good. Not only did ABC report their news as an exclusive lead story, but Peter Jennings said my statement sounded misleading. "We're going to begin this evening with what we believe is a meaningful lead in the most sensitive anthrax case so far," Jennings said, "despite a very recent denial by the White House. ABC News has learned what made the anthrax so dangerous in the letter to Senator Tom Daschle was a particular additive which only one country, as far as we know, that's a very important caveat, only one country as far as we know, has used to produce biological weapons. We'll go to the White House in just a moment, but first with what we do know, ABC's Brian Ross. Brian:"

The camera zoomed in on the leader of ABC's investigative unit.

"Peter, from three well-placed but separate sources tonight, ABC News has been told that initial tests on the anthrax sent to Senator Daschle have found a telltale chemical additive whose name means a lot to weapons experts. It is called bentonite."

Bentonite, Ross explained, helps keep anthrax particles floating in the air by preventing them from sticking together. The more they float, the more dangerous they are. As the cameras showed a tape of Iraqi soldiers marching in the streets, Ross continued, "It's possible other countries may be using it, too, but it is a trademark of Saddam Hussein's biological weapons program."

The former UN weapons inspector Tim Trevan was then shown saying, "It does mean for me that Iraq becomes the prime suspect as the source for the anthrax used in these letters." Ross then added, "It's important to stress that these are the findings of initial tests," and that government investigators would double- and triple-check them. After Ross was finished, Jennings called on Terry Moran at the White House, where Jennings told viewers, "There is a battle about Iraq that's been raging in the administration." He was alluding to an argument the President had settled one month earlier when he decided to retaliate against the Taliban in Afghanistan, rejecting advice to attack Iraq as well.

"Terry, just before we went on the air, the White House denied this," Jennings said.

"They did, Peter," Terry reported. "In the strongest terms, White House Press Secretary Ari Fleischer saying flat out it's not bentonite." He reported my conversation in which I told him researchers did not find any bentonite in the anthrax.

"I—I don't wish to downplay the denial at all," Jennings said, downplaying my denial, "but there is this raging argument in the administration about going after Saddam Hussein. Is this denial in any way connected?" I almost jumped out of my chair. The anchorman of

ABC's evening news was implying to millions of people that I would falsify information because the White House did *not* want to go after Saddam Hussein. I thought we were the administration that *wanted* to attack Iraq. If my statements were driven by the administration's alleged objectives in Iraq, I would have loved the ABC story. I wouldn't have denied it. I'd have let ABC blame Saddam for us.

My obligation was to tell the truth, and I provided it to ABC.

Later that night, I spoke to Jennings. I told him the story was wrong at its core. Our researchers, I said, had found no bentonite in the anthrax. He couldn't have been more polite and promised me he would look into it, and if ABC was wrong, they would correct it.

Over the next several days, I dug deep into the story. I spoke not only to officials at the NSC but to the researchers themselves at the Armed Forces Institute of Pathology. They told me the Daschle anthrax contained silicon and oxygen but not aluminum. Since bentonite contains aluminum, if there's no aluminum, they said, there's no bentonite. They also informed me that when UN inspectors had analyzed Iraqi's anthrax stocks in the nineties, the bentonite in the Iraqi anthrax contained aluminum.

No aluminum, they concluded, no bentonite. No bentonite, it's not Iraq.

I continued to badger a variety of people at ABC to see if they were going to correct the story. Finally, on October 31, six days after the story was aired, ABC backtracked.

At the end of a story about anthrax attacks, Jennings asked Brian Ross one of those scripted questions which had a scripted answer. "Brian, what's the latest we know about the additive called bentonite in the anthrax which made it allegedly dangerous?"

"Well, Peter, today the White House said that despite initial test results which we reported suggesting the presence of a chemical called bentonite, a trademark of the Iraqi weapons program, a further chemical analysis has ruled that out," Ross said. "The White House says there are chemical additives in that anthrax, including one called silica. Now, that's not a trademark of any country's weapons program, but it is known to be used, Peter, by Iraq, Russia and the U.S. in making a military-style anthrax." The White House said *today*? I had said it the night ABC broke the story.

On November 1, ABCNews.go.com ran a long follow-up story headlined TERROR TESTS: ADDITIVE SEARCH REQUIRES MORE STUDY.

The web story concluded, "Sources privy to the federal investigation say the tests on the Daschle sample are still under way. Even if these tests ultimately find bentonite, as well as silica, they will not prove Iraqi involvement."

It took almost a week, but ABC backed off their finding of a "smoking gun, a meaningful lead, and Saddam's trademark." But I still wonder how such a report made it on the air in the first place. I'm sure Brian Ross accurately reported the information he was given, but when I issued a clear denial, why didn't the network pull the story until they could more deeply investigate the facts? The allegation that Iraq was the likely source of the anthrax is too serious for a network to make on the basis of an anonymous source or three. The pressure to break news, the bigger the better, is sometimes so great that accuracy and thoroughness get sacrificed in exchange for exclusivity and speed.

AS OCTOBER ENDED, the President traveled to New York to throw out the ceremonial first pitch for the Yankees' World Series home opener in the Bronx. At a time when our nation was still reeling from the effects of the September 11 attack, Bush gave the country a reason to cheer.

Standing atop the pitching mound, sixty feet, six inches away from his target at home plate, the President threw a fastball with a little heat on it straight over the heart of the plate. The sellout crowd broke into tumultuous cheering, roaring, "USA, USA, USA." There wasn't a Democrat in the crowd, there wasn't a Republican in the crowd, there were simply fifty thousand Americans who wanted nothing more than to feel good about our nation. The pitch was a metaphor for our country. A nation which had rallied around the flag stood as one, cheering for America. I had a terrible cold and decided not to go on the trip, but from my couch at home that night, it sure felt good.

It almost wasn't that way.

Before the pitch, the President warmed up his throwing arm in an indoor bull pen underneath the right-field stands at Yankee Stadium. As he was tossing practice pitches, the Yankees' famous shortstop, Derek Jeter, approached him. Jeter saw the President was warming up from the base of the mound instead of standing on the pitching rubber. The base of the mound is closer to the plate, and it's an easier throw. Seven months earlier the President had thrown out the first pitch for the Milwaukee Brewers from the rubber, and he threw it in the dirt in front of home plate. He didn't want to make the same mistake twice.

"Mr. President, are you going to throw from the base of the mound, or are you going to take the rubber?" Jeter asked.

"From the base of the mound," Bush said.

"I wouldn't do that if I were you," Jeter told the surprised President.

"Why not?" Bush asked.

"This is New York," the shortstop explained. "If you throw from the base of the mound, they're going to boo you."

No politician wants to get booed, especially on national TV.

"Do you really think they'll do that?" Bush asked.

"This is New York. They'll boo you," Jeter repeated.

"I guess I'll take the mound," Bush said.

A few minutes later, the President stood on the steps of the Yankees dugout. Just as he was about to take the field, he heard Derek Jeter coming up to him from behind. "If you take the rubber, Mr. President, don't bounce it. They'll boo you." Seconds later, the President took the mound and threw that perfect strike.

The next day the President popped his head into the morning senior staff meeting and said that the reaction from the crowd, the calls of "USA USA, USA," would remain with him forever. He said he could feel the stadium shake with the cries of the crowd. It would be one of the highlights of his presidency, he said. The Yankees won the game and trailed in the best of seven World Series two games to one. "The Yankees will win" the World Series, Bush predicted to me on the phone later that afternoon. I wish he'd been right. They lost, four games to three.

IT HAD BEEN just over three weeks since the first bombs were dropped in Afghanistan.

"Ari, there has been some criticism of the war the last couple of days, especially, some comparisons of the administration's actions to those that were taken during Vietnam," Keith Koffler of *Congress Daily* said to me.

I was glad to have a chance to address the angle.

"This is a new type of war, that is totally different from anything our nation has faced before. And he [the President] understands that there will always be people who fight the last wars, whether they are Kosovo, whether they're the Persian Gulf, or whether they're Vietnam. He's not. He's learned lessons from those . . . when you're dealing with people who hide out in caves, when you're dealing with people who don't have standing armies . . . it's very different from that."

Keith pressed his point. He pointed out the Taliban had a standing army. "And the question a lot of people have is, Why aren't we going after that army which we are, indeed, fighting, massively? We seem to be engaged in a similar type of incrementalism—we're stepping up, we're starting to put people on the border, stepping up the air attacks—similar type of incrementalism we saw in Vietnam."

In Afghanistan, and later in Iraq, I thought that many White House reporters had no patience for war. If it wasn't over in a week or two, the United States must again have done something wrong, gotten itself stuck in a quagmire, as the *New York Times*'s Johnny Apple wrote in his front-page analysis of the war, just like Vietnam all over again. It was the press's Vietnam reflex, and I was increasingly being hit with it.

The anthrax situation worsened. Another woman in New York City, Kathy Nguyen, died, and the State Department, the Vice President's home, and the CIA all reported finding trace amounts of anthrax. Although billions of pieces of mail were processed and delivered without problems, official Washington seemed to find anthrax almost everywhere. The White House press corps's pessimism grew about the President's handling of his duties. Routine announcements were interpreted as signs of trouble.

To help spread America's message around the world, the White House announced the creation of an office of global communications, with a particular focus on how we were perceived in Muslim countries. When I entered the briefing room, I was hit by a triple dose of skepticism.

"Ari, we're in the middle of a major public relations blitz by the White House. You've got this new war room that's being set up with satellites in London and Pakistan, and now we've got Condoleezza Rice telling us about a series of major speeches next week. Is there a feeling in the administration that the President is losing a propaganda war?" NBC's David Gregory asked.

"We have [French President] Chirac and [British Prime Minister] Blair coming next week, the speech to Central European nations next week about the war effort. Does the President feel like some, particularly European allies, are going wobbly on him here at an important time?" he followed up.

"The President's address to the nation next week," asked CBS's John Roberts, "can you tell us what day that's going to be, and him coming out and talking about homeland security, is that an indication that he doesn't believe that the people who have been out there already talking about it have been doing a good enough job, that he's got to take up the mantle and do it himself?"

It was hard and tiring to remain calm and optimistic in a sea of skeptics, but that's the nature of the White House briefing room. It's just the way it works. The press has its job to do and I have mine.

"Ari, to get back to the allies, it is a fact that surveys of public opinion in Britain, France, Germany, and elsewhere show that support for military action in Afghanistan is waning, substantially and markedly," said ABC News's Terry Moran. "The President has said this is going to be a long campaign, hard, slogging. Is the President willing to continue military operations in Afghanistan in the face of declining support in Europe?"

The President was aware of the growing criticism in the press. Watching him, I realized one of his greatest strengths was his ability to ignore the day-to-day criticisms of the media. He had faith and confidence in the mission and the abilities of our military to carry it out. He didn't waver in the face of skeptical questioning. He kept his sights on the long-term goal of defeating the Taliban and routing Al Qaeda, no matter how long it took. He didn't like the press's impatience, but he never let it get to him. He wouldn't let it change his policies.

Bush believed that one of the lessons of Vietnam was that the president should give the military its mission and then let the generals run the war. He thought slowing down or speeding up the military action in response to daily pressures from the press was one of the mistakes during the Vietnam conflict. He was determined not to be that type of president. As the press's criticism grew, Bush stuck to his guns.

A PARADE OF foreign leaders streamed into the Oval Office throughout the fall of 2001. They pledged solidarity with the United States in our war on terror. Invariably, the President would bring up the peace process between the Israelis and the Palestinians. Suicide bombings were on the rise, and Israeli retaliatory strikes were growing bolder and tougher.

Bush thought Europe's leaders could do more to influence the peace process. "If Arafat thinks the European Union is leaning against Israel, he won't act responsibly. We need to continue to pressure both sides" to get back to the peace process, he told one European leader. "Sharon is the only democratically elected person in the region," he said. "I don't trust Sharon," the head of state replied.

In another meeting with a European leader, Bush again brought up the Middle East and his view that European policies were tilted against Israel. "The more the E.U. pressures Israel, the more Sharon will dig in," he said. Bush believed that European praise for Arafat gave the Chairman a way out of working for peace. He was prepared, as a strong supporter of Israel, to push Israel toward peace. He grew frustrated with European leaders who wouldn't do the same with Arafat.

In early November, Bush traveled to New York for a meeting of the UN General Assembly. Yasir Arafat was there as the leader of the Palestinian people. After a lunch meeting of all the world's leaders broke up, Arafat spied President Bush across the room and made a bee-line for him, seeking a presidential handshake. Bush had no desire to send Arafat any signal other than that he needed to crack down on the terrorists who were killing hundreds of Israelis through suicide bomb-ings. Until the Chairman took meaningful action, he wasn't welcome in the Bush White House. As Bush was engrossed in a conversation with another leader, Colin Powell glimpsed Arafat approaching. Powell put his hands on Bush's back, gave him a small shove, and said, "Mr. Pres-ident, speed it up." He ushered the President out of the way before Arafat could get his handshake.

In the afternoon of November 10, Bush met with Pakistani Presi-dent Pervez Musharraf. He expressed his appreciation for Pakistan's as-sistance in defeating the Taliban and Al Qaeda. The two leaders pledged to keep working together.

An hour later, and eleven days after I had been asked about the war turning into a Vietnam-like quagmire, the press asked the President whether the Northern Alliance, which had just captured the town of Mazar-e-Sharif, would enter Kabul, the Afghani capital. Our military strategy was succeeding; the Taliban and Al Qaeda were on the run.

ELEVEN

FALL BECOMES WINTER

VETERANS DAY 2001 was a federal holiday. The federal government and most banks were closed. Even though I was going to work, there was to be no briefing. I looked forward to a quiet day at the office.

As I entered the now closed to the public E Street entrance on the south side of the White House, my car radio reported that American Airlines Flight 587 from New York to Santo Domingo had crashed shortly after taking off from JFK Airport. City officials had immediately closed all the bridges and tunnels to Manhattan, fearing they were in the middle of another terrorist strike.

I went directly to the Situation Room below the West Wing to learn what was happening. A meeting was already under way involving officials from the National Security Council, the FBI, the Federal Aviation Administration, and the Office of Homeland Security. The President, who was in the middle of a meeting of his National Security Council, had already been informed of the crash.

I listened and watched as the professionals gathered information and did their work. A 100 percent baggage match had been done, although they couldn't be certain that all the bags went through a CAT scan. There had been no unusual communication to or from the cockpit. The cockpit door was a new one, reinforced since September 11. The

FBI said there were no reports of an explosion until the plane hit the ground. Fighter planes had been launched.

In the press office, reporters were hollering for me. They needed a reaction from the White House. Reporters, and many others, feared the worst and demanded answers to their questions. I instructed my staff to tell the press I was in the Situation Room and would have nothing to say until I had sufficient information to brief them. That's not good enough, the press said. But there was no way I was going to meet with them until I was satisfied that the first reports of this story were accurate enough to discuss publicly. If that meant the White House press would be angry with me, I was prepared to pay that price. I knew they were under tremendous pressure from their editors to learn what was going on, but how could I take their questions until I knew what was going on myself?

The President was back in the Oval Office, receiving updates and conducting other business. As I left the Situation Room to join him in the Oval, a report came in to a Sit Room officer about another plane crash in Chicago. Somehow, I just couldn't believe 9/11 was happening all over again. I asked a Sit Room staffer to let me know immediately if anything else developed on the Chicago story. When I got to the Oval, I asked the President if he had heard anything about a crash in Chicago. He hadn't, and I noticed my pager wasn't going off. If there had been a crash, the news would have been on the air instantly and my pager would have been vibrating.

In an echo of September 11, the President called Mayor Giuliani and Governor Pataki, pledging once again to help New York City deal with the consequences of the crash. Federal teams were already on the ground and en route to the scene, Bush said. "This may be mechanical. We don't know yet. We're waiting for the fog to lift, but nothing indicates anything out of the normal."

I got ready to brief the surly, growing pack of White House reporters, who were arriving for work on what they too had thought would be a day off. I spoke with Jane Garvey, the head of the Federal Aviation Administration, to make certain we both had the same facts, and I entered the briefing room shortly after noon. The networks took the briefing live.

"Good afternoon," I began. "This morning, as the President was convening a meeting of his National Security Council to go over the latest developments in the war against terrorism, he received a note handed into the meeting at 9:25 A.M., informing him of the crash of an American Airlines flight at JFK Airport in New York City."

I explained that security officials immediately began a conference call to monitor events and receive the latest information and respond. The President, I said, spoke with Mayor Giuliani and Governor Pataki, and the federal government would do everything it could to help.

"The National Transportation Safety Board has a team of investigators on site already, and they have an additional go-team of a larger number of investigators that are en route. The National Transportation Safety Board is the lead investigating agency."

You could almost hear the sigh of relief when I said the NTSB, not the FBI, which investigates terrorism and crime, was in charge. I couldn't yet say whether it was or was not terrorism, and I was going to be cautious. I simply sent a signal by highlighting the role of the NTSB, and I counted on the press to pick it up.

"The fact that the NTSB is the lead on this, is this an indication that you believe it was an accident as opposed to a criminal act?" came the first question, from John Roberts of CBS.

"I want to be very cautious at this early time about what is the cause of this. As you know, first facts are often facts that are subject to greatest change. But the National Transportation Safety Board is the lead government agency doing the investigating."

"Is there any evidence of terrorism at this point?"

"First information is always subject to change," I repeated. "We have not ruled anything in, ruled anything out."

"You can't say what other officials have said on background, there is no evidence of terrorism?"

I was on camera, speaking for the President, live on the networks.

"I'm aware of what the other officials have said, and I understand why they're saying it. Just simply, from the White House point of view, where we always maximize caution at a time like this, the White House will continue to gather the facts and review the information."

The press, and the public, got the hint, and fears faded.

IN MID-NOVEMBER, President Putin of Russia came to Washington, and then he accompanied President Bush to his Texas ranch. During their meeting in the White House, the two discussed the war on terror. Referring to Afghanistan's border with Pakistan, Putin said, "It's impossible to seal the border. The only solution is to destroy them like rats." Bush told Putin, banging his forefinger on the table for emphasis, "Until Al Qaeda is brought to justice, we're not leaving. As great nations, we're most vulnerable targets. You're the kind of guy I like to have in the foxhole with me."

The war in Afghanistan was going well. Teamed with the Northern Alliance, the United States was routing the Taliban and Al Qaeda, as one town fell after another. In the briefing room, the subject shifted to Iraq.

"Ari, Condi Rice yesterday said that we didn't need September 11 to tell us that Saddam Hussein was a bad man. Is that a signal that we might be heading into Iraq at some point?"

Appearing on *Meet the Press,* the President's national security adviser had been asked about America's intentions toward Iraq. "We didn't need September 11 to tell us that Saddam Hussein is a very dangerous man," she said.

"What Dr. Rice is indicating," I answered, "is that Saddam Hussein presented problems for the United States prior to September 11. Saddam Hussein has been someone that we have kept a careful eye on before September 11, as well as after September 11." I said the war in Afghanistan was phase one in the global war on terror, and that was where the President was concentrating, on phase one.

"Should we expect Iraq to be phase two or phase three? Should we be preparing for that at some point down the road?" I was asked, seventeen months before the war with Iraq began.

"If there is any indication of that, you will hear from the President," I said. "And I'm not leaning one way or another on that, but the President is involved deeply in phase one."

Right after Thanksgiving, the President welcomed to the Rose Garden two Christian missionaries who were held prisoner by the Taliban and later rescued by American troops. After his remarks, the press asked him about Iraq.

"What would you say about Iraq, as you begin to look at the next steps in the campaign against global terrorism? What message would you like to send to them now?"

"Well, my message is, is that if you harbor a terrorist, you're a terrorist. If you feed a terrorist, you're a terrorist. If you develop weapons of mass destruction that you want to terrorize the world, you'll be held accountable. And I also have said, as I recall at the White House, we're going to make sure that we accomplish each mission that we tackle. First things first."

The President's reply dominated my briefing.

"Can you tell me specifically when and where the President included in his definition of terrorist-aiding states any country that produces weapons of mass destruction that can be used by terrorists?" asked AP's Ron Fournier.

"And to focus on Iraq for a minute, which it seems [is] where the President is focused," asked one reporter—who failed to mention that the press, not the President, had raised the topic of Iraq—"he has said now a couple of times over the past few days that Saddam Hussein must allow UN inspectors back in to make sure that there is no development of weapons of mass destruction. Is that a hard demand by this administration? Should this be seen as the next phase in the war on terrorism?"

"In this question on what ought to be done with Iraq, has the administration essentially settled on an ultimatum, allow weapon inspectors back in or face the consequences?" ABC's Terry Moran asked.

I kept explaining the President was focused on Afghanistan and he was concerned about Iraq's potential to share weapons of mass destruction with terrorists.

Helen Thomas didn't like even the notion of a phase two involving Iraq. "Does the President feel the United States has the right to bomb or invade any country harboring terrorists?" she asked. "Is he going to invade Spain?" I couldn't figure out why she asked that about Spain, but I kept moving.

"The President is focused on phase one of the war against terrorism. But the President has made it plain to the American people that this is a long-term war," I said.

"Answer the question," Helen demanded. "What right do we have to invade any country?"

"I'm not aware that we are invading Spain," I said with a straight face.

I took thirty-four questions that day about Iraq, mostly asking whether he was sending a signal that Iraq was next, or whether the President was stepping up his rhetoric against Saddam's regime. Many in the White House press corps argued they had never previously heard the President say that sharing weapons of mass destruction with terrorists was tantamount to harboring terrorists, and thereby Bush had expanded the so-called Bush doctrine, clearly signaling his intention to turn up the heat on Iraq. I argued that this was nothing new; the President had earlier warned that Al Qaeda wanted to obtain weapons of mass destruction and he was determined never to let it happen.

About two weeks later, Helen returned to the topic of Iraq, and her line of inquiry bore a powerful resemblance to events that would unfold one year later.

"You said the world stands together on the war in Afghanistan. And that's true, the President had been on the phone since September 12, lining up allies and friends. This would not be true," Helen argued, "if he decides, as some of his advisers want, to go into Iraq, Somalia, every other country they've named on their target list. Would the United States still move unilaterally if it did not have UN and key ally backing?"

"Helen," I replied, "I'm just not going to speculate about anything hypothetical of that nature." In the fall of 2001, an invasion of Iraq was exactly that, hypothetical.

"Well, I think it's very valid," she pushed back. "It's a very valid question, because the UN has come out—the UN Secretary-General has come out and said he would not support it, and France and Britain, apparently, are not supporting." One year later Helen turned out to be two-thirds right, at least as far as who was supporting the United States.

"Well, again, it's a hypothetical, and I don't think anybody is in a position to tell you who will do what for something that's not defined."

"It's not so hypothetical when your advisers are calling for widening the war every day," she said.

"I'm not sure our advisers are calling for widening the war every day," I rebutted.

AS THE END of the year approached, both the war in Afghanistan and the anthrax crisis started to fade from daily front-page coverage. Although we didn't catch the anthrax suspect, there were no additional attacks and the press stopped asking me about it. The war in Afghanistan was proceeding well, and the media's attention grew to cover many new subjects.

By late in the year, it became official—our nation was in recession. The slowdown of 2000 had turned into a recession that was estimated to have begun in March 2001, forty days after President Bush took office.

"Is this his recession?" a reporter asked me at one briefing.

"The President understands this recession doesn't belong to any politician. This is the country's recession, because it's the people of our country who are unemployed as a result of an economic downturn. And this President has no interest in placing blame or pointing fingers at anybody for economic circumstances. His intention is to bring people together to solve it, not divide people by pointing fingers."

The President had proposed an economic stimulus plan, but it was languishing in the Senate. The House had passed it, but privately, the President was concerned that nothing was going to happen on Capitol Hill. He had been told that the Democratic leadership in the Senate wouldn't pass any economic measures that couldn't get at least a two-thirds vote among Democratic senators. In other words, if the liberals, who dominated the ranks of the Senate Democrats, wouldn't go along, nothing could get done.

Frustrated, the President complained that the White House didn't write legislation, the Congress did. His job was to lead and fight for action. The Senate had the power to block action; it didn't seem to have the will to take action.

Unemployment was now projected, under a worst-case scenario, to hit 7 percent. The same scenario, the President was advised, indicated that the economic recovery would kick in during the second half of 2002. I worked in the White House for two and a half years, or five halves. I must have heard five times that the recovery would take place in the next half. Only once did that projection turn out right. It wasn't the fault of the economists. The country was indeed going through a time of change, when old models that had reliably predicted economic behavior failed almost all economists, including the best experts in the private sector. We were at war, we were in the middle of a recession, and we had a growing budget deficit. What a way to end the first year in office, I thought.

EVERY FRIDAY it was my job as the President's spokesman to give a report on his "week ahead." One Friday in early December, I took to the podium and informed the press about the routine meetings the President had coming up during the week of December 10 to 14, 2001. When I got to Thursday, December 13, I stopped, stepped back, and refused to do my job. My deputy, Scott McClellan, took the podium to announce that the World Champion Arizona Diamondbacks would visit the White House to celebrate their World Series win over my New York Yankees. It was the one time I publicly split with the President on an important matter of policy.

The following week, as my December 13 briefing came to an end, I started walking off the podium, as I always do, but this time a man in a suit came around the corner and got onto the stage just as I was leaving it.

Who could that be and why is he taking the podium? I wondered. My first thought was whoever it was had the podium reserved, which made no sense. No one else could use the room without my authorization.

Then another person in a suit entered the room, this one a six-foot-ten, skinny guy whom I instantly recognized as Randy Johnson, the Diamondback pitcher who, along with Curt Schilling, had led the team to victory against the Yankees. I retreated to the podium to take my lumps, with the cameras still rolling.

"Congratulations," I muttered.

"Can somebody call in Mayor Giuliani, quick?" I cried, seeking help.

Johnson looked down at me, took out a Diamondback hat, and said, "We were told we couldn't leave until you've actually had this on," he said, putting his hat on my embarrassed, bald head.

"Congratulations. It was a great World Series, and you guys really deserved it," I stammered. I turned to the press and said, "These are the world champion Arizona Diamondbacks, I'm chagrined to report."

Then Johnson looked at me again, took the hat off my head, and said, "It may be just a rumor, but I heard if we rub your head, we'll be back here next year," and he began rubbing my bald head.

All I could think was that Yankee Manager Joe Torre might be watching. I mustered my courage, looked up at Johnson, and replied, "I suspect I'll have even less hair next year, and the Yankees will be back."

Later that evening, when it was time for the news, I didn't watch the usual cable TV shows; I didn't even watch the broadcast network news. Instead, I tuned in to ESPN's *SportsCenter,* where I saw the scene from the briefing repeated a dozen times. Almost one year into the job, I had been on cable TV hundreds of times, I had been on the broadcast networks dozens of times, but that night, I made *SportsCenter*. Amid all the pomp and circumstance, the trips abroad, the things I've seen, and the meetings I've been in, that day became one of my most enjoyable memories of having worked in the White House.

Unfortunately, I was wrong, and the Anaheim Angels were the next world champions to pay a visit. A group of Angels that included the manager, Mike Scioscia, and the players Troy Percival, Tim Salmon, and Scott Spiezio came to see me as well, this time off camera, and they gave me a framed edition of the *Los Angeles Times* headlined THE YANKEE RIPPERS after the Angels beat the Yankees in the 2002 playoffs.

The White House at all times is a serious place, but when those few less than serious moments roll around, it can also be a wonderful, amusing, lighthearted place.

MEANWHILE, the situation in the Middle East was growing increasingly serious. The suicide bombings continued unabated, despite the President's phone calls and meetings with Israeli and Arab leaders, despite the work of retired general Anthony Zinni, a special envoy sent to the region by the President.

Bush blamed Yasir Arafat. During one meeting with a foreign leader, he said, in the privacy of the Oval Office, "Arafat has shown us what happens when you don't lead. Five years ago, few followed Hamas. Now half think violence is right. My job is to show we must not waiver, for if we do, more evildoers will fill the vacuum." Bush compared Arafat unfavorably to Pakistani President Musharraf, who took strong action despite warnings there would be mass protests in the streets if he sided with the United States. "Musharraf was firm," Bush said. "He led, then there were no protests."

The cleanup of Ground Zero continued as the year wound down. The President had been told in November by Joe Allbaugh, the head of the Federal Emergency Management Agency (FEMA), that it would take until Labor Day 2002 for the entire cleanup to finish. In late December, Allbaugh told the President work would be done in early summer.

"You previously said Labor Day," Bush observed.

Allbaugh told Bush that the workers were so intent on doing their job quickly and professionally that they were ahead of schedule. He also informed the President that on day ninety, workers had found one perfectly preserved body, and they kept finding pieces of people's bodies three months after the attack.

It struck me that the President, in the middle of a war, a recession, and everything else on his mind, remembered Allbaugh's previous Labor Day prediction. The President received dozens of briefings a week on countless topics, hearing hundreds of facts, some important and some obscure. He noticed the change in this timetable and wanted to know what had caused it. One of the reasons Bush is such a good manager is that he hires good people and gives them room to do their jobs, but he holds people accountable for their actions. When a staffer changed stories in a presidential briefing, the President wouldn't let it slide. He wanted to know what had caused the change, drilling in to make sure a mistake wasn't made. It's a great way to make people think carefully when they brief him, to be certain they're as accurate as they can be, because he'll pin you down and demand to know why something has changed since your last briefing.

A few days before Christmas, the President visited Capitol Hill in an attempt to salvage his economic stimulus proposal. He met with Louisiana Senator John Breaux and other Democratic members of Congress, including Senators Zell Miller of Georgia and Ben Nelson of Nebraska. They often provided the key swing votes on close issues. They promised the President they would vote for his plan. One of the Democrats told him, "This gives us momentum to get something done. We have an agreement—we'll see if we have the votes." Their support, together with Republican support, meant there was more than a majority prepared to pass the President's economic stimulus plan, even in the Democratic-controlled Senate. Bush told the press an agreement had been reached on a bipartisan stimulus package. Senate Majority Leader Tom Daschle hadn't signed on, but the votes were there if Daschle would allow a vote to take place.

At my briefing, I took a pounding from the White House press.

"Has Tom Daschle signed on to this agreement?" was the first question.

"The agreement was reached by the President, the Republican Congressional leaders, and the centrists in both the House and in the Senate. The President would be delighted if Senator Daschle would sign on. The President will be delighted if Senator Daschle would even just allow it to come to a vote," I said.

"After weeks of working, essentially behind the scenes, with meetings on the Hill at night or the breakfasts here with the leaders, this is really an 'in your face, Tom Daschle' move, isn't it?" asserted ABC's Terry Moran.

"No," I rebutted, "this is an achievement, an agreement with the key people on the Hill who can deliver the votes in the center. This is the center speaking out. And this is an agreement that the American people, particularly those who worry about whether they're going to keep their jobs, can be proud of."

"Well, why shouldn't the American people see this as a return to the partisan wrangling over the nation's business, a return to very sharp-edged, in-your-face politics?"

I couldn't believe how vehement so many reporters were about *Bush* being partisan, just moments after he had found the bipartisan center and forged an agreement with it.

"Well, I think when you hear Democrats and Republicans alike sitting in a room at a common table saying, we have an agreement, that's the definition of bipartisanship," I rebutted. "Senator Breaux, Senator Nelson, Senator Miller, Congressman [Ken] Lucas were all in the meeting," I said, naming the Democrats who were prepared to deliver a majority for the Bush plan.

The press would have none of it. If Daschle wasn't for it, it couldn't be called an "agreement," and if Daschle wasn't for it, Bush must be the partisan. After fifteen minutes of arguing about who was and was not partisan, I said, "I just find it a curious line of thought that suggests when the President of the United States, a Republican, enters into an agreement with several key Democratic centrists, that that is anything other than bipartisan."

"He's stiffing the Democratic leader," a reporter stated.

If President Clinton had gone to Capitol Hill and met with a group of centrist Republicans and announced an agreement that Newt Gingrich and Bob Dole opposed, I believe the Washington press corps would have called Gingrich and Dole partisans and obstructionists. Clinton, they would have written, went the extra mile, rounded up moderate Republican support, only to be thwarted by partisan Republican leaders. But now, Bush, despite securing enough Democratic votes for the stimulus to pass, was somehow the partisan. All I could do was shake my head and wonder how different news coverage would be if newsrooms were more ideologically diverse. Senator Daschle ended up blocking consideration of the agreement, and a thinned-down stimulus package had to await passage until the following year, as the economy limped along.

Shortly after the New Year began, I was at home on a Sunday evening watching my favorite football team, the Miami Dolphins, when I got a phone call from Chief of Staff Andy Card and the White House physician, Richard Tubb, an Air Force colonel. The President, they told me, had fainted a little while ago while eating a pretzel. He must have hit the floor pretty hard, because he had an ugly scrape on his cheek, I was told.

Oh boy. The press is going to need a full briefing about this, I thought. It's a Sunday night, and they're scattered everywhere. I asked the doctor if he would mind doing a conference call with the wire reporters, the best way I figured I could get the story out. He said he'd do it. Two and a half hours after the President hit the floor, his doctor hit the phones to tell the press, and the American people, that the most powerful man in the world "fainted due to a temporarily decreased heart rate brought on by eating a pretzel." The President told Tubb the pretzel didn't feel like it went down right.

As soon as the story hit the wires, my home phone lit up. For the next hour, virtually every White House reporter called me, and I repeated what Tubb had told the wires. The President called me to fill me in on his bout with a pretzel and to express his sympathy to me on the Dolphins' loss in the playoffs. When I took this job, I thought some interesting adventures might come with it; I never thought presidential pretzel-fainting would be one of them.

ISRAEL AND TO SOME DEGREE Iraq were on the radar in early 2002. On January 3, 2002, Israeli commandos intercepted a ship, the *Karine A,* loaded with fifty tons of mortars, rockets, rocket-propelled grenades, small arms, and explosives. The ship had been sent from Iran to Palestinian terrorists, and Israel claimed that Yasir Arafat had knowledge of the shipment and was involved in its delivery. Arafat denied the charge in public and in private, but evidence came in showing he lied.

As problematic as Arafat, a lying leader who sponsors terror, was, many of the President's critics thought *Bush* was the problem because, they claimed, he wasn't engaged enough in the peace process, despite twelve summit meetings he held with Israeli, Egyptian, Jordanian, and other Arab leaders his first eleven months in office.

I told the press that progress was being made in the Middle East when the President became the first American president to call publicly for the creation of an independent Palestinian state alongside Israel, a visionary inducement if only the Palestinian people had a leader capable of seizing it. The President had dispatched General Zinni, his special envoy, to the region to help the parties reach agreements, and then the Palestinian Authority had derailed any signs of progress when they ordered up and paid for the weaponry aboard the *Karine A.*

My statement alarmed Helen Thomas, who holds strong views on the Middle East. "Where do the Israelis get their arms?" she asked.

"There's a difference, Helen, and that is—"

"What is the difference?" she demanded.

"The targeting of innocents through the use of terror, which is a common enemy for Yasir Arafat and for the people of Israel, as well as—"

"Palestinian people are fighting for their land—" Helen protested, interrupting me.

"I think killing of innocents is a category entirely different," I said. "Justifying killing of innocents for land is an argument in support of terrorism."

When Turkish Prime Minister Bulent Ecevit came to see Bush in the Oval Office, the President thanked him for having diplomatic relations with Israel, a rare act by a Muslim nation, and said, "We were watching until Arafat foolishly ordered up weapons from Iran. Tell Arafat the United States has trouble dealing with him because of his decision to support terror. . . . He claims he doesn't know about it, but the world thinks he does." Arafat clearly wasn't listening to the United States, but Bush hoped that if other nations turned up the heat on him, the violence could be reduced. Nevertheless, Bush told congressional leaders that Israel "has to be careful not to pour kerosene on the fire."

The President also told his Turkish guest what he thought about

Saddam Hussein: "As long as he's in power, he will present trouble. I have no plans at this time beyond diplomatic. If we take action, we'll consult." In what became a constant refrain to leaders urging them to think long term and to think tough, Bush added, "We have a chance to purge the world of terrorism. If you lead, people will follow. If you hesitate, people will become nervous."

When the press came in for a brief news conference with the two leaders, Bush was asked about Iraq. "I expect Saddam Hussein to let inspectors back into the country. We want to know whether he's developing weapons of mass destruction. He claims he's not; let the world in to see," the President said. "And if he doesn't, we'll have to deal with that at the appropriate time."

In another meeting early in 2002 with a leader from the Arab world, Bush was advised to be careful he didn't push Palestinians toward the extreme.

"Forgive me for interrupting," he said, "but we weren't pushing anyone, and he [Arafat] shows up with a shipment of arms. Here's the problem—we can't be hypocrites in the war on terror. We need to destroy this faceless army now. We have to act consistently. This man [Arafat] is obviously siding with groups of terror."

The suicide bombings in Israel continued unabated, and tensions in the region rose. They also rose in the press room when I foolishly took the bait on the type of question I usually avoided. At the end of February, reporters at the gaggle were pressing me on why Bush wouldn't meet with Arafat and what exactly he wanted from the Palestinian Chairman.

He wants Arafat to make a 100 percent effort to stop the violence, I said, adding that Arafat had a large security force that needed to arrest terrorists and keep them behind bars.

American Urban Radio's April Ryan joined the debate. "But, Ari, on the Middle East, it seems that the violence was quelled a lot when former President Clinton had both at the table, had both parties at the table. And now he's leaving Arafat out and dealing with Israel. I mean do you see something wrong here?"

I knew that after years of Middle East calm, violence broke out in

September 2000, during the Camp David peace process when the status of Jerusalem was put on the negotiating table, and it had continued unabated since. I thought the premise—that the violence was quelled when both parties were at the table—was false, and I wanted to set the record straight. To my ears, the question implied the violence had begun only under President Bush's watch.

I replied, "Actually, I think if you go back to when the violence began, you can make the case that in an attempt to shoot the moon and get nothing, more violence resulted; that as a result of an attempt to push the parties beyond where they were willing to go, that it led to expectations that were raised to such a high level that it turned into violence."

"Do you at least agree that the violence was quelled during at least the last few months of the Clinton administration, it wasn't as bad, and now since the Bush administration, since things have been different the way things are handled there, the violence has escalated?" April followed up.

"If what you're asking me, do I attribute the violence to President Bush taking office, the answer is no."

The press moved on, and I didn't think much more about what I'd said until I saw an Associated Press story headlined BUSH SPOKESMAN SAYS EX-PRESIDENT CLINTON TO BLAME FOR TODAY'S MID-EAST VIOLENCE, and I hit the roof. That's not what I said, I told myself. I wasn't blaming Clinton. I was defending President Bush by pointing out that the violence *didn't* begin on his watch. Of course, I glossed over my colorful language about shooting moons and pushing the parties too far. I may never have said anything about former President Clinton or even used the words *former administration,* but I didn't have to; I gave the press enough to work with so they could write a blame story.

I marched into the Oval Office and showed the President the story. I didn't say this, I protested, knowing I should make him aware of the problem before he heard about it from someone else. If you didn't say it and the story is wrong, call the reporter who wrote it and fix it, the President told me.

When my afternoon briefing began, reporters bore in, trying to get me to repeat what I'd said, this time for the cameras.

"Can you amplify in your comments today that you believe that President Clinton may have actually unleashed, through his summitry, the wave of violence at the end of 2000?" NBC's David Gregory asked.

"That's a mischaracterization of what I said," I declared, trying to defend myself. "In fact, I don't think I ever used the words *President Clinton* when I talked this morning." I tried my best to explain that all I wanted to do was set the record straight and establish that the violence didn't begin under President Bush.

Who was I referring to when I said "shoot the moon"? a number of reporters, including AP's Ron Fournier, cleverly asked. I felt I was one move away from being checkmated. If I said President Clinton, the story would be justified. I ducked and dodged, trying not to answer, kicking myself for having said "shoot the moon" in the first place. I had let April's question get to me and gone too far in explaining my position. The press always wanted me to blame former President Clinton for one thing or another, and this time I fell into the trap—this time, I belly flopped into it.

I gamely refused to specify who I was referring to, mumbling something about the President believed it was important to learn lessons from all his predecessors. I refused to repeat my "shoot the moon" comment or say to whom it applied, but I also told the press I wasn't backing off. The press had me—they knew it and so did I.

While I was dealing with the press, President Clinton's national security adviser, Sandy Berger, was calling Condi Rice, outraged that I had blamed Clinton for the violence.

"You have to issue a retraction," she told me.

"For what?" I demanded. I was defending the President, I started to argue, realizing I didn't have firm ground to stand on. Blaming President Clinton is not the President's policy, Condi reminded me, and despite sticking to my guns for a few more minutes, I realized she was right—it had sounded like I was blaming President Clinton.

The TV stations and wires were becoming increasingly crowded with Bush blames Clinton stories when I released my statement.

"Earlier today, in response to a question, I stated that violence in the Middle East began at the end of 2000 and accelerated in 2001. I mistakenly suggested that increasing violence in the Middle East was attributable to the peace efforts that were under way in 2000. That is not the position of the administration. As President Bush has consistently said, he supported President Clinton's efforts, at the behest of the parties, to achieve a comprehensive peace in the Middle East.

"No United States President, including President Clinton, is to blame for violence in the Middle East. The only people to blame for violence are the terrorists who engage in it.

"I regret any implication to the contrary."

Ouch. If the stories were bad before, they were terrible now.

"This was a rare and pointed war of words between the President's spokesman and former President Clinton," NBC's David Gregory reported. "And tonight, the White House, fearing the impact on the current Middle East process, is backing down."

"Presidential Press Secretary Ari Fleischer ended up having to eat his words when he said off camera, to a group of reporters this morning . . . ," Brit Hume told Fox's viewers.

The problem with being the White House press secretary is if you do your job right, you typically leave the press corps in various states of dissatisfaction by refusing to give direct answers to some of their questions. And if you're not careful and you give an answer that's too colorful—those "shoot the moon" words—you get to see your mistakes on the network news and read about them in the newspapers. But that's the job I signed up for, and February 28 wasn't a good day at the office.

The next morning, I went to give a speech in Florida, and I was glad to be out of Washington. The President, meanwhile, had a trip of his own and, not realizing that I was out of town, sent word that he was looking for me. He wanted me to walk next to him as he crossed in front of the TV cameras on the South Lawn to board Marine One. He knew it couldn't have felt good for me to issue that retraction, and he wanted to show the press, and everybody else, that I was still his man. One of the reasons the staff is so good to President Bush, and so loyal to him, is that he is so good and loyal to us. He demands accountability from his staff, but we all found him to be so likable that we were driven to do our jobs well, determined not to let him down.

TWELVE

LIFE RESUMES, BUSH KNEW, ARAFAT'S GONE, AND THE MARKET TUMBLES

B Y THE SPRING OF 2002, the mood in Washington was markedly different than it had been six months earlier. The President remained extraordinarily popular with the American people, as slowly and surely life moved on. The trauma of September 11 was fresh in people's minds, but the pall it had cast upon the nation began to lift. People resumed their routines, the Taliban and Al Qaeda were on the run even though we hadn't captured Osama bin Laden. Meanwhile, the usual partisanship that marks discourse in Washington seeped back in. The agenda shifted to the usual assortment of domestic issues—the economy, campaign finance reform, energy independence, immigration reform, judicial nominations, and trade. The White House press, and the Democrats, were looking hard to change the story line, frustrated that the President had remained so popular for so long.

In March, President Bush met with Republican congressional leaders in the Cabinet Room and summed up his approach to the war on terrorism.

"The American people are not impatient," he said. "If we find Al Qaeda, we'll go after them and bring them to justice. If we blink, the rest of the world will go to sleep. My nightmare scenario is that we allow them to get weapons of mass destruction. If people want, they can put someone else here who will wring their hands, and the world will suffer."

Iraq remained on the President's mind as well. In an Oval Office meeting with a visiting European head of state, Bush said, "I have no plans on my desk to attack Iraq, yet they're on my radar scope. He [Saddam] said he'd let inspectors in, and he thumbed his nose at the world. Those days are over."

More than one year before the invasion of Iraq, the issue was heavily debated in public. On March 13, the President called a news conference in the briefing room. He was asked if he would take unilateral action against Iraq.

"One of the things I've said to our friends is that we will consult, that we will share our views of how to make the world more safe," he said. "In regards to Iraq, we're doing just that. Every world leader that comes to see me, I explain our concerns about a nation which is not conforming to agreements that it made in the past; a nation which has gassed her people in the past; a nation which has weapons of mass destruction and apparently is not afraid to use them. . . . Again, all options are on the table, and— But one thing I will not allow is a nation such as Iraq to threaten our very future by developing weapons of mass destruction. They've agreed not to have those weapons; they ought to conform to their agreement, comply with their agreement."

Another reporter pressed the President again on whether, after consultations, he might take action on his own.

"We are going to consult. I am deeply concerned about Iraq. And so should the American people be concerned about Iraq. And so should people who love freedom be concerned about Iraq.

"This is a nation run by a man who is willing to kill his own people by using chemical weapons; a man who won't let inspectors into the country; a man who's obviously got something to hide. And he is a problem, and we're going to deal with him. But the first stage is to consult with our allies and friends, and that's exactly what we're doing."

In a revealing moment that captured the President's approach to how and why the military should be used in the war on terror, he was asked by Knight Ridder's Ron Hutchinson whether, as a member of the Vietnam generation, he worried that dispatching military advisers to the Philippines, the Georgian Republic, and other places would, like Vietnam, put the United States into direct conflicts that escalated. Under Bush, the United States had sent advisers to each of those places to help in their fight against terrorism.

He answered, "I believe this war is more akin to World War II than it is to Vietnam. This is a war in which we fight for the liberties and freedom of our country. Secondly, I understand there's going to be loss of life and that people are going to— And the reason I bring that up is because for a while, at least for a period it seemed to be that the definition of success in war was nobody lost their life. Nobody grieves harder than I do when we lose a life. I feel responsible for sending the troops into harm's way. It breaks my heart when I see a mom sitting on the front row of a speech and she's weeping, openly weeping for the loss of her son. It's—it's just— I'm not very good about concealing my emotions. But I strongly believe we're doing the right thing.

"And, Hutch," the President continued, "the idea of denying sanctuary is vital to protect America. And we're going to be, obviously, judicious and wise about how we deploy troops. I learned some good lessons from Vietnam. First, there must be a clear mission. Secondly, the politicians ought to stay out of fighting a war. There was too much politics during the Vietnam War. There was too much concern in the White House about political standing."

Hutch, or Ron Hutchinson, is one of the most thoughtful reporters I've ever met. I viewed his question as a savvy way to test the President, to measure how President Bush thinks as he approaches matters of war and peace. But I also thought that too many other reporters were like old generals, constantly fighting the last war, in this case a combination of Vietnam and the First Gulf War. They had a maddening tendency to shoehorn all military conflicts into a Vietnam-like mind-set, full of quagmires and quicksand, because of their expectation that modern wars would all be fast, with little loss of life, like the First Gulf War. The problem with much of the press and war, I thought, was that, for many reporters, if a military conflict wasn't over right away, with little loss of life, then it must be Vietnam all over again.

A week after the news conference, I entered the briefing room and was quickly confronted by reporters seeking confirmation that Abu Anas Liby, a most wanted terrorist, had been arrested in Sudan. I didn't know if that was true or not. If I told the press I didn't know, they would have asked me to look into it.

"I have nothing to discuss on that topic," I said.

Why not? reporters demanded. There were many conflicting reports about his capture, and the press thought they were entitled to a straight answer.

"Anything on this would necessarily involve intelligence, and that would involve either a confirmation or a denial of something, which I'm just not going to be able to do."

Reporters kept pushing for an answer.

"When you released this list of twenty-two Most Wanted, you were asking the public and all of us to try to help find these people. And now that there have been reports, television, newspaper, saying he's in custody, you can't confirm or deny?" asked Campbell Brown of NBC.

"There's just no information I have that I can share with you on that topic," I said again.

Reporters pressed several more times, and each time I refused to budge.

Exchanges like this began to wear on me. These White House reporters weren't asking about intelligence out of the blue. There were indeed conflicting press reports about his capture, and the reporters thought it quite reasonable to rely on the White House press secretary to help them report accurately. But from my point of view, it wasn't that simple, especially when it came to national security. If I thought something might be classified, my rule was simple—I would not talk about it. As much as finding the right balance about when I could and could not help the press was part of my job, national security always came first.

As a general matter, acknowledging a prominent capture might be good PR for the administration, but winning the war on terror was more important. Sometimes, when a bad guy was captured, we wanted to keep the news secret, preventing other bad guys from knowing one of their associates had been wrapped up. We *wanted* the arrested terrorist's cell phone or satellite phone to ring again. We *wanted* him to get e-mails that we could trace. Keeping news of an arrest secret would keep the trail alive, enabling us to arrest more bad guys. There was no question in my mind I wouldn't answer any questions about such matters, but to many in the press, it was another example of the secretive White House refusing to answer straightforward questions about events in the news. Given the day's focus on this one terrorist, I couldn't even explain why I couldn't answer their questions—doing so would have sent them a signal that we might have taken someone into custody. I couldn't answer the question. I couldn't help the press.

AT THE END OF MARCH, the President traveled to Mexico, El Salvador, and Peru, becoming the first sitting American President to visit Peru. His goal was to discuss trade and showcase El Salvador's and Peru's successes as new democracies in Central and South America. When we arrived in Lima, it quickly became apparent something was wrong. Everywhere he travels in the United States or around the world, the roads around the President are closed as his limo and the motorcade speed toward our destination, but this time, the local police, who had no experience with American-size presidential visits, had failed to close any intersections. No sooner had we left the airport than cars were careening into and out of the motorcade, joining it as some points, cutting it off at others. The press bus in the back of the motorcade was hopelessly cut off. It was mayhem. The Secret Service agents around the President, notably the counterassault team, were visibly tense as they watched every car for potential trouble. We arrived safely at the American embassy, where the President made a speech and prepared to reboard the motorcade for our next destination.

Andy Card approached Karen Hughes saying he wanted to talk to her during the ride and asked her to hop into his vehicle, an armored one. Karen and I, as well as several other staffers, usually rode in a van labeled "support." I always knew ours was the first car cut off from what's called the "secure package," the series of cars that are driven and protected by Secret Service agents, ready to break from the rest of the motorcade in times of trouble to whisk the President, the military aide with the nuclear football, and other top staff off to a safe location. Andy was being diplomatic, but I knew he was putting Karen into the secure package in case there was more trouble in the streets. As the motorcade pulled out, I looked at the bumper of the Secret Service vehicle in front of me and joked that we should get a good look at it now because if there was a problem, our only view of it would be from behind, way behind. After a few minutes, we arrived at our destination safe and sound.

International trips were always enjoyable and typically more relaxing for me than a day at the White House. I never had to do formal on-camera briefings for the press; instead I would ask a senior foreign-policy specialist to brief reporters on summit meetings. Secretary of State Powell or National Security Adviser Rice would also hold news conferences. I sat in on almost all the summit meetings, hearing firsthand the President's approach to foreign policy. I traveled to more than thirty foreign countries and took in their most treasured tourist spots and prized palaces, such as the inner rooms of the Kremlin, the Great Hall of the People in China, and Chequers, the British Prime Minister's Camp David. I attended many dinners or lunches with foreign leaders, including a small, private dinner between President Bush and President Chirac at Paris's Elysée Palace. We may have disagreed with France over Iraq, but there's a lot to agree with when it comes to their cuisine.

As we left El Salvador to return to the United States, I arrived at the helicopter departure site a half hour before the President. It was a moment I had long planned on. On Sundays in Washington, I played hardball in the Ponce de León league. You had to be thirty or older to play, thirty-six or older to pitch, and our first game was coming up. One of my assistants in the press office, Reed Dickens, also played in a baseball league, and we both had brought our gloves. Standing on a ridge a few hundred feet from Marine One, Reed and I took out our gloves and played catch. It wasn't exactly spring training, but it sure felt that way to me as Reed and I warmed up our arms in the warm Salvadoran sun.

THE CLIMATE IN WASHINGTON, thanks to events in the Middle East, wasn't as warm. It was bad and getting worse. Following a string of suicide bombings that took more than one hundred Israeli lives in the spring of 2002, Ariel Sharon ordered tanks into the West Bank as the Israelis occupied almost every Palestinian town, large and small. Secretary Powell visited the region but made little headway in reducing the violence, which seemed to be spiraling out of control. The President urged Sharon to withdraw from the West Bank and to give Palestinians room to breathe, but the Prime Minister was a hard man to influence. He began to withdraw slowly, and only eventually withdrew entirely after imposing a severe blow on the Palestinian capacity to inflict terror on the Israeli people.

In the spring, President Bush met in the Oval Office with a respected Arab leader to talk about peace in the Mideast and Iraq.

"Arafat can't get a damn thing done," Bush complained. "Israel has created a martyr out of that guy." The President thought it best if Arafat, who was now holed up and besieged in his mostly destroyed compound, was simply ignored for being a failed nonleader who incited terrorism. The American President repeatedly told that to Sharon. Bush was frustrated that Israel's focus on Arafat made him a hero to the Palestinian people. The most influential Arab states that could help achieve peace, Bush thought, were Saudi Arabia, Jordan, and Egypt. He also told his guest, "I believe there are people in your part of the world who want to destroy Israel."

"I agree," came the answer, "but there are people in Israel who want to get rid of the Palestinians." His guest also told Bush that, as bad as Arafat was, there was no alternative to him.

"What do you mean there's no alternative?" Bush demanded. "Of course there is."

"I'm sorry, Mr. President, there is no alternative. He's the best we have."

At that point, Bush leaned forward on the edge of his chair, pointed at his guest, and with his knees almost touching the knees of his Arab guest, he exclaimed, "What do you mean, there's no alternative to Arafat? *I* have more faith in the Arab people than you do. Surely there's a Palestinian leader better than Yasir Arafat. Of course there is."

"If there's an alternative, Mr. President, who is he, then?"

"I don't need to know his name," Bush replied. "I just need to know that an alternative exists and your job, and my job, is to create the environment necessary for that alternative to emerge."

I sat back in amazement.

The President had just told a respected Arab leader that he, the American from Texas, had more faith in the Arab people than an Arab did. Why? Because the Arabs were clinging to a failed status quo personified by Yasir Arafat. Bush had an ability to challenge people's fundamental premises, to recast stale debates so new solutions could be found. He later would talk publicly about his belief that God empowers each individual everywhere with a desire for freedom and that the Arab world wasn't immune to democracy and liberty. His belief that a better Palestinian leader could emerge if only the environment would change was rooted in his abiding faith in freedom. Arafat and his immediate, corrupt circle were the real problems, Bush thought—not the Palestinian people and not Ariel Sharon. The seeds of the President's June 24, 2002, Rose Garden speech declaring the United States would no longer work with Arafat were planted in that meeting.

On Iraq, Bush told his guest, "If the light goes green, [Hussein] is gone. He's like a three-cent cigar. Put him in the air and he'll unravel. A decisive win in Iraq will make your neighborhood a lot more peaceful. We're thinking beyond the current turmoil."

As the meeting broke up, the President told his guest, "I want everyone who visits me to feel comfortable expressing frustration. But I also want them to focus on the future, on what's realistic and what's doable, what can be accomplished."

One month later, Egyptian President Hosni Mubarak came to a private meeting at Camp David, and Bush warned him, "If Arafat doesn't perform, it's time for the Arab world to say enough is enough. Palestinians hurt and I know that. My view is that if the Palestinian people have a government that is open, transparent, and willing to serve the people, [the region] will be better off.... There's plenty of talent among the Palestinians, and that talent will emerge once there's a state. The people deserve hope. This is bigger than one person," Bush said, referring to Arafat.

That same spring, the President told a visiting Ariel Sharon, "I firmly believe we need two states side by side. I don't see how Israel can exist long term without it." He also told the retired general, "You don't want to expel Arafat. You want to expose him for what he is. The Arabs understand this. It's a breakthrough—you don't want to make him a martyr." He added, "If the Arabs feel they own a piece of the future, they'll be more likely to help stop terror."

The other bad news that spring was the economy and the deficit. Revenues continued to plunge, and with the April 15 end-of-tax-filing-season data in hand, we could see that the fiscal situation was getting worse. The deficit for 2002 might now be $150 billion, the President was advised, caused by the lingering effects of the recession. "Last year's economy is showing up in this year's revenues," his budget director, Mitch Daniels, said. The unemployment rate was rising too, hitting 6 percent.

ON MAY 15, David Martin of CBS News aired a report that caused a political earthquake. "The Central Intelligence [Agency's] daily brief to the President weeks before 9/11 specifically alerted him of a possible airliner attack in the United States, David Martin reports tonight," the story began before flashing to Martin.

"The President's daily intelligence brief is delivered to the President each morning, often by the Director of Central Intelligence himself. In the weeks before 9/11 it warned that an attack by Osama bin Laden could involve the hijacking of a U.S. aircraft," Martin reported.

Barely a minute after the report aired, AP's Ron Fournier stood outside my office. "Is the story true?" Ron asked.

I had never heard about any of this before and had no idea. I never saw a presidential daily brief and knew I was going to have to dig hard and fast to find out the facts.

Before the CBS story, the only person who had alleged Bush knew about the September 11 attack, yet let it happen anyway, was a left-wing congresswoman from Georgia, Cynthia McKinney. She was so radical she lost her seat later that year in a Democratic primary. (She was reelected to her seat in 2004.) But now, the White House press corps were in a feeding frenzy.

"Throughout the summer," I explained at my on-camera briefing the next day, after having been briefed by Andy Card and Condi Rice, "the administration received heightened reporting on threats on U.S. interests and territories, most of it focused on threats abroad. As a result, several actions were taken to button down security. All appropriate action was taken based on the threat information that the United States government received.

"The possibility of a traditional hijacking, in the pre–September 11 sense, has long been a concern of the government, dating back decades. The President did not—not—receive information about the use of airplanes as missiles by suicide bombers. This was a new type of attack that had not been foreseen."

For four frustrating days, the story dominated everything. Why didn't the President warn the American people in August that Al Qaeda wanted to hijack aircraft? the press demanded. Why didn't the administration connect the dots? Why didn't Bush level with the public?

Some in the press challenged my credibility too.

"Why, on September 11, did you tell the pool in response to a direct question whether the President had a warning, you said no warnings?"

"The President did not have any warnings, as I indicated, about the possibility of people using airplanes as missiles," I replied.

"He knew in August that this situation was possible," a reporter protested.

"What's 'this situation'?" I asked.

"That a terrorist hijacking was possible."

"Hijackings have been possible in the United States for decades," I said.

"He knew in August," a reporter concluded. "But on September 11 . . . in response to a direct question from the pool, 'Did the President get any warnings?' a general question about general warnings, you said, No warnings."

"If you can imagine the context of any question on September 11, it's warnings about the attack on New York, the Pentagon, the use of airplanes as missiles. I think it's impossible to interpret that question in any other context than warnings about what had just taken place literally moments and hours ago," I said angrily.

The story raged for days and began to fade only after the Democrats made a series of attacks on the President that went too far, questioning whether he was warned about the September 11 attack, but knowingly and deliberately allowed the attack to happen.

Senator Hillary Clinton gave a speech on the floor of the Senate in which she declared, "We learn today something we might have learned at least eight months ago; that President Bush had been informed last year, before September 11, of a possible Al-Qaeda plot to hijack a U.S. airliner." Then she held up an inflammatory front-page story from the tabloid *New York Post* headlined, BUSH KNEW.

"The President knew what?" the senator asked cleverly, knowing the question would cause the press to throw more oil onto the fire. The President faced down his critics by declaring, "Had I known that the enemy was going to use airplanes to kill on that fateful morning, I would have done everything in my power to protect the American people," he said in the Rose Garden. The allegations did, however, give momentum to demands for a full-blown review of all the events that led up to September 11, a review that led to the creation of the September 11 Commission.

Later, I spoke to David Martin about his CBS report and what it unleashed. He told me he was surprised it had created such an uproar. He didn't view his story as an indication that Bush knew, or could have known, about the September 11 attack. He saw it as one possible missed clue, but not a smoking gun pointed at September 11.

I found the attacks on President Bush frustrating and hard to understand. Richard Clarke, the President's former counterterrorism chief, told the September 11 Commission that Bush failed to make terrorism an urgent priority and put much of the blame for the attack on the President. Yet just four days after the attacks, Clarke had briefed me on a series of aggressive actions the administration had taken in the spring and summer of 2001 to counter the threat from Al Qaeda and its host, the Taliban.

Many in the White House press faulted as useless and vague the color-coded warnings that describe terrorist threats, yet now they demanded to know why we didn't warn the American people about the possibility of airplane hijackings in August 2001, instead of just warning the airlines, as the Federal Aviation Administration did. It seems to me that warnings about hijackings are just as vague as warnings about threats to unknown bridges, or reservoirs, or nuclear power plants, the types of warnings many in the press lampooned.

In the aftermath of September 11, the public *was* warned about such vague threats, yet many reporters ridiculed the announcements, skeptically asking what people were supposed to do with such nonspecific information. With the benefit of hindsight, however, the press asked why the public *wasn't* warned about hijackings, when if the government *had* issued a public report in August 2001, I doubt any network or major newspaper would have paid it much attention, given how generalized the information was.

The press has the advantage of twenty-twenty hindsight. The government doesn't.

THREE STRANGE EVENTS OCCURRED within a twenty-four-hour period on June 19, making for an odd day at the briefing room podium. At 8:00 that night, the White House received information about a small aircraft that had entered the temporary flight-restricted area of Washington, D.C. The plane did not enter the permanently closed airspace closer to the White House, but it did raise alarms. A Secret Service officer jumped the gun and gave an order to evacuate his area of the

White House, which included the cubes in which the press work. "The White House is being evacuated, the White House is being evacuated!" the press reported.

Other than the press and some staff on the South Lawn being told to leave, no one was sent packing, and the President wasn't notified or moved. It really wasn't any big deal, but because the press were ordered to leave, it became a big deal. It didn't take long for the Secret Service to let the press back in, and the story faded as the plane never came close to the White House.

Moments before this happened, the President was attending a fundraiser at the Washington Convention Center, and his motorcade was parked, as usual, in the center's garage. As the press were escorted into their vans, a reporter spotted a bullet on the floor of the garage and informed a White House aide. This too turned out to be no big deal—a law enforcement officer had somehow dropped it.

While all this was going on, the Federal Reserve was evacuated after suspicious items were found in a garbage can by an explosive-seeking police dog. That too turned out to be a false alarm.

One briefing, three false alarms, none of them serious, but any one of them could have made for a bad news day. Once again I thought, You never know what's going to happen when you show up for work as the White House press secretary.

THE PRESIDENT'S FRUSTRATION with the lack of progress in the Middle East, the constant suicide bombings, and his belief that Arafat was a major cause of the problem led to a profound change in American policy. In a major address in the Rose Garden on June 24, 2002, President Bush said, "I call on the Palestinian people to elect new leaders, leaders not compromised by terror. I call upon them to build a practicing democracy, based on tolerance and liberty. If the Palestinian people actively pursue these goals, America and the world will actively support their efforts. If the Palestinian people meet these goals, they will be able to reach agreement with Israel and Egypt and Jordan on security and other arrangements for independence.

"And when the Palestinian people have new leaders, new institutions, and new security arrangements with their neighbors, the United States of America will support the creation of a Palestinian state whose borders and certain aspects of its sovereignty will be provisional until resolved as part of a final settlement in the Middle East."

I thought Bush once again went beyond the accepted status quo and used America's authority, moral and political, to force change on those who didn't want it. His own nature, and the events of September 11, led him to believe that the United States harbors immense influence, and he didn't hesitate to use it, even in bold and controversial ways, if he thought doing so would advance the mission of peace long term. The amazing thing about his pronouncement that Arafat had to go was his successful cultivation of Arab leaders who quietly agreed. Many, including the President, thought that if Arafat were genuinely interested in peace, he would have accepted the agreement that President Clinton tried to broker in late 2000. Arafat couldn't accept Israel's offer of Palestinian control over 95 percent of the West Bank; he lacked the vision, the strength, and the ability to be a peacetime leader who acknowledged Israel's right to exist. Arafat was a failed leader who could stay in power only if he fermented dissent and turmoil below him.

One month later, Bush met in the Oval Office with the foreign ministers of three Arab nations.

"Arafat can't lead," the President told them. "The irony is the attitude that there's no one else. The Palestinian people can produce leaders; people who can lead who love peace will emerge. The path to peace can unleash a lot of money. There won't be money if people think it's going to be stolen," he said, alluding to corruption in the Palestinian Authority. Addressing the needs of the Palestinian people, he added, "We cry over the humanitarian plight. It's a blight on all of us." Then Bush referred to the Israelis and the suicide attacks from which they were suffering daily. "You know me," he told his Arab guests, "if somebody bombs *us,* we're going to kick their ass. You need to know that's how I feel."

I thought the President's June 24 speech was one of the most significant, and realistic, uses of American power in a generation. As a

Jew, I was moved by his commitment to Israel. It struck me his motivation was simple—Israel, Bush thought, was doing the same thing the United States was doing in the face of terror, namely, defending itself. He knew what he would do to protect the United States from attack, and Israel was living under the same threat, if not a worse one. Bush was consistent in his war on terror, and his consistency applied to Israel's actions as well. I think the President was also motivated by a common bond with Israel, recognizing that the Jewish nation was a democracy. Finally, the President, being a man of faith, had a profound respect for and commitment to the Jewish people's right to exist safely in their own homeland. One of his first acts as President, early in 2001, was to visit the Holocaust Memorial Museum in Washington, just as he had toured Yad Vashem as a governor in 1998. I thought Jews could have no better friend in the Oval Office than George W. Bush.

BEGINNING LATE IN 2001 and continuing into the new year, a series of corporate scandals rocked the nation, led by the unexpected collapse of the Houston-based energy giant Enron Corporation. The head of Enron, Ken Lay, had been a major donor to the Bush campaign, and when his company tanked, many Democrats tried to tie Bush to Lay, somehow blaming the President for the collapse. Enron engaged in questionable, potentially criminal financial practices, as did a number of other major companies, including WorldCom and Tyco.

In July 2002, Bush met with Republican congressional leaders to discuss the war on terror and a number of domestic initiatives. When it came to some people on Wall Street, the President said, "they'll buy you or sell you as long as they make money. All of us should feel the same sense of outrage. Business should be about honesty and integrity. I'm plenty hot about this," he said. One congressman told the President, "There's no such thing as business ethics. Just ethics."

Two days later, the President called the first meeting of the newly formed Corporate Fraud Task Force, chaired by Deputy Attorney General Larry Thompson and led by FBI Director Robert Mueller and other top officials. In the Roosevelt Room, named after the Roosevelt Presidents, one of whom was a trustbuster, Bush told the group of prosecutors, "I appreciate your willingness to pursue those who violate public trust. It's important to restore confidence. When everyone gets rich, they let their guard down. It's time to remind everybody they have ethical responsibilities."

The President also described to these seasoned law enforcement officers a conversation he'd had about ethics with a fellow on a rope line, the barrier that separates him from the public at his speeches. "The best ethics course is to handcuff one of the bastards," Bush was told. The prosecutors loved it, and indeed they did arrest and successfully prosecute many of those involved. By July 2004, two years after the task force was launched, prosecutors and investigators had obtained over five hundred corporate fraud convictions or guilty pleas and had charged over nine hundred defendants and over sixty corporate CEOs and presidents with criminal charges, including thirty-one people at Enron, twenty-one of them former Enron executives.

To underscore his commitment to fighting corporate fraud, Bush traveled to Wall Street to give a speech about ethics and fraud. A week before, the White House had to relive a ten-year-old controversy over the President's sale of Harken stock, because his attorneys had failed to file all the necessary paperwork when Bush sold his shares in the company. When the President began his remarks, the Dow Jones Industrial Average stood at 9274; when the trading day was over, the market had fallen, big time, to 9096. The market didn't rise on Bush's remarks—no one had said it would—instead it fell, so some reporters interpreted the President's remarks as a flop and blamed him for the decline.

Reporters typically carry a large dose of mistrust for corporate America, and pretty soon Harken, Enron, Bush, Halliburton, and Dick Cheney all got rolled into one ongoing controversy about whether the administration was out of touch with ordinary Americans and too closely in line with corporate America. Reporters were on the hunt for a scandal, even though there was no case for any of them to make.

After a week's worth of scandal-like questions, I got fed up. "After a week of noise about nothing," I exclaimed, "people are seeing a scandal-seeking Washington that's out of touch with a solution-seeking nation. And that's what this President is focused on: solving the problems that have been created, that have been growing up for a considerable number of years as a result of the bubble in the markets and the corporate excesses that took place as a result of that; and targeting the wrongdoers and people who engage in fraud so that the country can have confidence in the free enterprise system and those people who are responsible in corporate America."

Corporate America's excesses and crimes took a real toll on the stock market that summer. On Memorial Day 2002, the Dow Jones Industrial Average stood at 10,104. By Labor Day it had tumbled to 8663. *Someone* had to be blamed for the drop, and for the cable news shows, the blame fell on President Bush.

As the twenty-four-hour-a-day cable news networks put out their live reports, the bottom right hand corner of the screen displays a small arrow that points up or down, tracking the stock market throughout the day. It's a helpful guide for viewers; they can listen to the news and glance down at the small arrow to see how the market is doing.

But in the summer of 2002, whenever the market's slide coincided with a Bush speech, the cable TV blame game reached new lows. The President's speeches were shown on one side of the screen, but the small down arrow had morphed to take up the entire other half of the screen! It infuriated me that CNN, MSNBC, and Fox were suggesting by this juxtaposition that Bush's speech had caused the slide. I called the presidents of all the cable news departments to complain. Each admitted it was poor journalism, and they all stopped doing it, but the damage was done. The economy was bad, the market was tanking, there was corruption in parts of corporate America, and somehow it was all President Bush's fault. A year later, when the economy began its boom and the market soared, I wondered if any of the cable networks would juxtapose the President's speeches with huge up arrows. None of them did, of course.

At the final cabinet meeting that summer, the President talked about the need to pass trade promotion authority; he heard Treasury Secretary Paul O'Neill predict that the economy was about to grow by 3.0 to 3.5 percentage points. Unfortunately, that prediction was off by about a year. The President also gave an update on Iraq, telling the group, "We're plenty patient and will use all the tools at our disposal. I've asked Rumsfeld to look at every angle for how to remove Hussein. Now is the time—we can't wait ten years. Our intent is serious. We do believe there is a *causa belli* already that allows for the doctrine of pre-emption. If we're tough and firm, the world will follow. If we're successful, I know they'll follow."

THIRTEEN

HELEN THOMAS

HELEN IS A LEGEND.

My sparring partner in the briefing room, Helen Thomas is an icon in American journalism, deservedly so. When I began my job as White House press secretary, I invited Helen into my office for a private meeting. We talked about the White House press, the White House staff, and the way things worked. She started working as a White House reporter in 1961 for United Press International, and she had seen it all. I thought there might be a few things I could learn from her, and I also wanted to pay her my respects. I had never met her before.

She gave me a copy of her book *Front Row at the White House*. On its inscription page she wrote, "To Ari, Who holds the second toughest job in the White House. With my very best wishes. Tell the truth—and you will never go wrong." It was the best advice I ever received. As Helen knows, the job of the White House press secretary isn't to *say* everything you know to be true, but everything you *say* had better be true. In other words, you can remain silent on some things, but if you speak, you'd better tell the truth.

One of the little secrets about Helen and me is how well we got along on a personal level. While we clashed mightily in the briefing room, especially on Arab-Israeli affairs, she was doing her job and I was doing mine. She didn't care for the President and once called him the worst president in the history of our country. When I called her to ask if the press report quoting her as saying that was true, she simply said yes. I didn't care for her politics, she didn't care for mine, but she was in her eighties, she showed up for work every day, and she kept me on my toes.

Unlike virtually everyone else in the briefing room, Helen wasn't really a reporter any longer. She was a columnist for the Hearst Newspapers, having resigned from United Press International in 2000, freeing her up to give her opinions and not have to act like a neutral reporter who simply asked tough questions. If you asked some of the old-timers in the briefing room, they'll tell you she gave her opinions plenty even when she was a wire reporter—that's just Helen. Today, she's the only columnist in the United States with an assigned seat in the briefing room, a front-row seat. As long as I was the press secretary, she was going to keep it and be welcome in it. I'm willing to bet as long as she wants to work, she's going to be in that seat, giving her opinion, putting the press secretary in the hot seat.

In June 2003, Hart Seely, an award-winning journalist at the *Syracuse Post-Standard,* wrote an op-ed in the *New York Times* that amusingly highlighted some of my answers to Helen's questions.

"Helen, Bonjour; I like your chapeau."

"I'm happy to take your questions. Helen."

"Always interested in your opinion, Helen." And so on.

I asked Helen how she liked the piece, and she said she didn't like it at all. "I think it was very unfair because they should have had *my* comments," she exclaimed.

Here for the record are *both* sides of some of Helen's and my greatest exchanges. Sometimes I got the better of her. Sometimes she got the better of me. More often than not, she growled her questions at me and I did my best to smile, or laugh, although sometimes I snapped back at her. Every once in a while, I left the podium and winked at her, as if to say, Don't let anyone know we get along.

July 11, 2001

HELEN: The President has been in office six months now. He's had only three news conferences here. When can we expect another news conference, so we can put him on the pan, instead of you? (Laughter)

ARI: Helen, some days I'm very much in favor of that.

Q: Only two news conferences.

Q: Two? Is it only two?

ARI: Three, he's had three formal news conferences here in the briefing room. And, of course, he had five in a row on the last trip to Europe.

HELEN: That was nice, but—(Laughter)

ARI: We'll keep you advised when he has news conferences. Will you be joining us on the next trip to Europe?

HELEN: Will you take me along on Air Force One?

ARI: No. (Laughter) [Only pool reporters could be seated on Air Force One. Columnists took the press charter.]

Q: How about news organizations that don't have enough money to join you on all those [foreign] press conferences?

ARI: I highly recommend you make more money. (Laughter)

December 19, 2001

This exchange came after the capture and detention of John Walker Lindh, a twenty-year-old American found in Afghanistan among Taliban fighters, who had surrendered after a violent revolt at Qala-i-Jangi prison.

HELEN: Are we so primitive that we would ship this man in a box, deny him legal rights, deny him the right to see a lawyer, deny him the right to see his parents? I mean, is that America?

ARI: Helen, under the Geneva Convention regarding treatment of prisoners of war, the military and intelligence agencies may question prisoners for information—that's [of] military value—in the conduct of war without the presence of a lawyer. That is what the Geneva Convention calls for—

HELEN: You ship him in a box?

ARI:—and the Geneva Convention is being followed in this case.

HELEN: So it trumps his constitutional right to—

ARI: No, this is done consistent with the Constitution . . .

HELEN: He can't see his parents? He's not allowed to see his parents?

ARI: Again, Helen, I think they are moving forward with a review of the facts in this matter. But he is being treated under the Geneva Convention. He is being protected. He has been given medical care—which he was not receiving under the Taliban . . .

HELEN: And he's being interrogated without a lawyer. Is that fair?

ARI: He is being given all his rights, which are far more than the rights the Taliban or the Al Qaeda extended to anyone living there.

HELEN: We're not comparing ourselves, are we?

She got me on that one.

February 12, 2002

Helen was one of the first reporters to aggressively question the President's approach to Iraq. This exchange came more than one year before the war.

HELEN: Is the President ready to go to war with Iraq?

ARI: Helen, as the President said in his State of the Union, the President is prepared to take whatever action is necessary to protect the United States, protect our allies, and to protect peace internationally. And I can assure you no decisions have been made beyond the first phase of the war on terrorism. The President has been very plainspoken with the American people about the need to fight the war on terrorism wherever terrorism is. And he's focused right now on Afghanistan, but the President has been very clear that time is not on our side because of the threats posed by nations and terrorists against the United States.

HELEN: Does he know of any connection with the current fight against terrorism by Iraq? Does he have any evidence?

ARI: Well, when the President referred to the axis of evil, and identified North Korea, Iran, and Iraq, what the President was referring to is their—not only their support of terrorism, which is plain—they are on the State Department list of terrorist states—but also their development of weapons of mass destruction, their willingness in the case of several of those nations to export technology and material and provide weapons of mass destruction. And the President does fear the marrying of any of these nations with terrorist organizations.

HELEN: Well, we have weapons of mass destruction and we don't permit inspection.

ARI: Helen, if you're suggesting that there's a moral equivalence of the United States's success in keeping the peace for sixty years with our weapons and the actions of terrorists, I would urge you to reexamine that premise. I see no moral equivalence.

March 7, 2002

HELEN: Back to the Middle East. Does the President think that his hands-off policy has contributed in any way to the hopelessness and the rising violence in the Middle East? And anticipating your answer, I have a follow-on. (Laughter)

ARI: Why don't you just get it all out of the way, Helen? (Laughter)

HELEN: Well, American weaponry is being used. So why are we so passive in this conflict where people are dying on both sides?

ARI: Well, I just have to disabuse you of your premise that the United States is hands off, the United States is not involved. The United States has been deeply involved. The United States is always deeply involved.

HELEN: How? I mean, the President has never met a Palestinian. And he is—he seems to be so detached. Let's hear something positive.

ARI: The President has spoken out on this on any number of occasions. As you know, he just welcomed [Egyptian] President Mubarak at the White House.

HELEN: I know, everybody's for peace.

ARI: And he's talked with President Mubarak as he's talked with the

Crown Prince of Saudia Arabia, and any number of others in the Middle East about how to achieve peace.

HELEN: Well, you know how that's been interpreted? As rejection.

ARI: But, Helen, the premise of your question is that the United States is to blame for events on the ground in the Middle East—

HELEN: No, that's not the premise at all. I'm just saying—

ARI: —and I don't accept that.

HELEN: —by not participating in any sort of—as a mediator, as we've always been since the forties, how come—I mean, of course—why are we really not actively involved?

ARI: The United States has been, will be, and continues to be. So we disagree on the premise of it.

April 1, 2002

HELEN: Ari, does the President think that the Palestinians have a right to resist thirty-five years of brutal military occupation and suppression?

ARI: Helen, the President believes that as a result of a process that has got to focus on peace between Israel and the Palestinians, the President was the first to go to the United Nations and call for a Palestinian state. That remains the President's hope. That remains the President's vision. And, obviously, events in the Middle East have grown very violent. But that is the vision that the President continues to hold out for.

HELEN: But he does think they have a legitimate right to fight for their land?

ARI: Helen, I do not accept the premise of your question, and the manner that you asked it.

HELEN: Occupation, thirty-five years.

May 1, 2002

HELEN: What is the President's rationale for invading Iraq? I've been reading stories every day of preparations, no set plan yet, I admit, but anyway, all of the senior administration officials talk all the

time, including the President, about a change of regime. What is the
rationale for that?

ARI: Well, Helen, the President does believe that the people of Iraq, as
well as the region, would be better off without Saddam Hussein in
charge of Iraq.

HELEN: A lot of people would be better off in a lot of places.

ARI: Can I continue? And if you recall, Helen, the Congress passed last
year—or in a previous administration—legislation that made regime
change the official policy of the government. And that was signed
into law by President Clinton. So President Bush is continuing—

HELEN: What law was that?

ARI: It's called the Iraqi Liberation Act, signed—passed by—

HELEN: Did it say we were going to overturn—

ARI: —passed by the House and the Senate, signed into law by President Clinton. Regime change, in whatever form it takes, is the
policy of the United States government, under President Clinton,
continued under President Bush.

HELEN: So what is President Bush's rationale for that?

ARI: As I indicated, that the President believes that the people of Iraq,
as well as the region, will be more peaceful, better off without Saddam Hussein in charge of Iraq, given the fact that Saddam Hussein
has invaded two of his neighbors.

HELEN: That's not a reason. There are a lot of people all over the world—

ARI: Helen, if you were the President, you could have vetoed the law.
(Laughter) President Clinton signed it, and the President will keep
it enforced.

HELEN: That's not an answer either.

July 10, 2002

This exchange, which is mightily embarrassing to Helen, began when I
called on Raghubir Goyal, of the *India Globe*.

ARI: Goyal.

GOYAL: A comment and a question.

ARI: I'm sorry?

GOYAL: A comment, she asked me not to do, but I'm taking the liberty, the grand lady of the front row [Helen]—we had a great date at the Bombay Palace Restaurant on Tuesday, in Washington. She had a lot of good things to say about you. (Laughter)

ARI: Must have been a case of food poisoning. (Laughter)

September 4, 2002

HELEN: Beyond his opinion that the world will be better off, did he [Bush] present any concrete evidence of Iraq on the verge of nuclear planning, nuclear bombs, or any other thing that would really be different than what Israel has today?

ARI: Helen, first of all, I don't think it's fair to compare Israel to Iraq.

HELEN: Why not? It's the only nuclear power in the Middle East.

November 6, 2002

The night before this briefing, Republicans made history in midterm elections by winning back the Senate and gaining seats in the House of Representatives. Helen wasn't pleased.

HELEN: Does the President consider this a mandate to fulfill his agenda? Going to war with Iraq, privatizing Social Security, weakening the Civil Service Commission, and so forth?

ARI: Helen, you sound like a [political] commercial that didn't work. (Laughter)

December 2, 2002

HELEN: Does the President hope that there will be no weapons there [Iraq]?

ARI: The President wants—

HELEN: I mean, everything you say is so negative. It doesn't sound like you people really want to not find anything there.

ARI: I think everything *Saddam Hussein* has done has been so negative that this President is accurately and realistically describing facts to the world. And as a result of the President accurately describing facts to the world—

HELEN: But you're going in with such a negative attitude.

ARI: Well, I think it's fair to say the President has gone into this with a can-do attitude to preserve the peace, and if it hadn't been for the President's efforts and leadership and willing[ness] to state facts realistically, there would be no inspectors inside Iraq, would there be? There wouldn't have. It was the President who caused this to happen.

HELEN: Have they ever threatened the United States? Has Iraq ever threatened the United States?

ARI: Only when they shoot at our pilots. Only when they attack their neighbors and America's interests abroad.

HELEN: During the Gulf War when we were shooting at them.

ARI: They were shooting at our pilots just recently.

January 6, 2003

HELEN: At the earlier briefing, Ari, you said that the President deplored the taking of innocent lives. Does that apply to all innocent lives in the world? And I have a follow-up.

ARI: I refer specifically to a horrible terrorist attack on Tel Aviv that killed scores and wounded hundreds. And the President, as he said in his statement yesterday, deplores in the strongest terms the taking of those lives and the wounding of those people, innocents in Israel.

HELEN: My follow-up is why does he want to drop bombs on innocent Iraqis?

ARI: Helen, the question is how to protect Americans, and our allies and friends—

HELEN: They're not attacking you.

ARI: —from a country—

HELEN: Have they laid the glove on you or on the United States, the Iraqis, in eleven years?

ARI: I guess you have forgotten about the Americans who were killed in the First Gulf War as a result of Saddam Hussein's aggression then.

HELEN: Is this revenge, eleven years of revenge?

ARI: Helen, I think you know very well that the President's position is that he wants to avert war, and that the President has asked the United Nations to go into Iraq to help with the purpose of averting war.

HELEN: Would the President attack innocent Iraqi lives?

ARI: The President wants to make certain that he can defend our country, defend our interests, defend the region, and make certain that American lives are not lost.

HELEN: And he thinks they are a threat to us?

ARI: There is no question that the President thinks that Iraq is a threat to the United States.

HELEN: The Iraqi people?

ARI: The Iraqi people are represented by their government. If there was regime change, the Iraqi—

HELEN: So they will be vulnerable?

ARI: Actually, the President has made it very clear that he has no dispute with the people of Iraq. That's why the American policy remains a policy of regime change. There is no question the people of Iraq—

HELEN: That's a decision for them to make, isn't it? It's their country.

ARI: Helen, if you think that the people of Iraq are in a position to dictate who their dictator is, I don't think that has been what history has shown.

HELEN: I think many countries don't have—people don't have the decision—including us.

February 24, 2003

HELEN: Ari, why is the President pushing the world into war when millions, and people all over the world are against this war? The Turks are 95 percent against it, even though their leaders are being bought.

ARI: Helen, I think this falls right back into the category of subjects that we will not agree on, you and me, or you and the President—and you and most Americans, frankly. The fact of the matter is that—

HELEN: Maybe it doesn't matter whether all the world is against this?

ARI: If your perception is—if your reporting indicates to you all the world is against this, then I don't think you've lent too much reporting to it.

February 26, 2003

This exchange occured before the President made a speech to scholars, friends, and supporters of the American Enterprise Institute. The President outlined his vision of a peaceful Middle East and the role a regime change in Iraq could have in planting the seeds of democracy in the region.

HELEN: Then why are you going to bomb them? (Laughter) I mean, how do you bomb people back to democracy? This is a question of conquest. They didn't ask to be liberated by the United States. This is our self-imposed political solution for them.

ARI: Let me guess that you will not be at the speech tonight. Helen, the President is going to—

HELEN: I'll be very interested in what the President has to say because I don't think— I think if you ask five people anywhere, what's the reason the President wants to go to war, you'll get five different answers. Usually there's one defining moment and solution.

ARI: Tonight, the President is going to discuss this. I think you will hear the President tonight talk about the threat of Saddam Hussein and how he poses a danger to the American—

HELEN: In twelve years he [Hussein] hasn't done anything.

ARI: We will temporarily suspend the Q and A portion of today's briefing to bring you this advocacy minute. (Laughter)

March 14, 2003

HELEN: Will you ask— Ari, will you ask the President for me and for many, many others, has he really weighed the human cost on both sides, starting a war to go after one man?

ARI: Helen, this is not a war to go after one man. This is a war, if there is a war, to go after one regime led by Saddam Hussein that possesses weapons of mass destruction that can take the lives of millions. That's why the United Nations called on Saddam Hussein to disarm. It is because Iran—Iraq possesses weapons of mass destruction and that is the core of the issue. They have not disarmed.

HELEN: How do you know they do, when they haven't been discovered? We've had inspections, and so forth—and many other countries have weapons of mass destruction, including us.

ARI: And under Resolution 1441, Saddam Hussein was compelled by the United Nations Security Council to immediately, without condition, and without restriction disarm. He has not done so.

HELEN: You haven't found anything yet in the—

ARI: That doesn't prove that he doesn't have it, Helen, it just proves that he's able to hide it.

HELEN: But that doesn't prove they are either.

May 20, 2003

HELEN: Does the President think that it is a more dangerous world because of our invasion of Iraq and the upswing in terrorism which seems to be really more rampant now since— Do our policies have anything to do with that?

ARI: Helen, you may have missed the fact that the bombing in Bali took place before the war in Iraq, or the attempted attacks on the consulate took place before the war in Iraq.

HELEN: You don't see it as a more dangerous world today?

ARI: No. I think the President sees the world more safe today as a result of removing the threat of Saddam Hussein to the region and to people in that region who want to work for peace.

HELEN: Well, was it Saddam Hussein who caused the terrorism?

ARI: Yes, but not the attacks in Saudi Arabia. But that's why I made the point to you now that even before the war in Iraq there were terrorist attacks in other parts of the world that took great tolls.

HELEN: But you never linked them totally to Saddam.

ARI: That's correct. So why are you?

HELEN: Why am I? I think that there is a whole—there's a turmoil in the Arab world, obviously, from all the things we've been doing.

ARI: I think there's a lot of silent rejoicing in the Arab world that Saddam Hussein is gone.

FOURTEEN

IS THE NEWS ACCURATE?

REPORTERS DID IT at the *New York Times, USA Today,* and the British Broadcasting Corporation: they made things up—facts, events, and quotes—reported them as gospel, and later, much later, got fired once they were caught. At CBS, Dan Rather aired forged documents about President Bush's service in the National Guard. He stood by the accuracy of his story for a week, originally defending his reporting from those he accused of being "partisans." Only after pressure mounted did CBS admit they were duped and hadn't performed proper due diligence before putting the inflammatory story on the air. Of course, the networks botched their coverage of the 2000 election, wrongly reporting Al Gore the winner in Florida, later calling Bush the winner, then finally, and accurately, reversing both their calls by declaring no one the winner. Do reporters often make things up or air bogus stories? I don't think so, in fact I rather doubt it, but it's impossible to say. Each of these news organizations was shocked it occurred at all, and the top editors at the *Times, USA Today,* and the BBC lost their jobs in the wake of the controversies that followed.

According to a survey of journalists taken by the Pew organization, journalists are increasingly questioning the accuracy of their own work. The study found that 45 percent of the national media in 2004 believed that "news reports are full of factual errors," that's up from 30 percent in 1995.

A Gallup poll taken in September 2004 showed the press was suffering from an ongoing decline in public trust.

"In general, how much trust and confidence do you have in the mass media—such as newspapers, TV and radio," Gallup asked American adults, "when it comes to reporting the news fully, accurately and fairly: a great deal, a fair amount, not very much or none at all?"

Forty-four percent said either a great deal or a fair amount, while 55 percent said not very much or none at all. In 1972, according to Gallup, 68 percent had a great deal or a fair amount of trust in the press, and only 30 percent had not very much or none at all. The public's frustration with the press runs deep, and it's getting deeper.

How can readers or viewers know if the news they're getting is accurate? White House reporters, it seems to me, absolutely do their best to report accurately what they see and hear. We're a better and stronger country because every day the press in general, and the White House press corps in particular, publish or air thousands of facts that *are* true and accurate. Yes, they make mistakes, but they also get many things right, and that's why Americans by the tens of millions watch the news and buy their local papers. Readership, viewership, and trust in the press are declining, but the media is still a dominant force in our society. As press secretary, I had the advantage of catching mistakes that otherwise might have gone unnoticed. I also spent a career working with reporters and have a certain amount of sympathy and understanding for how hard it is to do their jobs. As much as I focus here on their mistakes, it's important to remember they get a lot of things right.

Under tremendous pressure from their editors to beat their competitors, White House reporters have a hard job as they struggle with deadlines and the need to find news. News organizations themselves are under pressure to make money. That's the likely reason that the Tribune Company, the nation's second-biggest newspaper chain, in June 2004 acknowledged that it improperly exaggerated its circulation figures for two publications, *Newsday* and a Spanish-language paper.

In 2004, Pulitzer Price finalist Jack Kelley was forced to resign from his job at *USA Today*. His newspaper later determined he had made up parts of at least twenty stories over ten years. According to the *Washington Post*, "*USA Today* editors ignored repeated warnings about problems with Kelley's reporting, including from government officials, while a newsroom 'virus of fear' deterred many staffers from challenging what became the worst scandal in the Gannett's paper's history."

The *Columbia Journalism Review* is a prestigious magazine that focuses on the inner workings of the industry. Ariel Hart, whom the *CJR* describes as a "free-lance fact-checker and a stringer for the *New York Times*," wrote in the July–August 2003 issue, "Journalists surely make mistakes often, but I think we don't—or can't admit it to ourselves because the idea of a mistake is so stigmatized. It's a Catch-22. I think some reporters and their editors start to believe that unless a reader or listener telephones with a correction, they've made no mistakes. Then enough time goes by and they think they've gotten beyond mistakes. So then why double-check facts, especially the most basic ones? Why look for mistakes in reporting they know is good, when mistakes are so bad? In a perverse turn-about, the intense fear of mistakes just makes for more mistakes."

Journalists, just like people in government, are human and prone to error, not out of malice but because of mistakes made by their sources, pressures from their editors and deadlines, preformed points of view that reflect bias, and good old-fashioned goofs. Buried on the second pages of many newspapers are corrections, acknowledgments by the editors that mistakes happen. The networks have no such corrections boxes—if and when they err, they're more reluctant to admit it.

After more than twenty years as a government spokesman and source of news, I've concluded that the press's worst mistakes derive from their drive to find conflict anywhere and everywhere; their tendency to hype the news or simplify the story line so subtleties and mitigating factors are lost or diminished; their tilt toward commentary instead of straight reporting; and a subtle but important liberal bias that helps Democrats more than Republicans.

I'm still an avid reader of the news, often reading three or four newspapers a day, but I increasingly rely on the Internet to find out what's happening in the political world. With alarming frequency, different newspapers will send reporters to cover the same event, and their headlines will describe totally opposite facts to their readers, making people wonder how you can really know what's going on.

I like going online to see what the President said himself before I read it in the newspapers, where often the coverage includes just two or three sentences from a much longer presidential address. After I read his remarks (www.whitehouse.gov), I enjoy seeing how they're interpreted in the press. The *Washington Post* (www.washingtonpost.com) allows readers to watch or download newsworthy congressional testimony from its website, affording the ability to see for themselves what's said, without the filter of the media. Other websites, such as www.pollingreport.com and www.realclearpolitics.com, let readers see the latest data from a variety of polling sources without the usual commentary from the pundits. Newslink.org provides access to hundreds of newspapers across the country, as well as radio and TV stations, so you can find more than one source if you really want to read up on the news.

WHEN THE BOSTON RED SOX all-star pitcher Curt Schilling showed up for spring training in 2004, he hung a T-shirt in his locker that read, "You have the right to remain silent. Anything you say will be misquoted, and then used against you." It's not just people in politics and government who complain about the press; it's many people whose paths have been crossed by the media.

In December 2003, President Bush met with Jordan's King Abdullah in the Oval Office to talk about the prospects for peace in the Middle East. A reporter asked him what he thought about the Geneva Accord, an informal "agreement" on the terms for Palestinian-Israeli peace worked out by people who weren't in the Israeli government and therefore had no power. Ariel Sharon's government had denounced the so-called accord.

Bush began his answer with the declaration "Everybody knows where I stand," and he reminded the press of his June 24, 2002, speech that outlined his terms for peace. He repeated his message—the Palestinians needed to fight terror and live in peace with Israel. He said, again, that Israel had to create an environment for a Palestinian state to emerge. He also reiterated the need for all the Arab nations to do their part in the peace process. In other words, he said nothing new.

A reporter pushed again. "This is a productive process, the Geneva Accords?"

"I think it's productive, so long as they adhere to the principles I just outlined," Bush said.

The next day's *Washington Post* hyped his answer and took it way out of context. BUSH SAYS PEACE PLAN MAY BE "PRODUCTIVE" declared the large-print headline. "President Bush said yesterday that an unofficial peace plan denounced by the Israeli government is a 'productive' contribution to ending the long conflict between Israelis and Palestinians," the story began. Three paragraphs later it added, "It was not clear yesterday whether Bush's comments were intended as a slap at Sharon. He avoided mentioning the Geneva Accord by name, and his remark that it is productive appeared to be off the cuff and open to interpretation."

If that's the case, why did the *Post* lead with their interpretation and make it a headline? In addition to the Israeli government, Jewish groups, especially Jewish backers of the President, rejected the Geneva Accord, but a headline like that could stir up a controversy. I thought the story's headline and lead weren't an accurate portrayal of what the President said.

Too often, the drive to make news, create conflict, and find a compelling lead causes reporters to add a little "oomph" to a quote, making it sound more significant than it really is. In January 2003, the President had not yet decided whether he would seek a second United Nations resolution, this time directly authorizing the use of force in Iraq. If and when Bush made that decision, it would clearly be a significant development.

At my briefing, I was asked if there was support for a second resolution and whether the President would welcome it.

"It's desirable, but it is not mandatory," I replied.

A few minutes later, the Bloomberg wire service ran a story headlined U.S. WANTS UN RESOLUTION SUPPORTING IRAQ ATTACK, FLEISCHER SAYS. The story began, "The U.S. wants the United Nations to pass a new resolution that authorizes the use of force to disarm Iraq, White House spokesman Ari Fleischer said."

The story made my nuanced answer starker than what I really said. Why didn't the headline and the lead simply report what I said— "desirable but . . . not mandatory"? The extra oomph Bloomberg gave my quote made the story misleading. Headlines have room for only a few words, and those words too often reflect hype and controversy, less often what a source *actually* said.

The press can change quotes in small, seemingly insignificant ways that make events more dramatic than they really are.

I was with the President outside the Oval Office when Baghdad fell and jubilant Iraqis took to the streets to beat a fallen statue of Saddam with their shoes. When I briefed the press, they asked if the President had watched events in Baghdad that morning. I said he did watch parts of the coverage; he was also in meetings, and when the statue fell, he remarked, "They got it down." I told the press, "He continued to watch *with interest* [emphasis added] for a few moments. His reaction was, 'This remains a time of the utmost caution, and he also noted the power of freedom.'"

A few minutes later, CNN told its viewers that the President had watched "with *great* [emphasis added] interest." Fox reported, "Bush was thrilled," and the *New York Times* the next day told its readers that the President was "elated." In the scheme of things, those upgrades to Bush's emotions aren't very significant, but they show how the press can take a little license in their reporting.

In the spring of 2003, the *Los Angeles Times* ran an editor's note that said, "On Monday, March 31, the *Los Angeles Times* published a front-page photograph that had been altered in violation of Times policy." The *Times* told its readers that a photo of a British soldier in Iraq directing civilians to take cover from Iraqi fire had been changed by the photographer to "improve its composition." In other words, to create a more intense-looking photo—to hype the news—an image was altered. The *Times,* to its credit, caught the mistake and fired the photographer, plus it told its readers about the deceptive photo in a visible and prominent way.

In July 2003 the President visited Botswana as part of a five-day tour of Africa. His remarks there focused on the nation's emergence as a democracy and its fight against AIDS; the President was upbeat about Botswana's prospects. Good news and favorable exhortations aren't the stuff of lead stories, so the press asked him about Iraq.

"There's no question we've got a security issue in Iraq," Bush said. "And we're going to have to deal with it person by person. We're going to have to remain tough."

Two months earlier, aboard the *Abraham Lincoln,* the President had said Iraq remained "dangerous" and ten days earlier, during a reenlistment ceremony in the East Room of the White House, he said, "At present, 230,000 Americans are serving inside or near Iraq. Our whole nation, especially their families, recognizes that our people in uniform face continuing danger. We appreciate their service under difficult circumstances, and their willingness to fight for American security and Iraqi freedom. As Commander in Chief I assure them, we will stay on the offensive against the enemy. And all who attack our troops will be met with direct and decisive force."

The *Washington Post* hyped his comments from Africa and found them newsworthy. BUSH ACKNOWLEDGES TROOPS FACE DANGER, the headline blared. The story's lead sentence said Bush's comments represented an "upgrading" of his previous threat assessments in Iraq. Upgrade? It was a repeat. Sometimes when the news is slow, it's easier for the hype to slip in.

I was talking with Martha Brant, a reporter from *Newsweek,* in my office one day, and she prefaced her question by saying it fell into the "too good to check" category. I had never heard that phrase before, so I asked her what it meant. Sometimes reporters get a tip, she said, that is so juicy and they want it to be true so badly, it's "too good to check." Being a thorough reporter, she *did* check her information with me (I don't recall the specific topic), and I gave her whatever guidance I could.

I believe CBS aired the bogus document about Bush and the National Guard because it was too good to check, at least to check carefully. I think the people involved in putting the show together, including Dan Rather, thought it was probably true about Bush and let themselves be duped because they *wanted* the damaging information to be true. I believe if CBS had more Republicans in their newsroom, there would have been a greater tendency to check the story carefully before putting it on the air. After all, conservative bloggers caught the document's phony type almost right away. It's again why the field of journalism only hurts itself when so many people who enter it come from a similar ideological point of view. Balance and ideological diversity in the newsroom are good for the news business. They will only make the press better at what they do and give the public more confidence that what is reported is the actual truth.

In January 2003, *Time* magazine wrote a story alleging that President Bush had "quietly reinstated" a tradition of having the White House deliver a floral wreath to the Confederate Memorial at Arlington National Cemetery—a practice, *Time* pointed out, that his father had halted in 1990. A member of my staff, Ashley Snee, was called by *Time* before the story ran and asked for comment. She looked into it, told the reporter it was wrong, Bush didn't reinstate such a policy, and said they shouldn't print the story. *Time* didn't believe her and ran the story anyway. A week later the magazine issued a retraction. "The story is wrong," *Time* told its readers, after the damage was done.

Time's editor apologized to me, after I called him to complain. I appreciated his reaction, but the story never should have run in the first place. Just like CBS with the bogus National Guard documents, reporters sometimes want so badly to *believe* something is true that they ignore facts to the contrary. In this case, the subtext was that Bush, being a white, conservative Texan, would of course pander to redneck, Confederate-sympathizing voters, particularly those in South Carolina who'd helped him defeat John McCain in the Republican primary. Democrats and liberals are fond of that story line; Republicans would likely challenge it. The liberal columnist Maureen Dowd picked up the *Time* allegation and repeated it in her column, even though it was wrong.

Sometimes the press's errors are caused by the need to report complicated matters instantly. This is particularly a problem for the cable news shows.

In June 2003, the U.S. Supreme Court handed down its ruling in a landmark affirmative action case dealing with the admissions policies of the University of Michigan and the University of Michigan's Law School. As soon as the ruling was released, the cables sprinted into action, posting banners on the bottoms of their screens alerting viewers to the news.

SUPREME COURT ALLOWS UNIV. AFFIRMATIVE ACTION RULES, CNN's banner declared.

HIGH COURT RULES IN FAVOR OF U. OF MICHIGAN ADMISSIONS POLICY, reported MSNBC.

SUPREME COURT UPHOLDS U OF MI LAW SCHOOL AFFIRMATIVE ACTION, said Fox's banner.

None of those first reports accurately summarized the court's verdict, although Fox was literally correct, albeit too narrow in its breaking report. As news of the complicated decision sank in, the cables rushed to reverse themselves. The Court had upheld an affirmative action program at the University of Michigan Law School but reversed the school's undergraduate program that awarded extra points to minority students.

RACE FACTOR UPHELD, POINT SYSTEM THROWN OUT, CNN's banner later noted.

SUPREME COURT SPLIT DECISION OF U OF MICHIGAN AFFIRM. ACTION POLICY, said MSNBC.

COURT STRUCK DOWN U OF M UNDERGRAD POINT SYSTEM, Fox later reported.

Sometimes the press just miss the news—they forget to put it in the paper. On June 25, 2003, the CIA confirmed that an Iraqi scientist had been found with parts of a gas centrifuge used to enrich uranium buried in his front lawn. The scientist had hidden the material from UN weapons inspectors. The story was reported prominently on all the network news shows and the next day in the nation's leading daily newspapers—except the *New York Times*. When I realized that my home edition of the *Times* said nothing about this important discovery, I called the paper's D.C. bureau chief, Jill Abramson, one of the most serious and responsible people I've ever met in the news business, or any business for that matter.

We should have had this story, she told me, and she noted that a Reuters' story was included in the late editions of the *Times* after its omission had been discovered. It was a difficult day, she explained. Do I think the *New York Times,* whose editorial page stridently opposed the war, left it out on purpose? No. Mistakes do happen. I only wish that when people in government make mistakes the press wouldn't accuse us of bad motives when we're all prone to errors. It's what makes us all human, after all.

Sometimes the press get facts wrong—just plain wrong.

On November 14, 2003, Defense Secretary Donald Rumsfeld began a six-day tour of Asia during which he met with foreign leaders to discuss U.S. military deployments in their region. "In his *first trip to Asia* [emphasis added] since returning to the Pentagon for a second tour as defense secretary, Mr. Rumsfeld stressed that he was carrying no formal proposals for discussion in coming days with the leaders of Japan and South Korea," reported the *New York Times.*

One day later, the *Times* corrected their story. "An article yesterday about Defense Secretary Donald H. Rumsfeld's current visit to Asia misstated his recent travel history. He had previously visited several parts of Asia since joining the present Bush administration. This is not his first trip there."

In July 2003, the *Times* wrote a story about Bush's efforts to woo voters when he visited Pittsburgh to speak to the National Urban League. The story mentioned criticisms of the President by members of the Congressional Black Caucus. Almost at the bottom of the story, readers were told, "Mr. Bush has never met with the caucus."

He did meet with the caucus, on January 31, 2001. A LexisNexis search revealed that the *Times* never corrected its mistake.

Sometimes the press make mistakes that are too small to correct, but they're mistakes nonetheless. This one, I suspect, was nothing more than a typo.

On November 1, 2003, the President was about to leave a speech in Southaven, Mississippi, when a woman drove her car through police lines and crashed it into a loading dock not far from the President's limousine. It made for some momentary excitement, even though she was later judged not to be a threat to the President.

In a small article in the next day's *Washington Post,* readers were told, "Roads are typically closed for blocks around the president's *250-vehicle* [emphasis added] motorcade." Two hundred and fifty? A typical motorcade is twenty to twenty-five vehicles.

In early April 2003, a pileup of media errors relating to the war in Iraq took place. At the morning senior staff meeting, Andy Card was so fed up with the mistakes the newspapers were making, he asked me if there was some way I could bring attention to the fact that many newspapers were getting things wrong—just plain wrong—about the war. I told him I'd see what I could do.

The staff often complained to me about the press, and the President did so every now and then. Often I would take the press's side, thinking my co-workers, and sometimes the President, were being too sensitive if they didn't like the way the press covered an issue in which they were immersed. But I looked at the examples Andy cited and about hit the roof. Over a two-day period, the *New York Times,* the *Washington Post,* and *USA Today* ran the following four corrections:

New York Times, April 2, 2003:

A front-page news analysis article on Sunday about the political perils faced by President Bush over the war with Iraq misattributed a comment about Saddam Hussein's government being a "house of cards." While some American officials used the phrase to predict a shorter conflict and a quick collapse of the Iraqi leadership, Vice President Dick Cheney was not among them.

New York Times, April 3, 2003:

A front-page article on Tuesday about criticism voiced by American military officers in Iraq over war plans omitted two words from an earlier comment by Lt. General William S. Wallace, commander of V Corps. General Wallace said [with the omission indicated by uppercasing] "The enemy we're fighting is A BIT different from the one we war gamed against."

Washington Post, April 3, 2003:

An April 2 article incorrectly stated that Deputy Secretary of State Richard L. Armitage "made calls" to Capitol Hill regarding funds for relief and reconstruction in Iraq in the Bush Administration's supplemental spending proposal. Armitage made no such calls.

USA Today, April 4, 2003:

Wednesday's 1A cover story reported that Commerce Secretary Don Evans had said President Bush believes he was called by God to lead the nation at this time. Evans, in fact, said only that the president believes he was called to lead at this time. The story also said Evans talks with the president every day. Evans says he talks with the president often, but not every day.

I told Brian Bravo, my aide in the press office who prepared the White House clips, to place all four corrections on the front page of the White House clips on Friday, April 4, so that the senior staff, and as many other people as possible, could see the corrections for themselves. I was glad the media did the right thing and corrected their errors, but after something appears on the front page, no corrections box is big enough to set the record straight.

Another reason the public sometimes wonder where they can go to *really* find out what's going on are contradictory headlines that describe a common event. Sometimes it's baffling enough that you never do learn the truth.

GREENSPAN HINTS AT LOWER RATES—*New York Times,*
    November 7, 2003
GREENSPAN SUGGESTS CONTINUED PATIENCE ON RATES—
    Wall Street Journal, November 7, 2003

BUSH OPPOSES BILL FOR PATIENTS' RIGHTS—*USA Today,*
March 22, 2001

BUSH SEEKS COMPROMISE ON PATIENTS' RIGHTS—*Washington
Post,* March 22, 2001

BUSH VOWS TO PUSH FOR PATIENT BILL OF RIGHTS—*New York
Times,* March 22, 2001

GOP RIFT COULD DELAY EDUCATION PLAN—Associated Press,
April 27, 2001

REPUBLICANS FORCE DEBATE ON BUSH EDUCATION PLAN—
Reuters, April 27, 2001

ENERGY EXECUTIVES LIKE PROPOSALS—*New York Times,* May
18, 2001

BUSH PLAN DRAWS MIXED REACTION FROM ENERGY EXECS
—Reuters, May 18, 2001

EXPERTS CONCLUDE OIL DRILLING HAS HURT ALASKA'S NORTH
SLOPE—*New York Times,* March 5, 2003

MIXED VERDICT OFFERED ON ALASKA OIL DRILLING—*Washington
Post,* March 5, 2003

ABORTION PILL SLOW TO WIN USERS AMONG WOMEN AND THEIR
DOCTORS—*New York Times,* September 25, 2002

ABORTION PILL SALES RISING, FIRM SAYS—*Washington Post,*
September 25, 2002

LARGE TRIAL FINDS AIDS VACCINE FAILS TO STOP INFECTION—
New York Times, February 24, 2003

VACCINE FOR AIDS APPEARS TO WORK—*USA Today,* February
24, 2003

NATIONS LINING UP TO BACK U.S. WAR—*Dallas Morning News,*
February 9, 2003

KEY ALLIES WIDEN RIFT WITH U.S.—*USA Today,* February 10, 2003

U.S. HOLDS BACK FROM ATTACKING REBELS IN NAJAF; ABRUPT
   REVERSAL OF PLAN—*New York Times,* August 12, 2004
MARINES OPEN BIG ASSAULT; U.S. ENTERS 8TH DAY OF FIGHTING IN
   NAJAF—*USA Today,* August 12, 2004

Sometimes the problem isn't just the headline, it's the story:

Even as the U.S. prepares for possible war against Iraq, there is
late word tonight of a major escalation in the U.S. war on
terror. President Bush is sending about three thousand troops to
the southern Philippines to fight Muslim militants.
                                    —CBS News, February 20, 2003

NBC News has learned the Pentagon is sending 750 U.S.
troops to the Philippines, where they will hunt Abu Sayaf
terrorist guerrillas there who are aligned with Al Qaeda.
                                    —NBC News, February 20, 2003

US COMBAT FORCE OF 1,700 IS HEADED TO THE PHILIPPINES
                            —New York Times, February 21, 2003

The independent commission charged with investigating the
Sept. 11, 2001, terrorist attacks said it hasn't received adequate
support from the White House, and raised the possibility that it
may not finish its work by a May 2004 deadline.
                            —Wall Street Journal, July 9, 2003

Although their intent today was clearly to create discomfort for
the White House, [Commission Chairmen] Mr. Kean and Mr.
Hamilton said repeatedly that they were optimistic that the
panel could complete its work on time and that it would offer
the most complete account available of the events that led to
the terrorist attacks.   *—New York Times,* July 9, 2003

Sometimes the contradiction is found on different pages of the same paper:

The sudden resignation of Mahmoud Abbas as prime minister of the Palestinian Authority stunned Bush administration officials today.
—*New York Times,* September 7, 2003, by Steven R. Weisman

White House officials said today that it had become clear within the last few weeks that Mr. Abbas would not survive as prime minister.
—*New York Times,* September 7, 2003, by James Bennett

Here are two prominent papers' take on the same development:

The United States agreed to hold informal one-on-one discussions with North Korea next month during multilateral talks about Pyongyang's nuclear weapon program.
—*Washington Post,* August 2, 2003

North Korea and the United States announced today that they had agreed to hold regional talks over North Korea's nuclear weapons program, in a victory for the Bush administration, which resisted 10 months of pressure to hold one-on-one talks with the North. —*New York Times,* August 2, 2003

And finally . . .

AT GOP DEBATE, A UNIFIED BLAST AT BUSH—*Washington Post,*
    October 23, 1999
5 GOP HOPEFULS KICK OFF DEBATES; THEY ATTACK THE PRESIDENT
    [CLINTON] BUT LARGELY IGNORE AN ABSENT BUSH—*New*
    York Times, October 23, 1999

FIFTEEN

GOING TO THE UNITED NATIONS

I N MID-AUGUST 2002, Condi Rice and I met for dinner at Diamond Back's Restaurant in Waco, Texas, a steak place forty minutes from the President's ranch. The pace of business in Washington didn't lend itself to relaxing evenings with the national security adviser, but life in Crawford afforded us the chance to kick back and talk. A table of Secret Service agents protecting Condi sat nearby. Also a few tables away sat a group of about a dozen White House reporters who had traveled to Texas with the President. Both tables kept an eye on us, the agents to keep the national security adviser safe, the press, wondering what we were talking about.

I asked Condi what the President was going to speak about in his address to the UN General Assembly, scheduled for September. The Middle East, she said, and values, with a heavy emphasis on the Israeli-Palestinian dispute and the potential to achieve democracy in the region. In the wake of a constant stream of stories describing potential war plans for Iraq, and following former National Security Adviser Brent Scowcroft's op-ed in the *Wall Street Journal* opposing military action there, I suggested that the focus of the world would be on Iraq and the President's intentions. If he doesn't address the issue, I said, the press will ask visiting heads of state what they think about Bush's threats against Iraq and that will be the news, no matter what Bush says.

After nearly a year's worth of tough talk from the President, Iraq was almost the only issue on the press's minds that August. I also asked her about reports that Saddam had weapons of mass destruction. He does, she said. He has biological and chemical weapons. She said he didn't have nuclear weapons.

The next morning the President called me to say Condi had filled him in on what I was thinking. He thought it was an interesting approach. I wasn't the only one urging an address on Iraq at the General Assembly—several others in the administration thought it was the best course of action as well.

When the President returned to Washington, the administration was in the middle of an uncomfortable dispute between the secretary of state and the Vice President. Secretary Powell, echoing the President's call for a return of inspectors to Iraq, was taken by surprise when the Vice President made a speech on August 26 stating, "A return of inspectors would provide no assurance whatsoever of his [Saddam's] compliance with U.N. resolutions. On the contrary, there is a great danger it would provide false comfort that Saddam was somehow 'back in the box.'" Three days later, the Vice President gave another speech about the threat from Iraq, but this time he softened his statement about inspections and omitted the line about "false comfort."

Reporters drilled in on the split.

"Is the President disturbed to see the kind of stories that suggest Colin Powell is not onboard with administration policy? And how can the President let these—his administration figures speak so differently about something that's such a priority for him?"

"Well, they haven't spoken differently. They've spoken the same," I said, thinking of the Vice President's second speech, not his first one. "I think this is much ado about no difference."

"So the President agrees with Secretary Powell that there must be an international consensus before there is any attack on Iraq?"

"The President has always said he will consult," I answered. "The President has always said that through leadership, others follow. That creates coalitions and that continues to be the President's view and the secretary's view and the administration's view." I was doing my best to find the links that united Bush, Cheney, and Powell.

"And Vice President Cheney agrees that there—with Secretary Powell on the need for inspectors to go back in?"

"The American position, as the Vice President said in his remarks, and Secretary Powell said, and as the President said, is that arms inspectors in Iraq are a means to an end, but the end is knowledge that Iraq has lived up to its promises that it made to end the Gulf War, that it has in fact disarmed, that it does not possess weapons of mass destruction."

"So hundreds of reporters are wrong? We're seeing a gap that doesn't exist?"

"I think it's much ado about no difference," I replied.

The White House press corps love stories about splits between administration officials. Publicity about a split only makes the split worse. President Bush believed the place to resolve differences was in front of him or in private, not in the press. No one in any walk of life wants family fights to go public. It's like pouring oil on a fire, and the White House press corps never minded watching a good fire burn. The press had good reason to see a difference of approach between Powell and Cheney; I had good reason to see the areas where their views were unified. The President's instructions to me were to do my best to stop the feuds from breaking out in public, but there was only so far I could go. A split is a split is a split, and the press are going to write about it if they find out about it. This split played out before their very eyes. I didn't need to make it worse by acknowledging it at the briefing, but I had to be careful about how far I went denying it. Thank goodness the Vice President gave that second speech, otherwise I wouldn't have had much of a leg to stand on.

At the next day's briefing, reporters bore in again on the Powell-Cheney split.

"A follow-up, Ari. Yesterday you said that all the players in the cabinet are singing from the same page about Iraq, but the perception—using that word, perception out there is there is a difference between what Secretary [sic] Cheney has been saying and Secretary of State Powell has been saying. You claim there's no difference."

"That's correct," I said, as the room burst into laughter.

"Can you elaborate? Because as far as the perception again," it sounds as if "there is some controversy there. As far as inspectors entering Iraq."

"Let me go back to the drawing board on the question of inspectors and remind you of something that the President of the United States has said. This is quoting from the President on January 16th of this year, early this year. And he said, 'I expect Saddam Hussein to let inspectors back into the country. We want to know whether he's developing weapons of mass destruction. He claims he's not; let the world in to see.'"

ON SEPTEMBER 4, the President met in the Cabinet Room for just under an hour with House Speaker Dennis Hastert and Minority Leader Richard Gephardt, Senate Majority Leader Tom Daschle and Minority Leader Trent Lott, and other congressional leaders. Throughout August, many Democrats were critical of Bush's intentions toward Iraq, and they demanded he consult with them. If the United States was going to war, the Congress must have a say, argued the Democrats, as did a few Republicans.

If they wanted a role, Bush was about to give it to them.

Bush began the meeting, seated in the middle of the long table in the President's chair, the one with a higher back than all the rest, and didn't stop talking for ten minutes. I took notes.

"Saddam Hussein is a serious threat to the United States, to his neighbors, and to the people who disagree with him inside Iraq," the President said, just warming up. "Before I arrived, regime change was policy. It was overwhelmingly supported in Congress, even more so since 9/11. No one thought at the time of that vote that the U.S. could be a battlefield. But we're vulnerable. Israel our friend is vulnerable. I want to start a dialogue in America [and] in the U.S. Congress.

"Doing nothing is not an option and I hope Congress agrees. That's an important debate, a good, honest debate.

"When a decision is made, I will come to Congress for a resolution," the President declared, throwing down the gauntlet. If you want a role—you'll have a role. I want you to vote, Bush was saying. "The American people want that to happen and I want that to happen. [We'll have] an honest debate about an incredibly serious threat.

"Saddam Hussein has stiffed the United Nations Security Council," Bush continued. "He sidestepped, he crawfished. He has no intention to comply. If the UN wants to be relevant, they need to do something about it. The fact that the world has not dealt with him has created a bigger monster. The Congress is going to be at our side as we make this decision. I will continue to make this case to the world.

"That's why I called you here," Bush concluded.

The room sat silent for a moment, and then the members started to do the talking.

"What new, tangible evidence is there?" asked one of the Democrats. "Who leads the new regime, how do we do it logistically if there's no support from the region? Will this be a worldwide effort or unilateral?" he continued.

We want to work with the UN, Bush said, otherwise we will have to act unilaterally.

The President also told the group he believed Iraq could eventually be a democracy. One leading Democratic senator who later voted to authorize the use of force against Iraq told the President, "I will be with you on condition we level with the American people—we'll have to stay [in Iraq] awhile."

"You're right," Bush said.

"If you can get it done without staying, we'll give you the Nobel Peace Prize," the senator said. "I'll support you for President," he added.

"I don't know whether that will help me or hurt me," Bush said to the room's amusement.

A Democratic senator who voted against the war cautioned the President. "Senior military officials have concerns about an attack," he said. "Saddam Hussein is a survivalist."

"He's an invader," Bush rebutted. "He has power beyond his borders. It's more complex than either/or. What will he be like in five years from now?"

The press were let in the room, and the President gave it to them straight.

"One of the things I made very clear to the members here is that doing nothing about that serious threat is not an option for the United States," he said, referring to Saddam. "I also made it very clear that we look forward to an open dialogue with Congress and the American people about the threat, and that not only will we consult with the United States Congress—we, being the administration—but that my administration will fully participate in any hearings that the Congress wishes to have on this subject, on the subject about how to make America a more secure country, how to best protect the American families in our country.

"At the appropriate time, this administration will go to the Congress to seek approval for [any action] necessary to deal with the threat."

Three hours later, the President met with his economic team in the Oval Office to get an update on the budget and economy. Revenue was dropping off at an astounding rate, he was told. Contrary to previous projections, there was now no chance the budget would be in balance by 2005. One of his advisers said he might need to propose an additional stimulus plan to kick-start the weak economy. No need, said Treasury Secretary O'Neill, who believed the economy was already on its way to recovery.

The next day Bush began a series of phone calls to world leaders, especially those on the Security Council, to tell them he would be giving an important speech at the United Nations and he hoped they would listen carefully. He told several of them that Saddam was a threat but he had made no decision yet about the use of military force. He promised to consult.

Shortly before his speech to the United Nations, Bush met in the Oval Office with Portuguese Prime Minister Durao Barroso, and he gave him a sneak preview of his upcoming address.

"I'm seeking a global solution at the UN. The truth is if I was a unilateralist, I'd have attacked already. But I agree with you that we need an internationalist solution."

When Saddam is gone, Bush added, "we'll invite the UN in to work on a confederation. Iraq's government is going to form, but freedom is their direction." His guest, who supported the attack, admonished the President that he needed to lead the world by being *with* the world. "Some of your friends are skeptical," the President was told.

"I have a coalition that wants to attack immediately," Bush replied. "I have a different coalition than you do," he added, referring to different camps in his own administration. "I'm not anxious for a fight. It's a tough decision. I had to hug the moms and dads who lost their sons in Afghanistan. It's conceivable that he [Saddam] will honor commitments and that would be wonderful. Anything short of that is unacceptable."

The next day, September 11, 2002, marked the sad one-year anniversary of the attack. The President visited the Pentagon, then traveled to the field in Pennsylvania where Flight 93 crashed to honor the heroism of the passengers who gave their lives so others might live. That plane had been destined for the White House, or perhaps the Capitol. I stood in the open field with my co-workers, and once again, a heavy sadness descended. I watched in silence as the President, again, hugged every soul he could find. The Secret Service stood back and let him be alone with the family members of those who lost their lives. We left the field and went to the site of the remaining two attacks, Ground Zero in Manhattan. This time there was no smell, no mountain of collapsed steel, no families wondering if their relatives might get out alive. The President walked down a ramp into the cleaned up pit where the Twin Towers once stood, hugging and consoling the families of those whose lives were taken in the first two attacks on that terrible morning just one year before.

Later that night, the President addressed the nation from Ellis Island.

"September 11, 2001, will always be a fixed point in the life of America. The loss of so many lives left us to examine our own. Each of us was reminded that we are here only for a time, and these counted days should be filled with things that last and matter: love for our families, love for our neighbors, and for our country; gratitude for life and to the Giver of life.

"There is a line in our time, and in every time, between those who believe all men are created equal, and those who believe that some men and women and children are expendable in the pursuit of power. There is a line in our time, and in every time, between the defenders of human liberty and those who seek to master the minds and souls of others. Our generation has now heard history's call, and we will answer it."

The next day, the President crossed midtown Manhattan to deliver his second major address to the nation in a twenty-four-hour period, this one before the United Nations General Assembly.

Before his address, the President met privately with UN Secretary-General Kofi Annan. Bush told him he wanted the UN to be relevant, and as they talked, the President reached for a bottle of Poland Spring water. Watching him, Secretary Powell took the bottle from his hands, remembering that the President once drank directly from his water bottle during a NATO meeting in Brussels, apparently offending some of his hosts.

"He's afraid I'll drink out of the bottle," Bush said with a smile. "Remember those stories of the Texas cowboy—it's true," he added as he took his bottle of water back from the secretary of state. He poured it into his glass as the room broke into laughter.

A minute later he told the Secretary-General that the UN was important. He also said, "I love my country. I'm going to do what's right for America."

The meeting concluded, and the President left to address the General Assembly, where he made his case against Iraq, calling on the UN to at long last enforce its own oft-violated resolutions.

"We know that Saddam Hussein pursued weapons of mass murder even when inspectors were in his country. Are we to assume that he stopped when they left?" Bush asked. "The history, the logic, and the facts lead to one conclusion: Saddam Hussein's regime is a grave and gathering danger. To suggest otherwise is to hope against the evidence. To assume this regime's good faith is to bet the lives of millions and the peace of the world in a reckless gamble. And this is a risk we must not take.

"All the world now faces a test, and the United Nations a difficult and defining moment. Are Security Council resolutions to be honored and enforced, or cast aside without consequence? Will the United Nations serve the purpose of its founding, or will it be irrelevant?"

And then the President pledged, "My nation will work with the U.N. Security Council to meet our common challenge. If Iraq's regime defies us again, the world must move deliberately, decisively to hold Iraq to account. We will work with the U.N. Security Council for the necessary resolutions. But the purposes of the United States should not be doubted. The Security Council resolutions will be enforced—the just demands of peace and security will be met—or action will be unavoidable. And a regime that has lost its legitimacy will also lose its power."

His speech concluded, the President boarded his motorcade, drove less than one block across First Avenue, and by the time his limo arrived at the U.S. Mission, across from the UN, the last car in his motorcade hadn't even left the UN. Security being security, he wasn't allowed to walk across the street.

At the U.S. Mission, he met with President Hamid Karzai of Afghanistan and reflected on his speech. "It's like speaking to the wax museum," Bush noted. "No one moves."

But the President's speech did move people; it moved the world. In characteristic Bush style, he threw down the gauntlet using plain language and direct terms, calling on the UN to mean what it says or risk becoming a meaningless debating society, going the way of the failed League of Nations.

An international organization that excelled in providing relief aid, food aid, and condemnations of Israel, the UN had failed to take action against genocide in Rwanda, and it couldn't even authorize military action against Serbia after its campaign of ethnic cleansing. But Bush, the so-called Texan unilateralist, woke the UN and caused it to look in the mirror, and many didn't like what they saw. Whether they could do anything about it remained to be seen.

One week after his speech in the UN, the President met in the Oval Office with the Czech Republic's famed leader Vaclav Havel, a former dramatist and essayist who had courageously criticized the Communist Party during the Cold War.

"You were the first leader to support me," Bush told his guest, referring to a NATO meeting early in 2001 when Havel had spoken out in favor of the President's plans for a missile defense. "I've learned lessons from you," Bush continued. "It's important to speak with moral clarity and when you see wrong, speak about the wrong you see."

Havel told the President, "If evil had been confronted in 1938, maybe there would have been no World War II." It wasn't the only time the President would hear that message.

As the meeting between the two similar-minded leaders broke up, Bush told Havel, "Behind my tough talk is peace. I long for peace. But we can't compromise with terror. I truly believe we will achieve peace in the Middle East. The catalyst for democracy is going to be a Palestinian state. When the Palestinian people move beyond Arafat, I personally will weigh in heavy with the Israelis to promote democracy and relieve the suffering of the Palestinian people. I won't stop until they throw me out of office or my time runs out."

SIXTEEN

JUST ONE BULLET;
ELECTION DAY, 2002;
AND THE INSPECTIONS RESUME

I N THE FALL OF 2002, the President gave the United Nations "weeks, not months" to come up with a resolution that authorized the return of weapons inspectors to Iraq, this time carrying out their mission in a forceful manner, with the right to search anywhere and everywhere, even inside Saddam's palaces, plus the right to question Iraqi scientists without the presence of Iraqi officials, outside Iraq if necessary.

Secretary Powell turned his efforts to the difficult diplomacy that ensued, working to secure the votes of reluctant nations, four of whom could veto the resolution if they chose. Tensions escalated as diplomats clashed and Bush made clear that Saddam was going to be removed, one way or another.

German Chancellor Gerhard Schroeder, running uphill for reelection in a difficult economy, found a rallying cry among the German people by opposing Bush's efforts in Iraq. He made it clear, after assuring the President privately that he understood Bush's objectives and would not stand in the way, that Germany would oppose the American effort to remove Saddam. Nor, he said, would it ever send troops to support the United States. One of his ministers compared Bush's actions to Adolf Hitler's, further inflaming a growing split between the United States and Germany. France, under President Jacques Chirac, seemed to be enjoying their role as an obstacle to the one remaining superpower in the world, putting them on a worldwide stage as they used their leverage to influence the outcome at the UN.

At the same time, Congress debated a resolution authorizing the use of force in Iraq, and passions were running hot on the Hill. Republicans were largely in favor of Bush's efforts, while Democrats were deeply split.

Bush, having made the decision to go to the UN, stuck with it. He grew frustrated with the pace of action there, but he never changed his mind that it was the right thing to do. His critics called him dangerously prone to unilateral action, while many conservative Republicans didn't trust the UN and were uncomfortable with his decision to go there at all. None of this deterred Bush. As much as he disliked the UN process, he wanted the body's support. Looking ahead at the role of the UN, the President told a group of newspaper owners during a meeting in the Roosevelt Room in late September, "If we have to use military force, it will be fast, furious, and we'll win. If Saddam Hussein goes, we will clean that country out of weapons of mass destruction and the UN will have a role in creating a post-Saddam government."

A few days later, the President received an update in the Oval Office on the likelihood of Congress passing a resolution authorizing military action. At one point in the meeting, Karl Rove told Bush that media polls showed the American people increasingly supported the use of force.

"If it were 20–80 against the use of force," Bush snapped at Karl, "I'd still go after the guy. That's what you need to know about me. Is he a threat to the country, and do we need to deal with him now, instead of five years from now?" The President wasn't asking Karl, or anyone else on the domestic staff, for an opinion; instead, he seemed to be summing up the essence of the decision he was weighing—is this war better fought now, or later, when Saddam is stonger?

On October 1, during my televised briefing, I was asked about a recent estimate by the Congressional Budget Office that showed the cost of war would be between $9 and $13 billion.

"The President has not made any decisions about military action or what military option he might pursue," I said. "And so I think it's impossible to speculate."

Instead of stopping right there, my brain and mouth somehow got disconnected. I continued, "I can only say that the cost of a one-way ticket is substantially less than that," meaning that Saddam could choose to leave the country voluntarily. "The cost of one bullet if the Iraqi people take it on themselves," I added, "is substantially less than that."

At first, the press corps didn't seem to notice what I'd said. They went on to other topics. But after a few minutes, an astute reporter, Jeanne Cummings of the *Wall Street Journal,* followed up.

"Is the White House advocating assassination as a possible option for Saddam Hussein?"

Uh-oh. I had stepped in it, I realized.

The press, for some odd reason, asked only one or two more questions about my "one bullet" theory, and I muddled through them simply by saying regime change was our policy.

As soon as the briefing was over, I entered the Oval Office to turn myself in. I told the President what I'd said, and he wasn't pleased. That's *not* our policy, he admonished me, saying I had better fix it.

I spent the rest of the day on the phone with reporters, telling them I had misspoken; what I said was not an expression of administration policy. Just when I thought I'd got the genie back into the bottle, Lloyd Grove of the *Washington Post* called me, intrigued with my interest in bullets, and he asked me what types of guns I owned and which ones were my personal favorites.

Growing up in Westchester, I never owned a gun, not even one with BBs in it. I went skeet shooting once with a friend from West Texas, and those skeets could not have been safer than when I held the shotgun. It was one of only two times in my life I had ever even *touched* a firearm.

"Lloyd," I said, "you got it wrong. Let me put it to you this way. I had only one bullet to give my country, and I used it to shoot myself in the foot."

THE NEXT DAY, the President announced a bipartisan agreement on the terms of a joint congressional resolution authorizing the use of armed force against Iraq. He was joined for a Rose Garden announcement by House Democratic leader Dick Gephardt and Senator Joe Lieberman, as well as Speaker Dennis Hastert and Senator John McCain. The President was leading, the Congress was agreeing, and the country seemed to be rallying.

The press increasingly sensed we were going to war, and some of their questions became repeats of the ones I had refused to answer in the lead-up to military action in Afghanistan, questions about specific military plans.

"I would assume that when the military goes in there," asked CBS's John Roberts, "they're not going to start hunting around for all of the chemical and biological weapons factories first, they're going to go for the head, correct?"

"I'm just not in a position to give you an indication of what a potential military tactic may or may not be," I said.

"I'm not asking about tactics, I'm asking about policy," John followed up.

IN MID-OCTOBER, I traveled to my alma mater, Middlebury College in Vermont, to receive an alumni achievement award. A reporter told me that they were expecting a large number of demonstrators at my speech, and Vermont being Vermont, I knew it would be true.

Middlebury is a wonderful place, a great school, and home to a little more than two thousand students. When we got to town, my fiancée, Becki Davis, and I went straight to a little deli for lunch; there I bumped into a large fellow in a police uniform. He told me it was lucky timing that we'd met, explaining he would be one of the people protecting me that night. Protecting me, I thought. This was getting interesting.

As Becki and I walked around the campus, we saw flyers everywhere urging students to protest my receiving the award. The Middlebury campus is not exactly a hotbed of activism, but I knew Burlington and Montpelier weren't too far away. Vermont, after all, did elect a socialist to Congress, and George W. Bush is not very popular in the Green Mountain State.

I arrived for my speech to a capacity crowd of seven hundred students and townspeople in the school's Mead Chapel, while an estimated fifteen hundred protesters marched outside, declaring their opposition to "Bush's war." Several protesters screamed at me during my remarks and were escorted out by campus security. The students were polite; a few said they supported Bush's position, and many others asked tough questions and stated their opposition to war. Even with the protests, it was great to be back in Middlebury, and I enjoyed the give-and-take with the students, during which I defended the President's approach to ousting Saddam Hussein. When it was time to go, a large group of protesters moved from the front of the chapel to the back door, knowing I would leave from there. The town police, augmented by the state police, formed a protective circle around me and escorted me through an angry crowd that formed long lines on both sides of the sidewalk where I passed.

"Baby killer," they screamed. "Warmonger," some yelled. I didn't let it get to me. I believed in President Bush, believed what I told the students, and no matter what, it was good to be back at Middlebury.

ON OCTOBER 16, Ariel Sharon visited with the President in the Oval Office. Bush pressed the Prime Minister on his intentions toward Arafat. "The key is to help new leadership emerge," the President said. "We must work to make the new institutions and developing state work. Arafat is on his way out," Bush added. "Don't make him a big shot. He's a little shot. Just let him fade away."

On Iraq, Bush said, "My first choice is to avoid military action, but if there is military action, I expect you to keep the neighborhood quiet. You need to protect yourself, but you need to work with us."

Sharon replied, "We understand the sensitivity. The Jewish people have struggled to avoid extermination for thousands of years. It's my job as leader of the Jewish state in Jerusalem to defend the Jewish people. We'll take every step to make it easy for you, and us."

NEGOTIATIONS OVER the resolution at the UN continued to drag on. The President's "weeks, not months" time line was being tested. Five weeks after he had announced his schedule, Bush told Lord Robertson, the NATO Secretary-General, that working with the UN was like being in a mosh pit, where you get passed from one set of hands to another, unsure of your own destiny. The President was certain of the outcome he sought—a tough UN resolution—he just didn't like the messy process of getting there. He also told the NATO leader, "This can be done peacefully—it's remote. I'm the guy who makes the decision, but I'm also the guy who gets to hug the widows. I take this seriously." Countless times I heard the President privately hope for a peaceful solution so he wouldn't have to commit our military to war. He knew if war came, there would be more widows he would have to console.

Election Day was approaching, making reporters' political antennae go up. In a sign of how the press are expert at finding politics in whatever actions the administration takes, or doesn't take, I was asked by a reporter from the *New York Times* about the timing of the vote in the United Nations.

"Are you waiting for the midterm elections to be over before you bring this UN resolution to a vote?" Elisabeth Bumiller asked me.

"The timing," I said, "is ultimately going to be decided by the diplomats who are involved in it. And this will take place this week or next, depending on what the status of the talks is."

"So domestic politics are not at all a concern?"

"If somebody wants to say, Why are you voting on it the week before the election, if the vote *is* the week before the election—they're going to ask that question. If they want to say, Why are you voting on it the week *after* the election, if it's voted on the week after the election, they're going to ask *that* question. I fail to see how anybody can make the case that voting on it before or after benefits one party or another. The vote will be decided by the diplomats in accordance with the progress of the talks. It just so happens there is an election at the same time."

"You don't think forcing a vote on a UN resolution before an election might scare off some voters, make voters nervous?" Bumiller pressed.

"It's not the United States that's dragging its feet," I pointed out. "The United States went up to the United Nations on September 12. If this could have been resolved weeks ago, I think the President would have been very satisfied."

As the election approached, the President traveled extensively to campaign for Republican candidates. Because we were on the road so much, I had fewer on-camera briefings to do, and instead, I briefed the smaller press pool in the back of Air Force One each day. Listening to the President's speech from the back of an airplane hangar or hotel ballroom wasn't exactly heavy lifting.

A few days before the election, the President's traveling party spent the night in Florida, after Bush had campaigned earlier in the day in Tennessee, as well as Atlanta and Savannah, Georgia. The next morning, as the motorcade pulled up to Air Force One for a flight to Illinois, Minnesota, South Dakota, and Iowa, I noticed that Karl Rove had left his laundry bag in the car. I grabbed it to give to him.

But when I arrived under the wing of Air Force One, where Karl and the press corps were standing waiting for the President to board the plane, I told Karl that I now possessed his "dirty laundry" and would release it to the media. He took off after me, and for a few moments, the two of us were running around like fools under Air Force One's wing, with Karl demanding the return of his laundry. We were all in a good mood, and it showed.

Karl and I did a joint briefing to the press about the election from the back of Air Force One, and we were asked about the Dirty Laundry caper by Associated Press's Scott Lindlaw. "There was some interesting horseplay out on the tarmac. I can only attribute that to this punishing schedule. Is the President getting stir-crazy at all with all this travel and all these hours?"

Karl went first, jokingly responding, "I would say that the horseplay on the tarmac—which was completely inappropriate—did not involve the President, but instead involved the President's chief communicator attempting to air the dirty laundry of another member of the President's traveling party in front of the press. And I think this is reprehensible conduct. And I know the President feels strongly about this serious divide among members of the senior staff."

"Let me— Hold on here for a second," I butted in. "There has been a serious accusation by the press, that this is a tight-lipped White House. As part of our new sunshine policy to let the press into things that previously [were] unseen, it's important for [Karl's] dirty laundry to be aired."

Karl then got serious and told the press how close we expected the election to be, and that anything could happen.

On Election Day, November 5, Republicans made history. Historically, the party in the White House loses seats in its first midterm election. Instead, we regained control of the Senate, making it the first time ever that a President's party took the Senate in his first off-year election. Only twice since the Civil War had an incumbent President's party gained seats in the House during his first off-year election. Republicans gained House seats as well. The President, who usually goes to bed around 10:00, stayed up until 1:00 A.M., monitoring the results and calling winners, and a few losers, from the residence. It was a great day, and a great night.

The President invited me to the third-floor residence of the Mansion to watch the election results come in. I loved being there. After the contested 2000 election, 2002 seemed like sweet vindication. I remembered well when Republicans took control of the House for the first time in forty years in 1994. Eight years later, watching events from the President's residence was a rare and wonderful moment.

The next day, the press asked me about the election results and what they meant for the future.

"Is this the end of checks and balances for the moment, and is the President poised to govern by fiat?" someone asked.

What a ridiculous question, I thought.

I controlled myself and replied, "Our system is built with checks and balances in mind. And that is the genius of our founding fathers." I also pointed out that with Republicans having such slender control in the House and Senate, it remained important to work with Democrats.

To me, this was another example of the briefing losing some of its relevance. Half the briefing is informative, with serious questions that *can* be answered. But overwrought questions like that can't be taken too seriously. Republicans held a one-vote margin in the Senate, where sixty votes are needed to get things done. Yet a reporter, the transcript doesn't indicate who, wanted to know if checks and balances had come to an end. Reporters must always have the right to ask whatever they want; but sometimes the briefing room made the questions a little less than penetrating. There were just some questions you couldn't take seriously, but my job was to stand there and take them.

At my Election Day briefing, I was asked an interesting question about the war on terror. Earlier that day, the press had reported that the United States government, working with Yemeni officials, had killed a senior associate of Al Qaeda who was also a suspect in the bombing of the USS *Cole*. I wouldn't confirm or deny it.

"By not addressing the specifics, are you saying that the United States will engage in a shadowy war, that there will be killings around the world using military equipment and personnel in the name of the American people that the American people will not be told about?"

"The President has made very plain to the American people that the United States is going to bring to justice the terrorists, Al Qaeda terrorists particularly, as our way of protecting the country," I replied.

"Secretly, if necessary?" a reporter asked, sounding alarmed.

"The President has said very plainly to the American people that this is a war in which there will sometimes be visible moments and sometimes there are going to be long lulls. And there are going to be things that are done that the American people may never know about. That is the very nature of the war on terror. And the President makes no bones about it, he will protect the American people in this war."

"Ari, shouldn't justice involve a judge, a jury, a prosecution, a defense?"

"Absolutely," I replied. "When it's a case of American citizens and when it's a case of anything covered under America's laws and our—

America's constitutional protections for America's citizens. When it comes to terrorists who seek to kill us, the President will defend and protect America."

ON THURSDAY, NOVEMBER 7, I took a brief vacation to get married to Becki Davis, who worked in the White House at the Office of Management and Budget. We had met in April 2001, became engaged one year later, and at the age of forty-two, I had finally met the woman I wanted to marry. I said "I do" in Indianapolis, Indiana, on November 9, 2002.

We traveled to the small, beautiful, and quiet island of Nevis in the British West Indies for our honeymoon. The Secret Service advised me to use a fake name when I checked into my hotel there, and I realized this was my chance to be whoever I wanted to be. That meant I was going to be a New York Yankee.

I thought about registering as Derek Jeter, but that would be too obvious a name. I also thought about becoming the Yankees' second baseman at the time, Alfonso Soriano, but I realized I didn't look much like an Alfonso. Then it hit me—I became Bernie Williams, the Yankee's all-star center fielder. He had one of those all-purpose, common names, so I could easily be a Bernie Williams. For me, it was enjoyable being the Yankees' center fielder, until everyone on staff at the hotel kept calling Becki Mrs. Williams. I had to wait until we got back to the States to hear my wife called Mrs. Fleischer.

The morning after Becki and I returned from our restful one-week honeymoon, it was off to accompany the President on a five-day visit to east Europe. While I was out to dinner with a group of reporters in Prague, the *Post*'s Lloyd Grove tracked me down, having heard that I became Bernie Williams during my honeymoon. He wanted to know if it was true. It was, I confessed. He asked me why I didn't use George Steinbrenner's name. The whole point, I said, was *not* to become a target.

JUST BEFORE MY WEDDING, the UN had unanimously passed a Security Council resolution to send weapons inspectors back into Iraq. In Prague, the President met with Czech President Vaclav Havel and reiterated his concerns about Saddam Hussein being a danger.

"Contrary to my image as a Texan with two guns, I'm more comfortable with a posse," Bush said in Havel's office inside Prague Castle. "In order to make words effective, there must be a strong sense of purpose, and I'm not going to yield in that strong sense of purpose.

"Our nation loves freedom—[it's a] God-given gift, and we worry about the plight of the Iraqi people. He [Saddam]'s dangerous to peace, he's a killer and there will be rejoicing in the streets when we free the Iraqi people, one way or another."

The President was in Prague for a NATO summit in which the ranks of the organization grew by seven, as Bulgaria, Estonia, Latvia, Lithuania, Romania, Slovakia, and Slovenia were admitted to the Western alliance. He met privately with France's President Chirac, and as the two leaders discussed Iraq, Bush said, "We're prepared to stay. The UN will play a role. Iraq needs to be whole and pluralistic. We have no desire to impose our will or pick winners and losers. I presume you want a role in post-Saddam Iraq and we'll work together."

The President also traveled to Lithuania, where he met with four presidents of the newly free nations of the Baltic, and then to Romania. All these nations used to live under Communism, and now they were members of NATO. Hundreds of thousands of people poured into the streets of Lithuania and Romania to greet the President and to cheer for him, and the United States. Whenever President Bush heard that Europe was against him, or that he was a unilateralist, he thought of those who had just escaped oppression and took solace in the fact that Europe was *not* against him; it was split. The American press typically simplified and overstated the case about Bush and Europe, or they ignored the leaders of those western European nations who supported the President. There *was* a split, with the leaders of France, Germany, Belgium, and Luxembourg against Bush's plans for Iraq, and the United Kingdom, Spain, Italy, and virtually all the leaders of east Europe with the President. Polls showed the people of Europe largely opposed Bush's policies, but they had also opposed President Reagan's. Protesters should never stop a leader from doing what he or she thinks is right. Reagan's policies turned out to be right and led to a more peaceful world. I believe that as Iraq increasingly becomes peaceful and free, no matter how long it takes, Bush too will be proven right.

ON DECEMBER 4, 2002, the President met in the Oval Office with a group of Jewish leaders to discuss Iraq, Israel, and peace in the Middle East.

"The best thing we can do for Israel," Bush said, "is to rid the world of Saddam Hussein." The President thought that was true for the rest of the world as well. He said he wasn't sure when that would happen and added that, in building an international coalition, he lost some control of the process. The UN inspections of Iraq had just begun. He also wondered aloud how the United States could flex its military muscles without them atrophying over time.

As for the Palestinians, Bush said, "The irony is I'm the best friend for the Palestinians because I'm the one guy who had the courage to blow the whistle on Palestinian leaders."

When it was time to go, he summed things up, saying, "I believe two-thirds of the axis of evil will become the axis of good," expressing his faith that peaceful change would come to Iran given the clamoring for reform by the nation's young people. As for North Korea, the prospect of fundamental change in its totalitarian government wasn't as bright, the President thought.

The UN inspectors were settling into Iraq as American opinion increasingly favored military action. The year ended with many people thinking war was around the corner.

SEVENTEEN

GROUNDHOG DAY

THE FIRST CABINET MEETING of 2003 took place on January 6. "I'm incredibly upbeat about the future of our country," the President said, kicking off the meeting. Later he added about Iraq, "If we don't have a case to make, I won't send in the troops." For the next month, the President told his guests that he was prepared to use force, but that he would seek whatever means he could to avoid it. From my point of view, it seemed clear he had crossed the threshold and was personally prepared to take military action, but he hoped for a reason not to.

The next day, Bush met in the Cabinet Room with the bipartisan leadership of the House and Senate. "I understand there are differences," the President said. "Half the Senate is running for President and that's okay. There's politics and we have to work through it and work together." Turning to Iraq, he told his visitors, "Sometimes it takes a little muscle to secure good diplomacy. Before I make a decision, I will make the reason known to Congress and everyone in America." None of the congressional leaders, including the Democrats, challenged him. If they had misgivings, they kept them to themselves.

Later that day, Bush met in the residence with Republican lawmakers and went a little further. "There's a chance, a good chance, I'll have to address the nation and commit troops to war. It's clear Saddam Hussein is not disarming. I want the process to work before I ratchet up the noise."

The process was the work of the inspectors and the reports they made to the United Nations, principally by Dr. Hans Blix, the chief United Nations weapons inspector. The world tuned in when Blix addressed the UN, and the White House was very sensitive to his findings, paying close attention to his presentations. In early January, Blix told the UN that after two months of searching, inspectors hadn't found any "smoking guns."

On January 9, I was asked about Blix's report.

"Can we presume that the President is very happy that Mr. Blix says there is no smoking gun in the search for weapons in Iraq?"

"The problem with guns that are hidden is you can't see their smoke," I replied, believing full well that Saddam had weapons of mass destruction and the inspectors were simply not able to find them. I also pointed out the job of the inspectors was not suddenly to find a cache of prohibited matériel; it was to evaluate evidence that Saddam had destroyed his weapons of mass destruction.

On January 10, I went into the Oval Office for an unusual meeting with the President and a group of Iraqi dissidents who were living in the United States and badly wanted Bush to attack Iraq and get rid of Saddam Hussein. Many of these people had had family members killed by Saddam or were themselves witnesses to chemical attacks.

"I believe in freedom and peace," Bush said, beginning the meeting. "I believe Saddam Hussein is a threat to America and to the neighborhood. He should disarm, but he won't, therefore we will remove him from power," the President said, overstating his intentions, at least at the time. "We can't make him change his heart. His heart is of stone."

The President listened as these Iraqis told their stories. A doctor from Tikrit, Hatem Mukhlis, told the President that Saddam had killed his father. "All the Iraqis are ready to get rid of Saddam Hussein," he told Bush. "The fear is what comes after. The difference is the participation of the Iraqi people. Iraq had democracy in the fifties. My job is to save lives. I'd like to save Iraqi and American lives. They're both my people."

The President asked if average Iraqis hated Israel.

No, they don't, he was told. The Iraqi people are self-absorbed, inward looking.

Kanan Makiya, with the Iraq Research and Documentation Project at Harvard University, told the President, "You're going to break the mold. You will change the image of the United States in the region. Democracy is truly doable in Iraq. The force for destruction can be turned to a force for construction." He explained that the Iraqi people, unlike the "oil-rich mullahs" of other Arab nations, were literate, with electricity in their villages. Iraqi society was different from other Arab societies, Bush was told.

"We're planning for the worst," the President said.

"People will greet the troops with flowers and sweets," he was told.

"How do you know?"

People on the inside of Iraq were passing that word along, he was told.

"What will the Iraqi people need for their future?" Bush asked.

"Currency, medical facilities, and an immediate humanitarian effort" was the answer.

"Is there starvation?"

"No, there is malnutrition."

The longer the meeting went, the more information the Iraqis started to volunteer.

"The Sunni-Shiite conflict is top-down driven," one of Bush's guests said, implying that, without Saddam playing one group against the other, the prospects for internal peace were not as daunting as they seemed.

"What are the elite like?" the President asked. "Are they well educated? Are there many left or have they been purged like in China? Let's say Saddam Hussein is gone. Now there's a void. What's your vision? The human condition? How does it evolve?"

"You need to find the right people now," he was advised.

"Will the diaspora head back?" he inquired, referring to Iraqis who had fled the country, many of whom now lived in democracies either in western Europe or in the United States.

"Yes," he was told.

"The democratization of Iraq will be more likely if Iraqis who understand and live under democracy flood back," Bush said. "How long will the military have to stay?"

"Two or three years."

"How do you deal with the impression the United States is bringing a leader in, imposing our will?" the President wanted to know.

"That's an outside issue, not internal."

As the meeting ended, the President told the group, "We haven't reached conclusions," backing off his opening statement. "I view you in the diaspora as partners. Your job is to gather the people who want to help and rally their hearts and souls. My job is to rally the world and win the war. I'm not sure my job is to pick," Bush said, meaning pick Iraq's next leader.

"I truly believe out of this will come peace between Israel and the Palestinians. Maybe one year from now we'll be toasting victory and talking about the transition to freedom," the President said, bringing the remarkable meeting to an end.

As the son of a Hungarian immigrant who fled persecution in 1939 to come to America, I was touched by the stories of these Iraqis and thought about how much the Iraqi people were suffering under Saddam. I was proud of President Bush for giving these people reason to hope, and I thought how America before had answered the call and how our nation, despite the criticisms directed at us, was the reason tens of millions of people around the world enjoy freedom and democracy.

The briefing room, meanwhile, was starting to feel like the movie *Groundhog Day*. Nothing had changed, and nothing was changing. The inspections inside Iraq were continuing, but no weapons had been found. Our troops were flowing to the region, increasingly ready for combat, but the President hadn't yet decided that war would begin. Presentations continued to be made to the UN, but minds didn't seem to be changing.

Reporters wanted the story line to change, and so did I. They wanted to know when something—*anything*—would happen.

On January 13, the Bloomberg reporter Dick Keil asked me, "Getting back to the Iraq question for a minute, if and when the time comes where the President has to explain his case to the public, will it be a sort of furry, fuzzy reiteration of past reports—"

"Did you say fuzzy?" I asked.

"Fuzzy—furry," Dick replied to the press's amusement.

"Furry, furry, and fuzzy," other reporters chimed in.

"Not feel good, just furry and fuzzy—reliance on past reports," Dick continued, reclaiming his time. "Or will it be new evidence gathered recently that will close the loop in the minds of Americans who are saying, What is the compelling urgency, what is the new evidence that makes this a risk that's—"

"I'm not going to speculate about events that are not yet taking place," I said, an unsatisfying answer for both the press and me, but it was the only accurate answer I could give at that time.

"With inspectors talking of up to a year to complete this work," asked AP Radio's Mark Smith, "and you're saying the President has not put a timetable on it, does that mean that the troops that he is sending overseas, he's willing to have them sit in their tents and on their— on their planes and ships and stuff for that length of time? He's not ruling out leaving them in the field for up to a year?"

"It means just as I said, the President has not put a timetable on it. And if the President hasn't put a timetable on it, I certainly won't."

The President had made a decision to pursue two approaches to Iraq, one diplomatic and the other military. Often I heard him say privately that he hoped the pressure of the military would lead to a diplomatic success. He lamented frequently that Germany's and France's opposition to our plans made it *harder* for the diplomatic mission to succeed. He thought if these two European nations had shown a willingness to use force, Saddam might have given up peacefully; instead Saddam may have taken false solace in his belief that the United States would never act militarily if these two important allies weren't with us.

But so long as Bush was pursuing both courses, there was little to say to the press, other than that he was pursuing both courses. Every day seemed like *Groundhog Day*.

The next day, January 14, the press got a small part of what they were hoping for—a timetable from the President.

Poland's President, Aleksander Kwasniewski, a principal ally in the war against Iraq, visited President Bush in the Oval Office for a private meeting. "Saddam Hussein is playing a game," Bush said. "In my judgment, it's time to move soon. We won't act precipitously, but time is running out."

When the meeting ended, the press came in for the usual question-and-answer session.

"The weapons inspectors say they need until March, maybe six months, maybe a year. Is this what you had in mind when you went to the UN back in September?" asked Steve Holland of Reuters.

"What I have in mind for Saddam Hussein is to disarm," Bush said. "The United Nations spoke with one voice. We said, we expect Saddam Hussein, for the sake of peace, to disarm. That's the question: Is Saddam Hussein disarming? He's been given eleven years to disarm. And so the world came together and we have given him one last chance to disarm. So far, I haven't seen any evidence that he is disarming.

"Time is running out on Saddam Hussein. He must disarm. I'm sick and tired of games and deception. And that's my view of timetables."

Naturally, the press wanted to know what that meant—*exactly* what that meant. Did that mean war would begin soon? Did that mean the inspectors would have to leave? How much more time did Saddam have? *When* would time run out?

There were no answers to these questions either. The President hadn't set a timetable, other than his attempt to turn up the heat by saying, amorphously, that time was running out. How much time was left became one more question whose answer I couldn't supply. The only person who could provide the answer was the President, and he hadn't given me any direction yet for how, or when, he would do that.

Eleven days before the State of the Union, the radio reporter Sarah Scott, asked me, "Will the President have a lot to say about Iraq in his State of the Union Message? And will you give us a sneak preview?"

"I will give you a sneak preview," I said on camera, "but not this previewy. This is a little early to do any sneaking."

Less than five minutes later, someone else asked, "Is the President planning on using the State of the Union as a platform for promoting Medicare reform and prescription drug coverage?"

"When I said I would provide the sneak preview later, I didn't literally mean five minutes later," I said to laughter, as that day's briefing came to a close. One thing for sure about the White House press corps—when I didn't answer a question, even for a *good* reason—it didn't guarantee the press wouldn't ask the same question, over and over again.

ON JANUARY 21, the President convened a meeting in the Roosevelt Room with a group of the nation's leading economists. The economy hadn't recovered yet, and Bush was worried.

"Controlling costs will be a big battle," he told the group, which included Martin Feldstein, Allen Sinai, Wayne Angell, and Allan Meltzer. "We have to be concerned about long-term deficits. The tax cuts, he said, "made the recession less than it would have been." Bush acknowledged to the group that the uncertainty caused by a potential war was taking its toll on the markets, and the economy. He called it a "risk premium," noting that business was sitting on its money, afraid to invest in new equipment or new hires given the possibility America might soon be at war.

"We're going to conduct our foreign policy according to security, not the stock market," he said. "The risk premium of Saddam Hussein launching an anthrax attack on America doesn't compare to the risk premium of removing Saddam Hussein."

The President barely traveled in January, meaning I was briefing four, often five days a week in the tension-filled air of the White House's James Brady Briefing Room. The job was tiring enough when I had *something* to say, but it became a real grind, when I had nothing new to say and the press had nothing new to ask.

Shortly before the State of the Union, the President took a day trip to St. Louis to talk about the economy, and I headed to the back of Air Force One to brief the press.

"Do you have any comment on a report out of Russia today that the United States has already declared—or given the order to go ahead and begin a war, I think it's in mid-February?"

"No, I have no comments on anything of that nature. The President has not made any final conclusions. And even if he had, if there was a discussion of the dates, I certainly would not discuss them."

"You know, that didn't really sound like much of a denial on the idea of an order being given for war."

"I've said that the President has not reached any final conclusions and that I don't talk about timetables. I'm never going to answer a question about a timetable—"

"Well, okay. I mean, I wasn't asking you to give a timetable. I was asking you for— Was the report accurate— Well, anyway, it doesn't matter. You're saying—"

"The only way to answer," I pointed out, "is to indicate a timetable about when—if or when the President is going to put America's troops into harm's way. And for the protection of the troops, that's a question that I don't think people would ever want me to answer directly."

ON JANUARY 27, Hans Blix was scheduled to return to the United Nations to give an update on what the inspectors were finding. The press wanted badly for someone to indicate that we would go to war based on his report. I kept telling them it was an important date, but I couldn't say what it might mean.

A couple days before the twenty-seventh, I was asked about this "important date."

"Does that mean it's a critical milepost in deciding whether we should go to war with Iraq? And if it's not, can you be more specific about what happens next and why it's important?"

"It's an important date," I replied. "And I can't be more specific until the date comes and we know what the inspectors say. It's important to hear what the inspectors have to report."

"Is it considered a milepost in deciding whether we go to war?"

"It's considered an important date," I repeated. "All the actions of the inspectors are part of what the President will evaluate because that's how the world will know whether Saddam Hussein is cooperating."

"Is the White House looking at it as a trigger point?"

"Important date," I said, again.

Groundhog Day repeated itself. The day before the State of the Union in late January, I was asked about Mohamed ElBaradei, the director general of the International Atomic Energy Agency, who said that his nuclear inspectors needed a few more months to complete their work. "Is the President willing to wait a few more months?" asked AP's Ron Fournier.

"The process is continuing," I said, "but the process is running out of time."

Since that approach didn't get me to change my answer, the press took a different tack.

"If you've concluded the Iraqis *aren't* complying with the inspectors, why not call a halt now, why not—you know, to get on with it?" asked Randy Mikkelsen, a Reuters correspondent.

"Because as the President said," I replied, "it's important to continue to consult, to work with world leaders about how to address the growing problem of Saddam Hussein's failure to comply with the inspectors; the problem of Saddam Hussein continuing to have in his possession biological weapons and chemical weapons which he has not accounted for. And we will continue to consult per the President's promise."

"How do you decide when he's run out of time?" followed up the CBS veteran Bill Plante.

"Well, that will be the judgment the President has to make."

Returning to the topic of when the military might attack, I was asked about the latest leaks out of the Pentagon.

"The Pentagon or some defense officials indicated on Friday that they won't be fully ready for a military action in Iraq until early March. Is that the White House view, as well?" asked Jim Angle of Fox News.

"I'm not going to discuss operational details of when the Pentagon will or won't be ready. All I know is if you read every account of when they will or won't be ready, you can pick any week beginning, basically, I guess, next week until March, because I've seen every week identified as when they'll be ready to go. So I think your guess is as good as—well, it's your guesses."

THE MORNING OF THE STATE OF THE UNION, the President met again with his cabinet.

"The world will follow us," he said. "It may not look like it now, but when it comes to keeping the peace and doing what is right, the world will follow us."

At lunchtime, the President met in the stately Family Dining Room in the Mansion with the anchors of the network news shows and several other leading news programs. It was the same room in which he held countless lunches and dinners with visiting heads of state. This time his guests were Dan Rather, Tom Brokaw, Peter Jennings, Ted Koppel, Brit Hume, and many other top anchors. They pressed him on Iraq and his intentions. There was no transcript of the meeting, but I took notes, although they don't reflect which anchor asked the questions.

Was he worried Saddam could attack the United States?

"I think he'd like to use Al Qaeda as a forward army," the President replied.

How much longer will the inspections last?

"I don't know when they'll end. Sooner rather than later."

What happens if Saddam attacks Israel?

"Holy hell will break out if he puts a weapon on Israel."

How are relations with the French?

"They're not going to run our foreign policy, but they'll remain our friend."

Is bin Laden dead or alive?

"Who knows?"

Is Iraq connected directly to 9/11?"

"No. There is no connection."

A year later, some of the President's critics argued that he tried to connect Saddam to the September 11 attack. I only wish his critics could have heard his one word answer to these anchors: "no," there is no connection between Saddam and the attack. I also wished these anchors would have reminded the critics that the President had firmly denied there was a connection. Saddam had links to Al Qaeda, Bush maintained, and the 9/11 commission found the same thing. The commission said they did not have a "collaborative relationship." After

September 11, the question Bush asked himself was, Could he afford to hope that the links never turned into active collaboration? Given Saddam's history of aggression, that was a chance the President wisely wasn't prepared to accept.

Soon it was time to address the nation. The State of the Union speech is watched by tens of millions of people; there's almost no forum where the American President can command a bigger audience. With a possible war on the horizon, the 2003 speech was watched by 62 million people. By comparison, the final episode of *Friends* was watched by 51 million, and the concluding episode of the first *Survivor* drew 52 million.

In his speech, the President said, "Today, the gravest danger in the war on terror, the gravest danger facing America and the world, is outlaw regimes that seek and possess nuclear, chemical, and biological weapons. These regimes could use such weapons for blackmail, terror, and mass murder. They could also give or sell those weapons to terrorist allies, who would use them without the least hesitation.

"Before September the 11th, many in the world believed that Saddam Hussein could be contained. But chemical agents, lethal viruses, and shadowy terrorist networks are not easily contained. Imagine those 19 hijackers with other weapons and other plans—this time armed by Saddam Hussein. It would take one vial, one canister, one crate slipped into this country to bring a day of horror like none we have ever known. We will do everything in our power to make sure that that day never comes.

"And tonight I have a message for the brave and oppressed people of Iraq: Your enemy is not surrounding your country—your enemy is ruling your country. (Applause.) And the day he and his regime are removed from power will be the day of your liberation."

The President also announced that Secretary Powell would go to the UN on February 5 to present information and intelligence about Iraq's illegal weapons programs and its attempts to hide them from inspectors.

At my briefing the next day, Condi Rice told me to say that we were now entering the "final phase." I added that during this phase the diplomatic window remained open, reflecting the President's serious desire to consult and reach agreements with our allies. The President still wanted to settle matters peacefully, I said, and the stronger the will of the international community, the greater the chance that the disarmament of Iraq could be done peacefully. I gave no indication of how long the window would remain open.

Two days after the State of the Union, the President and Italy's Prime Minister, Silvio Berlusconi, met in the Oval Office.

"We have not made up our mind on military action," Bush said. "I have made up my mind that one way or another Saddam Hussein will be disarmed. I have made up my mind to put troops in the region to show him [Saddam] we're serious. I did make up my mind to work with friends. We're beginning to make the case.

"We want to do everything we can to make your life easier," Bush added. "We will not bend over so far to let Saddam Hussein stay in power," he warned.

Referring to public opinion, Bush said, "This is going to change. You watch. Public opinion will change. We must lead our publics. We cannot follow our publics."

When the press entered the Oval, the President made news.

"Sir, are you open to giving Saddam a final deadline, are you willing to let him slip into exile—this, a man who recently said he wants to break the neck of our country?" asked AP's Ron Fournier.

"First, let me echo the comments of my national security adviser, who the other day in commenting about this process said this is a matter of weeks, not months. In other words, for the sake of peace, this issue must be resolved. Hopefully, it can be done peacefully. Hopefully, the pressure of the free world will convince Mr. Saddam Hussein to relinquish power. And should he choose to leave the country, along with a lot of the other henchmen who have tortured the Iraqi people, we would welcome that, of course."

A new timetable was established—weeks, not months.

ON SATURDAY, February 1, the space shuttle *Columbia* exploded, killing all seven astronauts aboard. Three days later, the President traveled to the Johnson Space Center in Houston, Texas, to console the bereaved and address the nation. It was sad that the President was getting so good at comforting families whose loved ones had been lost. He had done it on September 14, 2001, in New York City, at numerous military bases, and now at NASA's Mission Control.

In a private room, the President and Mrs. Bush slowly made their way from one grieving family to the next, expressing the country's thanks for their dedication to a mission they loved. Ilan Ramon was an Israeli astronaut and the son of a Holocaust survivor. He had fought for Israel in two wars and lost his life aboard the *Columbia*. He also flew on the Israeli mission in 1981 that successfully bombed the Osirak nuclear weapon facility near Baghdad, a mission that spared the world from Saddam obtaining nuclear weapons in the first place.

The President approached Ramon's young son to offer comfort. "He helped you out when he took out the Iraqi nuke plant," the son told Bush. The President asked Ramon's three sons if they wanted to grow up to be fighter pilots like their daddy. All three raised their hands, saying they did.

As the President went around the room, I spoke with the widow of Rick Husband, an astronaut from Amarillo, Texas. "My husband prayed for President Bush every day," she told me. She added, to my surprise, that she couldn't believe how tough the White House press corps was. She said she felt sorry for me, saying what a hard job I had. She also told me a reporter, after her husband's death, tried to get into her home dressed as a florist, presumably to take pictures.

I couldn't believe that someone who had just lost her husband could express such thoughts, when *she*, not I, deserved sympathy. The President left the room, saying how sorry he was to meet these brave families under such circumstances. He invited everyone there to the White House, a promise kept when they arrived in March for a private visit.

IN THE DAYS LEADING UP to Secretary Powell's UN presentation, there was little for the White House to say. The spotlight would soon be on the secretary, and his report would speak volumes. Back in the briefing room, the press were looking for something to do.

"Last week the President said, on Iraq, you are with us or with the enemy," a reporter said. "France and Germany are clearly not with us. Why aren't they with the enemy?"

I thought it was another example of an overwrought question, designed to see if I would start, or add to, international discord. It was trip the press secretary time.

"That's not true," I replied. "France and Germany *are* with us. They just, in the case of Germany, made a decision not to use military force; and in the case of France, I think France is still exploring what their ultimate position will be. But clearly, they're both with us. The question is the use of military force. So I don't think that's quite doing justice to what the President said."

On February 5, Colin Powell went to the UN. After holing himself up at the CIA to review its evidence against Saddam, Powell took what he viewed as the best of it and made America's case to the world.

"I cannot tell you everything that we know," he told the Security Council and tens of millions of Americas, "but what I can share with you, when combined with what all of us have learned over the years, is deeply troubling. What you will see is an accumulation of facts and disturbing patterns of behavior. The facts and Iraq's behavior demonstrate that Saddam Hussein and his regime have made no effort, no effort, to disarm, as required by the international community.

"Indeed, the facts and Iraq's behavior show that Saddam Hussein and his regime are concealing their efforts to produce more weapons of mass destruction."

For more than an hour, Powell captivatingly explained and showed evidence of Saddam's deceptions, using intercepted Iraqi communications, photographs, and charts. When he was finished, the tide had shifted. The American people thought Saddam was lying and the UN inspectors hadn't caught him, at least not yet.

I watched much of Powell's presentation with the President in his private study, just off the Oval Office. He was proud of his secretary of state. He thought he did a superb job. A year later, it became apparent that some of the information given to Powell may not have been accurate after all.

The day after the secretary's presentation, the President announced his intention to seek a second resolution at the UN, this one enforcing November's unanimous resolution demanding that Iraq disarm. In other words, authorizing the use of force to make Saddam disarm.

A couple of days later, John Howard, the Australian Prime Minister and a good ally, visited Bush in the Oval Office. "We're still in the mosh pit," the President complained. "But thanks to your strong resolve, we're finally getting clarity. Either he [Saddam] will leave or we'll get him." Moments later the President added, "Maybe we'll be blessed and there will be a peaceful resolution. The moral position is freeing people, as well as protecting ourselves.

"The infrastructure of Iraq will be preserved," Bush said, "with a bureaucracy that responds to the people."

ON FEBRUARY 11, I finished an otherwise unremarkable briefing, exited the podium, and walked up the ramp separating the lower press office from my office in upper press. As I opened the door to my office, a British reporter, Jamie Campbell, followed me in.

"Can I sit and ask you some questions? Is that all right?"

I had just concluded fifty minutes' worth of questions and didn't feel like answering any more, but since he was already in my office, there wasn't much I could do about it.

"What is it that persuades you that bin Laden isn't in the States?" Campbell asked me with a straight face.

"Well, I haven't heard that he is," I answered, thinking this was sounding a little odd already. "It sounds far-fetched, but if you have some evidence. . . . I think the burden's on you to provide evidence that he's in the States, otherwise it's a little far-fetched."

"I mean, if I showed you a photo like this, for example," he said, as he reached into his pocket and showed me a picture of a cleaned-up, good-looking man who bore a slight resemblance to Osama bin Laden, "what would you . . ."

Where in the world could this be going? I wondered.

He had a tape recorder with him (he later sent me a transcript of our conversation), and I told him he needed to talk to security experts, not me, about his picture. All I wanted to do was have lunch.

"Call the Department of Justice, call the Department of Homeland Security," I said. Call anybody but me, I thought. Bin Laden in the United States? That was something I had never heard before.

He thanked me for my time and politely departed. "Great to meet you. Cheers," he said.

You just never know what you're going to have to answer when you become the White House press secretary.

It didn't take long for *Groundhog Day* to resume, as reporters asked how long Bush was prepared to wait for a second resolution, and as the diplomats returned to center stage, privately debating terms of support for such a resolution.

"On a second resolution," I was asked by Fox News's Jim Angle at a mid-February briefing, "you're facing a little diplomatic headwind here from France, Germany, Russia, and it appears, China. What are the current plans for a second resolution? And what do you think its prospects are?"

"Resolutions at the United Nations are always matters that have headwinds and tailwinds," I answered. "It can often be a windy affair. That is the diplomacy."

On February 14, Hans Blix returned to the UN to report on Iraqi compliance with its disarmament obligations, and his report was read by the much of the White House press corps as a "brick wall of opposition" to the administration. Winning approval for a second resolution was proving extremely difficult.

While France certainly wasn't an "enemy," the French government was taking its differences with the United States to unusual lengths. President Chirac in mid-February publicly castigated the nations of east Europe that supported the American position, calling their actions "childish." "They have missed a good opportunity to remain silent," Chirac said. The press thought he was trying to blackball Romania and Bulgaria from entering the European Union as punishment for supporting the United States.

In the midst of the UN debate, the alert status went back up. The

Department of Homeland Security had advised people to keep supplies, including batteries and duct tape, in their homes in case of an attack. Sales of duct tape soared across the country. At a senior staff meeting, I facetiously suggested that Homeland Security advise people to buy durable goods, like cars and refrigerators, to see if that would jump-start the economy.

On February 19, Homeland Security Secretary Tom Ridge went to Cincinnati to speak about the threats at home and how people could protect themselves. Halfway through his speech, all the cable news stations, which had been covering him live, cut away from his remarks to show the rescue of a dog that was stranded on a block of frozen ice in the middle of New Jersey's Passaic River. It was pretty exciting footage; it was also an example of how the cable TV news shows conduct their affairs. The serious business of government took a backseat to a dramatic dog rescue. I must confess, I watched it pretty closely myself, pleased that the dog made it to safety.

As the press became convinced that war would take place in a matter of time, they started probing about the future of Iraq after an American military victory.

"It would be more persuasive for Americans to hear the President describe in more detail what U.S. involvement in a post-Saddam world would mean for the Iraqi people, what it would cost, how involved we would be," a reporter suggested.

"I think the President has talked about this in the past, when he talks about freedom and the fact that he is confident that any outcome in Iraq will lead to freedom for the Iraqi people.

"I would just remind you," I added, "when the Allies landed in France in June of 1944, we didn't know what the future government of Nazi Germany would be, but we knew the world would be a better place and a safer place as a result of beating the Nazis. . . . It's impossible to say with precision now what the future will hold, just as it was impossible to say on [D-Day] June 6, 1944."

The President also received a visit in February from NATO Secretary-General Lord Robertson, whose opinions he valued highly. Bush liked Robertson and enjoyed working with him. The Scotsman warned Bush that the way he spoke and the military flight jackets he wore were turning European opinion against him. When Bush spoke English, the President was told, Europeans heard Texan. It's your tone, Robertson advised. "Language that works here doesn't work in Europe. The same passion using a different effect can change public opinion," he said.

Robertson knew Bush wanted to avoid war, but other Europeans, he thought, feared the tone Bush used and the way he appeared in public. They concluded he was interested only in going to war. It was a problem, Bush's friend said.

The President listened carefully. He and the NATO leader usually saw eye to eye, and I could tell his words had an impact on the President. "I'm not going to change," Bush eventually told Robertson. "I am who I am." I could tell, however, that the President *did* think about whether he needed to adjust his approach and speak less declaratively, more subtly. The next morning the President told me he'd thought about his friend's message and no, he wouldn't change. All he could do was be himself, whether some in Europe liked it or not.

I suspect if he had tried to calibrate himself too carefully, it wouldn't have worked. One thing I've learned in this business—people may not agree with everything you do, but they want to know that you're sincere, you're acting on principle, and you're genuine. Politicians who are able to fine-tune their personae to appeal to different audiences risk turning themselves into weathervanes, always pointing in a different direction depending on the prevailing sentiments. President Bush is not like that. *He's* comfortable with who he is and what he seeks to do. And because he is comfortable, he makes millions of others comfortable—and millions of others uncomfortable—but that's what leadership is all about. Lord Robertson was right. The President's tone was not well received in Europe, but that didn't mean Bush was going to change his approach, nor did it mean he was wrong about the threat from Saddam's Iraq.

The issue of whether Turkey would allow access to the Fourth Infantry Division so a northern front could be opened against Iraq was a constant sore spot. The President met repeatedly with Turkey's various leaders, and it was hard to get a firm commitment either way from any of them.

I was asked about Turkey almost every day for five weeks.

"Anything new on Turkey?" I was asked aboard Air Force One in mid-February as the President flew to Georgia for a domestic event focused on the economy.

"There is nothing new to report on Turkey, except for the passage of time, and there is not a lot of time that can pass," I said. One way or another, the press kept asking. I pretty much gave the same nonanswer every time.

On February 24, the United States, Spain, and the United Kingdom offered the text of a second resolution to the United Nations Security Council. Its most important portion read, simply, "Iraq has failed to take the final opportunity afforded it in Resolution 1441." The President expressed his confidence the resolution would pass.

Two days later, Bush gave a rare prime-time address to a meeting of the American Enterprise Institute in Washington about the big picture and the goals of a potential war in Iraq, including the spread of democracy through the Middle East. I called the bureau chiefs for all the broadcast and cable news shows and filled them in. Dan Bartlett, the communications director, and I agreed not to ask for network coverage; instead I simply described the speech so each news division could make its own decision. I called it an "important speech" but deliberately did not call it "major." The cables always take the President's speeches live, but my approach put the broadcast networks in a tough spot.

If I had *asked* for live coverage, they all would have done it and told their viewers it was at the request of the White House. I didn't think the speech rose to that level, but I also thought that they should know in advance what the President was going to say in case they wanted to take it live. I hoped they would.

Five months earlier, the President had given a live prime-time address in Cincinnati about the possibility of war with Iraq, and all three broadcast networks—ABC, CBS, and NBC—reluctant to break into their lucrative prime-time sitcoms, reality shows, and newsmagazines chose not to air it live. Many press critics faulted the nets for not taking the address. This time, stung by the earlier criticism, they all decided to televise the President's remarks live.

Canceling regular programming, especially prime-time shows, with the millions of dollars they generate in commercials, and replacing it with a news event with no commercials is a huge decision for the networks. It is made not by the news division but by the corporate higher-ups. Ratings, and therefore money, are on the line. So too is their judgment about corporate responsibility and the definition of news.

There was considerable grumbling among the broadcast network higher-ups after this speech. The audience was friendly toward Bush and frequently interrupted his remarks with applause, which caused some of the network bosses to think they had been used by the White House in an effort to drum up public support for the war. If they hadn't aired the speech, the networks knew they would have been criticized again for putting money over the public interest. Having aired it, they had a case of buyer's remorse.

Less than one month later, however, with the nation at war, I noticed the broadcast networks were putting the President's midday speeches live on the air. When Bush traveled to a military base in Florida to meet with the troops, the speech was live on the cables *and* the broadcast networks. When the President met with veterans ten days after the war began, the networks again broke into daytime television to carry his remarks live from the Rose Garden. Both speeches were frequently interrupted with applause from these friendly groups, but no one at the networks complained. Was it because we were now at war and the threshold of newsworthiness had shifted? Perhaps. But the bigger reason was that the definition of news can also depend on the time of day it's made. It was easy for the broadcast networks to break into daytime television, which has far fewer viewers than their prime-time shows. If the President had given the same address to the same veterans and military groups in prime time, I can't imagine the broadcast networks would have covered it live.

Flash-forward one year, to May 2004. After a series of setbacks in the effort to rebuild Iraq, the President traveled to Carlisle, Pennsylvania, to reframe the postwar debate and describe a five-point approach to the future of Iraq. The address took place at 8:00 P.M., prime time. The White House promoted the speech but again did not request network coverage.

Natalie Morales, a news anchor for NBC's *Today* show, began the broadcast the morning of the President's speech by calling it "perhaps one of the most important of his career." Given that level of importance, did NBC or its counterparts, CBS and ABC, carry it live? No. Despite calling it "one of the most important of his career," they didn't deem it important enough to preempt their lucrative prime-time evening shows. The networks are in business to make money, a fact never lost on the top executives responsible for coverage decisions, and that too is how the news industry works. Reporters in news divisions would gladly have more time to air their stories, but they often run into resistance from higher-ups.

ON FEBRUARY 27, Elie Wiesel, the noted humanist, Nobel Peace Prize winner, and Holocaust survivor, came to see Condi Rice. Fifteen minutes after their meeting began, the President, interested in hearing Wiesel's thoughts about Iraq, entered the national security adviser's office.

Wiesel told Bush that if the allies had intervened in 1938, World War II and the Holocaust could have been avoided. "It's a moral issue," he said. "How can we *not* intervene?" Czech President Vaclav Havel had earlier told Bush the same thing.

The President said that he had read Wiesel's views on Auschwitz in Michael Beschloss's book *The Conquerors: Roosevelt, Truman and the Destruction of Hitler's Germany.* Wiesel wished in the book that the Allies had bombed Auschwitz, noting that he and his fellow inmates "were no longer afraid of death." Such an attack might have saved the lives of other Jews.

Bush expressed his frustration with the French government. "If the French had put pressure on him [Saddam], he'd have been gone."

Wiesel told the President, "I'm against silence. I'm against neutrality because it doesn't help the victim. It helps the aggressor."

After the meeting, Wiesel went to the microphones in front of the

White House and told the press what he had told the President. The cameras rolled, and his powerful message was captured on tape, where for the most part it remained. A LexisNexis search shows none of the TV networks covered the message from this Nobel Peace Prize winner. The next day's newspapers gave it scant coverage. Why? Because he agreed with President Bush. If he had disagreed with the war on Iraq, it would have been front-page, led the network news.

One month earlier, Nelson Mandela, the former President of South Africa, lit into the United States and President Bush, saying that Bush was undermining the United Nations. The contrast between how much of the press covered Mandela and Wiesel was stark.

"He [Bush] is acting outside it [the UN], not withstanding the fact that the United Nations is the idea of President Roosevelt and Winston Churchill," Mandela declared during an address in Johannesburg. "Both Bush as well as Tony Blair are undermining an idea which was sponsored by their predecessors. They do not care. Is it because the secretary-general of the United Nations is now a black man? (Applause) They never did that when secretary-generals were white."

Mandela the Nobel Peace Prize winner was just warming up.

"And if there is a country that has committed unspeakable atrocities in the world, it is the United States of America. (Applause) They don't care for human beings. Fifty-seven years ago when Japan was retreating on all fronts, they decided to drop the atom bomb in Hiroshima and Nagasaki. . . . What I'm condemning is that one power with a president who has no foresight, who can not think properly is now wanting to plunge the world (applause) into a holocaust, and I'm happy that people of the world, especially those of the United States, are standing up and opposing their own president." His remarks received considerable coverage on CBS and ABC and in the newspapers. It's another example of how the American people are often given the greatest *contrast* in the news but not *all* the news.

People deserved to hear what Wiesel thought, just as they deserved to hear what Mandela thought. But because of how the news business works, very few people heard Wiesel's pro-war message, while tens of millions heard Mandela's anti-American, anti-Bush screed.

I was particularly upset with ABC's coverage of Mandela's speech. Peter Jennings, in his news report that evening, shared only the anti-Bush portion of the South African leader's remarks with his viewers. Leaving out Mandela's over-the-top condemnation of the United States for "unspeakable atrocities" and his statement that Americans "don't care for human beings," Jennings focused his report solely on Bush.

"Now, a couple of other items in the 'Overseas Briefing,'" he began. "The former President of South Africa Nelson Mandela accused President Bush today of undermining the United Nations in his campaign against Iraq, and suggested Mr. Bush was doing it only because the UN Secretary-General was black. Mr. Mandela also described Mr. Bush as a president 'who can not think properly and wants to plunge the world into holocaust.'"

I complained to several people at ABC. Had the network's viewers, I argued, been aware of how anti-*American* Mandela's remarks were, they would have been in a more informed position to judge his anti-Bush views. Both Mandela's anti-Bush and his anti-American statements were covered by CBS, while NBC gave the speech no coverage at all. ABC, I complained, wasn't fair. Several people I spoke with at ABC, including some of the top brass in New York, agreed with me, but the damage was already done.

WAR

B Y MARCH 2003, fundamentally little had changed since the UN inspectors went to Iraq and the U.S. military buildup had begun late in 2002. The press still wanted to know when, not if, war would begin, and there was nothing I could tell them. They wanted to know if Turkey would cooperate; how come the inspectors hadn't found any weapons of mass destruction, even though the discovery of a drone created a stir; whether we had provided the inspectors with all the "actionable intelligence" we possessed; and now, when the vote would take place on the second UN resolution.

For five long months, every briefing seemed the same. It was a frustrating time for the press and for me.

It seemed to me that the President was heading toward war, but he always left himself an off-ramp in case Saddam fled the country or the inspectors reported a major discovery that would bring France, Germany, and Russia onboard, further increasing pressure on Iraq. I knew the President well enough to realize what his intentions were, but I also knew he wanted to avoid war if he could.

Groups that opposed the President sent people to Iraq to become human shields, and also in March, the Vatican weighed in against the war, which led to probably the oddest question I ever got from the press: "If the Pope was to be in Baghdad as a human shield, how might that affect the President's decision?" someone, I don't know who, asked me on camera. She wasn't a regular White House reporter. I said that wasn't an issue and moved on.

In early March I was asked if the President regretted his decision to involve the UN in the disarmament of Iraq.

"No," I said. "The President went into this knowing how the United Nations works and how slow the United Nations can be, but how important the United Nations is. . . . He created this process in the first place by asking the United Nations to get involved. And he's pleased they have gotten involved. He hopes they will play a productive role. But whether they agree or disagree, the President is determined to protect peace by making certain that, one way or another, Saddam Hussein is disarmed."

On March 7, the Department of Labor announced that the economy had lost 308,000 jobs the previous month. We were on the brink of war, and the economic news was awful.

One event that *did* change the atmosphere around the world, and in the briefing room, was when French President Chirac said in early March that France would veto any resolution authorizing the use of force, no matter what. His statement was particularly helpful to British Prime Minister Tony Blair, who faced an insurrection in his Labour Party over his pro-war position. Blair had promised to pursue a second UN resolution to authorize the use of force unless he was confronted with an "unreasonable veto" threat. France's veto-no-matter-what promise fit the category. There is still a good part of England that takes its disputes with France seriously. Chirac inadvertently helped rally the British people behind Blair. The French leader also set off a wave of anti-French sentiment in the United States whose depth caught me by surprise. I didn't like Chirac's bullying of east Europe, and I was obviously on the other side of the Iraq issue from the French leader. I remembered with some bitterness that France in 1986 wouldn't allow the United States overflight rights to bomb Libya in retaliation for the terrorist bombing of a West Berlin disco by Libyan agents that killed two American servicemen. But I also had been a French minor in college and a fan of French culture, and as much as I disliked French politics, I was struck by how dry the grass of anti-French sentiment was in America—it didn't take much for Chirac to ignite it.

At a mid-March briefing, I was asked about France's promise to vote no, no matter what.

"When it comes to the disarmament of Saddam Hussein," I said, "it is too risky to have a laissez-faire attitude about Iraq having weapons of mass destruction."

The briefing turned to other topics, and Helen Thomas and I resumed our clash over Iraq and Bush's intentions.

"Why is the President going through this charade of diplomacy when he obviously plans to go to war?" Helen demanded.

"When you use the word *charade,* which if I'm not mistaken, has French roots, you may want to address your question to those who say they will veto any resolution." Chirac, and my Middlebury education, was coming in handy as the briefing room broke out into laughter.

As much as France's intransigence played into American and British hands, I always tried to keep our disagreements at a reasonable level. At the same briefing where I tweaked France for *its* charade, I later said, "France has been a stalwart ally in the war on terror. Germany, as well. The information sharing, the working with the police agencies, and working together around the world to fight terrorism, is strong with those nations. So the issue should not be confused or broadened into something that it is not. We remain important nations and allies. We have differences. You are seeing those differences today."

I was asked about the growing call for boycotts of French products in the United States.

"I think you are seeing the American people speak spontaneously," I said. "And that is their right. It is the right of people in Europe to demonstrate. It is the right of people in Europe to speak their mind. So, too, is it the right of the American people to speak theirs."

Pretty soon in fact, Americans by the millions were boycotting French products, especially French wine.

On the afternoon of Friday, March 14, I began my briefing with an announcement.

"The President will travel to the Azores on Sunday to meet with Prime Minister Blair, Prime Minister Aznar [of Spain], Prime Minister Durao Barroso [of Portugal], to discuss how best to proceed to make it unequivocally clear to Saddam Hussein that there will be serious consequences if he fails to disarm."

It was a trip designed to help Tony Blair go the extra mile to win a vote in his Parliament. The so-called unilateralist President was willing to do all he could to help his coalition allies, whether they were Blair, Aznar, Italy's Berlusconi, Poland's Kwasniewski, or many others.

"The leaders will discuss all final diplomatic options," I said. A vote on the second resolution was still pending at the UN, although by this time prospects for its passage were slim to none.

I was asked what Bush hoped to accomplish in the Azores.

"I think there are still two issues that remain in play that have been at the core of this from the very beginning. One is the complete, total, and immediate disarmament of Saddam Hussein, exactly as called for in Resolution 1441. And the other is for Saddam Hussein and all his top leaders to leave the country."

"But realistically, at this point, at this late date, do you hold out any hope that Saddam Hussein is going to disarm—"

"The only person who can answer that question accurately is Saddam Hussein," I said. "The President hopes so. I think, realistically, the chances are slim."

One White House official involved in the planning of the Azores trip suggested we would be able to take only a small press pool with us. He said the complexity of getting a couple hundred reporters there— including building a filing center with phone lines over a weekend—on such short notice might be prohibitive. I objected. There's no way we can exclude the press from a meeting like this when we're on the verge of war, I argued. This is *exactly* why the press is supposed to be there. Thanks to the miraculously fast and hard work of the White House advance and travel offices, the entire press corps made the trip.

Maybe it was playing the devil's advocate, or maybe it's another example of the press placing blame on the President no matter what he does, but I was also asked on March 14 if Bush had a serious credibility gap because he'd let the diplomacy *continue* as long as he did. Two days before the trip, many in the White House press were tired of the diplomacy and wanted the story line to change.

"Ari, 182 days ago, the President told the United Nations: we expect a quick resolution to the issue of Iraq disarmament," a reporter said, twisting Bush's words. "And he set a deadline of days and weeks, not months and years. Six months later, he's still waiting. On January the fifteenth, he announced, Time is running out. On February the twenty-second, he announced, Time is short. My question is, since it is now March fourteenth, with no resolution in sight, how can you deny that the President has created a serious credibility gap?"

I answered, "Number one, I think you need to be precise in what you say the President said. On September twelfth, the President said that it should be weeks not months for the United Nations Security Council to act by passage of a resolution based on his September twelfth speech. That, indeed, happened when the Security Council, within weeks, not months, passed the resolution the President asked them to pass. On January thirtieth, when the President was asked how much longer will the current stage last, he said, Weeks, not months. I think what you've seen in both cases is the President is speaking precisely."

Only from the White House can a couple hundred people make a day trip to the Azores, located eight hundred miles off the coast of Portugal. I left early Sunday morning from Andrews Air Force Base, and I was back in Washington late that evening. The meeting, a last-minute discussion of what options—if any—were available to resolve the issue peacefully, went off without a hitch. It also gave Tony Blair additional help in winning a crucial vote in his Parliament to authorize the use of British troops in the disarmament of Saddam Hussein. For quite a while, Blair had feared he might lose the vote, and his Prime Minister position with it.

At a news conference following the summit, Bush summed up where matters stood. "Tomorrow is the day that we will determine whether or not diplomacy can work," the President declared. "And we sat and visited about this issue, about how best to spend our time between now and tomorrow. And as Prime Minister Blair said, we'll be working the phones and talking to our partners and talking to those who may now clearly understand the objective, and we'll see how it goes tomorrow.

"Saddam Hussein can leave the country, if he's interested in peace. You see, the decision is his to make. And it's been his to make all along as to whether or not there's the use of the military. He got to decide whether he was going to disarm, and he didn't. He can decide whether he wants to leave the country. These are his decisions to make. And thus far he has made bad decisions."

The President called it "a moment of truth for the world."

ON THE MORNING of Monday, March 17, the President called me into the Oval. We're pulling the plug on the diplomacy, he told me. He planned to address the nation that evening. He told me to announce the news at the morning gaggle. He had already spoken with Blair, Aznar, and Spanish King Juan Carlos I. Secretary Powell, who also worked the phones, gave Bush an update at the morning meeting of the National Security Council on the fruitless effort to secure the necessary votes to pass a second resolution.

It's finally coming to a head, I thought. Our nation will soon go to war.

At 10:12 A.M., I met with the press twenty-seven minutes late. I dispensed with my usual reading of the schedule and began the gaggle declaring, "The United Nations has failed to enforce its demands that Iraq immediately disarm. As a result, the diplomatic window has now been closed. The President will address the nation tonight at 8:00 P.M. He will say that, to avoid military conflict, Saddam Hussein must leave the country."

Reporters ran from the briefing room. It was like the old days in the movies, when men with hats on would sprint to phones to file their stories, only this time it was 2003 and they ran to their computers to file or hurried to the North Lawn to go live. The wire services and the larger TV networks kept reporters in their tiny booths in the back of the briefing room listening to the gaggle, ready to hit the news button if news was made. Their colleagues stayed in the room, and the rest of the gag-gle continued with the few reporters who remained. My statement was major news.

I told the press that the President intended to give Saddam an ulti-matum in his speech.

Right away they wanted to know if the war would begin that night.

"I will not get into any discussions of when hostilities may or may not begin," I replied. It was an answer I was used to giving by now.

Another reporter asked me if it was safe for the press to remain in Baghdad.

"Baghdad is not a safe place to be," I answered.

Later that afternoon, I spoke with the President in the Oval about his decision. He isn't one who dwells on his internal feelings, not even in private. I knew this decision weighed on him, however, so I asked him about it.

"The hardest part was making the decision that force *may* need to be used," he told me. "The decision to use it was not the hardest." The process the President had locked into place in his speech to the UN the previous September had come to its conclusion. He wanted diplomacy to succeed in forcing Saddam from power, but he also knew his threat to use the military had to be credible if the diplomatic option was to have meaning.

From the fall forward, the route he traveled began to have fewer and fewer exit ramps. The military was ready, diplomacy didn't work, and Saddam remained in place. There was no longer an exit ramp to take. The United States was going to war.

That night, from Cross Hall, the center of the Mansion, where the White House entrance crosses the hallway that runs the length of the President's residence, President Bush told the nation, "My fellow citi-zens, events in Iraq have now reached the final days of decision. . . . Peaceful efforts to disarm the Iraqi regime have failed again and again—because we are not dealing with peaceful men. Intelligence gathered by this and other governments leaves no doubt that the Iraq regime continues to possess and conceal some of the most lethal weapons ever devised.

"The United Nations Security Council has not lived up to its responsibilities, so we will rise to ours. . . . Saddam Hussein and his sons must leave Iraq within 48 hours. Their refusal to do so will result in military conflict, commenced at a time of our choosing."

The President also answered the question he had mused about in late September during a domestic policy briefing.

"We are now acting because the risks of inaction would be far greater. In one year, or five years, the power of Iraq to inflict harm on all free nations would be multiplied many times over. With these capabilities, Saddam Hussein and his terrorist allies could choose the moment of deadly conflict when they are strongest. We choose to meet that threat now, where it arises, before it can appear suddenly in our skies and cities."

Later that night, the security alert for the nation rose from yellow to orange, from elevated to high. At the gaggle on the eighteenth, I announced that the security perimeter around the White House had been extended. Pennsylvania Avenue in front of the Mansion was closed to pedestrians and all White House tours canceled. A heaviness was again setting in on life at the White House.

I was asked what the President was doing.

He's preparing for a possible war, I said.

The press wanted to know if military action could take place before the forty-eight-hour ultimatum expired. I wouldn't answer the question. "I think Saddam has to figure that out."

Turning to the issue of who was in or out of the coalition, Mike Allen of the *Washington Post* asked, "Secretary Powell said today that there is [*sic*] roughly 30 countries in the coalition of the willing. That leaves roughly 160 United Nations members in the coalition of the *unwilling*. Why is that?"

"That's, I don't think, a fair characterization of other nations to say that they're in a coalition of the unwilling," I countered. "Not every nation has the ability to contribute. Not every nation is in an area that is geographically advantageous concerning military operations or overflight or basing." By those criteria, I said, most nations opposed the First Gulf War as well.

The next morning, the communications staff vented their frustration with much of the press. During a routine communications planning meeting in Dan Bartlett's upstairs West Wing office, someone pointed out how muted the coverage was of Tony Blair's dramatic win in Parliament authorizing the use of force. After weeks of coverage about how much trouble Blair was in, his victory didn't get much press. Someone else pointed out that NBC's *Today* show, after reporting for months that the UN inspectors had found no proof that Saddam had biological or chemical weapons, had shifted gears. They were now reporting how vulnerable our troops were to a biological or chemical attack.

The on-camera briefing on the nineteenth was somber. The press knew war was around the corner and they wanted to know if any Iraqis had defected; what the future role of the UN would be; how much the war would cost; and what would happen when the ultimatum passed.

"At eight tonight," I said, referring to the President's pending address, "the American people will know Saddam Hussein has committed his final act of defiance."

My office was about thirty feet from the Oval Office, separated by one thick door from the hallway just outside the Oval. From that hallway to my desk, the distance was even less. I typically walked that hallway dozens of times a day, either to go to meetings in the Oval or somewhere else in the West Wing or sometimes just to pop into visit the staff in the outer Oval.

During the afternoon of the nineteenth, something was clearly up. The door to the Oval was closed, and it remained closed for a long, long time. Additional secure phones were brought into the Situation Room, and the atmosphere of the West Wing was more tense than normal. Late that evening, Andy Card called me to his office, where he shut the door and told me the war would begin that night. He didn't tell me much, but he said that the attack would begin and that the President would address the nation. He told me what time to expect the attack.

I had earlier prepared a two-sentence statement announcing the commencement of hostilities, patterned on Marlin Fitzwater's 1991 declaration that the liberation of Kuwait had begun. It was precleared and approved by the President. I showed it to Condi Rice, just to make sure it was still good to go, and she told me to run it past Secretary Rumsfeld. I called him, and he made a minor change and then said it was fine.

Gathered in Condi's large West Wing corner office, Andy Card, Karen Hughes, Dan Bartlett, Condi, and I anxiously watched TV, waiting for the antiaircraft fire to go off over Baghdad. The President was in the residence. We knew what time the F-117 stealth fighter was due to drop its bombs along with an accompaniment of cruise missiles, all brought to bear on Baghdad's Dora Farms, where Saddam and his two sons were believed to be. As soon as the first impact was made, we predicted Saddam's military would light up the skies with antiaircraft guns, causing the news shows to break in and show live the nighttime sky, illuminated by the burst of guns. As soon as it happened, I was supposed to read my statement to the press.

Then it happened. The skies lit up, I told my staff to give the press a two-minute warning that I was about to enter the briefing room, and we waited. Condi suggested, somewhat nervously, that we run the statement past Secretary Rumsfeld once again. She wanted to make certain that F-117 was safely out of the area before I announced anything. The standard two-minute warning stretched to almost fifteen minutes, and at 9:45 I stepped to the podium and said, "The opening stages of the disarmament of the Iraqi regime have begun. The President will address the nation at ten-fifteen." I departed instantly, without taking questions.

It was one of the few times at the White House that I was nervous as I approached that podium, knowing that my remarks confirmed we were at war and that my message was being watched live around the world. Normally, I never thought about who was watching, or how many people that might be. But that night felt different. It was only two sentences—but they were mine to read, and they told the world America was at war.

"MY FELLOW CITIZENS, at this hour, American and coalition forces are in the early stages of military operations to disarm Iraq, to free its people and to defend the world from grave danger," the President said, seated at his desk in the Oval Office.

"On my orders, coalition forces have begun striking selected targets of military importance to undermine Saddam Hussein's ability to wage war. These are opening stages of what will be a broad and concerted campaign. More than 35 countries are giving crucial support—from the use of naval and air bases, to help with intelligence and logistics, to the deployment of combat units . . .

"The people of the United States and our friends and allies will not live at the mercy of an outlaw regime that threatens the peace with weapons of mass murder. We will meet that threat now, with our Army, Air Force, Navy, Coast Guard and Marines, so that we do not have to meet it later with armies of fire fighters and police and doctors on the streets of our cities."

Our nation was at war for the second time in the twenty-six months I had worked in the White House.

THERE'S A SPOT on the South Lawn of the White House where Presidents can walk in peace, the only such open space at the White House. The entire North Lawn is open and visible, making it off-limits to the nation's leader because of security concerns. There was an informal agreement with all the shows to allow the President the use of that one spot where he could be private. On the morning of the twentieth, the morning after the war began, the President went to the South Lawn to play with his dogs. It was something he loved to do.

A few minutes later, a clip of the President at play aired on CNN. Of all mornings for the press to push the usual limits aside, this was it. I called CNN and the other news stations and asked them to grant the President the usual respect for his privacy on the South Lawn. To their credit, CNN was upset they had aired the footage. One correspondent, John King, assured me "operation castration" was under way, promising the footage would not be shown again.

The President called a cabinet meeting on the twentieth, which he began by stating, "We tried everything possible to solve this through peace. It was the absolute right decision to commit troops . . . the correct decision for peace and security." He described the horrible tortures Saddam and his sons had inflicted on the Iraqi people and said, "Of all things we stand for are human liberty and freedom."

Defense Secretary Rumsfeld told the group that the coalition was large and getting larger, and the pressure on the regime was growing. He said he couldn't guess how long the war would last or how much it would cost, but he hoped the regime would be toppled before the heavy air and ground war began.

Fearing possible attacks against the United States, the Vice President reviewed the presidential successor program known as Continuity of Government Operations and urged everyone to take it seriously. "The COG program can be a pain in the fanny," added the man who spent a good bit of his time living and working in secure, undisclosed locations so the government could continue if the President were killed.

The President said it was a "myth" to think the war would conclude quickly. "We won't act in a way that jeopardizes the mission or risks lives," he said, adding, "Iraq is a theater in the war on terror."

Secretary Powell talked about the problems we had with our allies and noted that, with France, "we've been in marriage counseling for 225 years."

MY WARTIME BRIEFINGS were a big disappointment for the White House press corps. White House reporters, often at the peak of their careers, want to be where the action is. To them, there's no place more important than their beat, and that's where they want the news to be made. Unfortunately for them, I was under orders from the President to have the Pentagon brief all operational details, just as I did in the war against the Taliban and Al Qaeda. In the Oval Office, the President once gently told a few White House reporters that they "were embedded in the wrong unit." If they wanted detailed coverage of the war effort, the White House wasn't the place to be, Bush said. Their colleagues at the Pentagon and those who risked their lives embedded with the military in the deserts of Iraq would get considerable airplay. White House reporters were not happy.

The first question I got at my first on-camera briefing after the bombing took place was one I wouldn't answer.

"Has Saddam Hussein or any of his leadership been killed or captured?"

Check with the Pentagon, I said.

The next day, after the President met with congressional leaders in the Oval Office, the press asked Bush the same, very logical question.

Ask Donald Rumsfeld, he said.

Our discipline made the press's job harder, but I can't imagine a better way to conduct military business. Old-timers in the press corps knew that was how the First Gulf War was briefed in 1991, but being used to it didn't mean the press liked it.

What intelligence did the President receive that led to the attack on Dora Farms? I was asked.

I can't tell you, I replied. I knew this wasn't easy for the White House press corps, and it certainly wasn't easy for me to stand up there for forty-five minutes, saying little to nothing at all.

Since there wasn't much we *could* talk about, some of the questions veered toward the bizarre.

"Ari, if the United States is at war, and if you assert that the United States has the right to target the Iraqi leader and his inner circle as part of command and control, does that make the President and the White House a legitimate target for Iraqis?"

"You can tell anybody who wants to know the answer to that to get their *own* international lawyer," I snapped. "I won't do it for them."

I was also asked how long the conflict might last.

"The President wants to prepare the country for the possibility that this may be longer and harder than some have suggested," I said.

On Friday, March 21, the bombing of Baghdad began in what the military dubbed a campaign of "shock and awe." The words seemed to imply that the Iraqi leaders would be overcome by such shock and awe that they would fold their tents and give up without a fight.

At my briefing that day, a reporter, watching TV coverage of the bombing, said to me, "There was a humanitarian crisis in Iraq even before the bombing began, in terms of food shortages. After what we saw today, this massive attack on Baghdad, that situation is clearly going to be much, much worse beginning tomorrow. What, specifically, is the administration planning to do when the sun comes up?"

White House reporters are as sharp as they come, but sometimes a good, compelling story line, like a looming humanitarian crisis, can trump reality. The fact was our bombing of military targets was so precise there was no humanitarian crisis, particularly in Baghdad.

"The destruction of a palace of Saddam Hussein's, the destruction of a military facility, may not have *anything* to do with the feeding of the Iraqi people," I replied. "You should not necessarily leap to that conclusion based on what you saw on TV today."

I was also asked how the administration expected allied forces to be greeted in Baghdad.

"That remains to be seen," I said, adding, "The President believes . . . that the Iraqi people are yearning to be free and to be liberated. The Iraqi people have lived under a brutal dictatorship led by Saddam Hussein, and the history of mankind shows people want to be free. And given the chance to throw off a brutal dictator like Saddam Hussein, people will rejoice."

I was asked if we expected evidence of chemical, biological, or nuclear weapons in Iraq.

"There is no question we have evidence and information that Iraq has weapons of mass destruction, biological and chemical particularly. This was the reason that the President felt so strongly that we needed to take military action to disarm Saddam Hussein, since he would not do it himself. As the military effort continues, I think you will see information develop for yourself, firsthand. This is one of the reasons that there are so many reporters present with the military. In many ways, you will have these answers yourselves. You are there, you are on the ground. And you will find the answers and they will speak volumes themselves," I said.

As well as the war had begun—with no humanitarian crisis, no destruction of dams by Saddam, no environmental destruction through widespread torching of oil fields, no intervention in the north by Turkey, and no serious military resistance—the first weekend of the war had its problems, as all wars must. The first American POWs were taken, a U.S. soldier threw a grenade at our own troops, and no weapons of mass destruction had been found. After a few days, the press started to bore in on the negative.

"If America cannot win the war in a short time, such as two or three weeks," I was asked on March 24, less than a week after the attack on Dora Farms, "or if Iraq has already used chemical weapons, will you think that the President will decide to use much more powerful weapons, such as nuclear weapons?"

"Well, number one, I'm not going to make any predictions about the length of the war," I replied, adding, "We do not discuss the type of weapons that we may use. We never have and we do not speculate about that." I'd given that response so many times that I hoped the press knew the answer by now. At the televised briefing, it didn't matter; it was a question that had to be asked even if the press knew the answer by heart. They wanted to get the answer on the record, or hoped I would announce a change in policy and make major news.

Pretty soon the press started drilling in, asking if military progress was slower than expected. It was a clever formulation, because the only way to rebut it was to explain what our expectations were, to discuss the timing of war plans which I wasn't privy to and wouldn't discuss even if I was.

When General William Scott Wallace, the commander of the Fifth Corps, said that "the enemy we're fighting is a bit different than the one we war-gamed against," the press seized on his remarks. They found his statement to be validation that the war wasn't going as well as the President and the Pentagon said it was.

The press were briefed about the war mostly by Central Command out of Doha, in the Arab nation of Qatar. Early one morning I was watching General Brooks on ABC's *Good Morning America* when he began showing a tape of Marines feeding Iraqis as part of the humanitarian effort. The clip was filmed by the United States military. As soon as the tape began to play, ABC cut away. The press didn't mind asking about the humanitarian situation in Iraq, but many media organizations apparently objected to showing any positive footage if its origin was the United States government.

On March 26th, the President traveled to Tampa, Florida, the base where the war had been planned. As usual I awoke at 5:00, enjoyed breakfast with my papers at home, and arrived at the White House to catch Marine One to Andrews Air Force Base, where I boarded Air Force One with the President. At the end of my briefing to the pool on the back of the plane, a reporter who must have carefully perused the airplane's breakfast menu asked me why the French toast had been re-named Freedom toast.

Since I had already eaten, I hadn't looked at the menu and had no idea what the reporter was talking about, although it wasn't too hard to guess.

Another reporter followed up, asking, seriously, if the White House was behind the decision to rename French toast.

"I'm not a hobbit, so I didn't have a second breakfast," I said, trying to avoid the topic without offending the French any further than they were already offended.

I asked if the menu had really been changed, and the press assured me it had.

"We're always proud of the men and women of our Air Force," I said, guessing the military crew aboard the plane made the change. Once again I realized that whatever the White House touches has the potential to become radioactive, even if we're not the ones responsible for it. Two days later a reporter asked me on camera if the President himself had ordered the menu to be changed. I gently replied that the President was focused on other matters.

BY LATE MARCH, many in the press were convinced the war was go-ing badly. Peter Jennings began the newscast one night reporting that the Army and Marines "struggled on towards Baghdad today." The *Washington Post* told its readers that the Army and Marines were "bogged down."

Three days before the war began, the Vice President had told Bob Schieffer on *Face the Nation* that the war might last "weeks, rather than months." Before the war had even gone *two* weeks, many in the press were quoting the Vice President's words back to me at the televised briefing, suggesting that he was wrong and that the war was taking longer than we thought.

Indeed, a major sandstorm swept southern Iraq, limiting and in some places halting ground operations, leading in part to the press's conclusions about the pace of the conflict. The military and the President were growing frustrated with the way the press portrayed the situation.

"I'm not paying attention to the press," the President told a group of veterans gathering in the Roosevelt Room nine days after the strike against Saddam, a mere seven days after ground forces started their major operations. "I get my information from Tommy Franks," he said, referring to the four-star general in charge of the war.

"Tommy gets what he needs," the President said. Stating again what he viewed as the lesson from Vietnam, he told the veterans, "We don't second-guess out of the White House. We don't adjust the plan based on editorials."

He was asked when the battle on the outskirts of Baghdad against the Republican Guard would begin. "I don't know. Tommy hasn't told me yet," he replied, underscoring his view that the best way to win a war was to define the mission to the military and then empower them to achieve it, without political interference.

Looking at the future, the President said, "The whole world is watching this. It will have an effect on whether people are friend or foe. The important thing is to win the peace. I don't expect Thomas Jefferson to come out of this, but I believe people will be free. The best thing we have going for us is that our values will unleash that freedom."

On March 31, the President visited a Coast Guard facility in Philadelphia to talk about homeland security and the war. As usual, protesters greeted him. Down the street from our destination at the Port of Philadelphia, about thirty protesters gathered, holding signs and shouting slogans. One sign read, "Mind Your Global Manners." Next to it a protester held up another sign with an expletive reading, "F——Bush." The two protesters must not have talked to each other, I figured.

ON APRIL 3, the President traveled to Camp Lejeune, North Carolina, a Marine base, for a speech to the troops and a meeting with several mothers and fathers, brothers and sisters, widows and children of those who had lost their lives in Iraq.

On the flight there, he walked two-thirds of the way toward the back of Air Force One to enter the guest cabin and greet the members of Congress who were accompanying him. He talked with his guests about the latest events in Iraq and described the situation there using the mathematical term *sine curve*. A sine curve is a wave that rises like an arrow until it slowly flattens out at its peak, then falls like an arrow, flattens out at its bottom, and rises again, wave after wave. "It's important we be steady through its ups and downs, although some try to surf it," he told the congressmen and congresswomen.

The speech to the troops was a rally-like affair, in front of twelve thousand Marines who wanted to fight in Iraq, cheering on their Commander in Chief. It felt like the top of a sine curve. The visit with the families of the fallen was the nadir, and it felt like one.

The President slowly worked the room, as he had now done many times before. He and Mrs. Bush were alone with each family, consoling and comforting them. Andy Card and I stood off to the side. "You're an inspiration—a tower of strength," the President said to one family. "God bless you. He's in heaven," the President said to another, as little children played nearby with their crayons. Many of the families wore pictures of their killed loved ones on their lapels. One father took his off and pinned it on the President.

The strength of the families was unbelievable. "He loved his country," the President was told by one of the fallen's relatives. "He loved being a Marine. He was proud to serve." I knew these families were suffering, but they also expressed their faith in their country, and the love their son or husband had for his military way of life. I wiped a tear from my eye.

The Commander in Chief also met seven-week-old twin girls who, because of the decision he had made to go to war, would never know their father. He was asked to pose for a picture with the twins. "This country loves you," he said to the girls. Then the President, the father of twin girls himself, left the room. He boarded Marine One where he sat, saying not a word, for the twenty-five-minute flight back to Air Force One. He looked out his window, alone with his thoughts.

SHORTLY BEFORE THE FALL OF BAGHDAD, the press asked me about the President's level of involvement in the war plan.

"Ari, you and Pentagon officials have emphasized that the President is not micromanaging this war, that he approved the overall war plan and has left the execution to the commanders. But now we're approaching the battle of Baghdad, with the prospect of not only heavy casualties—heavier casualties for coalition forces, for American troops but also for Iraqi civilians. At this point, will the President get more closely involved with the day-to-day decisions?"

"The President *is* closely involved in the day-to-day decisions," I said. "But to state the obvious, when the plan was written, it was anticipated that the plan would involve fighting in Baghdad. That's part of the plan. It was anticipated. And the plan is being implemented. And so General Franks will continue to make the tactical decisions, the timing decisions about the best way to conduct the plan, to implement that plan, which I assure you, includes how to deal with Baghdad."

The press also noted, by early April, the success of the military plan, and one reporter asked me about it.

"Last week," a reporter inquired, "the military plan that has been set in motion for a war in Iraq was very much criticized, including by many ex-generals and colonels and some in active duty in Iraq."

"I noticed," I said.

"Does the President feel that the quick taking of the airport and the closing in on the troops in Baghdad vindicates the plan?"

"The President has always felt that what is important," I said, "particularly in war, is to be steady at the helm and to lead and to do what he thought was right, and to implement the plan that he always felt was on progress. He understood there were going to be some criticisms."

I was also asked why we hadn't yet found any weapons of mass destruction and whether the war was justified without their discovery.

"I don't think that's going to happen," I said. "You've heard it repeatedly from DoD [Department of Defense] briefers that Iraq has weapons of mass destruction, biological and chemical. And we are confident that they will be found, and discovered, and seen."

"And even if they're not—the feeling is that the action was justified?"

"You're asking about a hypothetical that I just told you I don't think is going to happen."

In April, foreign leaders resumed their visits to the Oval Office. When President Rudolf Schuster of the central European Slovak Republic arrived for a private meeting on April 9, the American President told his guest, "The long-suffering people of Iraq will be free. A flower amid a troubled area will grow. You can take pride in doing what's right." Looking ahead, President Bush stated, "We trust the Iraqi people. They're plenty capable of governing themselves." It would, however, take a while, Bush added.

"I'm optimistic," he said. "The only time I've been pessimistic was trying to get a second resolution."

Later that day, Saddam's statue came down on live TV across the world, marking the fall of Baghdad and, for much of the press, the end of the war. While battles remained, the feeling in the White House press corps was the war was coming to a triumphant end. Dealing with the press was like dealing with a vise. They'd squeeze me on one side, declaring the war was going worse than expected and the military plan was a failure. Then they'd squeeze me on the other side, saying the war was over, it was an amazing triumph, why didn't we yet have a new government in place, and was Syria the next nation Bush would attack? I did my best to dial them back.

Within four hours of the White House press corps watching the amazing fall of the statue and the small but jubilant Iraqi crowds beating it with their shoes, I entered the briefing room.

"A lot of people are going to watch these events and assume the war is over," came the first comment. It was from AP's Ron Fournier.

"The war is not over," I said.

"Can you tell us the one, two, three, four, five, six things that need to happen before the President can address the country and say the war is over?" asked Fournier, following up.

"First of all, it's much too premature to even speculate about that."

"You've already said it's not over. I'm asking you what is it that would have to happen for him to be able to declare the war is over."

I said the response was twofold.

"The first is a message to the American people that we still need to be cautious because we still have our armed forces in harm's way; there still is fighting ahead of us.

"The President's second message is . . . that the long-suffering people of Iraq yearn to be free, and that this is an operation of liberation. And until the military situation is brought to an end . . . I make no predictions about what the President might say or when."

"Ari, how will we know when the regime is really toppled? Is it a matter of geography? Is it a matter of, we may not be able to find Saddam Hussein, but we know—the people we trust have control of all their weapons? How do we judge that?"

"I think from the President's point of view, one, he will be guided very much by the military analysis provided to him by General Franks, General Myers, and Secretary Rumsfeld. And by that I mean the President will be looking toward what indications do we have of resistance left in the country. And as I indicated, the President this morning cautioned that there are cities in the north that are not like cities in the south, where there still are pockets of resistance. We don't know how organized the resistance is. It may be organized."

I was later asked what the mood was in the West Wing. "There's been a lot of criticism and sniping from this room and elsewhere since the war began of the war plan, of the expectations before the war, and what officials are saying. Any feeling of vindication, or 'I told you so'?" asked ABC's Terry Moran.

"Well, from a personal point of view, all I can say is I'm always glad to be embedded with you," I said sarcastically.

The room groaned. Many reporters objected to my comment.

I should not have said it, but I was tired of the day-to-day combat with the press, and it was starting to show. I always did my best to keep it inside, but the constant conflict was wearing me down. The excitement of working in the White House, being around the President, and traveling on Marine One and Air Force One had worn off some time ago. I was mentally exhausted from the hours and the intensity of the job. But more than anything, the constant sparring with the press was getting to me. They *were* only doing their jobs, I told myself, but I was growing tired of doing mine.

The fallen-statue briefing continued, and so did the when-is-it-over questions. I didn't think anyone in the White House press corps was listening to my answers.

"Ari, so we are going to expect, we should expect a statement or a speech from the President declaring that the war is won?"

"No, I was asked about a speech by the President. I said I can't speculate about whether there would be a speech by the President or not."

"That's not a yes or a no. It's a maybe?" asked Elisabeth Bumiller of the *New York Times*.

"Just the President's reminder is that we're still in the middle of a war, and I think it's premature to get into that."

The fall of the statue also made many in the press think the entire city of Baghdad, 5 million strong, and the whole of the 24-million-person country had fallen with it.

"I have a question, too, about northern Iraq is going to be increasingly the focus of any further fighting. How much—"

"You cannot forget what you're watching in Baghdad is that which the camera lens can show you in Baghdad," I cautioned. "Baghdad is a large, large city in terms of people and size. There are other areas of Baghdad that are dangerous areas of Baghdad where fighting can still take place."

Further ignoring my cautions, I was asked about the future government of Iraq.

"At the moment, the coalition military, to the extent that it controls Iraq, is running Iraq. And the question is, When are they going to hand off to somebody else?"

"I don't think you should look at it as if it's that crisp a passing," I said. "This will be an important beginning, but it's a beginning on a continuum. It's not a stark beginning and end."

"How do you define winning the peace in Iraq?"

I said it would be measured by the emergence of the Iraqi people taking increased control of their lives and institutions.

"It is a process," I said. "And it is a process that will take some bit of time. And it's a process that can be marked by unsteady times, too. Nobody has said that as progress is made there won't be any setbacks in many areas of Iraq. There certainly will be."

ON APRIL 11, the President and Mrs. Bush went to Walter Reed Army Medical Center and the National Naval Medical Center in Bethesda, Maryland. For more than two hours the President visited wounded servicemen.

Marine Lance Corporal O. J. Santamaria of Daly City, California, a citizen of the Philippines, could barely stand his injuries were so bad, and he was hooked up to a portable IV unit. He sobbed heavily, from exhaustion and pain, but he was about to take his oath of citizenship. He fought for our country without even being a citizen, which is what our laws allow. Now, he was about to become an American. He had no family with him—only the President and First Lady. The director of the Bureau of Citizenship and Immigration Services, Eduardo Aguirre, Jr., read the oath, and Lance Corporal Santamaria struggled to repeat it.

"My fellow American," the President said, giving him a hug. "You're a good man. I'm proud of you."

"I'll never forget this moment," a tearful Bush said as he left to visit the next wounded serviceman.

From room to room he traveled, doing his best to cheer up the troops. Some had lost their legs to land mines. One Marine who couldn't talk as a result of a gunshot wound to his neck wrote the President a note. I didn't see what it said, but I watched the President read it, turn to the Marine, and say, "I'm here to thank *you*."

Bush entered another room with six Marines, five of whom were in wheelchairs. "The Marine Corps is awesome," he said. "Just ask the other side."

When Bush met a Marine who was wounded by a rocket-propelled grenade in An Nasiriyah, the Commander in Chief told him, "I'm in the presence of a hero."

"I want to thank you on behalf of every other Marine for letting us do our job," the wounded Marine told the President.

"Were you ready?" the President asked.

"Hell yes."

Then the Marine added, "I'll do it again when I'm ready."

The President turned to the Marine's mother and said, "You raised a good boy, Mom."

I noticed out of the corner of my eye that Bush's military aide, Major Paul Montanus, a stout, steady, smart, tough Marine himself—the man carrying the nuclear football—had tears running down his cheeks as he stood watching his wounded comrades meet their Commander in Chief. Once again I thought, These are great young men and women. We're a fortunate nation to have them.

Before the President left the hospital, he stopped to talk to the press. The statue had fallen two days earlier.

"Why shouldn't we say that the war is over except for pockets of resistance, sir? And do you feel any certain sense of vindication after all those people questioned the war plan?"

"This war will end when our commanders in the field tell me that the objective has been achieved. And Tommy Franks put together a great strategy. Wonderful thing about free speech and a lot of TV stations is you get a lot of opinions. Some of them were right, and some of them were really wrong. But that's okay. That's what we—that's what we believe; we believe in free speech, believe people ought to be able to express their opinion."

BY MID-APRIL, I could tell that most of the White House press corps thought the war was indeed over because the briefing returned to its usual pattern of foreign *and* domestic questions, including many on tax cuts, voting rights for the District of Columbia, and the state of the economy. Since Labor Day 2002, the briefing had been dominated by one topic—Iraq. Issues related to Iraq, such as looting and the search for weapons of mass destruction, were still raised, but one week after the statue fell, the White House press corps moved on to other things.

The President went to spend Easter at his ranch in Crawford, and I decided to stay in Washington. I was exhausted, although I didn't realize how tired I was until I arrived at my favorite restaurant, the Capital Grille on Pennsylvania Avenue. I met a dozen or so friends there who had nothing to do with my job. They were people I knew well before I entered the White House, and I looked forward to unwinding with them.

As I approached the bar to order a drink, I couldn't believe how simultaneously relaxed and burned out I felt. For the first time in seven months, with the exception of my honeymoon, I didn't worry about work, about frantic phone calls, or about the press. It felt so good to be normal. Since I joined the presidential campaign trail in March 1999, there had been only a few moments like this. I realized I had put large parts of my life on hold for four years. I was so glad to be married, but I realized how much of life Becki and I were missing. The war was tough enough, but the lead-up to the war, the dealings with the UN, the briefings that went nowhere, had really gotten to me.

Becki and I had first talked about my leaving the White House in February or March. I promised myself I wouldn't think about it again for all of April, and then I would revisit whether I wanted to stay or go. My mind wasn't yet made up, but inside, I knew which way I was leaning.

ON APRIL 25, I told the press that the President was going to travel the following week to San Diego and from there to the deck of the aircraft carrier *Abraham Lincoln* to welcome the ship and its sailors home.

"The President looks forward to the visit," I said. "He knows that the families will be waiting closely behind. And the President looks forward to being at sea to welcome these brave Americans home, and he looks forward then to them pulling into port so they can be reunited with their families."

The next Monday, April 28, the President visited Dearborn, Michigan, home to a large Arab American population. To a hero's welcome, he said to a group that included many Iraqis, "People who live in Iraq deserve the same freedom that you and I enjoy here in America. (Applause.) And after years of tyranny and torture, that freedom has finally arrived. (Applause.)

"I have confidence in the future of a free Iraq. The Iraqi people are fully capable of self-government. Every day Iraqis are moving toward democracy and embracing the responsibilities of active citizenship. Every day life in Iraq improves as coalition troops work to secure unsafe areas and bring food and medical care to those in need.

"America pledged to rid Iraq of an oppressive regime, and we kept our word. (Applause.) America now pledges to help Iraqis build a prosperous and peaceful nation, and we will keep our word again. (Applause.)"

The speech, and Bush's emotional, favorable reception by Arab Americans, got scant coverage on the evening news. Among the broadcast networks, ABC dedicated two sentences to it, while CBS didn't cover it at all.

I asked Terry Moran, ABC's White House correspondent, why the speech received so little attention. "I couldn't get it on the air," Terry told me. "If they had booed him, it would have led the news," he added.

On April 30 I was asked about the President's planned speech aboard the *Abraham Lincoln*.

"The President knows that while major combat operations have ended, and while the next phase has begun with the reconstruction of Iraq, there continue to be threats to the security and the safety of the American people. And he will describe that. There continues to be great progress in protecting the American people from those threats. But threats indeed do remain."

The press had already been told that the President would say major combat was over, but he would stop short of claiming victory.

"Why isn't this the time to legally declare that it's over?" CNN's Suzanne Malveaux asked me.

"Because as events are very visible, as you all have covered this morning, hostilities remain. There are pockets of resistance. There continue to be Iraqis who shoot at America's armed forces. It happened again in Fallujah.

"The President will fly out to the aircraft carrier on Navy One, after he departs Air Force One, lands in San Diego, and then transfers," I added, describing the plan to land aboard a fighter aircraft.

"The President's a former fighter pilot," Mark Smith of Associated Press Radio said. "Can you talk about the plane itself and where he's going to be?"

"The President will be sitting in the front seat," I said, "next to the pilot of the Navy aircraft. "He is a *former* pilot. For the sake of the landing, I'm sure he will be doing no piloting," I said, to the press's laughter. "I hope he's not watching today's briefing," I added, to even more laughter.

THE LANDING ON the USS *Abraham Lincoln,* CVN-72, was one of the most exciting days of my life. I had never before been on a carrier at sea, a mammoth floating city capable of bringing war or peace to people and places thousands of miles from America's shores.

The *Lincoln* set the record for the longest naval deployment by a nuclear-powered aircraft carrier in history, 290 consecutive days, in which it traveled more than 100,000 miles. It was at sea for so long that 150 babies were born to wives of sailors aboard the *Lincoln* while they were away. It's so large with such a big crew that it has a post office aboard with its very own zip code.

I had earlier told the press that one of the reasons the President would land aboard the *Lincoln* on a Viking fighter aircraft was that the *Lincoln* would be too far from shore to land there on his helicopter,

Marine One. Another reason, I said, was that the President *wanted* to land like a fighter pilot, having been one himself in the Guard.

Aboard Air Force One, as we flew to Naval Air Station North Island in San Diego, where the President would board the Viking, I also told the press pool that Bush would be wearing a flight suit. I don't know why they were so surprised to see him in one when he landed on the *Lincoln*, but surprised they were. The press also wanted to know how far the aircraft carrier would be from shore.

"I can't get accurate information. I've been asking for it. I don't have it yet," I responded. No one I asked at the White House could tell me. No one seemed to know. At the time, it didn't seem all that important, but a few days later it became a mini-imbroglio.

When Air Force One landed, the President's travel party split up. Along with a dozen or so staffers, I boarded a COD, a carrier-onboard-delivery aircraft. We were briefed by naval officials on what it would be like to fly at more than 300 miles per hour, then slow to a landing speed of 150 to 200 feet per second, only to be jerked to a sudden stop by a cable that snags a tailhook on the bottom of the plane. "I hope you didn't eat a lot, because you might lose your lunch," the briefer told us.

Unlike Air Force One, or civilian airplanes for that matter, the COD, being a military aircraft, wasn't known for its amenities. Its wires and exposed ceiling were visible to us, and since there were hardly any windows aboard, they were about all we could see from our uncomfortable, backward-facing seats. All aboard, including the White House staff, wore big, goofy-looking goggles, and we took pictures of one another, menacing civilians that we were.

It was a short flight that ended with a lurch, a short, sharp stop that was nowhere near as bad as they had made it out to be. I exited into a different world.

The deck of an active aircraft carrier is a sight to see, full of frenetic energy and bursts of sound, orchestrated with a precision and purpose that would make a symphony hall conductor proud. The ship's music, however, wasn't gentle, or even pretty; it was marked by an endless series of ear-piercing explosions of engines as jet aircraft took off and landed, surrounded by thousands of hands, seen and unseen, guiding every movement aboard the rolling runway. It seemed we were far out at sea, distanced from familiar surroundings, protected by a fierce warship.

I was introduced to Commander Ron Hughes, the officer assigned to be my guide aboard the ship. We hovered topside as I gazed up at the seven-story high "island," or tower, and down to the sea. Soon it was time for the President to land.

Much to the chagrin of his probably nervous pilot, the Viking carrying the Commander in Chief caught the fourth and final cable, and a picture made for television was beamed around the world. Looking perfectly comfortable and dashing in his flight suit, the President emerged to a hero's welcome. The sailors relished their opportunity to shake hands or slap backs with President Bush, and he was happy to oblige. The scene of his arrival and his jaunty walk from cockpit to flight deck was shown over and over again. I had no idea if anyone in the White House knew how dramatic that picture would be, or whether we ever intended to use it in a campaign commercial, but the talking heads on TV, who themselves understand the value of a good picture, instantly proclaimed we were *certain* to use the footage on the campaign.

In politics and government, no good event can last forever, and I should have known then and there that the press's euphoric coverage would somehow reverse itself, given their self-appointed role as a leveler in our society. The pictures were too beneficial to the President's image, and the press didn't think it was their job to show the President, any president, in a favorable light for any length of time. It didn't take long for the landing's success to turn into the landing's controversy.

But first, the President toured the ship in the company of its captain, and I toured it with Condi Rice and other officials.

We were shown the briefing room where the pilots received their assignments shortly before they launched their countless sorties into and over Iraq. During the windstorms that had temporarily halted the ground invasion, the pilots explained to us, they were watching live pictures on CNN showing the sands blowing and the Army temporarily halted, knowing they were the force that was going to provide protection for their "brothers below." Navy aviators, a very motivated crew to begin with, became even more motivated watching the news. For whatever problems or controversies live TV coverage can sometimes create, my visit to the ship's briefing room was an example of the media's power to do good in our society. News coverage helped us win a war as the Navy watched the Army and rose to their mission.

I waited my turn as Condi peered through a tiny, thick window way below the ship's deck to observe its nuclear reactor. "So that's what the North Koreans are after," the national security adviser wryly observed.

I ate dinner with a large group of officers and joined many of them for a cigar and a nonalcoholic beer on the ship's stern. I slept in the room of a squadron commander whose squadron had already left the ship for shore, a spacious quarters by ship standards, but perhaps one-fourth the size of a standard Holiday Inn room. What a thrill. What a day and what a night.

The President delivered his speech, declaring an end to major hostilities while warning that Iraq remained dangerous. A banner flew above him reading, "Mission Accomplished," and it surely seemed that way on May 1, 2003. Saddam was out of power and no longer a danger. That, to President Bush, was the core of the mission.

Many in the White House press corps wondered why it took the President *so long* to declare victory, even though I constantly reminded them, as the President had done, that Iraq remained dangerous. Had Bush waited any longer to declare an end to major hostilities, the press, who thought the conflict had largely ended three weeks earlier, when Saddam's statue fell, would have accused him of prolonging the war in an effort to gain politically. To me, the threat of Saddam was removed and everything seemed to be going well.

If my mood was good when I returned to Washington, it was matched by a sour one in the briefing room. Democrats, who realized the impact of a powerful speech following the President's dramatic landing, not to mention the seeming end of a successful war, were crying foul over the televised pictures of the President's landing, decrying them as political, demanding they not be used in campaign commercials. The Democrats would be free, of course, to criticize the President's conduct in war, and to run commercials against it, but the President, they argued, should be restrained in his ability to highlight success in war. It was now the White House press corp's chance to turn the tables, recognizing how favorable their coverage with the pictures had been, they now found reason to criticize the landing.

Helicopter-gate was born.

"On the visit to the aircraft carrier, I believe you told us from this podium that the reason the President had to take a jet out was because the carrier would be hundreds of miles offshore. As it turned out, it was way, way less than that. Were you misled?" I was asked on May 6.

"No, the original planning was exactly as I said. . . . The ship did make faster progress than anticipated. I asked about that when I was onboard. It's a factor of the weather. They were able to get closer to shore. But the bottom line remains the same, that the President wanted to arrive on it in a manner that would allow him to see an arrival on a carrier the same way pilots got to see an arrival on a carrier. As it did get closer, he could have taken a helicopter out there if he wanted to. He chose not to." I had also been told privately that it was safer to fly over water in a Viking than a helicopter because there are no ejection seats on Marine One.

The controversy of why Bush didn't land aboard the *Lincoln* on a helicopter instead of a fighter aircraft lingered for the next several days. Some reporters believed they were deliberately misled by the White House. To me, it was another example of how reasonable, innocent changes in circumstance aren't enough to mollify critics who are capable of creating conflict anywhere, for any reason. There was nothing I could say; to some reporters, the issue was the honesty of the White House.

Some reporters also claimed the President's speech actually delayed the arrival of the *Lincoln*'s crew into port. Given how long the ship had been at sea and how badly its sailors and Marines wanted to see their families, that was a serious charge to make. Indeed, given the progress the ship had made, it could have arrived one day *early* in port, but instead it arrived exactly on time, on May 2. If it *had* arrived one day early, I would have loved to have seen the press's stories about sailors stranded on the dock, since their families had long planned for a May 2 arrival and might not have been able, at the last minute, to arrive a day earlier. In the cycle of journalism, good news can't stay good for very long.

NINETEEN

SAYING GOOD-BYE

O N FRIDAY, MAY 16, I walked into the Oval Office and did something I had never done before. I closed the door behind me.

Alone with me, the President realized this was not going to be one of our usual conversations about the press or an issue I needed to review with him. It was different, and he sensed it.

I sat in the chair on his right side as he sat behind his desk. The President is a bottom-line guy, and I went straight to the bottom line. "Mr. President, I've come to the conclusion that my time has come to go."

Before I could say another word, he cut me off.

"Burnout?" he asked.

"Burnout," I said.

For almost three months, Becki and I had talked about whether I should leave the White House. I was increasingly tired and beginning to feel burned out. I still loved what I did, but I didn't think I would love it much longer if I kept doing it. Given the rigors of an upcoming campaign, I also knew that the spring-summer of 2003 would be my final off-ramp. If I stayed into the fall of 2003, it would only be right to stay through Election Day 2004. That would have meant almost six years on the campaign trail and the White House. I didn't think I had it in me.

Becki and I had also been talking about starting a family. There was no way I wanted to have a child in the middle of an election year. If I had a baby, I knew I would want to spend as much time as possible at the baby's side, and with Becki. A baby in any year is hard when you work at the White House, but during an election year I didn't want to have to make a choice between my child and my job. Plus, at the old age of forty-two, I didn't want to postpone starting a family any more than I already had.

In March, I told Becki that I wouldn't think about leaving or staying for all of April. I would take a month off from trying to figure it out. I'm typically very decisive and have a strong gut feel for what I want to do and when I want to do it. The decision to leave President Bush and walk away from the podium wasn't easy. I let it take its time, knowing that I'd come to a conclusion when I was good and ready.

I explained to the President that, as much as I enjoyed working for him and being a part of the White House, I was growing exhausted, and I didn't want to reach the point where I didn't want to show up for work. I liked my relationships with the press and still found satisfaction in our sparring sessions. But my job was wearing me down, and I knew it. The last thing I wanted to do was stay too long and not be good at what I was doing. We talked about who I thought should replace me, and that was that. When I stood up to leave, the President came over and gave me a big kiss on the head. He had done that once before, aboard Air Force One, when he heard Becki and I had become engaged. He was a hard man to leave, and I knew I was going to miss him.

I spent a good part of Sunday calling my family to let them know of my decision, and I also called the Vice President and about a dozen top aides to fill them in. I called top members of my staff, Scott McClellan, whom I had recommended to the President as my replacement; and Sean McCormack, and Claire Buchan, my other deputies. I couldn't have done my job without their amazing support and knowledge. They were friends as much as they were co-workers. Telling them I was leaving was hard, very hard to do. I asked them to keep it quiet so I could inform the press myself, and because they were part of the close-mouthed and secretive White House, I knew they wouldn't say a word.

On Monday, I announced my departure at the regular 7:30 senior staff meeting in the Roosevelt Room, and after that, word filtered out.

By the time I arrived in the briefing room for the 9:45 gaggle, the press had heard the news.

"So tell us. Tell us," CBS's John Roberts began.

"A round of applause here for a job well done," a reporter said, and the tough and grizzled White House press corps burst into applause. It was touching. As much as our jobs were to spar with one another, I liked them and was proud to have good relationships with almost every reporter in the room. The relationship between the press secretary and the press is complicated and fascinating. I don't know how I could have derived so much satisfaction and liked so much something that was so hard to do. The human side of the press corps was on display that morning, and I appreciated it—a lot.

"Leaving a man who you deeply believe in is not easy," I said. "Leaving the White House is hard. But I think in this business you really have to be guided by what's in your heart and know when the time is right, when your time has come. And I never meant to be a government for life type. I meant to come here after college for a couple years, and twenty years later, I'm still here."

I also talked about my wife. "I know I want to see more of Becki. Six months and ten days ago, I got married. And you do reach that point where your priorities really refocus. And a wonderful part of my refocusing my priorities now is going to be to see more of my wife."

Referring to the tension and the difficulties of serving both the President and the press corps, I said I was looking forward to doing something more relaxing. "I really want to unwind, do something more relaxing, like dismantling live nuclear warheads," I deadpanned.

True to form, the press later at the briefing asked me about the lowest moment on the job, not the best moment. I told them it was of course September 11, as well as the anthrax attacks.

April Ryan of American Urban Radio asked me, When is it too much spin?

"Well, you decide that," I said. "I mean, look, the job of anybody who is the White House press secretary is to faithfully articulate what the President is thinking and why he's thinking it. And that's what I do for a living. The job of the press corps is to find out everything you possibly can about everything under the sun. And I try to help you as much as I can, wherever I can. And my job is to represent the President, and that's what I always remember when I come to this podium."

Soon the briefing returned to the pressing issues of the day as I took questions about taxes, Israel, and the war on terror. It was business as usual, but already I could feel the pressures of the job lifting from my shoulders.

The next day my departure announcement was news on the front page of the *New York Times,* and I was interviewed live on all the broadcast and cable TV morning shows. I thought to myself how much my life had changed since I arrived in Washington, D.C., in early 1983, an unemployed political science major hoping to see what I could accomplish in the nation's capital. I realized that whatever I had done was thanks to people like former Congressman Norman Lent of New York, who gave me my first job on the Hill, Congressmen Joe DioGuardi, and Senator Pete Domenici, Congressman Bill Archer, Elizabeth Dole, and of course George W. Bush. It was quite a ride. I had loved it, but I was glad to be leaving it.

I wasn't leaving the White House for another two months, allowing me to go on the President's two upcoming foreign trips, one to Europe and the Middle East, the other to Africa. As much as I might be thinking about the future, I still had a day job to do.

ON MAY 30, the President left the United States for a visit to Poland, Russia, France, Egypt, Jordan, and Qatar.

At 8:00 in the morning on May 31, President Bush began a tour of Auschwitz, the concentration camp that took the lives of several of my mother's relatives. Being Hungarian, her favorite uncle and other relatives were shot on the banks of the Danube River in Budapest by the Nazis and their Hungarian hosts. Only a few of my great-uncles, great-aunts, and cousins made it as far as Auschwitz, most never to return. My uncle Laci, my grandmother's brother, was a Holocaust survivor, and when I met him in 1972, he had a number tattooed on his forearm, the notorious mark the Nazis left on their victims. He showed me the yellow Jewish star he was forced to wear.

The President entered the grounds of Auschwitz as Dr. Teresa Swiebocka, the senior curator, explained that Elie Wiesel had been sent there.

"He was a little boy," the President said aloud but almost to himself.

Bush entered the Extermination Building and stood under a sign that read, "Jews are a race that must be totally exterminated." Those were the words of Hans Frank, the Nazi governor-general in 1944.

The guide explained that prisoners entered Auschwitz not knowing their fate. Within fifteen to twenty minutes, they were suffocated to death by Zyklon B gas in rooms where they thought they would shower. Once dead, they were taken away, usually by other prisoners, and fed into ovens.

The President looked at a display of hair taken from the murdered victims, which sixty years later still looked, and presumably felt, like human hair. "What did they use it for?" he asked.

It was sold to the German textile industry.

He saw the suitcases the Jews brought with them to Auschwitz, thinking they could take their most sacred possessions to their newest place of settlement. He saw prayer shawls and artificial limbs.

"Powerful," he said, barely audible.

He stopped when he saw the display of baby shoes and shook his head. "So sad, all the little baby shoes."

The tour continued.

"You've done a good job recording history," the President told his guide. "How many people come here each year?"

Half a million.

"Where do they come from? Do they come from Germany?" Bush wanted to know.

He asked if visitors challenged the accuracy of the information his guide presented.

As a Jew, I marveled at what I was seeing. The tour group consisted of the President, the First Lady, and me. My job was to take notes on what he saw and what he said. A White House photographer was nearby, and of course so were the Secret Service. I stood there, as an aide, and as a Jew, watching the President of the United States visit the spot where my people were almost exterminated. I wondered what my relatives whom I never met would think if they knew I had returned to the place of their death as an aide to the President—a president who had emerged as Israel's best friend ever in the Oval Office, a president who has a profound warmth and respect for the Jewish people. I knew I would leave my job in a month, but few days left me as emotional and contemplative of how lucky I was to be an American, an American working for the President of the United States, particularly *this* President of the United States, as did that day at Auschwitz. The former President Bush's press secretary, Marlin Fitzwater, advised me when I took the job to stop and smell the roses. There were no roses to be found at Auschwitz, but on this day I stopped and took in every sight, every sound, every smell I could find.

The President was led into a small cell where a heavy wooden door was marked by claw marks just below eye level. Thirty-nine Jews had been stuffed into the tiny chamber, the guide explained. They could barely breathe or move. Sixty years later, the door bore a slightly hollowed out space from where they tried in vain to scratch their way through with their fingers.

He was shown another chamber, this one bearing a likeness of Jesus Christ etched into the wall. It was made by a Polish officer, his guide told him.

"Very sad," the President said quietly. He added, "History is a reminder of what's possible." I didn't know, and I didn't ask him, what he was thinking when he said that. Was it the ongoing threat to Jews in the Middle East and around the world? Was it the victims of Saddam's brutality, or was it fears of the next dictator who would rise up and kill hundreds of thousands or millions if the world let it happen? I didn't know. I did know that, as President, his job was to learn from history and prevent a Holocaust from happening again.

When his tour was over, the President addressed the press.

"Laura and I have just toured Auschwitz I, and what they call Auschwitz II, a place where millions were murdered. The sites are a sobering reminder that—of the power of evil and the need for people to resist evil. This site is a sobering reminder that when we find anti-Semitism, whether it be in Europe or anywhere else, mankind must come together to fight such dark impulses.

"And this site is also a strong reminder that the civilized world must never forget what took place on this site.

"May God bless the victims and the families of the victims, and may we always remember."

Later that day the President called me from his hotel room, asking if the press had picked up his remarks about the present need to fight anti-Semitism in Europe. He was traveling to France later in the week and wanted to make certain his message about fighting modern-day anti-Semitism, a topic he raised with President Chirac, was heard.

I told him the press weren't making a big deal of his remarks. He was disappointed to hear it.

IN RUSSIA, President Bush and President Putin signed the Treaty of Moscow, an agreement to reduce sharply the number of nuclear weapons in each nation's arsenal. As we prepared to leave, Putin approached me and asked what I was going to do when I left the White House. His staff told me my departure announcement had been news in Russia. He clasped my hand and said to me in English, "Best of luck."

We arrived in southeast France, in the small, lakeside town of Evian, on June 1 for a summit meeting with the world's largest and most powerful nations. That night I gathered for dinner with a small group of senior staffers at the Ermitage Hotel's outdoor terrace. We drank red wine, ate French cheese and lamb, and reminisced about the Bush presidency to date. Would the President make it through his September 14, 2001, speech at the National Cathedral without breaking down and crying? one aide remembered worrying about. Deputy Chief of Staff Joe Hagin described a disagreement among New York officials about which sites the President should visit on September 14, a fight so bad it almost derailed Bush's visit. We talked about September 11, 2001, and how much our world had changed since. It was a rare laid-back, contemplative night. Knowing I was leaving made nights like that even more special.

The President traveled to Egypt and Jordan to meet with Israeli and Arab leaders, including the new Palestinian Prime Minister, Mahmoud Abbas. In Aqaba, Jordan, when Abbas entered the room for a three-way summit with Bush and Israeli Prime Minister Ariel Sharon, Sharon rose and hugged him like a long-lost brother. For a few brief, shining moments, the prospects for peace in the Middle East appeared to be moving in the *right* direction.

Instead, Sharon may have hugged him, figuratively, a little too tight. The Palestinian people didn't think Abbas was tough enough. More important, his reformist efforts were rejected by Yasir Arafat, who forced Abbas's resignation, once again demonstrating that there could be no peace initiative Arafat wouldn't let, or make, fall apart.

From Jordan, Air Force One took us to the desert headquarters for the American military's efforts in Iraq, the Persian Gulf nation of Qatar. There, in 110-degree heat, I saw the most incredible palace I had ever seen. Through a shining marble entryway that soared six or seven stories, the President was led into the office of the Emir of Qatar, a friend of the United States whose efforts helped us to win the war in Iraq. After a visit with the troops based there to say thank you, the long voyage home began.

Shortly after Air Force One left Doha, the capital of Qatar, we were joined by fighter escorts because Air Force One's route home was straight over Iraq. We entered Iraqi airspace at 12:24 P.M. on June 5, and for the next hour and six minutes, we flew over a country that three months earlier had been ruled by Saddam Hussein. As we approached Baghdad, the President, his chief of staff, national security adviser and secretary of state knelt along the windows on the left side of the aircraft to stare at the sights below, places they had seen many times in classified photographs and maps. Now they were looking at Saddam's former home with their own eyes. The President knew the topography by heart. There's Saddam City, he said, pointing out a particular part of Baghdad. There's the airfield where our troops were stationed. Noting a bend in the river, the President said, There's Dora Farms, the site where the war began during the surprise air strike that attempted to kill Saddam and his two sons on March 19, 2003.

I thought it was a remarkable sight. The President of the United States flying over what I believed would become a free Iraq, a land where all my adult life a brutal killer had ruled, and now the President was studying the cityscape below, wondering what the future held for the nation he had attacked and liberated. There were many "pinch-me" moments working in the White House. This was one of them.

WHEN WE RETURNED to Washington, my mind was still on my job—it's the White House after all—but my heart was looking forward to a new life ahead. The questions in the briefing room were much the same. Where are the weapons of mass destruction? I don't know, but we're confident we'll find them. When will the economy recover? Soon. What's your reaction to what Governor Dean said? Ask the campaign.

The stock market surged in the summer of 2003, and the press asked me if Bush took credit. No, I said, his focus is on the overall economy, and, we hope, the better the economy does, the better the markets will do, but investors make those decisions.

I couldn't help myself, and I reminded reporters about the giant down arrows that accompanied the President's speeches on TV when the market was tanking. I said I hadn't noticed any gigantic up arrows now that the market was rising. The press laughed. They thought it was funny.

By July 1, the press coverage of Iraq was bad and getting worse. The focus was almost entirely on the violence and the killings of servicemen, newsworthy developments for certain but not the *only* news to be found there. The country was being rebuilt, schools being refurbished, hospitals reopened, electricity was increasingly coming online, and day-to-day life for the Iraqi people was improving. Money from Iraqi expatriates was flowing *into* the country, a good sign if ever there was one. Most of the press didn't see it that way, however.

After tough questioning by CBS's Bill Plante about faulty postwar preparations and conditions in Iraq, I fired back.

"I think what you're doing is you're ignoring the tremendous number of success stories that have taken place inside Iraq," I told him at the on-camera briefing.

"What success stories?" he retorted.

"I think this is one of those cases where if the glass of milk is nine-tenths full, you'll only see the one-tenth that is empty," I said.

"But I haven't heard any success stories. You got any?" Bill rebutted.

"You just haven't aired them, but there are many," I said. "And I think Ambassador Bremer [the U.S. administrator in Iraq] talks about them on a regular basis. The fact is, one of the reasons the Iraqi people are supportive of the efforts we've had there is because of the effort that's been done in the reconstruction phases."

I started to give examples.

"The children of Iraq have benefited tremendously, and that means their parents have also, from the health care systems that the United States has now got up and going—from immunization programs that are under way throughout Iraq; from the electricity that has now been restored in many places around Iraq . . . to the feeding of the Iraqi people—"

I interrupted myself. "I see your eyes are glazing over," I said to the CBS news veteran. "This is my point—that when the news is good, it's not something you pay much attention to."

The next day Bill Plante and I talked privately about our clash. On the one hand, he has a temper and is easy to rile, but on the other, he's a complete gentleman.

I complained to him about the negative tone of coverage.

"There's a concentration on the problem," he explained. "That's what the news is."

"No," I argued. "The news is the full context of facts, not just the bad ones."

At the same briefing where Bill and I clashed, another reporter cited a poll of how bad things where going in Iraq.

The poll showed, said the reporter, a sharp drop in the percentage of Americans who think things are going well in Iraq, from 70 to 50 percent. Thirty-seven percent think the administration misled them leading up to the war. The reporter added that there were also news stories quoting servicemen as saying we should get out of Iraq. Is the President concerned, I was asked.

"As for the poll you cited," I answered, "I had a feeling that this issue would be brought up, so I brought it with me." It was a *USA Today* poll.

"While the numbers have indeed declined, as you indicated, 69 percent say it was worth having—it is worth having U.S. troops in Iraq now; 63 percent say the administration did a good job in planning for the situation following major conflict in Iraq; 61 percent say the administration did not deliberately mislead the American people; 68 percent expressed confidence the United States can rebuild the Iraqi economy."

I knew those were good numbers, numbers I didn't think the press would bring up on their own at the briefing.

In reality, it didn't matter what I thought. The news is controlled by the news industry—the definition of what *is* news *is* up to them, not the government, and that's the way it must always be. I may disagree with their definition of news, but it's their decision to make.

The President, or anyone else in public life, can say something a million times. If the press don't cover it, very few people will hear it. And sadly, it's the good news that doesn't get covered. In a land as hopeful and optimistic as America, I refuse to believe that news is only, or mostly bad. Our lives are full of happy, good developments, yet the news we get is too full of sad, troubling reports. Even when things have gone wrong for our nation, we've always seen the bright side and found a way to forge ahead, to make things better, to fix and improve, and along the way America has excelled.

The press have a mission to find the bad, and in the process, they help us correct it. They're right to expose wrongdoing so it too can be seen and fixed. In doing so, they protect the Republic itself. But that shouldn't be their only mission. It shouldn't even be their main mission. The news should *not* be a concentration on the problem. It should be a concentration on failure *and* success. The bad *and* the good. The news, and all the news. The American people are plenty capable of handling it. I wish they could hear more of it.

AFTER A FIVE-DAY TRIP to Africa, I returned to the White House on July 14, 2003, for my final day of work. A controversy raged over the accuracy of a claim the President had made in his State of the Union address concerning Iraq's efforts to obtain uranium from Africa. For more than forty-five minutes, the press and I enjoyed our last clash, and then I was asked if I had any final thoughts to share.

I thanked my staff and the city of people at the White House who make the place go round but whose efforts aren't publicly recognized. When my long list of thank-yous was done, I thanked the press.

"As today shows, the relationship between the press secretary and the press corps is designed to be a relationship that has some levels of tension built into it. It is the press's job to ask anything about everything. I always do my best to give you the fullest answers from the President that I possibly can. And I hope that I've endeavored to do that and do it well in the course of our interaction.

"But one thing is for sure," I added. "As sometimes messy as it can be, in the 225-year history of our country, the fact that there is a free press who can ask whatever it wants and a government that is accountable has kept our nation strong and free. And it will forevermore."

Then I turned my focus elsewhere.

"The final person I want to thank is, of course, the President, a person who gave me this opportunity to serve my country, a person in whom I believe so deeply, both on policy and as a person, as a leader, and as somebody I've come to be very close to.

"There's one other thing the President did, by putting me here, that I will always remember and take with me from the White House, and that is, thanks to the President, I met my wife here, because she worked at the White House too. Becki is with us today. Becki, I can't wait to see you at regular hours."

It was my three hundredth briefing, and when the day was over, I said good-bye. I drove through the gates of the White House for the last time as press secretary. Through one gate, through another, until I neared the third and final barrier. I thanked the Secret Service Uniformed Division officer who was keeping watch, blended into the usual traffic, and headed for home.

EPILOGUE

WE NEVER DID find weapons of mass destruction in Iraq. Although we found old artillery shells with traces of sarin gas and other chemicals, we have yet to discover any of the chemical or biological stockpiles we thought we would discover there. Yet President Bush still won reelection.

We live today in an era of danger much like the Cold War. Except for a ten-year period between the fall of the Berlin Wall and the attack on the World Trade Center, foreign policy and defense-related issues have been a staple of American elections from World War II through the present. The nineties were a false respite when our elections turned mostly inward, with foreign affairs, terrorism, and defense spending relegated to second- or third-tier issues in the minds of the voters. September 11 changed our nation's focus much the way Pearl Harbor did.

In 2004, voters who worried about terrorism and keeping America safe voted overwhelmingly to reelect President Bush, despite our failure to find weapons of mass destruction in Iraq and despite numerous attacks on the President for deceiving our nation and lying our way into war.

I said, from the White House podium, on many occasions that we *knew* Saddam Hussein possessed chemical weapons. I said we *knew* Saddam possessed biological weapons.

Why did I say it?

I said it because it was the best judgment of the career intelligence analysts who serve our nation. I said it because my boss, President George W. Bush, said it, just as President Clinton had said it before him, and just as Vice President Gore said it. Senator John Kerry said it as well in a speech on the Senate floor in 2002. According to the arms inspector David Kay, France in the 1990s concluded Iraq had weapons of mass destruction, and so did Germany. The United Nations also thought it was true.

If we all said it, what happened? Where are these weapons of mass destruction?

It seems to me only four things could have happened. One is Saddam moved them out of Iraq before the war without us knowing it. Two is Saddam destroyed them and left no evidence behind. Three is that he hid them somewhere inside Iraq and we've yet to discover them. Four is that Iraq didn't have weapons of mass destruction and we were all wrong.

David Kay, the former UN chief weapons inspector and head of the Iraq Survey Group that was sent by the U.S. government to search for weapons of mass destruction after the war, said we may all have been wrong. He reported we had not found any stockpiles of weapons of mass destruction.

That was the honest assessment of an honest man. But it wasn't all that David Kay reported. His statement commanded attention, and it dominated the headlines. But as always, there was more to the news than the headlines. Here's what *else* David Kay said when he submitted his report to Congress in October 2003:

"We have discovered dozens of WMD-related program activities and significant amounts of equipment that Iraq concealed from the United Nations during the inspections that began in late 2002."

These included "a clandestine network of laboratories and safehouses maintained by the Iraqi intelligence service. 'Reference strains' of biological organisms, concealed in a scientist's home, including a live strain of deadly botulinum, and new research on Brucella, Congo Crimean Hemorrhagic Fever, ricin and aflatoxin.

"In the chemical and biological weapons area we have confidence that there were at a minimum clandestine on-going research and development activities that were embedded in the Iraqi Intelligence Service," Kay reported.

On January 28, 2004, when David Kay, the man who said we hadn't found any weapons of mass destruction, testified before the Senate Armed Services Committee, he said, "If you read the total body of intelligence in the last twelve to fifteen years that flowed out of Iraq, I quite frankly think it would be hard to come to a conclusion other than Iraq was a gathering, serious threat to the world with regard to WMD. . . . I think the world is far safer with the disappearance and the removal of Saddam Hussein. I have said I actually think this may be one of those cases where it was even more dangerous than we thought."

In other words, Kay said we did not find actual weapons of mass destruction. Instead, we found an ongoing, active research and development effort to create chemical and biological weapons, even while the UN inspectors were in Iraq, hidden in scientists' homes.

Charles Duelfer, who succeeded Kay, confirmed in October 2004 that no weapons of mass destruction were found. He reported, however, that at the beginning of 2003 Saddam probably had the capability to produce mustard agent within six months and nerve agents in significant quantities within two years.

What purpose could there be for Saddam to pursue these weapons in violation of international law? I don't think they were for "peaceful purposes," not in the hands of Saddam and his sons, Qusai and Odai.

Saddam pledged as the price for ending the 1991 Gulf War to abandon his pursuit of weaponry, particularly weapons of mass destruction. But he didn't.

The Bush administration may have been wrong about Saddam's actual capabilities, but we weren't wrong about his intentions. To this day, I believe it was only a matter of time before Saddam would have confronted the West, Israel included, with weapons of mass destruction. He had a history of using the weapons he possessed, and he had a history of aggression against his neighbors. He attacked Iran, Kuwait, Saudi Arabia, and Israel. I don't think he was contained or constrained; he was biding his time.

If this war wasn't fought in 2003, it was only a matter of time until it would have had to have been fought, this time against an enemy that probably *would* have had weapons of mass destruction and would have used them against our military forces. Critics who accept Kay's and Duelfer's conclusion that Saddam *didn't* have active weapons of mass destruction can't dismiss the findings that he was developing them.

Particularly after we learned, on September 11, how vulnerable we are to a surprise attack, could an American president take a chance that Saddam Hussein either had or was trying to obtain weapons of mass destruction *without* confronting him? If I and others in the administration had *never* said that Saddam had weapons of mass destruction, even though we had good reason to believe it at the time, and instead said he had an ongoing, active research and development effort to obtain chemical and biological weapons, that alone in my judgment would have been reason to go to war. For the safety of the American people, we couldn't let Saddam possess weapons of mass destruction, nor could we let him seek them, hoping that he somehow never obtained them, or once he obtained them he wouldn't use them. Saddam was a unique threat, and so were his ruthless sons. They're threats no more.

As divided as America became over the war, I think back to what Czech President Havel and the Holocaust survivor Elie Wiesel told the President. If only action had been taken in 1938 or 1939, World War II could have been averted, they said. Winston Churchill was seen by many in Europe at the time as a militarist not interested in peace. If the world *had* taken military action in the 1930s, I'm sure some would have said that Hitler wasn't the threat Churchill claimed him to be. They would have caviled: Lives would have been lost, and for what reason? Who will rebuild Germany? Isn't it a mess?

We'll never know if President Bush, along with Britain's Tony Blair and the leaders of Spain, Italy, Poland, Australia, and many of our east European allies, averted a third world war by deposing Saddam before he possessed and used weapons of mass destruction. It would have been fanciful to think in 1938 that World War II could have been averted had the Nazi threat been removed before it fully materialized.

We may not know, but I sleep better at night knowing that the risk posed by Saddam is gone and that the man who gave $25,000 to the families of Palestinian suicide bombers will never again be in a position to give them, or anyone, aid or comfort. The risk is gone, and I feel the world is better because of it.

As for the White House press corps, a significant part of me misses them. I enjoyed sparring with some of the nation's toughest, smartest people on behalf of a President in whom I believed. While I think they're too conflict-oriented and they only hurt themselves through their lack of ideological diversity, I found them to be an earnest group of people who believe in their mission—reporting the truth as they see it.

I don't miss the daily grind, and I don't miss the long hours. But I still believe that as messy as things are, our system, the press included, is the best on earth.

As in most markets whose success or failure is determined by competition, the problems of the media will sort themselves out over time. The emergence of Fox News, which for the first time outdrew the broadcast networks in viewers during the 2004 Republican Convention, is a reflection of the demands of the public. If the networks weren't perceived as so ideologically lopsided by a sizable amount of the public, Fox wouldn't have gotten off the ground. If Fox is seen as conservative, then the networks need to grapple with the fact that they're perceived as liberal.

I know they don't believe they're liberal, but TV markets vote with their remotes, and the broadcast networks are losing viewers. Until the networks and rest of the mainstream press corps realize the subtle ways their largely Democratic voting habits and attitudes shape policy coverage, polarization of the news industry will continue. The Internet and the rise of opinionated bloggers provide increasing numbers of Americans with places to find the news other than the mainstream media. As Republicans and conservatives leave the broadcast networks behind, the networks' viewers will increasingly be dominated by Democrats and liberals.

At the beginning of our Republic, that's the way news worked. The media were partisan, with one paper advocating for one party and another paper, a different party. To their credit, today's media hold themselves out as neutral and seek only to report the facts. I hope this book challenges reporters and journalism schools to think a little bit differently about how they report the facts, to accept the proposition that it's not healthy for journalism schools to graduate people from mostly one party or school of thought, and that newsrooms flourish when accepted ideas and ideals, particularly on policy matters, are challenged by people from the top editors down, owing to a healthy dose of ideological diversity. I believe readership and viewership will rise as well if the public is convinced that the mainstream media are more representative of society as a whole.

I loved my job in the White House, and I remain an avid follower of the news. Government service and journalism are both noble endeavors. Great institutions that last forever are made stronger by the reflections of those of us fortunate to have passed through. From my perch at the podium, I took a lot of heat. I hope I also shed some light.

INDEX